The Ketogenic Diet:
A complete guide for
dieters and practitioners

Lyle McDonald

This book is not intended for the treatment or prevention of disease, nor as a substitute for medical treatment, nor as an alternative to medical advice. It is a review of scientific evidence presented for information purposes, to increase public knowledge of the ketogenic diet. Recommendations outlined herein should not be adopted without a full review of the scientific references given and consultation with a health care professional. Use of the guidelines herein is at the sole choice and risk of the reader.

For information contact: Lyle McDonald, 500 E. Anderson Ln. #121-A, Austin, Tx 78752

ISBN: 0-9671456-0-0

FIRST EDITION
FIFTH PRINTING

Printed in the USA by

MP
MORRIS PUBLISHING

3212 East Highway 30 • Kearney, NE 68847 • 1-800-650-7888

Acknowledgements

Thanks to Dan Duchaine and Dr. Mauro DiPasquale, and before them Michael Zumpano, who did the initial work on the ketogenic diet for athletes and got me interested in researching them. Without their initial work, this book would never have been written.

Special thanks to the numerous individuals on the internet (especially the lowcarb-l list), who asked me the hard questions and forced me to go look for answers. To those same individuals, thank you for your patience as I have finished this book.

Extra special thanks go out to my editors, Elzi Volk and Clair Melton. Your input has been invaluable, and prevented me from being redundant. Thanks also goes out to everybody who has sent me corrections through the various printings. Even more thanks to Lisa Sporleder, who provided me valuable input on page layout, and without whom this book would have looked far worse.

Finally, a special acknowledgement goes to Robert Langford, who developed the 10 day ketogenic diet cycle which appears on pages 150-151.

Introduction

I became interested in the ketogenic diet two and one-half years ago when I used a modified form (called a cyclical ketogenic diet) to reach a level of leanness that was previously impossible using other diets. Since that time, I have spent innumerable hours researching the details of the diet, attempting to answer the many questions which surround it. This book represents the results of that quest.

The ketogenic diet is surrounded by controversy. Proponents of the ketogenic diet proclaim it as a magical diet while opponents denounce the diet because of misconceptions about the physiology involved. As with so many issues of controversy, the reality is somewhere in the middle. Like most dietary approaches, the ketogenic diet has benefits and drawbacks, all of which are discussed in this book.

The goal of this book is not to convince nor dissuade individuals to use a ketogenic diet. Rather, the goal of this book is to present the facts behind the ketogenic diet based on the available scientific research. While the use of anecdotal evidence is minimized, it is included where it adds to the information presented.

Guidelines for implementing the ketogenic diet are presented for those individuals who decide to use it. Although a diet free of carbohydrates is appropriate for individuals who are not exercising or only performing low-intensity aerobic exercise, it is not appropriate for those individuals involved in high-intensity exercise. In addition to the standard ketogenic diet, two modified ketogenic diets are discussed which integrate carbohydrates while maintaining ketosis.

The first of these is the targeted ketogenic diet, which includes the consumption of carbohydrates around exercise. The second, the cyclical ketogenic diet, alternates a span of ketogenic dieting with periods of high-carbohydrate consumption. In addition to an examination of the ketogenic diet, exercise is addressed, especially as it pertains to ketogenic diets and fat loss.

This book is divided into seven parts. Part I includes an introduction to the ketogenic diet and a history of its development. Part II presents the physiology of fuel utilization in the body, ketone bodies, the adaptations to ketosis, changes in body composition, and other metabolic effects which occur as a result of ketosis. Part III discusses the specific diets presented in this book. This includes a general discussion of dieting principles, including body composition and metabolic rate, as well as details of how to develop a standard, targeted, and cyclical ketogenic diet. Part IV completes discussion of the ketogenic diet with chapters on breaking fat loss plateaus, ending the diet, tools used to enhance the diet, and concerns for individuals considering using ketogenic diet.

Part V discusses exercise physiology, including aerobic exercise, interval training, and weight training. Additionally, the effects of exercise on ketosis and fat loss are discussed. Part VI develops general exercise guidelines based on the information presented in the preceding chapters. Part VII presents sample exercise programs, as well as guidelines for pre-contest bodybuilders. Finally, Part VIII discusses the use of supplements on the ketogenic diet, both for general health as well as specific goals.

This book is meant as a technical reference manual for the ketogenic diet. It includes information that should be useful to the general dieting public, as well as to athletes and bodybuilders. Hopefully, the attention to technical accuracy will make it useful to researchers and medical professionals. As such, technical information is necessarily presented although attempts have been made to minimize highly technical details. Over 600 scientific references were examined in the writing of this book, and each chapter includes a full bibliography so that interested readers may obtain more detail when desired. Readers who desire further in-depth information are encouraged to examine the cited references to educate themselves.

Lyle McDonald

Bio: Lyle McDonald received his B.S. from the University of California at Los Angeles in physiological sciences. He has written for several publications, including two web magazines (Cyberpump and Mesomorphosis), two print magazines (Hardgainer and Peak Training Journal), and two newsletters (Dave's PowerStore Newsletter and Dirty Dieting).

Foreword

<u>REGULATION OF KETOGENESIS</u>
(Sung to the tune of "Clementine")

In starvation, diabetes, sugar levels under strain
You need fuel to keep going saving glucose for your brain
Ketone bodies, Ketone bodies, both acetoacetate
And its partner on reduction, 3-hydroxybutyrate.

Glucagon's up, with low glucose, insulin is down in phase
Fatty acids mobilised by hormone-sensitive lipase
Ketone bodies, Ketone bodies, all start thus from white fat cell
Where through lack of glycerol-P, TG making's down as well.

Fatty acyl, CoA level, makes kinase phosphorylate
Acetyl-CoA carboxy-lase to its inactive state
Ketone bodies, Ketone bodies, because glucagon they say
Also blocks carboxylation, lowers Malonyl-CoA.

Malonyl-CoAs a blocker of the key CPT-1
Blocking's off so now the shuttle into mito's is begun
Now we've ß oxidation, now we've acetyl-CoA
But what's to stop it's oxidation via good old TCA?

In starvation, glucose making, stimulating PEP CK
Uses oxaloacetic, also lost another way
Ketone bodies, what is odd is that the oxidation state
Also favours the reduction of OA to make malate.

OA's low now, citrate synthase, thus loses activity
So the flux into the cycle cuts off (temporarily)
Ketone bodies, Ketone bodies situation thus is this
Acetyl-CoA's now pouring into Ketogenesis.

It's a tricky little pathway, it's got HMG-CoA
In effect it's condensation in a head-to-tailish way
Ketone bodies, Ketone bodies, note the ratio of the pair
Is controlled by NAD to NADH everywhere.

Don't despise them, they're good fuels for your muscles, brain and heart
When you're bodies overloaded though, that's when your troubles start
Ketone bodies, ketone bodies, make acetone, lose CO2
You can breath those out, but watch out - acidosis does for you!

Table of contents

Part I
Introduction

Chapter 1: Introduction to the ketogenic diet
Chapter 2: The history of the ketogenic diet

Prior to discussing the details of the ketogenic diet, it is helpful to discuss some introductory information. This includes a general overview of the ketogenic diet as well as the history of its development, both for medical conditions as well as for fat loss.

Chapter 1:
Introduction to the ketogenic diet

Many readers may not be familiar with the ketogenic diet. This chapter discusses some general ideas about ketogenic diets, as well as defining terms that may be helpful.

In the most general terms, a ketogenic diet is any diet that causes ketone bodies to be produced by the liver, shifting the body's metabolism away from glucose and towards fat utilization. More specifically, a ketogenic diet is one that restricts carbohydrates below a certain level (generally 100 grams per day), inducing a series of adaptations to take place. Protein and fat intake are variable, depending on the goal of the dieter. However, the ultimate determinant of whether a diet is ketogenic or not is the presence (or absence) of carbohydrates.

Fuel metabolism and the ketogenic diet

Under 'normal' dietary conditions, the body runs on a mix of carbohydrates, protein and fat. When carbohydrates are removed from the diet, the body's small stores are quickly depleted. Consequently, the body is forced to find an alternative fuel to provide energy. One of these fuels is free fatty acids (FFA), which can be used by most tissues in the body. However, not all organs can use FFA. For example, the brain and nervous system are unable to use FFA for fuel ; however, they can use ketone bodies.

Ketone bodies are a by-product of the incomplete breakdown of FFA in the liver. They serve as a non-carbohydrate, fat-derived fuel for tissues such as the brain. When ketone bodies are produced at accelerated rates, they accumulate in the bloodstream, causing a metabolic state called ketosis to develop. Simultaneously, there is a decrease in glucose utilization and production. Along with this, there is a decrease in the breakdown of protein to be used for energy, referred to as 'protein sparing'. Many individuals are drawn to ketogenic diets in an attempt to lose bodyfat while sparing the loss of lean body mass.

Hormones and the ketogenic diet

Ketogenic diets cause the adaptations described above primarily by affecting the levels of two hormones: insulin and glucagon. Insulin is a storage hormone, responsible for moving nutrients out of the bloodstream and into target tissues. For example, insulin causes glucose to be stored in muscle as glycogen, and FFA to be stored in adipose tissue as triglycerides. Glucagon is a fuel-mobilizing hormone, stimulating the body to break down stored glycogen, especially in the liver, to provide glucose for the body.

When carbohydrates are removed from the diet, insulin levels decrease and glucagon levels increase. This causes an increase in FFA release from fat cells, and increased FFA burning in the liver. The accelerated FFA burning in the liver is what ultimately leads to the production of ketone bodies and the metabolic state of ketosis. In addition to insulin and glucagon, a number of other hormones are also affected, all of which help to shift fuel use away from carbohydrates and towards fat.

Exercise and the ketogenic diet

As with any fat-loss diet, exercise will improve the success of the ketogenic diet. However, a diet devoid of carbohydrates is unable to sustain high-intensity exercise performance although low-intensity exercise may be performed. For this reason, individuals who wish to use a ketogenic diet and perform high-intensity exercise must integrate carbohydrates without disrupting the effects of ketosis.

Two modified ketogenic diets are described in this book which approach this issue from different directions. The targeted ketogenic diet (TKD) allows carbohydrates to be consumed immediately around exercise, to sustain performance without affecting ketosis. The cyclical ketogenic diet (CKD) alternates periods of ketogenic dieting with periods of high-carbohydrate consumption. The period of high-carbohydrate eating refills muscle glycogen to sustain exercise performance.

Chapter 2:
History of the Ketogenic Diet

Before discussing the theory and metabolic effects of the ketogenic diet, it is useful to briefly review the history of the ketogenic diet and how it has evolved. There are two primary paths (and numerous sub-paths) that the ketogenic diet has followed since its inception: treatment of epilepsy and the treatment of obesity.

Fasting

Without discussing the technical details here, it should be understood that fasting (the complete abstinence of food) and ketogenic diets are metabolically very similar. The similarities between the two metabolic states (sometimes referred to as 'starvation ketosis' and 'dietary ketosis' respectively) have in part led to the development of the ketogenic diet over the years. The ketogenic diet attempts to mimic the metabolic effects of fasting while food is being consumed.

Epilepsy (compiled from references 1-5)

The ketogenic diet has been used to treat a variety of clinical conditions, the most well known of which is childhood epilepsy. Writings as early as the middle ages discuss the use of fasting as a treatment for seizures. The early 1900's saw the use of total fasting as a treatment for seizures in children. However, fasting cannot be sustained indefinitely and only controls seizures as long as the fast is continued.

Due to the problems with extended fasting, early nutrition researchers looked for a way to mimic starvation ketosis, while allowing food consumption. Research determined that a diet high in fat, low in carbohydrate and providing the minimal protein needed to sustain growth could maintain starvation ketosis for long periods of time. This led to development of the original ketogenic diet for epilepsy in 1921 by Dr. Wilder. Dr. Wilder's ketogenic diet controlled pediatric epilepsy in many cases where drugs and other treatments had failed. The ketogenic diet as developed by Dr. Wilder is essentially identical to the diet being used in 1998 to treat childhood epilepsy.

The ketogenic diet fell into obscurity during the 30's, 40's and 50's as new epilepsy drugs were discovered. The difficulty in administering the diet, especially in the face of easily prescribed drugs, caused it to all but disappear during this time. A few modified ketogenic diets, such as the Medium Chain Triglyceride (MCT) diet, which provided greater food variability were tried but they too fell into obscurity.

In 1994, the ketogenic diet as a treatment for epilepsy was essentially 'rediscovered' in the story of Charlie, a 2-year-old with seizures that could not be controlled with medications or other treatment, including brain surgery. Charlie's father found reference to the ketogenic diet in the literature and decided to seek more information, ending up at Johns Hopkins medical center.

Charlie's seizures were completely controlled as long as he was on the diet. The amazing success of the ketogenic diet where other treatments had failed led Charlie's father to create the Charlie Foundation, which has produced several videos, published the book "The Epilepsy Diet Treatment: An introduction to the ketogenic diet", and has sponsored conferences to train physicians and dietitians to implement the diet. Although the exact mechanisms of how the ketogenic diet works to control epilepsy are still unknown , the diet continues to gain acceptance as an alternative to drug therapy.

Other clinical conditions

Epilepsy is arguably the medical condition that has been treated the most with ketogenic diets (1-3). However, preliminary evidence suggests that the ketogenic diet may have other clinical uses including respiratory failure (6), certain types of pediatric cancer (7-10), and possibly head trauma (11) . Interested readers can examine the studies cited, as this book focuses primarily on the use of the ketogenic diet for fat loss.

Obesity

Ketogenic diets have been used for weight loss for at least a century, making occasional appearances into the dieting mainstream. Complete starvation was studied frequently including the seminal research of Hill, who fasted a subject for 60 days to examine the effects, which was summarized by Cahill (12). The effects of starvation made it initially attractive to treat morbid obesity as rapid weight/fat loss would occur. Other characteristics attributed to ketosis, such as appetite suppression and a sense of well being, made fasting even more attractive for weight loss. Extremely obese subjects have been fasted for periods up to one year given nothing more than water, vitamins and minerals.

The major problem with complete starvation is a large loss of body protein, primarily from muscle tissue. Although protein losses decrease rapidly as starvation continues, up to one half of the total weight lost during a complete fast is muscle and water, a ratio which is unacceptable.

In the early 70's, an alternative approach to starvation was developed, termed the Protein Sparing Modified Fast (PSMF). The PSMF provided high quality protein at levels that would prevent most of the muscle loss without disrupting the purported 'beneficial' effects of starvation ketosis which included appetite suppression and an almost total reliance on bodyfat and ketones to fuel the body. It is still used to treat severe obesity but must be medically supervised (13).

At this time, other researchers were suggesting 'low-carbohydrate' diets as a treatment for obesity based on the simple fact that individuals tended to eat less calories (and hence lose weight/fat) when carbohydrates were restricted to 50 grams per day or less (14,15). There was much debate as to whether ketogenic diets caused weight loss through some peculiarity of metabolism, as suggested by early studies, or simply because people ate less.

The largest increase in public awareness of the ketogenic diet as a fat loss diet was due to "Dr. Atkins Diet Revolution" in the early 1970's (16). With millions of copies sold, it generated extreme interest, both good and bad, in the ketogenic diet. Contrary to the semi-starvation and very low calorie ketogenic diets which had come before it, Dr. Atkins suggested a diet limited only in carbohydrates but with unlimited protein and fat. He promoted it as a lifetime diet which would provide weight loss quickly, easily and without hunger, all while allowing dieters to eat as much as they liked of protein and fat. He offered just enough research to make a convincing argument, but much of the research he cited suffered from methodological flaws.

For a variety of reasons, most likely related to the unsupported (and unsupportable) claims Atkins made, his diet was openly criticized by the American Medical Association and the ketogenic diet fell back into obscurity (17). Additionally, several deaths occurring in dieters following "The Last Chance Diet" - a 300 calorie-per-day liquid protein diet, which bears a superficial resemblance to the PSMF - caused more outcry against ketogenic diets.

From that time, the ketogenic diet (known by this time as the Atkins diet) all but disappeared from the mainstream of American dieting consciousness as a high carbohydrate, lowfat diet became the norm for health, exercise performance and fat loss.

Recently there has been a resurgence in low carbohydrate diets including "Dr. Atkins New Diet Revolution" (18) and "Protein Power" by the Eades (19) but these diets are aimed primarily at the typical American dieter, not athletes.

Ketogenic diets and bodybuilders/athletes

Low carbohydrate diets were used quite often in the early years of bodybuilding (the fish and water diet). As with general fat loss, the use of low carbohydrate, ketogenic diets by athletes fell into disfavor as the emphasis shifted to carbohydrate based diets.

As ketogenic diets have reentered the diet arena in the 1990's, modified ketogenic diets have been introduced for athletes, primarily bodybuilders. These include so-called cyclical ketogenic diets (CKD's) such as "The Anabolic Diet" (20) and "Bodyopus" (21).

During the 1980's, Michael Zumpano and Daniel Duchaine introduced two of the earliest CKD's: 'The Rebound Diet' for muscle gain, and then a modified version called 'The Ultimate Diet' for fat loss. Neither gained much acceptance in the bodybuilding subculture. This was most likely due to difficulty in implementing the diets and the fact that a diet high in fat went against everything nutritionists advocated.

In the early 1990's, Dr. Mauro DiPasquale, a renowned expert on drug use in sports, introduced "The Anabolic Diet" (AD). This diet alternated periods of 5-6 days of low carbohydrate, moderate protein, moderate/high fat eating with periods of 1-2 days of unlimited carbohydrate consumption (20). The major premise of the Anabolic Diet was that the lowcarb week would cause a 'metabolic shift' to occur, forcing the body to use fat for fuel. The high carb consumption on the weekends would refill muscle carbohydrate stores and cause growth. The carb-loading phase was necessary as ketogenic diets can not sustain high intensity exercise such as weight training.

DiPasquale argued that his diet was both anti-catabolic (preventing muscle breakdown) as well as overtly anabolic (muscle building). His book suffered from a lack of appropriate references (using animal studies when human studies were available) and drawing incorrect conclusions. As well, his book left bodybuilders with more questions than it provided answers.

A few years later, bodybuilding expert Dan Duchaine released the book "Underground Bodyopus: Militant Weight Loss and Recomposition" (21). Bodyopus addressed numerous topics related to fat loss, presenting three different diets. This included his approach to the CKD, which he called BODYOPUS. BODYOPUS was far more detailed than the Anabolic Diet, giving specific food recommendations in terms of both quality and quantity. As well, it gave basic workout recommendations and went into more detail regarding the physiology of the diet.

However, "Bodyopus" left many questions unanswered as evidenced by the numerous questions appearing in magazines and on the internet. While Duchaine's ideas were accepted to a limited degree by the bodybuilding subculture, the lack of scientific references led health professionals, who still thought of ketogenic diets as dangerous and unhealthy, to question the diet's credibility.

A question

Somewhat difficult to understand is why ketogenic diets have been readily accepted as medical treatment for certain conditions but are so equally decried when mentioned for fat loss. Most of the criticisms of ketogenic diets for fat loss revolve around the purported negative health effects (i.e. kidney damage) or misconceptions about ketogenic metabolism (i.e. ketones are made out of protein).

This begs the question of why a diet presumed so dangerous for fat loss is being used clinically without problem. Pediatric epilepsy patients are routinely kept in deep ketosis for periods up to 3 years, and occasionally longer, with few ill effects (3,5). Yet the mention of a brief stint on a ketogenic diet for fat loss and many people will comment about kidney and liver damage, ketoacidosis, muscle loss, etc. If these side effects occurred due to a ketogenic diet, we would expect to see them in epileptic children.

It's arguable that possible negative effects of a ketogenic diet are more than outweighed by the beneficial effects of treating a disease or that children adapt to a ketogenic diet differently than adults. Even then, most of the side effects attributed to ketogenic diets for fat loss are not seen when the diet is used clinically. The side effects in epileptic children are few in number and easily treated, as addressed in chapter 7.

References cited

1. "The Epilepsy Diet Treatment: An introduction to the ketogenic diet" John M. Freeman, MD ; Millicent T. Kelly, RD, LD ; Jennifer B. Freeman. New York: Demos Vermande, 1996.
2. Berryman MS. The ketogenic diet revisited. J Am Diet Assoc (1997) 97: S192-S194.
3. Wheless JW. The ketogenic diet: Fa(c)t or fiction. J Child Neurol (1995) 10: 419-423 .
4. Withrow CD. The ketogenic diet: mechanism of anticonvulsant action. Adv Neurol (1980) 27: 635-642.
5. Swink TD, et. al. The ketogenic diet: 1997. Adv Pediatr (1997) 44: 297-329.
6. Kwan RMF et. al. Effects of a low carbohydrate isoenergetic diet on sleep behavior and pulmonary functions in healthy female adult humans. J Nutr (1986) 116: 2393-2402.

7. Nebeling LC. et. al. Effects of a ketogenic diet on tumor metabolism and nutritional status in pediatric oncology patients: two case reports. J Am Coll Nutr (1995) 14: 202-208.

8. Nebeling LC and Lerner E. Implementing a ketogenic diet based on medium-chain triglyceride oil in pediatric patients with cancer. J Am Diet Assoc (1995) 95: 693-697.

9. Fearon KC, et. al. Cancer cachexia: influence of systemic ketosis on substrate levels and nitrogen metabolism. Am J Clin Nutr (1988) 47:42-48.

10. Conyers RAJ, et. al. Cancer, ketosis and parenteral nutrition. Med J Aust (1979) 1:398-399.

11. Ritter AM. Evaluation of a carbohydrate-free diet for patients with severe head injury. J Neurotrauma (1996) 13:473-485.

12. Cahill GF and Aoki T.T. How metabolism affects clinical problems. Medical Times (1970) 98: 106-122.

13. Walters JK, et. al. The protein-sparing modified fast for obesity-related medical problems. Cleveland Clinical J Med (1997) 64: 242-243.

14. Yudkin J and Carey M. The treatment of obesity by a 'high-fat' diet - the inevitability of calories. Lancet (1960) 939-941.

15. Yudkin J. The low-carbohydrate diet in the treatment of obesity. Postgrad Med (1972) 51: 151-154.

16. "Dr. Atkins' Diet Revolution" Robert Atkins, MD. New York: David McKay Inc. Publishers, 1972.

17. Council on Foods and Nutrition A critique of low-carbohydrate ketogenic weight reducing regimes. JAMA (1973) 224: 1415-1419.

18. "Dr. Atkins' New diet Revolution" Robert Atkins, MD. New York: Avon Publishers, 1992.

19. "Protein Power" Michael R. Eades, MD and Mary Dan Eades, MD. New York: Bantam Books, 1996.

20. "The Anabolic Diet" Mauro DiPasquale, MD. Optimum Training Systems, 1995.

21. "BODYOPUS: Militant fat loss and body recomposition" Dan Duchaine. Nevada: Xipe Press, 1996.

Part II:
The Physiology of Ketosis

Chapter 3: Fuel utilization
Chapter 4: Basic ketone physiology
Chapter 5: Adaptations to ketosis
Chapter 6: Changes in body composition
Chapter 7: Other effects of the ketogenic diet

To address the physiology behind the ketogenic diet, a number of topics must be discussed. Chapter 3 discusses the utilization of various fuels: glucose, protein, fat, ketones. Although not specific to the ketogenic diet, this provides the background to understand the following chapters.

Chapters 4 and 5 address the topics of ketone bodies, ketogenesis, as well as the adaptations which are seen during the ketogenic diet. These two chapters are among the most technical in the book but are critical to understanding the basis for the ketogenic diet. Many of the adaptations seen are well-established, others less so. To avoid turning this into an undergraduate level biochemistry discussion, many of the smaller details have been omitted. Interested readers are encouraged to examine the references cited, especially the recent review papers.

Chapter 6 addresses the question of whether a ketogenic diet causes greater, weight, water, fat, and protein losses compared to a more traditional fat loss diet. Finally, chapter 7 addresses the other metabolic effects which occur during ketosis.

A note on nomenclature: Strictly speaking, the term 'ketone' refers to a general class of chemical compounds. However, the only three ketone bodies we are concerned with are acetoacetate (AcAc), beta-hydroxybutyrate (BHB) and acetone. To avoid confusion, and since we are only concerned with these three specific ketone bodies, the terms ketone bodies and ketone(s) are used interchangeably.

Chapter 3:
The basics of fuel utilization

Although this chapter does not discuss the ketogenic diet in great detail, the information presented is helpful in understanding the following chapters. There are four primary fuels which can be used in the human body: glucose, protein, free fatty acids, and ketones. These fuels are stored in varying proportions in the body. Overall, the primary form of stored fuel is triglyceride, stored in adipose tissue. Glucose and protein make up secondary sources. These fuels are used in varying proportions depending on the metabolic state of the body.

The primary determinant of fuel utilization in humans is carbohydrate availability, which affects hormone levels. Additional factors affecting fuel utilization are the status of liver glycogen (full or empty) as well as the levels of certain enzymes.

Section 1: Bodily Fuel Stores

The body has three storage depots of fuel which it can tap during periods of caloric deficiency: protein, which can be converted to glucose in the liver and used for energy ; carbohydrate, which is stored primarily as glycogen in the muscle and liver ; and fat , which is stored primarily as body fat. A fourth potential fuel is ketones. Under normal dietary conditions, ketones play a non-existent role in energy production. In fasting or a ketogenic diet, ketones play a larger role in energy production, especially in the brain. A comparison of the various fuels available to the body appear in table 1.

Table 1: Comparison of bodily fuels in a 150 lb man with 22% bodyfat		
Tissue	Average weight (lbs)	Caloric worth (kcal)
Adipose tissue triglyceride	33	135,000
Muscle protein	13	24,000
Carbohydrate stores		
Muscle glycogen (normal)	00.25	480
Liver glycogen	00.5	280
Blood glucose	00.04	80
Total carbohydrate stores	00.8	840

Source: "Textbook of Biochemistry with Clinical Correlations 4th ed." Ed. Thomas M. Devlin. Wiley-Liss, 1997.

The main point to take from this chart is that carbohydrate stores are minimal in comparison to protein and fat, sufficient to sustain roughly one day's worth of energy. Although stored protein could conceivably fuel the body for far longer than carbohydrate, excessive protein losses will eventually cause death. This leaves adipose tissue as the primary depot for long term energy storage (2). The average person has enough energy stored as bodyfat to exist for weeks or months without food intake and obese individuals have been fasted for periods of up to one year.

Section 2: Relationships in fuel use

Looking at table 1, it appears that there are least 4 distinct fuels which the body can use: glucose, protein, free fatty acids (FFA), and ketones. However when we look at the relationships between these four fuels, we see that only glucose and FFA need to be considered.

The difference in the proportion of each fuel used will depend on the metabolic state of the body (i.e. aerobic exercise, weight training, normal diet, ketogenic diet/fasting). Exercise metabolism is addressed in later chapters and we are only concerned here with the effects of dietary changes on fuel utilization.

In general, tissues of the body will use a given fuel in proportion to its concentration in the bloodstream. So if a given fuel (i.e. glucose) increases in the bloodstream, the body will utilize that fuel in preference to others. By the same token, if the concentrations of a given fuel decrease in the bloodstream, the body will use less of that fuel. By decreasing carbohydrate availability, the ketogenic diet shifts the body to using fat as its primary fuel.

Glucose and protein use

When present in sufficient quantities, glucose is the preferred fuel for most tissues in the body. The major exception to this is the heart, which uses a mix of glucose, FFA and ketones.

The major source of glucose in the body is from dietary carbohydrate. However, other substances can be converted to glucose in the liver and kidney through a process called gluconeogenesis ('gluco' = glucose, 'neo' = new, 'genesis' = the making). This includes certain amino acids, especially alanine and glutamine.

With normal glucose availability, there is little gluconeogenesis from the body's protein stores. This has led many to state that carbohydrate has a 'protein sparing' effect in that it prevents the breakdown of protein to make glucose. While it is true that a high carbohydrate intake can be protein sparing, it is often ignored that this same high carbohydrate also decreases the use of fat for fuel. Thus in addition to being 'protein sparing', carbohydrate is also 'fat sparing' (3).

If glucose requirements are high but glucose availability is low, as in the initial days of fasting, the body will break down its own protein stores to produce glucose. This is probably the origin of the concept that low carbohydrate diets are muscle wasting. As discussed in the next chapter, an adequate protein intake during the first weeks of a ketogenic diet will prevent muscle loss by supplying the amino acids for gluconeogenesis that would otherwise come from body proteins.

By extension, under conditions of low glucose availability, if glucose requirements go down due to increases in alternative fuels such as FFA and ketones, the need for gluconeogenesis from protein will also decrease. The circumstances under which this occurs are discussed below.

Since protein breakdown is intimately related to glucose requirements and availability, we can effectively consider these two fuels together. Arguably the major adaptation to the ketogenic diet is a decrease in glucose use by the body, which exerts a protein sparing effect (2). This is discussed in greater detail in chapter 5.

Free Fatty Acids (FFA) and ketones

Most tissues of the body can use FFA for fuel if it is available. This includes skeletal muscle, the heart, and most organs. However, there are other tissues such as the brain, red blood cells, the renal medulla, bone marrow and Type II muscle fibers which cannot use FFA and require glucose (2).

The fact that the brain is incapable of using FFA for fuel has led to one of the biggest misconceptions about human physiology: that the brain can only use glucose for fuel. While it is true that the brain normally runs on glucose, the brain will readily use ketones for fuel if they are available (4-6).

Arguably the most important tissue in terms of ketone utilization is the brain which can derive up to 75% of its total energy requirements from ketones after adaptation (4-6). In all likelihood, ketones exist primarily to provide a fat-derived fuel for the brain during periods when carbohydrates are unavailable (2,7).

As with glucose and FFA, the utilization of ketones is related to their availability (7). Under normal dietary conditions, ketone concentrations are so low that ketones provide a negligible amount of energy to the tissues of the body (5,8). If ketone concentrations increase, most tissues in the body will begin to derive some portion of their energy requirements from ketones (9). Some research also suggests that ketones are the preferred fuel of many tissues (9). One exception is the liver which does not use ketones for fuel, relying instead on FFA (7,10,11).

By the third day of ketosis, all of the non-protein fuel is derived from the oxidation of FFA and ketones (12,13). As ketosis develops, most tissues which can use ketones for fuel will stop using them to a significant degree by the third week (7,9). This decrease in ketone utilization occurs due to a down regulation of the enzymes responsible for ketone use and occurs in all tissues except the brain (7). After three weeks, most tissues will meet their energy requirements almost exclusively through the breakdown of FFA (9). This is thought to be an adaptation to ensure adequate ketone levels for the brain.

Except in the case of Type I diabetes, ketones will only be present in the bloodstream under conditions where FFA use by the body has increased. For all practical purposes we can assume that a large increase in FFA use is accompanied by an increase in ketone utilization and these two fuels can be considered together.

Relationships between carbohydrates and fat

Excess dietary carbohydrates can be converted to fat in the liver through a process called de novo lipognesis (DNL). However short term studies show that DNL does not contribute significantly to fat gain in humans. As long as muscle and liver glycogen stores are not completely filled, the body is able to store or burn off excess dietary carbohydrates. Of course this process occurs at the expense of limiting fat burning, meaning that any dietary fat which is ingested with a high carbohydrate intake is stored as fat.

Under certain circumstances, excess dietary carbohydrate can go through DNL, and be stored in fat cells although the contribution to fat gain is thought to be minimal (14). Those circumstances occur when muscle and liver glycogen levels are filled and there is an excess of carbohydrate being consumed.

The most likely scenario in which this would occur would be one in which an individual was inactive and consuming an excess of carbohydrates/calories in their diet. As well, the combination of inactivity with a very high carbohydrate AND high fat diet is much worse in terms of fat gain. With chronically overfilled glycogen stores and a high carbohydrate intake, fat utilization is almost completely blocked and any dietary fat consumed is stored.

This has led some authors to suggest an absolute minimization of dietary fat for weight loss (15,16). The premise is that, since incoming carbohydrate will block fat burning by the body, less fat must be eaten to avoid storage. The ketogenic diet approaches this problem from the opposite direction. By reducing carbohydrate intake to minimum levels, fat utilization by the body is maximized.

Summary

From the above discussion, we can represent the body's overall use of fuel as:

Total energy requirements = glucose + FFA

Therefore if energy requirements stay the same, a decrease in the use of glucose will increase the use of FFA for fuel. By corollary, an increase in the body's ability to use FFA for fuel will decrease the need for glucose by the body. This relationship between glucose and FFA was termed the glucose-FFA Cycle by Randle almost 30 years ago (17,18).

Section 3: Factors influencing fuel utilization

There are several factors which affect the mix of fuels used by the body. The primary factor is the amount of each nutrient (protein, carbohydrate, fat and alcohol) being consumed and this impacts on the other three factors (16). The second determinant is the levels of hormones such as insulin and glucagon, which are directly related to the mix of foods being consumed. Third is the bodily stores of each nutrient including fat stores and muscle/liver glycogen. Finally the levels of regulatory enzymes for glucose and fat breakdown, which are beyond our control except through changes in diet and activity, determine the overall use of each fuel. Each of these factors are discussed in detail below.

Quantity of nutrients consumed

There are four substances which man can derive calories from: carbohydrate, protein, fats, and alcohol. As stated above, the body will tend to utilize a given fuel for energy in relation to its availability and concentration in the bloodstream.

In general, the body can increase or decrease its use of glucose in direct proportion to the amount of dietary carbohydrate being consumed. This is an attempt to maintain body glycogen stores at a certain level (19). If carbohydrate consumption increases, carbohydrate use will go up and vice versa.

Protein is slightly less regulated (16). When protein intake goes up, protein oxidation will also go up to some degree. By the same token, if protein intake drops, the body will use less protein for fuel. This is an attempt to maintain body protein stores at constant levels.

In contrast, the amount of dietary fat being eaten does not significantly increase the amount of fat used for fuel by the body. Rather fat oxidation is determined indirectly: by alcohol and carbohydrate consumption (15).

The consumption of alcohol will almost completely impair the body's use of fat for fuel. Similarly the consumption of carbohydrate affects the amount of fat used by the body for fuel. A high carbohydrate diet decreases the use of fat for fuel and vice versa (15). Thus, the greatest rates of fat oxidation will occur under conditions when carbohydrates are restricted. As well, the level of muscle glycogen regulates how much fat is used by the muscle (20,21), a topic discussed in chapter 18. Using exercise and/or carbohydrate restriction to lower muscle and liver glycogen levels increases fat utilization (22).

Hormone levels

There are a host of regulatory hormones which determine fuel use in the human body. The primary hormone is insulin and its levels, to a great degree, determine the levels of other hormones and the overall metabolism of the body (2,16,23). A brief examination of the major hormones involved in fuel use appears below.

Insulin is a peptide (protein based) hormone released from the pancreas, primarily in response to increases in blood glucose. When blood glucose increases, insulin levels increase as well, causing glucose in the bloodstream to be stored as glycogen in the muscle or liver. Excess glucose can be pushed into fat cells for storage (as alpha-glycerophosphate). Protein synthesis is stimulated and free amino acids (the building blocks of proteins) are be moved into muscle cells and incorporated into larger proteins. Fat synthesis (called lipogenesis) and fat storage are both stimulated. FFA release from fat cells is inhibited by even small amounts of insulin.

The primary role of insulin is to keep blood glucose in the fairly narrow range of roughly 80-120 mg/dl. When blood glucose increases outside of this range, insulin is released to lower blood glucose back to normal. The greatest increase in blood glucose levels (and the greatest increase in insulin) occurs from the consumption of dietary carbohydrates. Protein causes a smaller increase in insulin output because some individual amino acids can be converted to glucose. FFA can stimulate insulin release as can high concentrations of ketone bodies although to a much lesser degree than carbohydrate or protein. This is discussed in chapter 4.

When blood glucose drops (during exercise or with carbohydrate restriction), insulin levels generally drop as well. When insulin drops and other hormones such as glucagon increase, the body will break down stored fuels. Triglyceride stored in fat cells is broken down into FFA and glycerol and released into the bloodstream. Proteins may be broken down into individual amino acids and used to produce glucose. Glycogen stored in the liver is broken down into glucose and released into the bloodstream (2). These substances can then be used for fuel in the body.

An inability to produce insulin indicates a pathological state called Type I diabetes (or Insulin Dependent Diabetes Mellitus, IDDM). Type I diabetics suffer from a defect in the pancreas leaving them completely without the ability to make or release insulin. IDDM diabetics must inject themselves with insulin to maintain blood glucose within normal levels. This will become important when the distinction between diabetic ketoacidosis and dietary induced ketosis is made in the next chapter.

Glucagon is essentially insulin's mirror hormone and has essentially opposite effects. Like insulin, glucagon is also a peptide hormone released from the pancreas and its primary role is also to maintain blood glucose levels. However, glucagon acts by raising blood glucose when it drops below normal.

Glucagon's main action is in the liver, stimulating the breakdown of liver glycogen which is then released into the bloodstream. Glucagon release is stimulated by a variety of stimuli including a drop in blood glucose/insulin, exercise, and the consumption of a protein meal (24). High levels of insulin inhibit the pancreas from releasing glucagon.

Under normal conditions, glucagon has very little effect in tissues other than the liver (i.e. fat and muscle cells). However, when insulin is very low, as occurs with carbohydrate restriction and exercise, glucagon plays a minor role in muscle glycogen breakdown as well as fat mobilization. In addition to its primary role in maintaining blood glucose under conditions of low blood sugar, glucagon also plays a pivotal role in ketone body formation in the liver, discussed in detail in the next chapter.

From the above descriptions, it should be clear that insulin and glucagon play antagonistic roles to one another. Whereas insulin is primarily a storage hormone, increasing storage of glucose, protein and fat in the body ; glucagon's primary role is to mobilize those same fuel stores for use by the body.

As a general rule, when insulin is high, glucagon levels are low. By the same token, if insulin levels decrease, glucagon will increase. The majority of the literature (especially as it pertains to ketone body formation) emphasizes the ratio of insulin to glucagon, called the insulin/glucagon ratio (I/G ratio), rather than absolute levels of either hormone. This ratio is an important factor in the discussion of ketogenesis in the next chapter. While insulin and glucagon play the major roles in determining the anabolic or catabolic state of the body, there are several other hormones which play additional roles. They are briefly discussed here.

Growth hormone (GH) is another peptide hormone which has numerous effects on the body, both on tissue growth as well as fuel mobilization. GH is released in response to a variety of stressors the most important of which for our purposes are exercise, a decrease in blood glucose, and carbohydrate restriction or fasting. As its name suggests, GH is a growth promoting hormone, increasing protein synthesis in the muscle and liver. GH also tends to mobilize FFA from fat cells for energy.

In all likelihood, most of the anabolic actions of GH are mediated through a class of hormones called somatomedins, also called insulin-like growth factors (IGFs). The primary IGF in the human body is insulin like growth factor-1 (IGF-1) which has anabolic effects on most tissues of the body. GH stimulates the liver to produce IGF-1 but only in the presence of insulin.

High GH levels along with high insulin levels (as would be seen with a protein and carbohydrate containing meal) will raise IGF-1 levels as well as increasing anabolic reactions in the body. To the contrary, high GH levels with low levels of insulin, as seen in fasting or carbohydrate restriction, will not cause an increase in IGF-1 levels. This is one of the reasons that ketogenic diets are not ideal for situations requiring tissue synthesis, such as muscle growth or recovery from certain injuries: the lack of insulin may compromise IGF-1 levels as well as affecting protein synthesis.

There are two thyroid hormones, thyroxine (T4) and triiodothyronine (T3). Both are released from the thyroid gland in the ratio of about 80% T4 and 20% T3. In the human body, T4 is primarily a storage form of T3 and plays few physiological roles itself. The majority of T3 is not released from the thyroid gland but rather is converted from T4 in other tissues, primarily the liver. Although thyroid hormones affect all tissues of the body, we are primarily concerned with the effects of thyroid on metabolic rate and protein synthesis. The effects of low-carbohydrate diets on levels of thyroid hormones as well as their actions are discussed in chapter 5.

Cortisol is a catabolic hormone released from the adrenal cortex and is involved in many reactions in the body, most related to fuel utilization. Cortisol is involved in the breakdown of protein to glucose as well as being involved in fat breakdown.

Although cortisol is absolutely required for life, an excess of cortisol (caused by stress and other factors) is detrimental in the long term, causing a continuous drain on body proteins including muscle, bone, connective tissue and skin. Cortisol tends to play a permissive effect in its actions, allowing other hormones to work more effectively.

Adrenaline and noradrenaline (also called epinephrine and norepinephrine) are frequently referred to as 'fight or flight' hormones. They are generally released in response to stress such as exercise, cold, or fasting. Epinephrine is released primarily from the adrenal medulla, traveling in the bloodstream to exert its effects on most tissues in the body. Norepinephrine is released primarily from the nerve terminals, exerting its effects only on specific tissues of the body.

The interactions of the catecholamines on the various tissues of the body are quite complex and beyond the scope of this book. The primary role that the catecholamines have in terms of the ketogenic diet is to stimulate free fatty acid release from fat cells.

When insulin levels are low, epinephrine and norepinephrine are both involved in fat mobilization. In humans, only insulin and the catecholamines have any real effect on fat mobilization with insulin inhibiting fat breakdown and the catecholamines stimulating fat breakdown.

Liver glycogen

The liver is one of the most metabolically active organs in the entire body. All foods coming through the digestive tract are processed initially in the liver. To a great degree, the level of liver glycogen is the key determinant of the body's overall trend to store or breakdown nutrients (25). Additionally, high levels of liver glycogen tends to be associated with higher bodyfat levels (19).

The liver is basically a short term storehouse for glycogen which is used to maintain blood glucose. The breakdown of liver glycogen to glucose, to be released into the bloodstream, is stimulated by an increase in glucagon as discussed previously.

When liver glycogen is full, blood glucose is maintained and the body is generally anabolic, which means that incoming glucose, amino acids and free fatty acids are stored as glycogen, proteins, and triglycerides respectively. This is sometimes called the 'fed' state (1).

When liver glycogen becomes depleted, via intensive exercise or the absence of dietary carbohydrates, the liver shifts roles and becomes catabolic. Glycogen is broken into glucose, proteins are broken down into amino acids, and triglycerides are broken down to free fatty acids. This is sometimes called the 'fasted' state (1).

If liver glycogen is depleted sufficiently, blood glucose drops and the shift in insulin and glucagon occurs. This induces ketone body formation, called ketogenesis, and is discussed in the next chapter.

Enzyme levels

The final regulator of fuel use in the body is enzyme activity. Ultimately enzyme levels are determined by the nutrients being ingested in the diet and the hormonal levels which result.

For example, when carbohydrates are consumed and insulin is high, the enzymes involved in glucose use and glycogen storage are stimulated and the enzymes involved in fat breakdown are inhibited. By the same token, if insulin drops the enzymes involved in glucose use are inhibited and the enzymes involved in fat breakdown will increase.

Long term adaptation to a high carbohydrate or low carbohydrate diet can cause longer term changes in the enzymes involved in fat and carbohydrate use as well. If an individual consumes no carbohydrates for several weeks, there is a down regulation of enzymes in the liver and muscle which store and burn carbohydrates (1,17,18). The end result of this is an inability to use carbohydrates for fuel for a short period of time after they are reintroduced to the diet.

Summary

Although there are four major fuels which the body can use, for our purposes only the interactions between glucose and free fatty acids need to be considered. As a general rule, assuming that the body's total energy requirements stay the same, an increase in glucose use by the body will result in a decrease in the use of fatty acids and vice versa.

There are four major factors that regulate fuel use by the body. Ultimately they are all determined by the intake of dietary carbohydrates. When carbohydrate availability is high, carbohydrate use and storage is high and fat use is low. When carbohydrate availability is low, carbohydrate use and storage is low and fat use is high.

The most basic premise of the ketogenic diet is that the body can be forced to burn greater amounts of fat by decreasing its use of glucose. The adaptations which occur in the body as well as the processes involved are discussed in the next chapter.

References Cited

1. "Textbook of Biochemistry with Clinical Correlations 4th ed." Ed. Thomas M. Devlin. Wiley-Liss, 1997.
2. Cahill G. Starvation in man. N Engl J Med (1970) 282: 668-675
3. "Textbook of Medical Physiology" Arthur C. Guyton. W.B. Saunders Company, 1996.
4. Owen O.E. et. al. Brain metabolism during fasting. J Clin Invest (1967) 10: 1589-1595.
5. Sokoloff L. Metabolism of ketone bodies by the brain. Ann Rev Med (1973) 24: 271-280.
6. Cahill G. Ketosis. Kidney International (1981) 20: 416-425.
7. Mitchell GA et. al. Medical aspects of ketone body metabolism. Clinical & Investigative Medicine (1995) 18: 193-216.
8. Swink TD et. al. The ketogenic diet: 1997. Adv Pediatr (1997) 44: 297-329.
9. Robinson AM and Williamson DH. Physiological roles of ketone bodies as substrates and signals in mammalian tissues. Physiol Rev (1980) 60: 143-187.
10. Nosadini R. et. al. Ketone body metabolism: A physiological and clinical overview. Diabet/Metab Rev (1989) 5: 299-319.
11. Krebs HA et. al. The role of ketone bodies in caloric homeostasis. Adv Enzym Regul (1971) 9: 387-409.
12. Elia M. et. al. Ketone body metabolism in lean male adults during short-term starvation, with particular reference to forearm muscle metabolism. Clinical Science (1990) 78: 579-584.
13. Owen OE et. al. Protein, fat and carbohydrate requirements during starvation: anaplerosis and cataplerosis. Am J Clin Nutr (1998) 68: 12-34.
14. Hellerstein M. Synthesis of fat in response to alterations in diet: insights from new stable isotope methodologies. Lipids (1996) 31 (suppl) S117-S125.
15. Flatt JP. Use and storage of carbohydrate and fat. Am J Clin Nutr (1995) 61(suppl): 952S-959S.
16. Flatt JP. McCollum Award Lecture, 1995: Diet, lifestyle, and weight maintenance. Am J Clin Nutr (1995) 62: 820-836.
17. Randle PJ. Metabolic fuel selection: general integration at the whole-body level. Proc Nutr Soc (1995) 54: 317-327.
18. Randle PJ et. al. Glucose fatty acid interactions and the regulation of glucose disposal. J Cell Biochem (1994) 55 (suppl): 1-11.
19. Flatt JP. Glycogen levels and obesity. Int J Obes (1996) 20 (suppl): S1-S11.
20. Schrauwen P, et. al. Role of glycogen-lowering exercise in the change of fat oxidation in response to a high-fat diet. Am J Physiol (1997) 273:E623-E629
21. Schrauwen P, et al. Fat balance in obese subjects: role of glycogen stores. Am J Physiol. (1998) 274: E1027-E1033.
22. Flatt JP. Integration of the overall response to exercise. Int J Obes (1995) 19 (suppl): S31-S40.
23. Cahill GF Jr. et. al. Hormone-fuel relationships during fasting. J Clin Invest (1966) 45: 1751-1769
24. Cahill GF. Banting Memorial Lecture 1971: Physiology of insulin in man. Diabetes (1971) 20: 785.
25. Foster D. Banting Lecture 1984 - From Glycogen to Ketones - and Back. Diabetes (1984) 33: 1188-1199.

Chapter 4:
Basic ketone physiology

To understand the adaptations which occur as a result of ketosis, it is necessary to examine the physiology behind the production of ketone bodies in the liver. As well, an examination of what ketone bodies are and what ketosis represents is necessary. Finally, concerns about ketoacidosis as it occurs in diabetics are addressed.

Section 1: Ketone bodies

What are ketone bodies?

The three ketone bodies are acetoacetate (AcAc), beta-hydroxybutyrate (BHB) and acetone. AcAc and BHB are produced from the condensation of acetyl-CoA, a product of incomplete breakdown of free fatty acids (FFA) in the liver. While ketones can technically be made from certain amino acids, this is not thought to contribute significantly to ketosis (1). Roughly one-third of AcAc is converted to acetone, which is excreted in the breath and urine. This gives some individuals on a ketogenic diet a 'fruity' smelling breath.

As a side note, urinary and breath excretion of acetone is negligible in terms of caloric loss, amounting to a maximum of 100 calories per day (2). The fact that ketones are excreted through this pathway has led some authors to argue that fat loss is being accomplished through urination and breathing. While this may be very loosely true, in that ketones are produced from the breakdown of fat and energy is being lost through these routes, the number of calories lost per day will have a minimal effect on fat loss.

Functions of ketones in the body

Ketones serve a number of functions in the body. The primary role, and arguably the most important to ketogenic dieters, is to replace glucose as a fat-derived fuel for the brain (3,4). A commonly held misconception is that the brain can only use glucose for fuel. Quite to the contrary, in situations where glucose availability is limited, the brain can derive up to 75% of its total energy requirements from ketone bodies (3).

Ketones also decrease the production of glucose in the liver (5-7) and some researchers have suggested that ketones act as a 'signal' to bodily tissues to shift fuel use away from glucose and towards fat (6). These effects should be seen as a survival mechanism to spare what little glucose is available to the body. The importance of ketones as a brain fuel are discussed in more detail in the next chapter.

A second function of ketones is as a fuel for most other tissues in the body. By shifting the entire body's metabolism from glucose to fat, what glucose is available is conserved for use by the brain (see chapter 5 for more detail) (6). While many tissues of the body (especially muscle) use a large amount of ketones for fuel during the first few weeks of a ketogenic diet, most of these same tissues will decrease their use of ketones as the length of time in ketosis increases (4). At this time, these tissues rely primarily on the breakdown of free fatty acids (FFA). In practical terms, after three weeks of a ketogenic diet, the use of ketones by tissues other than the brain is negligible and can be ignored.

A potential effect of ketones (discussed further in chapter 5) is to inhibit protein breakdown during starvation through several possible mechanisms, discussed in detail in the next chapter. The only other known function of ketones is as a precursor for lipid synthesis in the brain of neonates (4).

Section 2: Ketogenesis and the two site model

The formation of ketone bodies, called ketogenesis, is at the heart of the ketogenic diet and the processes involved need to be understood. As described in the previous chapter, the primary regulators of ketone body formation are the hormones insulin and glucagon. The shift that occurs in these two hormones, a decrease in insulin and an increase in glucagon is one of the major regulating steps regulating ketogenesis.

A great amount of research has been performed to determine exactly what is involved in ketogenesis. All the research has led to a model involving two sites: the fat cell and the liver. In addition, the enzyme mitochondrial HMG CoA reductase (MHS) has been suggested as a third site of regulation (4,8). For our purposes, MHS and its effects are unimportant so we will focus only on the first two sites of regulation: the fat cell and the liver.

The fat cell

As discussed in the previous chapter, the breakdown of fat in fat cells, is determined primarily by the hormones insulin and the catecholamines. When insulin is high, free fatty acid mobilization is inhibited and fat storage is stimulated through the enzyme lipoprotein lipase (LPL). When insulin decreases, free fatty acids (FFA) are mobilized both due to the absence of insulin as well as the presence of lipolytic (fat mobilizing) hormones such as the catecholamines (9,10). Glucagon, cortisol and growth hormone play additional but minor roles.

Insulin has a much stronger anti-lipolytic effect than the catecholamines have a lipolytic effect. If insulin is high, even though catecholamines are high as well, lipolysis is blocked. It is generally rare to have high levels of both insulin and catecholamines in the body. This is because the stimuli to raise catecholamine levels, such as exercise, tend to lower insulin and vice versa.

Breakdown and transport of Triglyceride (11)

When the proper signal reaches the fat cell, stored triglyceride (TG) is broken down into glycerol and three free fatty acid (FFA) chains. FFA travels through the bloodstream, bound to a protein called albumin. Once in the bloodstream, FFA can be used for energy production by most tissues of the body, with the exception of the brain and a few others.

FFA's not used for energy by other tissues will reach the liver and be oxidized (burned) there. If there is sufficient FFA and the liver is prepared to produce ketone bodies, ketones are produced and released into the bloodstream.

The fat cell should be considered one regulatory site for ketone body formation in that a lack of adequate FFA will prevent ketones from being made in the liver. That is, even if the liver is in a mode to synthesize ketone bodies, a lack of FFA will prevent the development of ketosis.

The liver

The liver is always producing ketones to some small degree and they are always present in the bloodstream. Under normal dietary conditions, ketone concentrations are simply too low to be of any physiological consequence. A ketogenic diet increases the amount of ketones which are produced and the blood concentrations seen. Thus ketones should not be considered a toxic substance or a byproduct of abnormal human metabolism. Rather, ketones are a normal physiological substance that plays many important roles in the human body.

The liver is the second site involved in ketogenesis and arguably the more important of the two. Even in the presence of high FFA levels, if the liver is not in a ketogenic mode, ketones will not be produced.

The major determinant of whether the liver will produce ketone bodies is the amount of liver glycogen present (8). The primary role of liver glycogen is to maintain normal blood glucose levels. When dietary carbohydrates are removed from the diet and blood glucose falls, glucagon signals the liver to break down its glycogen stores to glucose which is released into the bloodstream. After approximately 12-16 hours, depending on activity, liver glycogen is almost completely depleted. At this time, ketogenesis increases rapidly. In fact, after liver glycogen is depleted, the availability of FFA will determine the rate of ketone production. (12)

The Insulin/Glucagon ratio

With the two regulating sites of ketogenesis discussed, we can return to the discussion of insulin and glucagon and their role in establishing ketosis. When carbohydrates are consumed, insulin levels are high and glucagon levels are low. Glycogen storage is stimulated and fat synthesis in the liver will occur. Fat breakdown is inhibited both in the fat cell as well as in the liver (8).

When carbohydrates are removed from the diet, liver glycogen will eventually be emptied as the body tries to maintain blood glucose levels. Blood glucose will drop as liver glycogen is depleted. As blood glucose decreases, insulin will decrease and glucagon will increase. Thus there is an overall decrease in the insulin/glucagon ratio (I/G ratio) (8,14).

As insulin drops, FFA are mobilized from the fat cell, providing adequate substrate for the liver to make ketones. Since liver glycogen is depleted, CPT-1 becomes active, burning the incoming FFA, which produces acetyl-CoA. Acetyl-CoA accumulates as discussed in the section above and is condensed into ketones.

The liver has the capacity to produce from 115 to 180 grams of ketones per day once ketogenesis has been initiated (4,15-17). Additionally, the liver is producing ketones at a maximal rate by the third day of carbohydrate restriction (16). It appears that once the liver has become ketogenic, the rate of ketone body formation is determined solely by the rate of incoming FFA (12). This will have implications for the effects of exercise on levels of ketosis (see chapter 21 for more details). Figure 1 graphically illustrates the 2 site model of ketogenesis.

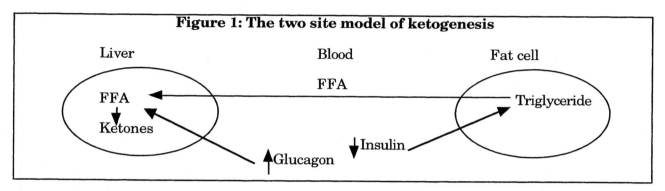

Figure 1: The two site model of ketogenesis

Summary

The production of ketone bodies in the liver requires a depletion of liver glycogen and a subsequent fall in malonyl-CoA concentrations allowing the enzyme carnitine palmityl tranferase I (CPT-1) to become active. CPT-1 is responsible for carrying free fatty acids into the mitochondria to be burned. At the same time CPT-1 is becoming active, a drop in blood glucose causes a decrease in the insulin/glucagon ratio allowing free fatty acids to be mobilized from fat cells to provide the liver with substrate for ketone body formation.

Technical note: Malonyl-CoA and Carnitine Palmityl Transferase-1 (CPT-1)

Rather than liver glycogen per se, the primary regulator of ketogenesis in the liver is a substance called malonyl-CoA (8,13). Malonyl-CoA is an intermediate in fat synthesis which is present in high amounts when liver glycogen is high. When the liver is full of glycogen, fat synthesis (lipogenesis) is high and fat breakdown (lipolysis) is low (8).

Malonyl-CoA levels ultimately determine whether the liver begins producing ketone bodies or not. This occurs because malonyl-CoA inhibits the action of an enzyme called carnitine palmityl tranferase 1 (CPT-1) both in the liver and other tissues such as muscle (8,13).

CPT-1 is responsible for transporting FFA into the mitochondria to be burned. As FFA are burned, a substance called acetyl-CoA is produced. When carbohydrate is available, acetyl-CoA is used to produce more energy in the Krebs cycle. When carbohydrate is not available, acetyl-CoA cannot enter the Krebs cycle and will accumulate in the liver (figure 2).

As Malonyl-CoA levels drop and CPT-1 becomes active, FFA oxidation occurs rapidly causing an increase in the level of acetyl-CoA. As discussed in the next section, when acetyl-

CoA levels increase to high levels, they are condensed into acetoacetic acid which can further be converted to beta-hydroxybutyrate and acetone, the three major ketone bodies.

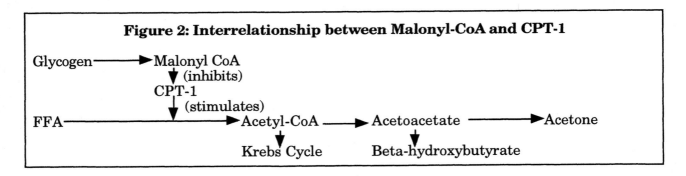

Figure 2: Interrelationship between Malonyl-CoA and CPT-1

Section 3: Ketosis and Ketoacidosis

Having discussed the mechanisms behind ketone body production, we can now examine the metabolic state of ketosis, and what it represents. Additionally, ketosis is contrasted to runaway diabetic ketoacidosis.

What is ketosis?

Ketosis is the end result of a shift in the insulin/glucagon ratio and indicates an overall shift from a glucose based metabolism to a fat based metabolism. Ketosis occurs in a number of physiological states including fasting (called starvation ketosis), the consumption of a high fat diet (called dietary ketosis), and immediately after exercise (called post-exercise ketosis). Two pathological and potentially fatal metabolic states during which ketosis occurs are diabetic ketoacidosis and alcoholic ketoacidosis.

The major difference between starvation, dietary and diabetic/alcoholic ketoacidosis is in the level of ketone concentrations seen in the blood. Starvation and dietary ketosis will normally not progress to dangerous levels, due to various feedback loops which are present in the body (12). Diabetic and alcoholic ketoacidosis are both potentially fatal conditions (12).

All ketotic states ultimately occur for the same reasons. The first is a reduction of the hormone insulin and an increase in the hormone glucagon both of which are dependent on the depletion of liver glycogen. The second is an increase in FFA availability to the liver, either from dietary fat or the release of stored bodyfat.

Under normal conditions, ketone bodies are present in the bloodstream in minute amounts, approximately 0.1 mmol/dl (1,6). When ketone body formation increases in the liver, ketones begin to accumulate in the bloodstream. Ketosis is defined clinically as a ketone concentration above 0.2 mmol/dl (6). Mild ketosis, around 2 mmol, also occurs following aerobic exercise. (4). The impact of exercise on ketosis is discussed in chapter 21.

Ketoacidosis is defined as any ketone concentration above 7 mmol/dl. Diabetic and alcoholic ketoacidosis result in ketone concentrations up to 25 mmol (6). This level of ketosis will never occur in non-diabetic or alcoholic individuals (12). A summary of the different ketone body concentrations appears in table 1.

Table 1: Comparison of ketone concentrations under different conditions

Metabolic state	Ketone body concentration (mmol/dl)
Mixed diet	0.1
Ketosis	0.2
Fasting 2-3 days	1
Post-exercise	Up to 2
Fasting 1 week	5
Ketogenic diet	5-6
Fasting 3-4 weeks	6-8
Ketoacidosis	8+
Diabetic ketoacidosis	Up to 25

Note: Ketone body concentrations are higher in fasting than during a ketogenic diet due to the slight insulin response from eating.

Data is from Mitchell GA et al. Medical aspects of ketone body metabolism. Clinical & Investigative Medicine (1995) 18:193-216 ; and Robinson AM and Williamson DH. Physiological roles of ketone bodies as substrates and signals in mammalian tissues. Physiol Rev (1980) 60: 143-187.

Ketonemia and ketonuria

The general metabolic state of ketosis can be further subdivided into two categories. The first is ketonemia which describes the buildup of ketone bodies in the bloodstream. Technically ketonemia is the true indicator that ketosis has been induced. However the only way to measure the level of ketonemia is with a blood test which is not practical for ketogenic dieters.

The second subdivision is ketonuria which describes the buildup and excretion of ketone bodies in the urine, which occurs due to the accumulation of ketones in the kidney. The excretion of ketones into the urine may represent 10-20% of the total ketones made in the liver (4). However, this may only amount to 10-20 grams of total ketones excreted per day (17). Since ketones have a caloric value of 4.5 calories/gram, (17) the loss of calories through the urine is only 45-90 calories per day.

The degree of ketonuria, which is an indirect indicator of ketonemia, can be measured by the use of Ketostix (tm), small paper strips which react with urinary ketones and change color. Ketonemia will always occur before ketonuria. Ketone concentrations tend to vary throughout the day and are generally lower in the morning, reaching a peak around midnight (6). This may occur from changes in hormone levels throughout the day (18). Additionally, women appear to show deeper ketone levels than men (19,20) and children develop deeper ketosis than do adults (5). Finally, certain supplements, such as N-acetyl-cysteine, a popular anti-oxidant, can falsely indicate ketosis (4).

The distinction between ketonuria and ketonemia is important from a practical standpoint. Some individuals, who have followed all of the guidelines for establishing ketosis will not show urinary ketones. However this does not mean that they are not technically in ketosis. Ketonuria is only an indirect measure of ketone concentrations in the bloodstream and Ketostix (tm) measurements can be inaccurate (see chapter 15 for more details).

What does ketosis represent?

The development of ketosis indicates two things. First, it indicates that the body has shifted from a metabolism relying primarily on carbohydrates for fuel to one using primarily fat and ketones for fuel (4). This is arguably the main goal of the ketogenic diet: to cause an overall metabolic shift to occur in the body. The reasons this shift may be desirable are discussed in the next chapter.

Second, ketosis indicates that the entire pathway of fat breakdown is intact (4). The absence of ketosis under conditions which are known to induce it would indicate that a flaw in fat breakdown exists somewhere in the chain from fat breakdown, to transport, to oxidation in the liver. This absence would indicate a metabolic abnormality requiring further evaluation.

Blood pH and ketoacidosis

A major concern that frequently arises with regards to ketogenic diets is related to the slight acidification caused by the accumulation of ketone bodies in the bloodstream. Normal blood pH is 7.4 and this will drop slightly during the initial stages of ketosis.

While blood pH does temporarily decrease, the body attains normal pH levels within a few days (21) as long as ketone body concentrations do not exceed 7-10 mmol (22). Although blood pH is normalized after a few days, the buffering capacity of the blood is decreased (21), which has implications for exercise as discussed in chapters 18 through 20.

There is frequent confusion between the dietary ketosis seen during a ketogenic diet and the pathological and potentially fatal state of diabetic ketoacidosis (DKA). DKA occurs only in Type I diabetes, a disease characterized by a defect in the pancreas, whereby insulin cannot be produced. Type I diabetics must take insulin injections to maintain normal blood glucose levels. In diabetics who are without insulin for some time, a state that is similar to dietary ketosis begins to develop but with several differences.

Although both dietary ketosis and DKA are characterized by a low insulin/glucagon ratio, a non-diabetic individual will only develop ketosis with low blood glucose (below 80 mg/dl) while a Type I diabetic will develop ketosis with extremely high blood glucose levels (Type I diabetics may have blood glucose levels of 300 mg/dl or more) (12).

Additionally, the complete lack of insulin in Type I diabetics appears to further increase ketone body formation in these individuals. While a non-diabetic individual may produce 115-180 grams of ketones per day (4,16), Type I diabetics have been found to produce up to 400 grams of ketones per day (22,23). The drop in blood pH seen in DKA is probably related to the overproduction of ketones under these circumstances (12).

This increase in ketone formation is coupled with an inability in the Type I diabetic to use ketones in body tissues (12). Presumably this occurs because blood glucose is present in adequate amounts making glucose the preferred fuel. Thus there is a situation where ketone body formation is high but ketone body utilization by the body is very low, causing a rapid buildup of ketones in the bloodstream.

Additionally, in non-diabetic individuals there are at least two feedback loops to prevent runaway ketoacidosis from occurring. When ketones reach high concentrations in the bloodstream (approximately 4-6 mmol), they stimulate a release of insulin (8,12). This increase in insulin has three major effects (24). First, it slows FFA release from the fat cell. Second, by raising the insulin/glucagon ratio, the rate of ketone body formation in the liver is decreased . Third, it increases the excretion of ketones into the urine. These three effects all serve to lower blood ketone body concentration.

In addition to stimulating insulin release, ketones appear to have an impact directly on the fat cell, slowing FFA release (12,22). This would serve to limit FFA availability to the liver, slowing ketone body formation. Ultimately these two feedback loops prevent the non-diabetic individual from overproducing ketones since high ketone levels decrease ketone body formation.

Type I diabetics lack both of these feedback loops. Their inability to release insulin from the pancreas prevents high ketone body levels from regulating their own production. The clinical treatment for DKA is insulin injection which rapidly shuts down ketone body formation in the liver, slows FFA release from fat cells, and pushes ketones out of the bloodstream (12). Additionally, rehydration and electrolyte supplementation is necessary to correct for the effects of DKA (12).

The feedback loops present in a non-insulin using individual will prevent metabolic ketosis from ever reaching the levels of runaway DKA (12). Table 2 compares the major differences between a normal diet, dietary ketosis and diabetic ketoacidosis.

Table 2: Comparison of Dietary Ketosis and Diabetic Ketoacidosis (DKA)			
	Normal diet	Dietary ketosis	DKA
Blood glucose (mg/dl)	80-120	~ 65-80	300+
Insulin	Moderate	Low	Absent
Glucagon	Low	High	High
Ketones production (g/day)	Low	115-180	400
Ketone concentrations (mmol/dl)	0.1	4-10	20+
Blood pH	7.4	7.4	<7.30

One additional pathological state which is occasionally confused with dietary ketosis is alcoholic ketoacidosis. Alcoholic KA occurs in individuals who have gone without food while drinking heavily (4). Ethanol also has effects on ketone body formation by the liver, causing a runaway ketotic state similar to DKA (25). In contrast to DKA, alcoholic ketoacidosis can be easily reversed by eating carbohydrates as this increases insulin and stops ketone formation (4).

Summary

Ketosis is a metabolic state where ketones and FFA replace glucose as the primary fuel of the body in most tissues. The presence of ketosis indicates that fat breakdown has been activated in the body and that the entire pathway of fat degradation is intact. The lack of ketosis in states such as fasting and a ketogenic diet known to induce ketosis would indicate the presence of a metabolic abnormality.

Ketosis can be delineated into ketonemia, the presence of ketones in the bloodstream, and ketonuria, the presence of ketones in the urine. Clinically, ketosis is defined as a ketone concentration of 0.2 mmol. A ketogenic diet or fasting will result in ketone levels between 4 and 8 mmol. Ketoacidosis is defined as 8 mmol or higher and pathological ketoacidosis, as in diabetic ketoacidosis, can result in ketone concentrations of 20 mmol or greater. Ketoacidosis, as it occurs in Type I diabetics and alcoholics and which is potentially fatal, will not occur in non-diabetic individuals due to built in feedback loops whereby excess ketones stimulate the release of insulin, slowing ketone body formation.

References Cited

1. Nosadini R. et. al. Ketone body metabolism: A physiological and clinical overview. Diabet/Metab Rev (1989) 5: 299-319.
2. Council on Foods and Nutrition. A critique of low-carbohydrate ketogenic weight reducing regimes. JAMA (1973) 224: 1415-1419.
3. Owen OE et. al. Brain metabolism during fasting".J Clin Invest (1967) 10: 1589-1595.
4. Mitchell GA et. al. Medical aspects of ketone body metabolism. Clinical & Investigative Medicine (1995) 18:193-216.
5. Haymond MW et. al. Effects of ketosis on glucose flux in children and adults. Am J Physiol (1983) 245: E373-E378
6. Robinson AM and Williamson DH. Physiological roles of ketone bodies as substrates and signals in mammalian tissues. Physiol Rev (1980) 60: 143-187.
7. Miles JM et. al. Suppression of glucose production and stimulation of insulin secretion by physiological concentrations of ketone bodies in man. J Clin Endocrin Metab (1981) 52: 34-37.
8. Foster D. Banting Lecture 1984 - From Glycogen to Ketones - and Back. Diabetes (1984) 33: 1188-1199.
9. Wolfe RR et. al. Effect of short-term fasting on lipolytic responsiveness in normal and obese human subjects. Am J Physiol (1987) 252: E189-E196.
10. Jenson MD et. al. Lipolysis during fasting: Decreased suppression by insulin and increased stimulation by epinephrine. J Clin Invest (1987) 79: 207-213.
11. "Textbook of Biochemistry with Clinical Correlations 4th ed." Ed. Thomas M. Devlin. Wiley-Liss, 1997.
12. "Ellenberg and Rifkin's Diabetes Mellitus: Theory and Practice 5th ed." Ed. Porte D and Sherwin R. New York: Appleton and Lange, 1997.
13. McGarry JD et. al. Regulation of ketogenesis and the renaissance of carnitine palmitoyltransferase. Diabetes/Metab Rev (1989) 5:271-284.
14. Fery F et. al. Hormonal and metabolic changes induced by an isocaloric isoprotienic ketogenic diet in healthy subjects. Diabete Metab (1982) 8: 299-305.

15. Flatt JP. On the maximal possible rate of ketogenesis. Diabetes (1972) 21: 50-53.
16. Garber A.J. et. al. Hepatic ketogenesis and gluconeogenesis in humans. J Clin Invest (1974) 54: 981-989.
17. Reichard GA et. al. Ketone-body production and oxidation in fasting obese humans. J Clin Invest (1974) 53: 508-515.
18. Ubukata E et. al. Diurnal variations in blood ketone bodies in insulin-resistant diabetes mellitus and noninsulin-dependent diabetes mellitus patients: the relationship to serum C-peptide immunoreactivity and free insulin. Ann Nutr Metab (1990) 34: 333-342.
19. Merimee T.J. et. al. Sex variations in free fatty acids and ketones during fasting: evidence for a role of glucagon. J Clin Endocrin Metab (1978) 46: 414-419.
20. Merimee TJ and Fineberg SE. Homeostasis during fasting II: Hormone substrate differences between men and women. J Clin Endocrinol Metab (1973) 37: 698-702.
21. Withrow CD. The ketogenic diet: mechanism of anticonvulsant action. Adv Neurol (1980) 27: 635-642.
22. Balasse EO and Fery F. Ketone body production and disposal: Effects of fasting, diabetes and exercise Diabetes/Metabolism Reviews (1989) 5: 247-270.
23. Misbin RI. et. al. Ketoacids and the insulin receptor. Diabetes (1978) 27: 539-542.
24. Keller U. et. al. Human ketone body production and utilization studied using tracer techniques: regulation by free fatty acids, insulin, catecholamines, and thyroid hormones. Diabetes/Metabolism Reviews (1989) 5: 285-298.
25. Cahill G. Ketosis. Kidney International (1981) 20: 416-425.

Chapter 5:
Adaptations to Ketosis

Having discussed the basics of fuel utilization, ketone body formation and ketosis, it is now time to examine in detail the adaptations which occur in shifting the body away from glucose and towards fat metabolism. The primary adaptation occurs in the brain although other systems are affected as well.

There is a common misconception, especially among bodybuilders, that ketosis is indicative of protein breakdown when in fact the exact opposite is the case. The development of ketosis sets in motion a series of adaptations which minimize body protein losses during periods of caloric deprivation. In fact, preventing the development of ketosis during these periods increases protein losses from the body.

The adaptations to ketosis are complex and involve most systems of the body. As with the previous sections, smaller details are ignored for this discussion and interested readers should examine the references provided. Rather, the major adaptations which occur in the body's tissues, especially the brain, liver, kidney and muscle are described

The adaptations to ketosis have been studied in great depth during periods of total starvation. While this is an extreme state, the lack of food intake makes it simpler to examine the major adaptations. To help individuals understand the adaptations to ketosis, the metabolism of the body is examined during both short and long term fasting. The next chapter discusses the effects of food intake on ketosis, as well as body composition changes. The following sections address in detail the effects of ketosis on glucose/protein requirements as well as the effects on fat and ketone use.

Section 1: An overview of starvation

Starvation and the ketogenic diet

In one sense, the ketogenic diet is identical to starvation, except that food is being consumed. That is, the metabolic effects which occur and the adaptations which are seen during starvation are roughly identical to what is seen during a ketogenic diet. The primary difference is that the protein and fat intake of a ketogenic diet will replace some of the protein and fat which would otherwise be used for fuel during starvation.

The response to total starvation has been extensively studied, arguably moreso than the ketogenic diet itself. For this reason the great majority of data presented below comes from studies of individuals who are fasting. With few exceptions, which are noted as necessary, the metabolic effects of a ketogenic diet are identical to what occurs during starvation.

Although it is discussed in greater detail in a later section, the critical aspect of developing ketosis is the quantity of carbohydrates in the diet and carbohydrate restriction mimics the response seen with total fasting (1-3). The amounts of protein and fat are less critical in this regard (see chapter 9 for more details).

A brief overview of the adaptations to starvation (4)

Before looking in detail at the adaptations to starvation, we will briefly discuss the major events which occur. Starvation can be broken into 5 distinct phases. In the first phase, during the first 8 hours of starvation, the body is still absorbing fuel from previous meals. Within 10 hours after the last carbohydrate containing meal, roughly 50% of the body's total energy requirements are being met by free fatty acids (FFA).

In the second phase, the first day or two of starvation, the body will rely on FFA and the breakdown of liver glycogen for its energy requirements. Liver glycogen is typically gone within 12-16 hours.

In the third phase, during the first week of starvation, the body will drastically increase the production of glucose from protein and other fuels such as lactate, pyruvate and glycerol. This is called gluconeogenesis (the making of new glucose) and is discussed in detail below. At the same time, tissues other than the brain are decreasing their use of glucose, relying on FFA and ketones instead. This helps to spare what little glucose is available for the brain. During this phase, protein breakdown increases greatly.

The fourth phase of starvation is ketosis, which begins during the third or fourth day of starvation, and continues as long as carbohydrates are restricted. The major adaptations during ketosis is increased utilization of ketones by the brain. The final phase, which begins in the second week, is marked by decreasing protein breakdown and gluconeogenesis, as the major protein sparing adaptations to ketosis occur. With the exception of the initial hours of carbohydrate restriction (phases 1 and 2), each of the above phases is discussed in more detail below.

Changes in hormones and fuel availability

Although some mention is made in the discussions below of the adaptations seen during this time period, most of the major adaptations to ketosis start to occur by the third day, continuing for at least 3 weeks (4-6). During the first 3 days of fasting, blood glucose drops from normal levels of 80-120 mg/dl to roughly 65-75 mg/dl. Insulin drops from 40-50 μU/ml to 7-10 μU/ml (5,7,8). Both remain constant for the duration of the fast. One thing to note is that the body strives to maintain near-normal blood glucose levels even under conditions of total fasting (5). The popularly held belief that ketosis will not occur until blood glucose falls to 50 mg/dl is incorrect. Additionally, the popular belief that there is no insulin present on a ketogenic diet is incorrect (7).

One difference between fasting and a ketogenic diet is that the slight insulin response to dietary protein will cause blood glucose to be maintained at a slightly higher level, approximately 80-85 mg/dl (1). This most likely occurs due to the conversion of dietary protein to glucose in the liver.

39

At the same time that insulin and glucose are decreasing from carbohydrate restriction, other hormones such as glucagon and growth hormone are increasing, as are the levels of adrenaline and noradrenaline (7,10-12). Cortisol may actually decrease (13). This increases the rate of fat breakdown and blood levels of FFA and ketones increase (6,8,10,14,15).

Although the liver is producing ketones at its maximum rate by day three (14), blood ketone levels will continue to increase finally reaching a plateau by three weeks (6). The decrease in blood glucose and subsequent increase in FFA and ketones appear to be the signal for the adaptations which are seen, and which are discussed below (16).

In addition to increases in FFA and ketones, there are changes in blood levels of some amino acids (AAs). Increases are seen in the the branch chain amino acids, indicating increased protein breakdown (1, 17-19). As well, there are decreases in other AAs, especially alanine (1, 10,17-19) This most likely represents increased removal by the liver but may also be caused by decreased release of alanine from the muscles (16). This is discussed in further detail in section 3. Changes in levels of the other amino acids also occur and interested readers should examine the references cited. Blood levels of urea, a breakdown product of protein also increase (1). All of this data points to increased protein breakdown during the initial stages of starvation.

By the third day of carbohydrate restriction, the body is no longer using an appreciable amount of glucose for fuel. At this time essentially all of the non-protein energy is being derived from the oxidation of fat, both directly from FFA and indirectly via ketone bodies (20).

Section 2: Changes in ketone and fat usage during starvation

The changes which occur in ketone and FFA utilization during starvation are different for short and long term starvation. Both are discussed below.

Fat and ketone use during short term starvation

Measurements of fuel use show that approximately 90% of the body's total fuel requirements are being met by FFA and ketones by the third day (20). After three weeks of starvation, the body may derive 93% of its fuel from FFA (10, 21).

For an individual with a metabolic rate of 2700 calories per day, roughly 2400 calories of FFA (approximately 260 grams of fat) are used to fuel the body. Considering that one pound of fat contains 3,500 calories, this represents a loss of almost two-thirds of a pound of fat per day. Smaller individuals with lower metabolic rates will use proportionally less fat. While this extreme rate of fat loss makes starvation attractive as a treatment for obesity, the problems associated with total fasting (especially body protein loss) make it unacceptable.

The main point is that the metabolic state of ketosis causes a large scale shift from glucose to fat metabolism resulting in a much larger oxidation of fat than is seen on a more 'balanced' diet. The ketogenic diet is an attempt to harness this shift to cause maximum fat loss and minimum muscle loss, as discussed in greater detail in the upcoming sections.

Fat and ketone use during long term starvation

Most tissues except the brain, stop using ketones for fuel after the third week of ketosis. This is especially true for skeletal muscle. While muscle initially derives up to 50% of its energy requirements from ketones (22), this drops to 4-6% by the third week of ketosis. (22, 23). This is thought to occur for the following reason.

During the first few days of ketosis, the brain is incapable of using ketones for fuel. By using a large amount of ketones for fuel, skeletal muscle prevents a rapid increase in blood ketone levels, which might cause acidosis. As time passes and the brain adapts to using ketones for fuel, skeletal muscle must stop using ketones for fuel, to avoid depriving the brain of fuel. For all practical purposes, with long term starvation, the primary fuel of all tissues except the brain (and the others mentioned in section 3) is FFA, not ketones.

Section 3: Changes in Glucose and Protein Use During Starvation

At the same time that FFA and ketone use is increasing, the body's use of glucose and protein are going down. This is a critical adaptation for two reasons. First and foremost, there are tissues in the body which can not use FFA for fuel, requiring glucose. By decreasing their use of glucose, those tissues which do not require glucose for energy spare what little is available for the tissue which do require it. Thus, there is always a small requirement for glucose under any condition. As we shall see, this small glucose requirement can easily be met without the consumption of carbohydrates.

The second reason is that a reduction in protein losses is critical to survival during total starvation. The loss of too much muscle tissue will eventually cause death (6). From a fat loss standpoint, the 'protein sparing' effect of ketosis is also important to prevent lean body mass losses.

To examine the adaptations to ketosis in terms of glucose and protein, we first need to discuss which tissues do and do not require glucose. Then the adaptations which occur during starvation, in terms of the conservation of glucose, can be examined.

Which tissues use glucose?

All tissues in the body have the capacity to use glucose. With the exception of the brain and a few other tissues (leukocytes, bone marrow, erythrocytes), all tissues in the body can use FFA or ketones for fuel when carbohydrate is not available (5,23).

Under normal dietary conditions, glucose is the standard fuel for the brain and central nervous system (CNS) (24,25). The CNS and brain are the largest consumers of glucose on a daily basis, requiring roughly 104 grams of glucose per day (5,25).

This peculiarity of brain metabolism has led to probably the most important misconception regarding the ketogenic diet. A commonly heard statement is that the brain can only use glucose for fuel but this is only conditionally true. It has been known for over 30 years that, once ketosis has been established for a few days, the brain will derive more and more of its fuel requirements from ketones, finally deriving over half of its energy needs from ketones with the remainder coming from glucose (6,26,27).

As a few tissues do continue to use glucose for fuel, and since the brain's glucose requirement never drops to zero, there will still be a small glucose requirement on a ketogenic diet. This raises the question of how much glucose is required by the body and whether or not this amount can be provided on a diet completely devoid of carbohydrate.

How much carbohydrate per day is needed to sustain the body?

When carbohydrate is removed from the diet, the body undergoes at least three major adaptations to conserve what little glucose and protein it does have (5). The primary adaptation is an overall shift in fuel utilization from glucose to FFA in most tissues, as discussed in the previous section (5,6). This shift spares what little glucose is available to fuel the brain.

The second adaptation occurs in the leukocytes, erythrocytes and bone marrow which continue to use glucose (6). To prevent a depletion of available glucose stores, these tissues break down glucose partially to lactate and pyruvate which go to the liver and are recycled back to glucose again (5,6). Thus there is no net loss of glucose in the body from these tissues and they can be ignored in terms of the body's carbohydrate requirements.

The third, and probably the most important, adaptation, occurs in the brain, which shifts from using solely carbohydrate for fuel to deriving up to 75% of its energy requirements from ketones by the third week of sustained ketosis. (5,6,26) As the brain is the only tissue that continues to deplete glucose in the body, it is all we need concern ourselves with in terms of daily carbohydrate requirements.

The brain's glucose requirements

In a non-ketotic state, the brain utilizes roughly 100 grams of glucose per day (5,25). This means that any diet which contains less than 100 grams of carbohydrate per day will induce ketosis, the depth of which will depend on how many carbohydrates are consumed (i.e. less carbohydrates will mean deeper ketosis). During the initial stages of ketosis, any carbohydrate intake below 100 grams will induce ketosis (28). As the brain adapts to using ketones for fuel and the body's glucose requirements decrease, less carbohydrate must be consumed if ketosis is to be maintained.

The question which requires an answer is this: What sources of glucose does the body have other than the ingestion of dietary carbohydrate? Put differently, assuming zero dietary carbohydrate intake, can the body produce enough glucose to sustain itself?

Please note that the following discussion is only truly relevant to individuals on a Standard Ketogenic Diet (SKD) who are not exercising. However the same information also applies to individuals using a TKD or CKD as some period is spent in ketosis. The impact and implications of exercise on carbohydrate requirements is discussed in later chapters.

Sources of glucose in the body during short term ketosis

The easiest way to examine the body's requirements for glucose is to look at the effects of complete fasting in both the short term (a few hours to 3 weeks) and the long term (3 weeks and up). The few differences between complete fasting and a ketogenic diet are discussed afterwards.

Liver glycogen and gluconeogenesis

The initial storage depot of carbohydrate in the body is the liver, which contains enough glycogen to sustain the brain's glucose needs for approximately 12-16 hours (4). We will assume for the following discussion that liver glycogen has been depleted, ketosis established, and that the only source of glucose is from endogenous fuel stores (i.e. stored bodyfat and protein). The effects of food intake on ketosis is discussed in chapter 9.

After its glycogen has been depleted, the liver is one of the major sources for the production of glucose (gluconeogenesis) and it produces glucose from glycerol, lactate/pyruvate and the amino acids alanine and glutamine (5,6,25) The kidney also produces glucose as starvation proceeds (8).

Glycerol comes from the breakdown of adipose tissue triglyceride, lactate and pyruvate from the breakdown of glycogen and glucose, and alanine and glutamine are released from muscle. Since we are ultimately concerned with the loss of muscle tissue during ketosis, gluconeogenesis from alanine and glutamine are discussed further.

Protein breakdown

With the induction of starvation, blood alanine/glutamine levels both increase significantly, indicating an increase in muscle protein breakdown (6,19). Alanine is absorbed by the liver, converted to glucose and released back into the bloodstream. Glutamine is converted to glucose in the kidney (8). There are also increases in blood levels of the branch-chain amino acids, indicating the breakdown of skeletal muscle (18).

During the initial weeks of starvation, there is an excretion of 12 grams of nitrogen per day. Since approximately 16% of protein is nitrogen, this represents the breakdown of roughly 75 grams of body protein to produce 75 grams of glucose (6). If this rate of protein breakdown were to continued unchecked, the body's protein stores would be depleted in a matter of weeks, causing death.

After even 1 week of starvation, blood alanine levels begin to drop and uptake by the kidneys decreases, indicating that the body is already trying to spare protein losses (19). During longer periods of starvation, blood levels of alanine and glutamine continue to decrease, as does glucose production by the liver (6,21). As glucose production in the liver is decreasing, there is increased glucose production in the kidney (21).

Because of these adaptations, nitrogen losses decrease to 3-4 grams per day by the third week of starvation, indicating the breakdown of approximately 20 grams of body protein (6). With extremely long term starvation, nitrogen losses may drop to 1 gram per day (7), indicating the breakdown of only 6 grams of body protein. However at no time does protein breakdown decrease to zero, as there is always a small requirement for glucose (10). As we shall see in a later section, the development of ketosis during starvation is critical for protein sparing.

Fat breakdown

The glycerol portion of triglycerides (TG) is converted to glucose in the liver with roughly ten percent of the total grams of TG broken down (whether from bodyfat or dietary fat) appearing as glucose (25,29). An average sized individual (150 lbs) may catabolize 160-180 grams of fat per day which will yield 16-18 grams of glucose (10). Obviously a larger individual would oxidize more fat, producing more glucose. The amount of glycerol converted to glucose is fairly constant on a day to day basis and will depend primarily on metabolic rate.

Protein and fat

Excluding the glucose made by recycling lactate and pyruvate, the body will produce the 100 grams of glucose which it needs from the breakdown of approximately 180 grams of TG and 75 grams of muscle protein (see Table 1) (6).

Table 1: Sources of glucose during the initial stages of starvation	
Source	Glucose produced (grams)
Amount of carbohydrate required by brain	~100
Breakdown of 180 grams of TG	18
Breakdown of 75 grams of protein	75
Total carbohydrate produced per day in the liver	93

Production of glucose during long term starvation

As long term adaptation to ketosis continues, there are a number of adaptations which occur to further spare glucose. From the third day of ketosis to three weeks of fasting, the brain gradually increases its use of ketones for fuel, ultimately deriving up to 75% of its total energy from ketones (6,26). This shift to using ketones by the brain means that only 40 grams of glucose per day is required, the remaining 60-75 grams of energy being provided by ketones (26). This means that less protein must be broken down to produce glucose. Since TG breakdown will still provide 18 grams of glucose per day, protein breakdown will only be 20 grams per day (see table 2 on the next page) (6). As stated previously, is appears the primary purpose of ketones in humans is to provide the brain with a non-glucose, fat-derived fuel for the brain (27,30).

Summary

The implication of the adaptations discussed above is that the body does not require dietary carbohydrates for survival (exercise and muscle growth are a separate issue). That is, there is no such thing as an essential dietary carbohydrate as the body can produce what little glucose it needs from other sources.

Of course, the price paid is the loss of body protein, which will ultimately cause death if continued for long periods of time. This loss of body protein during total starvation is unacceptable but the above discussion only serves to show that the body goes through a series of adaptations to conserve its protein. As we see later in this chapter, the addition of dietary protein will maintain ketosis, while preventing the breakdown of bodily protein. In brief, rather than break down bodily protein to produce glucose, the body will use some of the incoming dietary protein for glucose production. This should allow maximal fat utilization while sparing protein losses.

Table 2: Sources of glucose during long term starvation	
Source	Glucose produced (grams)
Amount of carbohydrate required by brain	~40
Breakdown of 180 grams of fat	18
Breakdown of 20 grams of protein	20
Total carbohydrate produced per day in the liver and kidney	38

Section 4: Ketosis and protein sparing

Having quantitatively examined the adaptations which occur in terms of glucose use and nitrogen losses during starvation, the mechanisms behind the 'protein sparing' effect of ketosis can now be discussed.

The question which needs to be answered is what mechanisms exist for ketones (or ketosis) to spare protein. There are at least four possible mechanisms through which ketogenic diets may spare protein, three of which are well established in the literature, the fourth less so. They are discussed in more detail below.

Decreasing the body's glucose requirements

This is arguably the primary mechanism through which ketosis spares nitrogen losses. This adaptation is discussed in detail in the previous sections and is well established in the literature. To briefly recap, by shifting the body's overall metabolism to fat and ketones (especially in the brain), less protein is converted to glucose and protein is spared (6,27). This mechanism is not discussed in further detail here.

It should be noted that preventing the development of ketosis, either with drugs or with the provision of too much dietary carbohydrate, maintains the nitrogen losses during starvation (31).

That is, the development of ketosis is a critical aspect of preventing excessive nitrogen losses during periods of caloric insufficiency. This suggests that non-ketogenic low-carbohydrate diets (frequently used by bodybuilders) may actually cause greater protein losses by preventing the body from maximizing the use of fat for fuel, which is addressed in chapter 6 .

Decreased nitrogen excretion via the kidney

The kidney is a major site of ketone uptake and the buildup of ketones in the kidney has at least two metabolic effects (32). The first is an increase in urinary excretion of ketones, which can be detected with Ketostix (tm). The second is an impairment of uric acid uptake, which is discussed in chapter 7.

The excretion of ketones through the kidneys has an important implication for nitrogen sparing. The kidney produces ammonia, which requires nitrogen, as a base to balance out the acidic nature of ketones and prevent the urine from becoming acidic. This is at least one possible site for an increase in protein losses during ketosis (32). In all likelihood, the increased excretion of ammonia may be the basis of the idea (long held in bodybuilding) that ketone excretion is indicative of protein loss.

As ketosis develops, however, there is an adaptation in the kidney to prevent excessive ammonia loss. As blood ketone concentrations increase, the kidney increases its absorption of ketones. If this increased absorption was accompanied by increased ketone excretion, there would be further nitrogen loss through ammonia production.

However urinary excretion of ketones does not increase, staying extremely constant from the first few days of ketosis on. Therefore, most of the ketones being absorbed by the kidney are not being excreted. The resorption of ketones appears to be an adaptation to prevent further nitrogen losses, which would occur from increasing ammonia synthesis (16,32). This adaptation has the potential to spare 7 grams of nitrogen (roughly 42 grams of body protein) per day from being lost (32).

Directly affecting protein synthesis and breakdown.

As stated, it is well established that protein breakdown decreases during the adaptation to total starvation and one of the mechanisms for this decrease is a lessening of the brain's glucose requirements. It has also been suggested that protein sparing is directly related to ketosis (5,26). As well, many popular authors have suggested that ketones are directly anti-catabolic but this has not been found in all studies.

As described previously, muscles will derive up to 50% of their energy requirements from ketones during the first few days of ketosis. However this drops rapidly and by the third week of ketosis, muscles derive less only 4-6% of their energy from ketone bodies (22). This becomes important when considering the time course for nitrogen sparing during ketosis.

Infusion studies

Several studies have examined the effects on protein breakdown during the infusion of ketone bodies at levels that would be seen in fasting or a ketogenic diet. Of these studies, three have shown a decrease in protein breakdown (33-35) while two others have not (36,37). One study suggested that ketones were directly anabolic (38). One oddity of these studies is that the infusion of ketones (usually as a ketone salt such as sodium-acetoacetate) causes an increase in blood pH (36,38), contrary to the slight drop in blood pH which normally occurs during a ketogenic diet.

At least one study suggests that the rise in pH is responsible for the decrease in protein breakdown rather than the ketones themselves (36); and sodium bicarbonate ingestion can reduce protein breakdown during a ketogenic diet (39). However, since blood pH is normalized within a few days of initiating ketosis, while maximal protein sparing does not occur until the third week, it seems unlikely that changes in blood pH can explain the protein sparing effects of ketosis.

It should be noted that these studies are different than the normal physiological state of ketosis for several reasons. First and foremost, the mixture of ketone salts used is not chemically identical to the ketones that appear in the bloodstream. Additionally, the increase in pH seen with ketone salt infusion is in direct contrast to the drop in pH seen on a ketogenic diet suggesting a difference in effect. Therefore, ketones produced during metabolic ketosis may still have a direct anti-catabolic effect.

Possibly the biggest argument against the idea that ketones are directly anti-catabolic is the time course for changes in nitrogen balance. Most of the infusion studies were done on individuals who had been fasting for short periods of time, overnight or a few days. The major decrease in nitrogen sparing does not occur until approximately the third week of ketosis, at which time muscles are no longer using ketones to any significant degree (22,40). All of the above data makes it difficult to postulate a mechanism by which ketones directly affect muscle protein breakdown. In all likelihood, contrary to popular belief, ketones are not directly anti-catabolic.

Affecting thyroid levels

A fourth possible mechanism by which ketosis may reduce protein breakdown involves the thyroid hormones, primarily triiodothyronine (T3). T3 is arguably one of the most active hormones in the human body (42-44). While most think of T3 simply as a controller of metabolic rate, it affects just about every tissue of the body including protein synthesis. A decrease in T3 will slow protein synthesis and vice versa. As a side note, this is one reason why low carbohydrate diets are not ideal for individuals wishing to gain muscle tissue: the decrease in T3 will negatively affect protein synthesis.

The body has two types of thyroid hormones (42). The primary active thyroid hormone is T3, called triiodothyronine. T3 is responsible most of the metabolic effects in the body. The other thyroid hormone is T4, called thyroxine. Thyroxine is approximately one-fifth as metabolically active as T3 and is considered to be a storage form of T3 in that it can be converted to T3 in the liver.

T3 levels in the body are primarily related to the carbohydrate content of the diet (44-46) although calories also play a role (47-49). When calories are above 800 per day, the carbohydrate content of the diet is the critical factor in regulating T3 levels and a minimum of 50 grams per day of carbohydrate is necessary to prevent the drop in T3 (44,48,49). To the contrary, one study found that a 1500 calorie diet of 50% carbohydrate and 50% fat still caused a drop in T3, suggesting that fat intake may also affect thyroid hormone metabolism (50).

Below 800 calories per day, even if 100% of those calories come from carbohydrate, T3 levels drop (47). Within days of starting a ketogenic diet, T3 drops quickly. This is part of the adaptation to prevent protein losses and the addition of synthetic T3 increases nitrogen losses during a ketogenic diet (1). In fact the ability to rapidly decrease T3 levels may be one determinant of how much protein is spared while dieting (51).

Hypothyroidism and euthyroid stress syndrome (ESS)

There are two common syndromes associated with low levels of T3 which need to be differentiated from one another. Hypothyroidism is a disease characterized by higher than normal thyroid stimulating hormone (TSH) and lower levels of T3 and T4. The symptoms of this disease include fatigue and a low metabolic rate.

The decrease in T3 due to hypothyroidism must be contrasted to the decrease seen during dieting or carbohydrate restriction. Low levels of T3 with normal levels of T4 and TSH (as seen in ketogenic dieting) is known clinically as euthyroid stress syndrome (ESS) and is not associated with the metabolic derangements seen in hypothyroidism (1). The drop in T3 does not appear to be linked to a drop in metabolic rate during a ketogenic diet (17,52).

As with other hormones in the body (for example insulin), the decrease in circulating T3 levels may be compensated for by an increase in receptor activity and/or number (1). This has been shown to occur in mononuclear blood cells but has not been studied in human muscle or fat cells (53). So while T3 does go down on a ketogenic diet, this does not appear to be the reason for a decrease in metabolic rate.

Summary

The primary adaptation to ketosis (as it occurs during total starvation) is a gradual decrease in the body's glucose requirements with a concomitant increase in the use of free fatty acids and ketones. The main adaptation which occurs is in the brain which shifts from deriving 100% of its fuel from glucose to deriving as much as 75% of its total energy requirements from ketones. Thus the commonly stated idea that the brain can only use glucose is incorrect.

A large increase in the breakdown of body protein during the initial stages of starvation provides the liver and kidney with the amino acids alanine and glutamine to make glucose. However, there is a gradual decrease in protein breakdown which occurs in concert with the decreasing glucose requirements.

Although the exact mechanisms behind the 'protein sparing' effect of ketosis are not entirely established, there are at least four possible mechanisms by which ketogenic diets may spare protein. These include decreased glucose requirements, decreased excretion of ketones from the kidneys, a possible direct effect of ketones on protein synthesis, and the drop in thyroid levels seen during starvation.

References Cited

1. Fery F et. al. Hormonal and metabolic changes induced by an isocaloric isoprotienic ketogenic diet in healthy subjects. Diabete Metab (1982) 8: 299-305.
2. Bloom W and Azar G. Similarities of carbohydrate deficiency and fasting. Part I: weight loss, electrolyte excretion and fatigue. Arch Intern Med (1963) 112: 333-337.
3. Azar G and Bloom W. Similarities of carbohydrate deficiency and fasting. Part II: Ketones, nonesterified fatty acids and nitrogen excretion. Arch Intern Med (1963) 112: 338-343.
4. Cahill G. Starvation. Trans Am Clin Climatol Assoc (1982) 94: 1-21.
5. Cahill G. Starvation in man. N Engl J Med (1970) 282: 668-675
6. Cahill G and Aoki TT. How metabolism affects clinical problems Medical Times (1970) 98: 106-122.
7. Cahill, G et. al. Hormone-fuel relationships during fasting. J Clin Invest (1966) 45: 1751-1769
8. Owen OE et. al. Liver and kidney metabolism during prolonged starvation. J Clin Invest (1969) 48: 574-583
10. Owen OE et. al. Protein, fat and carbohydrate requirements during starvation: anaplerosis and cataplerosis. Am J Clin Nutr (1998) 68: 12-34.
11. Wolfe RR et. al. Effect of short-term fasting on lipolytic responsiveness in normal and obese human subjects. Am J Physiol (1987) 252: E189-E196
12. Jensen MD et. al. Lipolysis during fasting: decreases suppression by insulin and decreased stimulation by epinephrine. J Clin Invest (1987) 79: 207-213.
13. Haymond MW et. al. Effects of ketosis on glucose flux in children and adults. Am J Physiol (1983) 245: E373-E378
14. Garber AJ et. al. Hepatic ketogenesis and gluconeogenesis in humans. J Clin Invest (1974) 54: 981-989.
15. Carlson MG et al. Fuel and energy metabolism in fasting humans. Am J Clin Nutr. (1994) 60: 29-36.
16. Robinson AM and Williamson DH Physiological roles of ketone bodies as substrates and signals in mammalian tissues. Physiol Rev (1980) 60: 143-187.
17. Phinney S.D. et. al. The human metabolic response to chronic ketosis without caloric restriction: physical and biochemical adaptations. Metabolism (1983) 32: 757-768.
18. Swendseid ME et. al. Plasma amino acid levels in subjects fed isonitrogenous diets containing different proportions of fat and carbohydrate. Am J Clin Nutr (1967) 20: 52-55.
19. Felig P. et. al. Amino acid metabolism during prolonged starvation. J Clin Invest (1969) 48: 584-594.

20. Elia M. et. al. Ketone body metabolism in lean male adults during short-term starvation, with particular reference to forearm muscle metabolism. Clinical Science (1990) 78: 579-584.

21. Felig P. et. al. Utilization of metabolic fuels in obese subjects. Am J Clin Nutr (1968) 21: 1429-1433.

22. Owen OE and Reichard GA Human forearm metabolism during progressive starvation. J Clin Invest (1976) 50: 1536-1545.

23. Mitchell GA et al. Medical aspects of ketone body metabolism. Clinical & Investigative Medicine (1995) 18: 193-216.

24. Sokoloff L. Metabolism of ketone bodies by the brain. Ann Rev Med (1973) 24: 271-280.

25. Felig P. et. al. Blood glucose and gluconeogenesis in fasting man. Arch Intern Med (1969) 123: 293-298.

26. Owen OE et. al. Brain metabolism during fasting. J Clin Invest (1967) 10: 1589-1595.

27. "Ellenberg and Rifkin's Diabetes Mellitus: Theory and Practice 5th ed." Ed. Daniel Porte and Robert Sherwin. Appleton and Lange, 1997.

28. Bistrian BR et. al. Effect of a protein-sparing diet and brief fast on nitrogen metabolism in mildly obese subjects. J Lab Med (1977) 89:1030-1035

29. Bortz WM et. al. Glycerol turnover in man. J Clin Invest (1972) 51: 1537-1546.

30. Balasse EO and Fery F. Ketone body production and disposal: Effects of fasting, diabetes and exercise. Diabetes/Metabolism Reviews (1989) 5: 247-270.

31. Flatt JP and Blackburn GL. The metabolic fuel regulatory system: implications for protein sparing therapies during caloric deprivation and disease. Am J Clin Nutr (1974) 27: 175-187.

32. Sapir DG and Owen OE. Renal conservation of ketone bodies during starvation. Metabolism (1975) 24: 23-33.

33. Sherwin RS et. al. Effect of ketone infusion on amino acid and nitrogen metabolism in man. J Clin Invest (1975) 55: 1382-1390.

34. Pawan GLS and Semple SJG. Effect of 3-hydroxybutyrate in obese subjects on very-low-energy diets and during therapeutic starvation. Lancet (1983) 1:15-17.

35. Beaufrere B et al. Effects of D-beta-hydroxybutyrate and long- and medium-chain triglycerides on leucine metabolism in humans. Am J Physiol. (1992) 262: E268-E274.

36. Fery F and Balasse EO. Differential effects of sodium acetoacetate and acetoacetic acid infusions on alanine and glutamine metabolism in man. J Clin Invest (1980) 66: 323-331.

37. Miles JM et. al. Failure of infused b-hydroxybutyrate to decrease proteolysis in man. Diabetes (1983) 32: 197-205.

38. Nair KS et. al. Effect of b-hydroxybutyrate on whole-body leucine kinetics and fractional skeletal muscle protein synthesis in humans. J Clin Invest (1988) 82: 198-205.

39. Gougeon-Reyburn R and Marliss EB. Effects of sodium bicarbonate in nitrogen metabolism and ketone bodies during very low protein diets in obese subjects. Metabolism (1989) 38: 1222-1230.

40. Hagenfeldt L and Wahren J. Human forearm metabolism during exercise VI. Substrate Utilization in Prolonged Fasting. Scand J Clin Lab Invest (1971) 27: 299-306.

41. "Werner and Ingbar's The Thyroid: A fundamental and clinical text" Lewis E. Braverman and Robert D. Utiger. Lipincott-Raven publishers, 1995.

42. Van Gall L.F. et. al. Factors determining energy expenditure during very-low-calorie diets. Am J Clin Nutr (1992) 56: 224S-229S.

43. Freake HC and Oppenheimer JH. Thermogenesis and thyroid function. Annual Rev Nutr (1995) 15: 263-291.

44. Pasquali R. et. al. Effects of dietary carbohydrates during hypocaloric treatment of obesity on peripheral thyroid hormone metabolism. J Endocrinol Invest (1982) 5: 47-52.

45. Fery F. et. al. Hormonal and metabolic changes induced by an isocaloric isoproteneic ketogenic diet in healthy subjects. Diabete et Metabolisme (1982) 8: 299-305.

46. Serog P. et. al. Effects of slimming and composition of diets on VO2 and thyroid hormones in healthy subjects. Am J Clin Nutr (1982) 35: 24-35.

47. O'Brian J.T. et. al. Thyroid hormone homeostasis in states of relative caloric deprivation. Metabolism (1980) 29: 721- 727.

48. Spaulding SW. et.al. Effect of caloric restriction and dietary composition of serum T3 and reverse T3 in man. J Clin Endocrin Metabolism (1976) 42: 197-200.

49. Pasquali R et. al. Relationships between iodothyronine peripheral metabolism and ketone bodies during hypocaloric dietary manipulations. J Endocrinol Invest (1982) 6: 81-89.

50. Otten M.H. et. al. The role of dietary fat in peripheral thyroid hormone metabolism. Metabolism (1980) 29: 930- 935.

51. Yang MU and Van Itallie TB. Variability in body protein loss during protracted severe caloric restriction: role of triiodothyronine and other possible determinants. Am J Clin Nutr (1984) 40: 611-622.

52. Acheson KJ and Berger AG. A study of the relationship between thermogenesis and thyroid hormones. J Clin Endocrin Metab (1980) 51: 84-89.

53. Matzen LE and Kvetny J. The influence of caloric deprivation and food composition on TSH, thyroid hormones and nuclear binding of T3 in mononuclear blood cells in obese women. Metabolism (1989) 38: 555-561.

Chapter 6:
Changes in body composition

Having discussed the primary metabolic adaptations which occur during ketosis in the previous chapter, we can now examine the effects of ketogenic diets on body composition. The first issue to examine is the effect of food intake on ketosis. This will lead into an examination of protein sparing on a ketogenic diet, as well as issues involving weight, water, and fat loss.

The question to be answered is whether a ketogenic diet does in fact cause greater fat loss with less loss of body protein than a more 'balanced' diet. Unfortunately, the lack of appropriate studies, as well as a high degree of variability in study subjects, make this a difficult question to answer unequivocally. Issues relating to water loss on a ketogenic diet are discussed as well.

Section 1: Macronutrients and Ketosis

Before discussing how to prevent nitrogen loss during starvation, we need to briefly discuss the effects of different nutrients on the development of ketosis. Both protein and carbohydrate intake will impact the development of ketosis, affecting both the adaptations seen as well as how much of a 'protein sparing' effect will occur.

Despite the generally 'high fat' nature of the ketogenic diet, or at least how it is perceived, dietary fat intake has a rather minimal effect on ketosis per se. Fat intake will primarily affect how much bodyfat is used for fuel. Although alcohol has been discussed within the context of ketoacidosis, the effects of alcohol intake on the state of ketosis are discussed again here.

The ketogenic ratio

Although its application for ketogenic dieters is somewhat limited, the simplest way to examine the effects of food consumption on ketosis is to look at the equation used to develop ketogenic diets for childhood epilepsy (figure 1).

Figure 1: The ketogenic ratio

$$\frac{\text{Ketogenic}}{\text{Anti-ketogenic}} = \frac{K}{AK} = \frac{0.9 \text{ fat} + 0.46 \text{ protein}}{1.0 \text{ carbohydrate} + 0.1 \text{ fat} + 0.58 \text{ protein}}$$

Note: Protein, fat and carbohydrates are in grams.

Source: Withrow CD. The ketogenic diet: mechanism of anticonvulsant action. Adv Neurol (1980) 7: 635-642.

This equation represents the relative tendency for a given macronutrient to either promote or prevent a ketogenic state (1). Recalling from the previous chapter that insulin and glucagon are the ultimate determinants of the shift to a ketotic state, this equation essentially represents the tendency for a given nutrient to raise insulin (anti-ketogenic) or glucagon (pro-ketogenic).

For the treatment of epilepsy, the ratio of K to AK must be at least 1.5 for a meal to be considered ketogenic (1). Typically, this results in a diet containing 4 grams of fat for each gram of protein and carbohydrate, called a 4:1 diet. More details on the development of ketogenic diets for epilepsy can be found in the references, as they are beyond the scope of this book.

Although this ratio is critically important for the implementation of the ketogenic diet in clinical settings, we see in chapter 9 that it is not as important for the general dieting public. Each macronutrient is now briefly discussed within the context of the equation in figure 1.

Carbohydrate

Carbohydrate is 100% anti-ketogenic. As carbohydrates are digested, they enter the bloodstream as glucose, raising insulin and lowering glucagon, which inhibits ketone body formation. In fact, any dietary change that raises blood glucose is anti-ketogenic.

As mentioned in the previous chapter, the brain is the only tissue which requires glucose in amounts of roughly 100 grams per day. If sufficient carbohydrate is consumed to provide this much glucose, the brain will have no need to begin using ketones. Therefore any diet which contains more than 100 grams of carbohydrate per day will not be ketogenic (2). After approximately three weeks, when the brain's glucose requirements have dropped to only 40 grams of glucose per day, carbohydrates must be restricted even further.

Additionally, from the standpoint of rapidly depleting liver glycogen, the more that carbohydrates are restricted during the first days of a ketogenic diet, the faster ketosis will occur and the deeper the degree of ketonemia. When examining the diet studies, any diet with more than 100 grams of carbohydrates is considered to be non-ketogenic (often called a 'balanced' diet) while any diet with less than 100 grams of carbohydrates is ketogenic (2).

Protein

Protein has both ketogenic effects (46%) and anti-ketogenic effects (58%). This reflects the fact that 58% of dietary protein will appear in the bloodstream as glucose (3), raising insulin and inhibiting ketogenesis. Note that the insulin response from consuming dietary protein is much smaller than that from consuming dietary carbohydrates. Consequently protein must be restricted to some degree on a ketogenic diet as excessive protein intake will generate too much glucose, impairing or preventing ketosis. Protein also stimulates glucagon release and has some pro-ketogenic effects.

The most critical aspect of protein intake has to do with preventing the breakdown of body protein. By providing dietary protein during starvation, the breakdown of body protein can be decreased or avoided entirely (4). The interactions between protein and glucose intake and protein sparing are the topic of the next section.

Fat

Fat is primarily ketogenic (90%) but also has a slight anti-ketogenic effect (10%). This represents the fact that ten percent of the total fat grams ingested will appear in the bloodstream as glucose (via conversion of the glycerol portion of triglycerides) (5,6). If 180 grams of fat are oxidized (burned) per day, this will provide 18 grams of glucose from the conversion of glycerol.

Alcohol

Although alcohol is not represented in the above equation, having no direct effect on ketosis, alcohol intake will have an impact on the depth of ketosis and the amount of body fat used by the body. As discussed in chapter 4, excessive alcohol intake while in ketosis can cause runaway acidosis to develop which is potentially very dangerous. Additionally as alcohol intake limits how much FFA can be processed by the liver, calories from alcohol will detract from overall fat loss.

Summary

The three macronutrients are carbohydrate, protein and fat. All three nutrients have differing effects on ketosis due to their digestion and subsequent effects on blood glucose and hormone levels. Carbohydrate is 100% anti-ketogenic due to its effects on blood glucose and insulin (raising both). Protein is approximately 46% ketogenic and 58% anti-ketogenic due to the fact that over half of ingested protein is converted to glucose, raising insulin. Fat is 90% ketogenic and ten percent anti-ketogenic, representing the small conversion of the glycerol portion of triglycerides to glucose. While alcohol has no direct effect on the establishment of ketosis, excessive alcohol intake can cause ketoacidosis to occur.

Section 2: Nitrogen sparing: A theoretical approach

The breakdown of body protein during total starvation to produce glucose ultimately led researchers to explore two distinctly different approaches to prevent this loss. The simplest approach was to provide glucose in order to eliminate the need for protein breakdown. However, this had a secondary effect of preventing the adaptations to ketosis. In some clinical situations such as post-surgical trauma, providing glucose or glucose with protein caused greater protein losses by preventing the adaptations to ketosis from occurring.

The second approach was to mimic the effects of starvation while consuming food. This allows ketosis to develop while limiting the loss of body protein. One approach was to simply consume high quality protein, which was called the protein sparing modified fast (PSMF).

After much research, it was concluded that a protein intake of 1.5-1.75 grams protein per kilogram of ideal body weight (ideal body weight was used to approximate lean body mass) would spare most of the nitrogen loss, especially as ketosis developed and the body's glucose requirements decreased. As we shall see below, providing sufficient protein from the first day of a low-carbohydrate diet should prevent any net nitrogen loss from the body. Of all aspects of the PSMF or ketogenic diet, adequate dietary protein is absolutely critical to the success of the diet in maximizing fat loss and sparing body protein.

The ketogenic diet as most consider it is simply a PSMF with added dietary fat. Note that the addition of dietary fat does not affect the adaptations or protein sparing effects of the PSMF. Only overall fat loss is affected since dietary fat is used to provide energy instead of bodyfat.

How much dietary protein is necessary to prevent nitrogen losses?

Without going into the details of protein requirements, which are affected by activity and are discussed in the next chapter, we can determine the minimum amount of protein which is necessary to prevent body protein losses by looking at two factors: the amount of glucose required by the brain, and the amount of glucose produced from the ingestion of a given amount of dietary protein.

Both of these factors are discussed in previous chapters and a few brief calculations will tell us how much protein is necessary. In the next section, these values are compared to a number of diet studies to see if they are accurate.

To briefly recap, during the first weeks of ketosis, approximately 75 grams of glucose must be produced (the other 18 grams of glucose coming from the conversion of glycerol to glucose) to satisfy the brain's requirements of ~100 grams of glucose per day. After approximately 3 weeks of ketosis, the brain's glucose requirements drop to approximately 40 grams of glucose. Of this, 18 grams are derived from the conversion of glycerol, leaving 25 grams of glucose to be made from protein.

Since 58% of all dietary protein will appear in the bloodstream as glucose (3), we can determine how much dietary protein is required by looking at different protein intakes and how much glucose is produced (table 1).

Table 1: Protein intake and grams of glucose produced *	
Protein intake (grams)	Glucose produced (grams)
50	27
100	58
125	72.5
150	87
175	101.5
200	116
* Assuming a 58% conversion rate	

Assuming zero carbohydrate intake, during the first 3 weeks of a ketogenic diet a protein intake of ~150 grams per day should be sufficient to achieve nitrogen balance. Therefore, regardless of bodyweight, the minimum amount of protein which should be consumed during the initial three weeks of a ketogenic diet is 150 grams per day.

After 3 weeks of ketosis, as little as 50 grams of protein per day should provide enough glucose to achieve nitrogen balance. The inclusion of exercise will increase protein requirements and is discussed in chapter 9.

Carbohydrate intake

The consumption of carbohydrate will decrease dietary protein requirements since less glucose will need to be made from protein breakdown. For example, if a person was consuming 125 grams of protein per day, this would produce 72 grams of glucose plus 18 more from the breakdown of glycerol for a total of 90 grams of glucose. To avoid any nitrogen losses, this individual could either consume 10 grams of carbohydrate per day or simply increase protein intake to 150 grams per day.

Summary

Looking at the topic of protein sparing from a purely theoretical standpoint, a protein intake of approximately 150 grams per day should be sufficient to prevent any nitrogen losses during the first three weeks of a ketogenic diet. After this time period, as little as 50 grams of protein should be necessary to prevent nitrogen losses. These values are examined by looking at specific studies in the next section.

Section 3: Nitrogen sparing: The studies

Having examined protein requirements from a theoretical standpoint, we can now see how the values determined previously compare to the studies done on ketogenic diets at varying calorie levels. Before examining some key studies, a discussion of nitrogen balance and how it is determined is necessary. Additionally, some of the problems with nitrogen balance are discussed.

Protein losses and nitrogen balance

There are many methods of measuring protein losses during dieting and starvation (7). Without exception all make assumptions and simplifications. From the standpoint of the ketogenic diet, some methods are better than others, but none are perfect.

Many early ketogenic diet studies simply subtracted muscle loss from total weight loss and assumed the difference represented fat loss. The problem with this method was that assessment of muscle loss can be seriously affected by the glycogen loss seen on a ketogenic diet (8).

Although newer methods are becoming available, most of the studies examined estimate body protein losses by performing a nitrogen balance study. Nitrogen is brought into the body in the form of dietary protein and is excreted from the body through a number of pathways including urine, feces and sweat (9). Generally estimations are made for fecal and sweat nitrogen losses and only urinary nitrogen excretion is measured.

Since it is easier to measure nitrogen than it is to measure protein directly, a nitrogen balance study compares the amount of nitrogen being lost in the urine to the amount of nitrogen being consumed in the diet. If less nitrogen is being excreted than consumed, the body is said to be in positive nitrogen balance meaning that protein is being stored. Since the body has a minimal store of non-tissue protein (9), it is assumed that this stored protein is being incorporated into muscle or other tissues. If more nitrogen is being excreted than is being consumed, the body is in negative nitrogen balance meaning that body protein is being broken down and excreted. A negative nitrogen balance generally indicates a loss of lean body mass and we will assume it to indicate a loss of muscle.

Problems with nitrogen balance

Although nitrogen balance is one of the best methods for determining muscle loss while dieting, there are still problems. First and foremost, there tends to be a great degree of variability in total nitrogen losses among subjects in diet studies. For example, one study found that daily nitrogen losses on a ketogenic diet varied among the subjects between 1 gram of nitrogen/day and 6 grams of nitrogen/day. This represents a difference in bodily protein breakdown of 6-36 grams of protein/day (10). Unfortunately most diet studies report nitrogen balances as average values for differing diet groups. This tends to overstate either how well or how poorly a diet works to spare protein. If one individual loses a significant amount of nitrogen while another loses very little, reporting an average does not provide accurate information.

An additional problem is that there is no easy way to tell where the protein is coming from or going to. In the case of a negative nitrogen balance, it is possible that liver proteins are being broken down, while muscle is spared and vice versa. To simplify matters, we will equate a negative nitrogen balance with a loss of muscle.

Why the variability?

The reason for such variability in nitrogen sparing is likely related to several factors. Obese individuals appear to better spare protein losses due to having a greater store of bodyfat to use as an alternate fuel (10). In contrast, higher levels of lean body mass appear to increase nitrogen losses (10). This may be part of the reason that heavily muscled individuals tend to lose muscle more easily. The ability to decrease insulin levels and establish ketosis may also play a role (11,12). Finally, the ability to rapidly down regulate the levels of thyroid hormones may play a role in nitrogen sparing (10).

Additionally, since the major adaptations to ketosis (especially with regards to protein sparing) take at least 3 weeks to occur, studies shorter than three weeks in duration may erroneously conclude that the ketogenic diet provides no benefit in terms of protein sparing compared to a balanced diet (13). Invariably these studies show a gradual improvement in nitrogen balance over three weeks suggesting that the ketogenic diet might have the benefit in terms of protein sparing in the longer term (13). Since most dieters do not diet for only three weeks, longer term changes in nitrogen balance are more important than short term.

Most diet studies are done at extremely low calorie levels, generally less than 800 calories per day (referred to as a very-low-calorie-diet or VLCD). Although the dietary fat intake has little effect on nitrogen sparing, the low calorie nature of most studies has an important implication: to keep calories very low, protein intake must also be low.

Research has established that a minimum protein intake of 1.5 grams protein/kg ideal body weight is necessary to achieve nitrogen balance (2,14). However, some studies provide as little as 50 grams of protein per day, drawing erroneous conclusions about the nitrogen sparing effects of ketogenic diets (15). When protein intake is inadequate to begin with, extra carbohydrate is significantly protein sparing, especially in the first three weeks while the adaptations to ketosis are occurring (15). But given adequate protein, carbohydrates appear to have no additional nitrogen sparing effect.

As the following data shows, providing adequate protein from the first day of even a VLCD ketogenic diet should prevent any loss of nitrogen. The calculations presented in the last section suggest that 150 grams of protein per day should be used during at least the first three weeks of a ketogenic diet. The available studies are examined to see if this value is correct.

How much protein is needed to prevent nitrogen loss?

Having examined this question theoretically in the previous section, we can examine a few studies to see if the suggested 150 grams of protein per day is correct. Since only a few studies provided an appropriate amount of protein to its subjects, we will look at these studies in detail.

In a maintenance calorie diet study, six subjects were given 2,800 calories with 135 grams of protein, 40 grams of carbohydrate and 235 grams of fat for a period of 6 days (15). This was compared to a diet containing 135 grams of protein, 40 grams of fat, and 475 grams of carbohydrate. Both diet groups were in positive nitrogen balance from the first day of the study. As well, the 40 grams of carbohydrate in the ketogenic group spared some protein breakdown. It would be expected that a lower carbohydrate intake would require a larger intake of protein to avoid nitrogen losses.

In a second maintenance calorie diet study, subjects received 1.75 g protein/kg ideal body weight daily (17). Nitrogen balance was attained in most subjects by the second week of the study. However, since the study did not list how many grams of protein were given to each subject, it is impossible to determine how much additional protein would have been needed to establish nitrogen balance from the first day. This study simply supports the idea that nitrogen balance can be attained quickly on a ketogenic diet, provided that sufficient protein is consumed

In another study, eight men were placed on diets of 1800 calories, containing 115 grams of protein for 9 weeks (18). Carbohydrate intake varied from 104 grams to 60 grams to 30 grams. Although all three groups were in ketosis to some degree (especially during the first three weeks), we will only consider that 30 and 60 carbohydrate gram diets as truly ketogenic diets.

Nitrogen balance was slightly negative during the first week of the diet. Approximately 2 grams of nitrogen were lost, equating to 13 grams of protein converted to glucose, meaning that 22 additional grams of protein would have been required to attain nitrogen balance. Added to the 115 grams of protein given, this yields a total of 137 grams of protein to prevent all nitrogen losses. Nitrogen balance was achieved during week 2 and became slightly positive during the third week.

In a third study, which examined the metabolic effects of a variety of different dietary approaches, subjects were studied under a total of 6 different dietary conditions (19). We are only concerned with three of them. The first was a 400 calorie diet consisting of 100 grams of protein. In this group the average negative nitrogen balance was -2 grams, the equivalent of 12 grams of body protein broken down to make glucose. An additional 20 grams of dietary protein (for a total of 120 grams/day) would have provided this amount of glucose and prevented any nitrogen losses. When you consider that even 100 grams of protein was unable to prevent nitrogen losses, it is no surprise that studies using less protein (often only 50 grams per day) than this fail to show nitrogen sparing with ketogenic diets.

The second dietary approach we are concerned with was a group given 800 calories as 200 grams of protein. In this group, there was a positive nitrogen balance of almost 8 grams/day, the equivalent of 48 grams of protein. This suggests that a protein intake of 152 grams would have been sufficient to achieve nitrogen balance, supporting the value of 150 grams from the previous section.

A third group was given 400 calories of protein and 400 calories of fat and showed the same negative nitrogen balance as the 400 calories of protein only. This points out that the fat intake/calorie level of a ketogenic diet does not affect nitrogen balance. Meaning that, protein calories are far more important than fat calories in terms of achieving nitrogen balance on a ketogenic diet.

This study is interesting as it shows that nitrogen balance can be attained essentially regardless of calorie level as long as sufficient protein intake is consumed, as has another study (20). The difference between the two values for protein intake determined in this study (120 grams and 152 grams) cannot be explained from the data presented.

Do ketogenic diets spare more nitrogen than non-ketogenic diets?

A lack of well done studies makes this question difficult to answer unequivocally. As mentioned above, the problem is that many studies are very short, generally a few days to a few weeks. As the studies discussed above show (and discussed in detail in chapter 5), a minimum of 3 weeks is required for the protein sparing adaptations to ketosis to occur.

Most studies comparing ketogenic to non-ketogenic diets are done at very low calorie levels (VLCD, below 600 cal/day). These have limited applicability to an individual dieting at 10-20% below maintenance levels as advocated in this book for reasons discussed in detail below.

All that can be said from most of these studies is that a non-ketogenic diet will spare nitrogen better than a ketogenic diet as long as the diet periods are less than three weeks (13,16,19,21). The problem being that diets are rarely used for a period as short as three weeks in the real world. Some studies show greater nitrogen sparing for the ketogenic diet (22-24) while others show no advantage (21,23,25) and others show less nitrogen sparing (13,15,26).

At higher calorie levels (maintenance to 1200 calories), there are few studies. One study at 1200 calories found less lean body mass (LBM) loss for the higher carbohydrate diets (27) while another found no difference in LBM losses (28). A final study done at 1800 calories found less nitrogen sparing for the ketogenic diet during the first three weeks of the diet but greater nitrogen sparing during the last three weeks of the diet (18).

Summary

Arguably the most critical aspect to prevent nitrogen losses on a ketogenic diet is the consumption of adequate protein. It should be noted that there is great variability in how well people spare protein on a ketogenic diet. On average it appears that a protein intake of at least 120-150 grams per day should be sufficient to maintain nitrogen balance, regardless of calorie levels. However, this value does not include any additional protein needed to cover exercise, and none of these studies have discussed weight training individuals. This topic of exercise and protein requirements is discussed in chapter 9.

It is difficult to draw any good conclusions about the relative effects on protein sparing for ketogenic versus non-ketogenic diets. The general study designs, incorporating very short study periods, very low calories and inadequate protein make it impossible to draw conclusions for an individual dieting at twenty percent below maintenance calories, with adequate protein, and who is exercising. The limited studies done at higher calorie and higher protein levels suggest that the ketogenic diet is no worse in terms of protein sparing than a non-ketogenic diet, assuming that adequate protein is given. One study suggests that protein sparing is better as long as adequate protein is given and the adaptations to ketosis are allowed to occur.

Anecdotal evidence suggests that there is great variety in muscle loss when individuals diet. Many individuals can avoid muscle loss effectively with any number of diets while others find that muscle losses are much less on a ketogenic diet compared to a more balanced diet. By the same token, some individuals find that their muscle loss is greater on a ketogenic diet versus a more traditional diet.

The implication of the above data is this: if an individual finds that they lose too much muscle on a balanced diet, with a reasonable deficit, and adequate protein, a ketogenic diet may be worth trying. By corollary, if an individual finds that they are losing lean body mass on a ketogenic diet (as indicated by changes in body composition measurements or consistent losses of strength in the gym), and protein intake is adequate, it should be concluded that the adaptations to ketosis are not sufficient to prevent protein losses and a more 'balanced' dietary approach should be tried.

Section 4: Water and weight loss

Having discussed the topic of nitrogen sparing we can finally examine the effects of ketogenic diets on the other aspects of body composition: water, weight and fat loss. The question then to be answered is whether a ketogenic diet will cause more weight and/or fat loss than a non-ketogenic diet with the same calories. As with the sections on protein sparing, study methodology makes makes it impossible to absolutely answer this question. Prior to discussing the effects of the ketogenic diet on body composition, a few comments about the various studies cited by both the pro- and anti-ketogenic groups are in order.

Problems with the studies

Most of the early ketogenic diet studies looked at weight loss only, making no distinction between fat, water and muscle loss. As discussed in chapter 8, a dieter's goal should be maximal fat loss with minimal muscle loss. Since water weight can be gained or lost quickly, it should not be used as the factor to determine whether a ketogenic or balanced diet is the optimal approach.

Likewise, many early studies, which are frequently cited by pro-ketogenic authors, confused water loss with fat loss due to methodological problems. These studies should not be considered as evidence either for or against a ketogenic diet.

Many early diet studies were extremely short in duration, five to ten days in some cases. This makes drawing valid conclusions about the effectiveness of a given diet approach impossible as results are confounded by the rapid water losses which occurs in the first few days. In very short term studies, a ketogenic diet will almost always show greater weight loss because of fluid losses. However, the amount of fat loss which can occur in this period of time is negligible in almost any diet study. As well, since few dieters pursue fat loss for only 10 days, studies of this duration have limited applicability.

The early studies

A number of studies done in the 50's and 60's showed almost magical results from low-carbohydrate, high-fat diets. The primary result was significantly greater weight loss for low versus high carbohydrate diets in obese subjects (29,30). This led researchers involved to conclude that there was an enhancement of metabolism with the high fat diets, a sentiment echoed by some popular diet book authors. It was suggested that ketogenic diets caused the secretion of a 'fat mobilizing substance' which enhanced fat loss (31,32), but this substance was never identified.

In these studies, obese subjects lost weight on a 2600 calorie high fat diet but lost no weight when put on a 2000 calorie higher carbohydrate diet (29,30). As these studies attempted to measure changes in lean body mass as well, they concluded that large amounts of fat were being lost on the high fat, but not the high-carbohydrate diets.

As would be expected, results of this nature were far too good to be true. The very short term nature of the studies, 9 days or less, as well as the rapid weight loss which occurred in the first few days of the high fat diets, indicate that the supposed fat loss which was occurring was coming primarily from changes in water balance (33,34), which can contribute anywhere from 5 to 15 lbs of weight loss within a few days (see next section). Later studies using the same experimental design, determined that the weight lost and counted as fat was water and that there was no 'metabolic advantage' to low carbohydrate diets in terms of weight loss (35,36).

Water loss on the ketogenic diet

A well established fact is that low-carbohydrate diets tend to cause a rapid loss of water in the first few days. This occurs for several reasons. First and foremost, glycogen is stored along with water in a ratio of three grams of water for every gram of stored carbohydrate (37). As glycogen is depleted, water is lost. For large individuals, this can represent a lot of weight.

Additionally, ketones appear to have a diuretic effect themselves causing the excretion of water and electrolytes (38). This includes the excretion of sodium, which itself causes water retention. Electrolyte excretion is discussed in greater detail in the next chapter.

Due to confusions about weight loss and fat loss (see chapter 8), many individuals are drawn to low-carbohydrate diets specifically for the rapid initial loss of water weight. During the first few days of a ketogenic diet, water loss has been measured from 4.5 to 15 lbs (17,39-41).

Although transient, this rapid initial weight loss can provide psychological incentive for dieters, which may mean greater compliance with the diet. In one study of subjects on a very-low-calorie ketogenic diet adhered to their diet much more than individuals consuming more carbohydrate, and who lost less weight (8).

Regardless of possible psychological benefits, it should be understood that the initial weight loss on a ketogenic diet is water. This is especially critical for when individuals come off of a ketogenic diet, either deliberately or because they 'cheated'. The rapid weight gain which occurs when carbohydrates are reintroduced into the diet, which can range from three to five pounds in one day, can be as psychologically devastating to dieters as the initial weight loss was beneficial. In the same way that fat cannot be lost extremely rapidly, it is physiologically impossible to gain three to five pounds of true bodyfat in one day. This is discussed in more detail in chapter 14 .

A final thing to note is that this water loss can be misinterpreted as a loss of protein-containing lean body mass (LBM), depending on the method of measurement. (8). This may be part of the reason that some studies find report a greater loss of LBM for ketogenic versus non-ketogenic diets.

Weight loss

The fact that the initial weight loss on a ketogenic diet is from a loss of water weight has led to a popular belief that the only weight lost on a ketogenic diet is from water, an attitude that makes little sense. The question then is whether more or less true weight (i.e. non-water) is lost on a ketogenic diet versus a non-ketogenic diet.

In most studies, a low-carbohydrate diet will show a greater total weight loss than a high-carbohydrate (8,18,19,25,26,35) but this is not always the case (10,13,15,22) . Once water loss has been taken into account, the rate of weight loss seen, as well as the total weight loss is generally the same for ketogenic versus non-ketogenic diets (35,40). That is, if individuals are put on a 1200 calorie per day diet, they will lose roughly the same amount of 'true' weight (not including water) regardless of the composition of the diet. As discussed in chapter 2, a loss of weight is not the sole goal of a diet. Rather the goal is maximization of fat loss with a minimization of muscle loss.

Section 5: Fat loss

The basic premise of the ketogenic diet is that, by shifting the metabolism towards fat use and away from glucose use, more fat and less protein is lost for a given caloric deficit. Given the same total weight loss, the diet which has the best nitrogen balance will have the greatest fat loss. Unfortunately a lack of well done studies (for reasons discussed previously) make this premise difficult to support.

Before discussing the studies on ketogenic diets, a related approach, called the protein sparing modified fast (PSMF) is discussed. Following that, changes in body composition are discussed at three calorie levels: maintenance calories, below 1200 calories per day, and finally between 10% below maintenance and 1200 calories per day.

The PSMF

The PSMF is a ketogenic regimen designed to maximize fat loss while minimizing protein losses. The sole source of calories are lean proteins which provide 1.5 grams of protein per kilogram of ideal body mass (which is used to estimate lean body mass) or approximately 0.7-0.8 grams of protein per pound. (14,20,42-44). Vitamins and minerals are given to avoid the problems discussed in chapter 7 and no other calories are consumed (42,44).

The total caloric intake of the PSMF is extremely low, generally 600-800 calories per day or less. Once the adaptations to ketosis have occurred, the remainder of the day's caloric requirements are derived from bodyfat. For an average size male, with a basal metabolic rate of 2700 calories per day, this may represent 2500 calories or 280 grams of fat (approximately 0.7 lb of fat) used per day.

Fat losses of 0.2 kilograms/day (0.45 lbs) in women and 0.3 kilograms/day (0.66 lbs) in men can be achieved and weight losses of three to five pounds per week are not uncommon (44,45). This can be achieved with only small losses of protein, which occur primarily during the first three weeks while the adaptations to ketosis are occurring.

Additionally, appetite tends to be blunted in some individuals, making adherence easier. Finally, there are typically improvements in blood pressure, blood glucose, and blood lipids while on the PSMF (44). These effects make the PSMF is a very attractive approach for fat loss.

However, the PSMF has drawbacks which make it unsuitable for do-it-yourself dieters.

First and foremost, the extremely low calorie nature of the PSMF makes medical supervision an absolute requirement as frequent blood tests must be performed to watch for signs of metabolic abnormalities (44). Additionally, the excessively low calories will cause a decrease in metabolic rate making weight regain more likely than if a more moderate approach is used.

Typically the PSMF is only used with cases of morbid obesity, when the risks associated with the PSMF are lower than the risks associated with remaining severely obese, and where rapid weight loss is required (44,45). In fact, the PSMF has been shown to be more effective in individuals who are obese versus those who are lean (43,46).

The ketogenic diet at maintenance calories

A popular belief states that fat can be lost on a ketogenic diet without the creation of a caloric deficit. This implies that there is an inherent 'calorie deficit', or some sort of metabolic enhancement from the state of ketosis that causes fat to be lost without restriction of calories. There are several mechanisms that might create such an inherent caloric deficit.

The loss of ketones in the urine and breath represents one mechanism by which calories are wasted. However, even maximal excretion of ketones only amounts to 100 calories per day (47). This would amount to slightly less than one pound of extra fat lost per month.

Additionally since ketones have fewer calories per gram (4.5 cal/gram) compared to free fatty acids (9 cal/gram), it has been suggested that more fat is used to provide the same energy to the body. To provide 45 calories to the body would require 10 grams of ketones, requiring the breakdown of 10 grams of free fatty acids in the liver, versus only 5 grams of free fatty acids if they are used directly. Therefore an additional 5 grams of FFA would be 'wasted' to generate ketones.

However, this wastage would only occur during the first few weeks of a ketogenic diet when tissues other than the brain are deriving a large portion of their energy from ketones. After this point, the only tissue which derives a significant amount of energy from ketones is the brain. Since ketones at 4.5 calories/gram are replacing glucose at 4 calories/gram, it is hard to see how this would result in a substantially greater fat loss. Anecdotally, many individuals do report that the greatest fat loss on a ketogenic diet occurs during the first few weeks of the diet, but this pattern is not found in research.

Only one study has examined a long term ketogenic diet at maintenance calories (17). Elite cyclists were studied while they maintained their training. Over the span of four weeks there was a small weight loss, approximately 2.5 kilograms (~5lbs) which was quickly gained back when carbohydrates were refed. This loss most likely represented water and glycogen loss, and not true fat loss. Whether this would be different with weight training is unknown. But it does not appear that a ketogenic diet affects metabolism such that fat can be lost without the creation of a caloric deficit.

Strangely, some individuals have reported that they can over consume calories on a ketogenic diet without gaining as much fat as would be expected. While this seems to contradict basic thermodynamics, it may be that the excess dietary fat is excreted as excess ketones rather than being stored. Frequently these individuals note that urinary ketone levels as measured by

Ketostix (tm) are much deeper when they over consume calories. Obviously at some point a threshold is reached where fat consumption is higher than utilization, and fat will be stored.

One study has examined the effect of increasing amounts of dietary fat while on a low-carbohydrate diet and found that up to 600 grams of fat per day could be consumed before weight gain began to occur (48). This effect only occurred in subjects given corn oil, which is high in essential fatty acids, but did not occur in subjects given olive oil, which is not. The corn oil subjects reported a feeling of warmth, suggesting increased caloric expenditure which generated heat. This obviously deserves further research.

The ketogenic diet at very low calorie levels (VLCD, below 1200 cal/day)

As with the studies on protein sparing, VLCD studies comparing ketogenic to non-ketogenic diets tend to be highly variable in terms of results. Some studies show greater weight/fat and less protein losses (19,24,46,49) while others show the opposite (10,15,21,23,25,26,50). The variability is probably related to factors discussed previously: short study periods, insufficient protein in many studies, and exceedingly low calorie levels.

Additionally, few studies incorporate exercise, which has been shown to improve fat loss while sparing muscle loss. Therefore, it is difficult to extrapolate from these studies to the types of ketogenic diets discussed in this book (with a moderate caloric deficit, sufficient protein, and exercise). Ultimately these studies should should not be used as evidence for or against ketogenic diets.

The ketogenic diet at low calorie levels (10% below maintenance to 1200 cal/day)

In contrast to the results seen with ketogenic VLCDs, there is slightly more evidence that a ketogenic diet will show greater fat loss and less muscle loss than a non-ketogenic diet at higher calorie levels. However, more research is needed at moderate caloric deficits. Since there are few studies done comparing fat loss/muscle loss at this caloric level, they are discussed in more detail.

In one of the earliest studies of low-carbohydrate diets, subjects were fed 1800 calories, 115 grams of protein, and varied carbohydrate from 104 grams to 60 grams to 30 grams (18). Fat was varied in proportion to carbohydrate to keep calories constant. The diet was fed for 9 weeks. Total fat loss was directly related to carbohydrate content with the highest fat loss occurring with the lowest carbohydrate content and vice versa. Since there were so few subjects in each group, the data for each subject is presented. The data from this study appears in table 2 on the next page.

By examining the data for each subject, some patterns emerge. First and foremost, there is a definite trend for greater fat loss and less LBM loss as carbohydrates are decreased in the diet. However, there is a large degree of variability (note that subject 3 in the medium carbohydrate group lost less muscle than subject 3 in the low carbohydrate group). Before drawing any ultimate conclusions from this study, it should be noted that the protein intake is still below what is recommended in this book, which might change the results in all diet groups. Additionally, the low carbohydrate nature of all three diets, relative to current dietary recommendations, makes it impossible to draw conclusions between a ketogenic diet and a more typical high-carbohydrate diet deriving 55-60% of its total calories from carbohydrate.

Table 2: changes in body composition

Group		Carb (g)	Protein (g)	Fat (g)	Weight loss (kg)	Fat loss (kg)	LBM loss (kg)
High	1	104	115	103	8.5	6.6	1.9
	2				13.9	10.2	2.7
Medium	1	60	115	122	13.4	9.9	3.5
	2				11.6	9.9	1.7
	3				11.8	10.9	0.9
Low	1	30	115	133	Not measured		
	2				15.3	14.7	0.6
	3				16.0	15.0	1.0

Source: Young CM et. al. Effect on body composition and other parameters in young men of carbohydrate reduction in diet. Am J Clin Nutr (1971) 24: 290-296.

Two recent studies, both at 1200 calories found no significant difference in the weight or fat loss between groups consuming high- or low-carbohydrate diets (27,28) However, an examination of the data shows a trend towards greater fat loss in the lower carbohydrate groups with less protein loss. The data is summarized below in table 3.

Table 3: Changes in body composition for high- and low-carbohydrate diets

Study	Length (weeks)	Carbs (g)	Protein (g)	Weight loss (kg)	Fat loss (kg)	LBM loss (kg)*
Golay (27)	12	75	86	10.2	8.1	2.1
		135	86	8.6	7.1	1.4
Alford (28)	10	75	90	6.4	5.7	0.7
		135	60	5.4	4.5	0.9
		225	45	4.8	3.7	1.1

*Determined as the difference between total weight loss and fat loss

Note: in both studies, the difference in weight, fat and LBM loss was not statistically significant, due to the high degree of variability among subjects.

Source: Golay A et al. Weight-loss with low or high carbohydrate diet? Int J Obes (1996) 20: 1067-1072 ; and Alford BB et. al. The effects of variations in carbohydrate, protein and fat content of the diet upon weight loss, blood values, and nutrient intake of adult women. J Am Diet Assoc (1990) 90: 534-540.

Why the discrepancy between VLCD research and moderate caloric deficits?

The discrepancy between research on diets with extreme caloric deficits versus those with more moderate deficits is perplexing. At first glance it would seem that the greater the caloric deficit, the more fat which should be lost. However in practice, even with sufficient dietary protein, this is rarely the case, especially in the first few weeks of a diet. Although the reasons for this discrepancy are unknown, some speculation is warranted.

It appears that there are certain caloric thresholds beyond which the physiological responses to diet and exercise change. As discussed in chapter 22, exercise has its greatest impact in increasing fat loss and decreasing muscle loss with moderate caloric deficits. (51) Once calories are reduced below a certain point, exercise generally stops having a significant effect.

It may also be that once calorie levels fall below a certain level, there is increased muscle loss regardless of diet, especially in the first few weeks. That is, for reasons which are not entirely understood, the body appears to be limited in the quantity of fat it can breakdown without some loss of protein (52). This makes it difficult to measure significant differences in bodyfat and protein losses, simply because they are so high in both ketogenic and non-ketogenic VLCDs.

This speculation is consistent with studies on metabolic rate showing a much larger decrease in metabolic rate once calories reach a certain low level (53,54). Hence this book's recommendation to use moderate caloric restriction with exercise. It is interesting that the study done with the highest caloric intake (1800 calories/day) showed the most significant differences in fat and weight loss ; but more research is needed at this calorie level.

Along with this is the issue of inadequate protein, discussed previously in this book. The low-calorie nature of the VLCD mandates low protein levels. With only 400 calories per day, the maximum amount of protein which could be consumed would be 100 grams, still lower than the 150 grams required to prevent all nitrogen losses determined in the last chapter. Low protein intake may be one cause of the decrease in metabolic rate with VLCDs (55) and it seems reasonable that this could have an impact on fat loss/LBM loss as well.

Summary

The effects of the ketogenic diet on weight and water loss are fairly established. In general, due to the diuretic nature of ketones, total weight and water loss will generally be higher for a ketogenic diet compared to a non-ketogenic diet. However, once water losses, which may represent a weight loss of 5 pounds or more, are factored out, the true weight loss from a ketogenic diet is generally the same as for a non-ketogenic diet of the same calorie level. This is especially true at low calorie levels.

The research on fat and LBM losses are more contradictory and may be related to calorie level. At maintenance calories, fat loss will not occur. At extremely low calorie levels, below 1200 per day and lower, there are some studies suggesting that a ketogenic diet causes more fat/less LBM loss than a non-ketogenic diet while other studies support the opposite. In all likelihood, the differences are due to variations in study design, protein intake, study length, etc. Because these studies do not mimic the types of ketogenic diets described in this book, with a moderate caloric deficit, adequate protein, and exercise, they should not be used as evidence for or against the ketogenic diet.

At more moderate caloric levels, one early study has shown that fat loss increased as carbohydrate intake decreased. Two recent studies showed no statistically significant differences, but there was a trend towards greater fat loss and less muscle loss as carbohydrate quantity came down. An important note is the high degree of variability in subject response to the different diets. None of these studies provided what this author considers to be adequate amounts of protein.

Perhaps the proper conclusion to be drawn from these studies is the variety of approaches which can all yield good results. At the very least, a properly designed ketogenic diet with adequate protein appears to give no worse results than a non-ketogenic diet with a similar caloric intake. Some research suggests that it may give better results. Anecdotally many individuals report better maintenance of lean body mass for a SKD/CKD compared to a more traditional diet. This is not universal and others have noted greater LBM losses on a ketogenic diet.

The definitive study comparing a ketogenic to a non-ketogenic diet has yet to be performed. It would compare fat loss/muscle loss for a ketogenic diet at 10-20% below maintenance calories, with adequate protein, and weight training to a higher carbohydrate diet with the same calories, protein intake, and exercise.

Ultimately, fat loss depends on expending more calories than are consumed. Some individuals have difficulty restricting calories on a high-carbohydrate diet. If lowering carbohydrates and increasing dietary fat increases satiety, and makes it easier to control calories, then that may be the better dietary choice. Other potential pros and cons of the ketogenic diet are discussed in the next chapter.

References Cited

1. Withrow CD. The ketogenic diet: mechanism of anticonvulsant action. Adv Neurol (1980) 27: 635-642.
2. Phinney S. Exercise during and after very-low-calorie dieting. Am J Clin Nutr (1992) 56: 190S-194S
3. Jungas RL et. al. Quantitative analysis of amino acid oxidation and related gluconeogenesis in humans Phys Rev (1992) 72: 419-448
4. Cahill G. Starvation. Trans Am Clin Climatol Assoc (1982) 94: 1-21.
5. Felig P. et. al. Blood glucose and gluconeogenesis in fasting man. Arch Intern Med (1969) 123: 293-298.
6. Bortz WM et. al. Glycerol turnover in man. J Clin Invest (1972) 51: 1537-1546.
7. Yang MU et. al. Estimation of composition of weight loss in man: a comparison of methods. J Appl Physiol (1977) 43: 331-338.
8. Krietzman S. Factors influencing body composition during very-low-calorie diets. Am J Clin Nutr (1992) 56 (suppl): 217S-223S.
9. Lemon P. Is increased dietary protein necessary or beneficial for individuals with a physically active lifestyle? Nutrition Reviews (1996) 54: S169-S175.
10. Yang MU and Van Itallie TB. Variability in body protein loss during protracted severe caloric restriction: role of triiodothyronine and other possible determinants. Am J Clin Nutr (1984)

40: 611-622.

11. Flatt JP and Blackburn GL. The metabolic fuel regulatory system: implications for protein sparing therapies during caloric deprivation and disease. Am J Clin Nutr (1974) 27: 175-187.

12. Blackburn GL et. al. Protein sparing therapy during periods of starvation with sepsis or trauma. Ann Surg (1973) 177: 588-594.

13. Hendler R and Bonde AA. Very low calorie diets with high and low protein contest: impact on triiodothyronine, energy expenditure and nitrogen balance. Am J Clin Nutr (1988) 48: 1239-1247.

14. Davis PG and Phinney SD. Differential effects of two very low calorie diets on aerobic and anaerobic performance. Int J Obes (1990) 14: 779-787.

15. Vazquez J and Adibi SA. Protein sparing during treatment of obesity: ketogenic versus nonketogenic very low calorie diet. Metabolism (1992) 41: 406-414.

16. Swendseid ME et. al. Plasma amino acid levels in subjects fed isonitrogenous diets containing different proportions of fat and carbohydrate. Am J Clin Nutr (1967) 20: 52-55.

17. Phinney SD et. al. The human metabolic response to chronic ketosis without caloric restriction: physical and biochemical adaptations. Metabolism (1983) 32: 757-768.

18. Young CM et. al. Effect on body composition and other parameters in young men of carbohydrate reduction in diet. Am J Clin Nutr (1971) 24: 290-296.

19. Bell J. et. al. Ketosis, weight loss, uric acid, and nitrogen balance in obese women fed single nutrients at low caloric levels. Metab Clin Exp (1969) 18:193-208.

20. Bistrian BR et. al. Effect of a protein-sparing diet and brief fast on nitrogen metabolism in mildly obese subjects. J Lab Med (1977) 89:1030-1035

21. Yang MU and VanItallie TB. Composition of weight lost during short-term weight reduction. Metabolic responses of obese subjects to starvation and low-calorie ketogenic and nonketogenic diets. J Clin Invest (1976) 58: 722-730.

22. Hoffer LJ et. al. Metabolic effects of very low calorie weight reduction diets. J Clin Invest (1984) 73: 750-758.

23. Golay A. et. al. Similar weight loss with low- or high-carbohydrate diets. Am J Clin Nutr (1996) 63: 174-178.

24. Morgan WD et. al. Changes in total body nitrogen during weight reduction by very-low-calorie diets. Am J Clin Nutr (1992) 56 (suppl): 26S-264S.

25. DeHaven JR at. al. Nitrogen and sodium balance and sympathetic-nervous-system activity in obese subjects treated with a very low calorie protein or mixed diet. N Engl J Med (1980) 302: 302-477.

26. Dietz WH and Wolfe RR. Interrelationships of glucose and protein metabolism in obese adolescents during short term hypocaloric dietary therapy. Am J Clin Nutr (1985) 42: 380--390.

27. Golay A et al. Weight-loss with low or high carbohydrate diet? Int J Obes (1996) 20: 1067-1072.

28. Alford BB et. al. The effects of variations in carbohydrate, protein and fat content of the diet upon weight loss, blood values, and nutrient intake of adult women. J Am Diet Assoc (1990) 90: 534-540.

29. Kekwick A and Pawan GLS. Metabolic study in human obesity with isocaloric diets high in fat, protein, and carbohydrate. Metabolism (1957) 6: 447-460.

30. Kekwick A and Pawan GLS. Calorie intake relation to bodyweight changes in the obese. Lancet (1956) 155-161.

31. Chalmers TM et. al. On the fat-mobilising activity of human urine Lancet (1958) 866-869.
32. Chalmers TM et. al. Fat-mobilising and ketogenic activity of urine extracts: Relation to corticotrophin and growth hormones. Lancet (1960) 6-9.
33. Grande F Letters to the editor: (Fasting versus a ketogenic diet). Nutr Rev (1967) 25:189-191
34. Grande F. Energy balance and body composition: a critical study of three recent publications. Ann Int Med (1968) 68: 467-480.
35. Werner SC Comparison between weight reduction on a high calorie, high fat diet and on a isocaloric regimen high in carbohydrate. New Engl J Med (1955) 252: 604-612.
36. Oleson ES and Quaade F. Fatty foods and obesity. Lancet (1960) 1:1048-1051
37. "Textbook of Biochemistry with Clinical Correlations 4th ed." Ed. Thomas M. Devlin. Wiley-Liss 1997.
38. Sigler MH. The mechanism of the natiuresis of fasting. J Clin Invest (1975) 55: 377-387.
39. Olsson KE and Saltin B. Variations in total body water with muscle glycogen changes in man. Acta Physiol Scand (1970) 80: 11-18.
40. Pilkington TRE et. al. Diet and weight reduction in the obese. Lancet (1960) 1: 856-858.
41. Kreitzman SN et. al. Glycogen storage: illusions of easy weight loss, excessive weight regain, and distortions in estimates of body composition. Am J Clin Nutr (1992) 56: 292S-293S.
42. Bistrian B. Recent developments in the treatment of obesity with particular reference to semistarvation ketogenic regimens. Diabetes Care (1978) 1: 379-384.
43. Palgi A. et. al. Multidisciplinary treatment of obesity with a protein-sparing modified fast: Results in 668 outpatients. Am Journal Pub Health (1985) 75: 1190-1194.
44. Walters JK et. al. The protein-sparing modified fast for obesity-related medical problems. Cleveland Clinical J Med (1997) 64: 242-243.
45. Bistrian BR Clinical use of protein-sparing modified fast. JAMA (1978) 2299-2302.
46. Iselin HU and Burckhardt P. Balanced hypocaloric diet versus protein-sparing modified fast in the treatment of obesity: A comparative study. Int J Obes (1982) 6:175-181.
47. Council on Foods and Nutrition. A critique of low-carbohydrate ketogenic weight reducing regimes. JAMA (1973) 224: 1415-1419.
48. Kasper H. et. al. Response of bodyweight to a low carbohydrate, high fat diet in normal and obese subjects. Am J Clin Nutr (1973) 26: 197-204.
49. Rabast U. et. al. Dietetic treatment of obesity with low and high-carbohydrate diets: comparative studies and clinical results. Int J Obes (1979) 3: 201-211.
50. Hood CE et. al. Observations on obese patients eating isocaloric reducing diets with varying proportions of carbohydrate. Br J Nutr (1970) 24: 39.
51. Saris WHM. The role of exercise in the dietary treatment of obesity. Int J Obes (1993) 17 (suppl 1): S17-S21.
52. Owen OE et al. Protein, fat and carbohydrate requirements during starvation: anaplerosis and cataplerosis. Am J Clin Nutr (1998) 68: 12-34.
53. Saris WHM. Effects of energy restriction and exercise on the sympathetic nervous system. Int J Obes (1995) 19 (suppl 7): S17-S23.
54. Prentice AM et. al. Physiological responses to slimming. Proc Nutr Soc (1991) 50: 441-458.
55. Whitehead JM et. al. The effect of protein intake on 24-h energy expenditure during energy restriction. Int J Obes (1996) 20: 727-732.

Chapter 7:
Other effects of the ketogenic diet

The ketogenic diet has numerous metabolic effects, many of which are discussed in the previous chapters. However there are numerous other metabolic effects that need to be discussed as well as concerns which are typically raised regarding the ketogenic diet.

This chapter is a catch-all to discuss any effects on the body that have not been discussed in previous chapters. It examines the effects (and side-effects) of the metabolic state of ketosis on the human body. As well, some of the major health concerns which have been voiced regarding the ketogenic diet are addressed here.

There are ultimately two main concerns regarding the ketogenic diet in terms of health risks. The first is the potential negative effects of the 'high protein' intake of the ketogenic diet. Additionally, there is the effect of high levels of ketones. They are discussed as needed below.

Please note that not all of the effects of ketosis on human physiology are known at this time. Ketosis has been studied for almost 100 years and will most likely continue to be studied so any information provided here represents only the current base of knowledge. For this discussion, no distinction is made, except as necessary, between starvation ketosis and dietary ketosis.

A note on long-term effects

There are few studies of the long term effects of a ketogenic diet. One of the few, which followed two explorers over a period of 1 year was done almost 70 years ago (1). Beyond that study, the two models most often used to examine the effects of the ketogenic diet are the Inuit and pediatric epilepsy patients. Epileptic children have been studied extensively, and are kept in ketosis for periods up to three years. In this group, the major side effects of the ketogenic diet are elevated blood lipids, constipation, water-soluble vitamin deficiency, increased incidence of kidney stones, growth inhibition, and acidosis during illness.

However, the pediatric epilepsy diet is not identical the the typical ketogenic diet used by dieters and healthy adults, especially in terms of protein intake, and may not provide a perfect model. While studies of epileptic children give some insight into possible long term effects of a ketogenic diet, it should be noted that there are no studies of the long-term effects of a CKD or similar diet approach. The consequences of alternating between a ketogenic and non-ketogenic metabolism are a total unknown. For this reason, it is not recommended that a CKD, or any ketogenic diet, be followed indefinitely.

Insulin resistance

Although low-carbohydrate diets tend to normalize insulin and blood glucose levels in many individuals, a little known effect is increased insulin resistance when carbohydrates are refed. There is little research concerning the physiological effects of refeeding carbohydrates after long-term ketogenic dieting although fasting has been studied to some degree. Early ketogenic diet literature mentions a condition called 'alloxan' or 'starvation diabetes', referring to an initial insulin resistance when carbohydrates are reintroduced to the diet following carbohydrate restriction (2).

In brief, the initial physiological response to carbohydrate refeeding looks similar to what is seen in Type II diabetics, namely blood sugar swings and hyperinsulinemia. This type of response is also seen in individuals on a CKD. It should be noted that this response did not occur universally in research, being more prevalent in those who had preexisting glucose control problems. As well, exercise appears to affect how well or poorly the body handles carbohydrates during refeeding.

One hypothesis for this effect was that ketones themselves interfered with insulin binding and glucose utilization but this was shown not to be the case (3,4). In fact, ketones may actually improve insulin binding (2). The exact reason for this 'insulin resistance' was not determined until much later. The change was ultimately found to be caused by changes in enzyme levels, especially in those enzymes involved in both fat and carbohydrate burning (5). High levels of free fatty acid levels also affect glucose transport and utilization (6).

Long periods of time without carbohydrate consumption leads to a down regulation in the enzymes responsible for carbohydrate burning. Additionally, high levels of free fatty acids in the bloodstream may impair glucose transport (6).

This change occurs both in the liver (5) and in the muscle (5,7). During carbohydrate refeeding, the body upregulates levels of these enzymes but there is a delay during which the body may have difficulty storing and utilizing dietary carbohydrates. This delay is approximately 5 hours to upregulate liver enzyme levels and anywhere from 24-48 hours in muscle tissue (8,9). While there is a decrease in carbohydrate oxidation in the muscle, this is accompanied by an increase in glycogen storage (7).

These time courses for enzyme up-regulation correspond well with what is often seen in individuals on a CKD, which is really nothing more than a ketogenic diet followed by carbohydrate refeeding done on a weekly basis. Frequently, individuals will report the presence of urinary ketones during the first few hours of their carb-loading period, seeming to contradict the idea that carbohydrates always interrupt ketosis. This suggests that the liver is continuing to oxidize fat at an accelerated rate and that ingested carbohydrates are essentially not being 'recognized' by the liver.

After approximately 5 hours, when liver enzymes upregulate, urinary ketone levels typically decrease as liver glycogen begins to refill. Another interesting aspect of carbohydrate refeeding is that liver glycogen is not initially refilled by incoming glucose. Rather glucose is released into the bloodstream for muscle glycogen resynthesis (especially if muscle glycogen stores are depleted) initially, refilling liver glycogen later.

In practice, many individuals report what appears to be rebound hypoglycemia (low blood sugar) either during the carb-up or during the first few days of eating carbohydrates when ketogenic eating is ended, for the reasons discussed above.

Ketones themselves do not appear to alter how cells respond to insulin (4) which goes against the popular belief that ketogenic diets somehow alter fat cells, making them more likely to store fat when the ketogenic diet is ended. Practical experience shows this to be true, as many individuals have little trouble maintaining their bodyfat levels when the ketogenic diet is stopped, especially if their activity patterns are maintained.

Appetite suppression

An unusual effect of complete fasting is a general decrease in appetite after a short period of time. Additionally, studies which restrict carbohydrate but allow 'unlimited' fat and protein find that calorie intake goes down compared to normal levels further suggesting a link between ketosis and appetite (10,11).

Since continued fasting causes an increase in ketone bodies in the bloodstream, achieving a maximum in 2-3 weeks, it was always assumed that ketones were the cause of the appetite suppression (12). As with many aspects of ketosis (in this case starvation ketosis), this assumption was never directly studied and propagated itself through the literature without challenge. Recent research indicates that ketones per se are most likely not the cause of the decreased appetite during ketosis.

As discussed in chapter 9, several studies have shown an automatic decrease in caloric intake (and presumably appetite) when individuals restrict carbohydrates to low levels, despite being told to eat 'unlimited' amounts of fat and protein. In one study the ketogenic diet suppressed appetite moreso than a balanced diet where an appetite suppressant was given (13).

Several studies have compared appetite on a very low calorie (below 800 calories/day) ketogenic diet versus appetite on a balanced diet with the same calories (14,15). In general, no difference was seen in appetite between the two diets. This leads researchers to think that ketones do not blunt appetite in and of themselves. Rather two possible mechanisms seem a more likely explanation for the appetite blunting seen with a ketogenic diet.

First, is the relatively higher fat content of the ketogenic diet compared to other diets. Fat tends to slow digestion, meaning that food stays in the stomach longer, providing a sense of fullness. The same has been shown to for protein (14). Additionally, protein stimulates the release of the hormone cholecystokinin (CCK) which is thought to help regulate appetite.

However, studies using very-low-calorie intake (and hence low dietary fat intakes) have documented this same blunting of appetite, suggesting a different mechanism. Rather than the effects of dietary fat, the researchers argue that what is perceived as a blunting of appetite is simply a return to baseline hunger levels.

That is, during the initial stages of a diet, there is an increase in appetite, which is followed by a decrease over time. It is this decrease which is being interpreted by dieter's as a blunting of appetite (14,15).

Overall, the data supporting an appetite suppressing effect of ketogenic diets points to a mechanism other than ketones. This is not to say that appetite may not be suppressed on a ketogenic diet, only that it is most likely not ketones or metabolic ketosis which are the cause of the suppression.

Anecdotally, some individuals have a strong suppression of appetite while others do not. This discrepancy can probably be ascribed to individual differences. If a dieter's appetite is suppressed substantially on a ketogenic diet, it may be difficult for them to consume the necessary calories. In this case, the use of calorically dense foods such as mayonnaise and vegetable oils can be used to increase caloric intake. If appetite is not suppressed on a ketogenic diet, less calorically dense foods can be consumed.

Cholesterol levels

The relatively high fat intake of the ketogenic diet immediately raises concerns regarding the effects on blood lipids and the potential for increases in the risk for heart disease, stroke, etc. Several key players in relative risk for these diseases are low density lipoproteins (LDL, or 'bad cholesterol'), high density lipoproteins (HDL, or 'good cholesterol') and blood triglyceride levels (TG). High levels of total cholesterol, and high levels of LDL correlate with increased disease risk. High levels of HDL are thought to exert a protective effect against cholesterol-related disease.

The overall effects of implementing a ketogenic diet on blood cholesterol levels are far from established. Early short-term studies showed a large increase in blood lipid levels (16,17). However, later studies have shown either no change or a decrease in cholesterol levels (18-20).

One problem is that few long term studies are available on the ketogenic diet, except in epileptic children. In this population, who are kept in deep ketosis for periods up to three years, blood lipid levels do increase (21,22). However, the ketogenic diet is not thought to be atherogenic due to the fact that any negative effects induced by three years in ketosis will be corrected when the diet is ended (22).

It has been shown that Inuits, who maintain a ketogenic diet for long periods of time every year, do not develop heart disease as quickly as other Americans (23), suggesting that there are no long term effects. However, this may be related to the fact that a ketogenic diet is not continued indefinitely. There may be a slow removal of cholesterol from the arteries during time periods when a more balanced diet is being followed (23).

Most of the degenerative diseases thought to be linked to high blood lipid levels take years (or decades) to develop. Unless an individual is going to stay on a ketogenic diet for extremely long periods of time, it is not thought that there will be appreciable problems with cholesterol buildup. From a purely anecdotal standpoint, some individuals who have undergone testing show a complete lack of cholesterol buildup in their arteries.

Another problem is that weight/fat loss per se is known to decrease cholesterol levels and it is difficult to distinguish the effects of the ketogenic diet from the effects of the weight/fat loss which occurs. A few well designed studies allow us to make the following rough generalizations:

1. If an individual loses weight/fat on a ketogenic diet, their cholesterol levels will go down (18,24,25) ;
2. If an individual does not lose weight/fat on a ketogenic diet, their cholesterol levels will go up (24,26).

As well, there can be a decrease followed by increase in blood lipid levels (27). This is thought to represent the fact that body fat is a storehouse for cholesterol and the breakdown of bodyfat during weight loss causes a release of cholesterol into the bloodstream (27). Additionally, women may see a greater increase in cholesterol than men while on the ketogenic diet although the reason for this gender difference in unknown (28). In practical experience however, there is a great range of responses among individuals on a ketogenic diet. Some show a drastic decrease in cholesterol while others shown an increase.

Changes in blood TG levels are also common on the ketogenic diet. Somewhat counterintiuitively, there is generally a decrease in blood TG levels, (28) which may indicate greater uptake of TG by tissues such as skeletal muscle.

Since no absolute conclusions can be drawn regarding cholesterol levels on a ketogenic diet, dieters are encouraged to have their blood lipid levels monitored for any negative responses. Ideally, blood lipid levels should be checked prior to starting the diet and again 6-8 weeks later. If repeat blood lipid tests show a worsening of lipid levels, saturated fats should be substituted with unsaturated fats or the diet should be abandoned.

Low energy levels

Carbohydrates are the body's preferred fuel when they are available (see chapter 4). As well, they burn more efficiently than fats. Many individuals voice concerns about drops in general energy levels (not including exercise) on a ketogenic diet due to the lack of carbohydrates.

Many subjects in early studies on ketosis or the PSMF noted transient lethargy and weakness. As well many studies noted a high occurrence of orthostatic hypotension which is a drop in blood pressure when individuals move from a sitting to standing position. This caused lightheadedness in many individuals. It was always taken for granted that ketosis caused this to happen.

However, later studies established that most of these symptoms could be avoided by providing enough supplemental minerals, especially sodium. Providing 4-5 grams of sodium per day (not much higher than the average American diet) prevents the majority of symptoms of weakness and low energy, possibly by maintaining normal blood pressure (26).

In most individuals fatigue should disappear within a few days to a few weeks at most. If fatigue remains after this time period, small amounts of carbohydrates can be added to the diet, as long as ketosis is maintained, or the diet should be abandoned for a more balanced diet.

The effects of ketogenic diets on exercise are discussed in chapter 22. To summarize, ketogenic diets can generally sustain low-intensity aerobic exercise without problem after a period of adaptation. However because carbohydrates are an absolute requirement to sustain high intensity exercise such as weight training or high-intensity aerobic exercise, a standard ketogenic diet is not appropriate.

Effects on the brain

A well known effect of ketogenic diets is the increased use of ketones by the brain (29). As well, some of the effects of the ketogenic diet in treating childhood epilepsy may be due to this increased extraction of ketones (30,31). Due to the changes which occur, a variety of concerns has been voiced in terms of possible side-effects. These include permanent brain impairment and short term memory loss.

These concerns are difficult to understand in terms of where they originated. What must be understood is that ketones are normal physiological substances. As discussed in great detail in chapter 4, ketones provide the brain with fuel when glucose (or food in general) is not available. The brain develops the enzymes to use ketones during fetal development and these enzymes are still present as we age (32), which should serve to illustrate that ketones are normal fuels, and not toxic byproducts of an abnormal metabolism.

Although not a perfect model, epileptic children provide some insight into possible detrimental long term effects of the ketogenic diet on brain function. Quite simply, there are no negative effects in terms of cognitive function (30). Except for some initial transient fatigue, similar to what is reported in adults, there appears to be no decrement in mental functioning while on the diet or after it is ended.

However, this is not absolute proof that the ketogenic diet couldn't have possible long-term effects on the brain ; simply that no data currently exists to suggest that it will have any negative effects. Anecdotally, individuals tend to report one of two types of functioning while in ketosis: excellent or terrible. Some individuals feel that they concentrate better and think more lucidly while in ketosis ; others feel nothing but fatigue. Differences in individual physiology may explain the difference.

With regard to short term memory loss, the only study which remotely addresses this point is a recent study which showed temporary decrements in a trail-making task (which requires a high degree of mental flexibility) during the first week of a low-calorie ketogenic diet as compared to a non-ketogenic diet (33). The majority of the effects were seen during the first week of the diet, and disappeared as the study progressed.

As stated previously, some individuals do note mental fatigue and a lack of concentration during the first 1-3 weeks of a ketogenic diet. In practical terms, this means that individuals who operate heavy machinery, or need maximum mental acuity for some reason (i.e. a presentation or final exam) should not start a ketogenic diet during this time period.

Uric acid levels

Uric acid is a waste product of protein metabolism that is excreted through the kidneys. Under normal circumstances, uric acid is excreted as quickly as it is produced. This prevents a buildup of uric acid in the bloodstream which can cause problems, the most common of which is gout. Gout occurs when urate cause deposit in the joints and cause pain.

High levels of uric acid in the bloodstream can occur under one of two conditions: when production is increased or when removal through the kidneys is decreased. The ketogenic diet has been shown to affect the rate of uric acid excretion through the kidneys.

Ketones and uric acid compete for the same transport mechanism in the kidneys. Thus when the kidneys remove excess ketone bodies from the bloodstream, the removal of uric acid decreases and a buildup occurs.

Studies of the ketogenic diet and PSMF show a consistent and large (oftentimes doubling or tripling from normal levels) initial increase in uric acid levels in the blood (24,26). In general however, levels return towards normal after several weeks of the diet (35). Small amounts of carbohydrates (5% of total daily calories) can prevent a buildup of uric acid (35). Additionally, in studies of both epileptic children as well as adults the incidence of gout are very few, and only occur in individuals who are predisposed genetically (12, 26,34).

Related to this topic, uric acid stones have occasionally been found in epileptic children following the ketogenic diet (36). This appears to be related to high levels of urinary ketones, low urinary pH and fluid restriction in these patients. It is unknown whether individuals consuming sufficient water on a ketogenic diet have any risk for this complication.

From a practical standpoint, individuals with a genetic predisposition towards gout should either include a minimal amount of carbohydrates (5% of total calories) in their diet or not use a ketogenic diet.

Kidney stones and kidney damage

A common concern voiced about ketogenic diets is the potential for kidney damage or the passing of kidney stones, presumably from an increase in kidney workload from having to filter ketones, urea, and ammonia. As well, dehydration can cause kidney stones in predisposed individuals. Finally, the 'high-protein' nature of ketogenic diets alarms some individuals who are concerned with potential kidney damage.

Overall there is little data to suggest any negative effect of ketogenic diets on kidney function or the incidence of kidney stones. In epileptic children, there is a low incidence (~5%) of small kidney stones (22,30). This may be related to the dehydrated state the children are deliberately kept in rather than the state of ketosis itself (22).

The few short term studies of adults suggest no alteration in kidney function (by measuring the levels of various kidney enzymes) or increased incidence of kidney stones, either while on the diet or for periods up to six months after the diet is stopped (26). Once again, the lack of any long term data prevents conclusions about potential long-term effects of ketosis on kidney function.

With regards to the protein issue, it should be noted that kidney problems resulting from a high protein intake have only been noted in individuals with preexisting kidney problems, and little human data exists to suggest that a high protein intake will cause kidney damage (37). From a purely anecdotal standpoint, athletes have consumed high protein diets for long periods and one would expect kidney problems to show up with increasing incidence in this group. But such an increase has not appeared, suggesting that a high protein intake is not harmful to the kidneys under normal circumstances (37).

However, much of this is predicated on drinking sufficient water to maintain hydration, especially to limit the possibility of kidney stones. Individuals who are predisposed to kidney stones (or have preexisting kidney problems) should consider seriously whether a ketogenic diet is appropriate for them. If they do choose to use a ketogenic diet, kidney function should be monitored with regular blood work to ensure that no complications arise.

Liver damage

Another concern often raised is for the potential negative effects of a ketogenic diet on the liver. In one of the few longer-term (4 weeks) studies of the ketogenic diet, liver enzymes were measured and no change was observed (26). Additionally, no liver problems are encountered in epileptic children. However, it is unknown whether negative effects would be seen in the longer term.

Constipation

Arguably one of the more common side-effects seen on a ketogenic diet is that of reduced bowel movements and constipation (30,34). In all likelihood, this stems from two different causes: a lack of fiber and increased gastrointestinal absorption of foods.

First and foremost, the lack of carbohydrates in a ketogenic diet means that fiber intake will be low unless supplements are used. There is no doubt that fiber is an important nutrient to human health. A high fiber intake has been linked to the prevention of a variety of health problems including some forms of cancer and heart disease.

To make a ketogenic diet as healthy as possible, some type of sugar-free fiber supplement should be used. In addition to possibly preventing any health problems, this will help to maintain bowel regularity. Many individuals find that a large salad containing fibrous vegetables may help with regularity and should fit easily with the 30 gram carbohydrate limit.

One interesting effect of the ketogenic diet is the typically reduced stool volume seen (30). Presumably this is due to enhanced absorption/digestion of foods which leads to less waste products being generated (22).

Vitamin/mineral deficiencies

The restricted food choices of a ketogenic diet raise concerns about possible deficiencies in vitamin and mineral intake. Any diet which is restricted in calories, whether ketogenic or not, will show a decrease in micro-nutrient intake compared to a similar diet at higher calories. So the question is whether the ketogenic diet is more or less nutritionally adequate compared to a 'balanced' diet at the same calorie level. While this is a fairly moot point for those who have already decided to use a ketogenic diet, it is important to examine, if for no other reason than to know what nutrients should be supplemented to the diet.

It is difficult, if not impossible, to obtain adequate micro-nutrients on any diet containing less than 1200 calories per day (37). To a great degree, micro-nutrient intake is affected by total caloric intake regardless of diet. That is, a diet containing 400 calories will have less micro-nutrients that one containing 2000 calories regardless of composition. Therefore, let us look at nutrient intake relative to caloric intake (amount of nutrient per calorie).

One researcher did exactly this, comparing nutrient intakes of his low-carbohydrate diet to the subject's normal diet (39). He then examined how much micronutrient intake would be affected if the subject's normal diets were reduced to the same caloric level as they consumed on the low-carbohydrate diet. As these studies demonstrated, there will obviously be a decrease in nutrient intake if a subject decreases caloric intake from 1900 to 1400 (39). The question therefore is whether a 1400 calorie ketogenic diet is more or less nutritionally complete than a 1400 calorie balanced diet.

On an absolute level, small decreases in thiamine, nicotinic acid, calcium and iron were noted while there were increases in vitamin D and riboflavin. When compared on a relative scale (amount of nutrient per 1000 calories), nutrient intake was actually higher on the low-carbohydrate diet (39). It should be noted that the diet studied was higher in carbohydrate (averaging 67 grams per day) than most ketogenic diets and contained milk. This provides only a limited model for a diet containing 30 grams of carbohydrate or less per day.

Another study examining nutrient intake of a ketogenic diet at 2100 calories found the ketogenic diet to provide greater than the RDA for Vitamin A, Vitamin C, riboflavin, niacin, and phosphorous. There were deficiencies in thiamine, Vitamin B-6, folacin, calcium, magnesium, iron, zinc and fiber (38).

It should be noted that current research into optimal health and prevention of diseases focuses on nutrients in vegetables called phytonutrients, which appear to play a protective role in many diseases. The limited vegetable intake on a ketogenic diet means that these nutrients will not be consumed to any appreciable degree. This once again points to the fact that the ketogenic diet should probably not be used long term (unless indicated for medical reasons), or that individuals on a ketogenic diet should use their small carbohydrate allowance to maximize vegetable intake.

Due to its restrictive nature, the ketogenic diet can be deficient in certain nutrients. However this is no different than any other calorically restricted diet in that any reduction in food intake will result in a reduction in nutrient intake. At the very minimum, a basic multi-vitamin/mineral (providing at least the RDA for all nutrients) should be taken daily to avoid deficiencies. Depending on the intake of dairy foods such as cheese, a calcium supplement may be warranted. Specific nutrients, especially electrolytes are discussed in the next section.

Electrolyte excretion/Death

The diuretic (dehydrating) nature of ketosis causes an excretion of three of the body's primary electrolytes: sodium, potassium, and magnesium (31,40). These three minerals are involved in many processes in the body, one of which is the regulation of muscle contraction, including the heart. Some studies show a net loss of calcium while others do not (31).

A severe loss of electrolytes is problematic. At the least, it can cause muscle cramping, which is often reported by individuals on a ketogenic diet. At the extreme, it can compromise normal heart function.

During the late 1970's, a large number of deaths occurred in individuals following a 300 calorie per day liquid ketogenic diet called "The Last Chance Diet" (41-43). This diet relied on a processed protein as its only source of calories and the protein, which was a hydrolyzed collagen protein with the amino acid tryptophan added to it, contained no vitamins or minerals. As well, mineral supplements were not given or suggested to individuals on the diet.

Several possible causes for these deaths have been suggested, including the direct breakdown of the heart due to the low quality of protein used (42). A second, and more likely cause was that the depletion of electrolytes caused fatal heart arrhythmias. As well, given high quality protein and adequate mineral supplementation, no cardiac abnormalities appear in individuals on a ketogenic diet (44).

"The Last Chance Diet" should be contrasted to a ketogenic diet based around whole foods. The intake of whole protein foods will ensure some intake of the three electrolytes. Even so, studies show that the amount of electrolytes consumed by most on a ketogenic diet is insufficient. Some of the fatigue which was demonstrated in early ketogenic diet studies may have occurred from insufficient mineral intake, especially sodium (26).

A known effect of ketogenic diets is a decrease in blood pressure, most likely due to sodium excretion and water loss. In individuals with high blood pressure (hypertension), this may be beneficial. Individuals with normal blood pressure may suffer from 'orthostatic hypotension' which is lightheadedness which occurs when moving from a sitting to standing posture (45). The inclusion of sufficient minerals appears to be able to prevent symptoms of fatigue, nausea and hypotension (26).

To counteract the excretion of minerals on a ketogenic diet, additional mineral intake is required. Although exact amounts most vary, suggested amounts for the three primary electrolytes appear below (26,46):

Sodium: 3-5 grams in addition to the sodium which occurs in food
Potassium: 1 gram in addition to the 1-1.5 grams of potassium which occur in food
Magnesium: 300 mg

Note: An excessive intake of any single mineral (especially potassium) can be just as dangerous as a deficiency. Although the values listed above are averages, individuals are encouraged to have mineral levels checked to determine the required level of mineral supplementation. At no time should mineral supplements be taken in excess.

Calcium loss/Osteoporosis

A general belief states that high protein diets may be a causative factor in osteoporosis but this is still highly debated (47,48). While studies have shown increased calcium excretion with high protein intakes, this was typically with 'purified' proteins (37). It is thought that whole-food proteins do not cause this to occur as the high phosphate content prevents calcium losses (37). In any event, the 'high protein' nature of the ketogenic diet raises concerns about calcium loss and osteoporosis. There is some evidence that the ketogenic diet causes disordered calcium metabolism, especially if it is combined with drug treatment for epilepsy (49). This effect is reversed when adequate Vitamin D is consumed. Additionally, depending on dairy intake, a calcium supplement may be necessary to ensure positive calcium balance. The current guidelines for calcium intake are 1200 milligrams/day for men and pre-menopausal women and 1500 mg/day for post-menopausal women.

Weight/Fat regain

It is well known that dieting alone shows extremely poor rates of long term success. Typically less than 5-10% of individuals who lose weight through dieting alone will maintain that weight loss in the long term. The effects and implications of coming off a ketogenic diet are discussed in chapter 14. In brief, any fat loss efforts based on caloric restriction alone are typically bound for failure, regardless of whether the diet used is ketogenic or not.

For some reason, there is a concern that weight regain is more of an issue on ketogenic diets than other diets. This most likely stems from the confusion between the loss of body weight and the loss of bodyfat (see chapter 8). The dehydration and glycogen depletion which occurs on ketogenic diets can be anywhere from 1 to 15 pounds of bodyweight. Thus it is to be expected that this weight will be regained when carbohydrates are reintroduced into the diet (either because the diet is being stopped, or for carb-ups as with a CKD).

For individuals who fixate on the scale as the only measure of their progress, this weight regain can be disheartening and may make the individual fear carbohydrates as the source of their excess body weight. Dieters must realize that the initial weight gain is water and glycogen (carbohydrate stored in the muscle) and move past it. Focusing on changes in body composition (see chapter 8) should avoid psychological problems with the weight regain from replenishing water and glycogen. Other issues pertaining to returning to a 'balanced' diet from a ketogenic (or cyclical ketogenic diet) are addressed in chapter 14.

Immune system

Anecdotally, there is a great deal of variety in individual response to ketogenic diets in terms of the immune system. Some individuals have reported a decrease in certain ailments, notably allergy symptoms, while others become more susceptible to minor sicknesses.

There is limited research into the effects of a ketogenic diet on the immune system with two studies showing decrements in some indices of immune system status (50,51). However, one of these studies (50) was done on epileptic children who may consume inadequate protein while the other was done during a PSMF (51). Therefore, it is difficult to be sure whether it is ketosis, a lack of protein, or a lack of calories which is causing these decrements in immune system status. Since no decrease in immune system status was seen when a maintenance calorie ketogenic diet was given, (26) it would seem that any negative immune systems effects in the other studies were caused by low calories and inadequate protein.

Optic neuropathy

One unusual side effect of ketogenic diets which has appeared in a few cases is the development of optic neuropathy, which is a dysfunction of the optic nerve. In all cases, the problem was linked to the fact that the individuals in question were not receiving calcium or vitamin supplements for periods of up to a year. Supplementation of adequate B-vitamins, especially thiamine, corrected all cases which were reported (52,53).

Hair loss/changes in finger and toenails

A final effect which has occasionally been noted, primarily during total fasting or the PSMF, is transient hair loss (34). In a related vein, some individuals have reported changes in the quality of their finger and toe nails. The cause of this phenomenon is unknown but could possible be related to protein or vitamin and mineral intake.

Summary

A number of metabolic effects have either been directly or anecdotally observed to occur in individuals who use the ketogenic diet. As well, a number of health concerns have been voiced, some valid, some invalid. This chapter addresses the main concerns surrounding the ketogenic diet, as well as other effects which can occur outside of the major metabolic effects discussed in the previous chapter.

References Cited

1. Lieb CW. The effects on human beings of a twelve months' exclusive meat diet. JAMA (1929) 20-22.
2. Robinson AM and Williamson DH Physiological roles of ketone bodies as substrates and signals in mammalian tissues. Physiol Rev (1980) 60: 143-187.
3. Kissebah AH. et. al. Interrelationship between glucose and acetoacetate metabolism in human adipose tissue. Diabetologia (1974) 10: 69-75.
4. Misbin RI et. al. Ketoacids and the insulin receptor. Diabetes (1978) 27: 539-542.
5. "Textbook of Biochemistry with Clinical Correlations 4th ed." Ed. Thomas M. Devlin. Wiley-Liss 1997.
6. Roden M et al. Mechanism of free fatty acid-induced insulin resistance in humans. J Clin Invest. (1996) 97: 2859-2865.
7. Cutler DL. Low-carbohydrate diet alters intracellular glucose metabolism but not overall glucose disposal in exercise-trained subjects. Metabolism: Clinical and Experimental (1995) 44: 1364-70.
8. Randle PJ Metabolic fuel selection: general integration at the whole-body level. Proc Nutr Soc (1995) 54: 317-327.
9. Randle PJ et. al. Glucose fatty acid interactions and the regulation of glucose disposal. J Cell Biochem (1994) 55 (suppl): 1-11.
10. Yudkin J. and Carey M. The treatment of obesity by a 'high-fat' diet - the inevitably of calories. Lancet (1960) 939.
11. Yudkin J. The low-carbohydrate diet in the treatment of obesity. Postgrad Med (1972) 151-154
12. Cahill G. Starvation. Trans Am Clin Climatol Assoc (1982) 94: 1-21.
13. Kew MC. Treatment of obesity in the Bantu: value of a low-carbohydrate diet with and without an appetite suppressant. South Africa Med Journal (1970) 44: 1006-1007.
14. Rosen JC et. al. Comparison of carbohydrate-containing and carbohydrate-restricted hypocaloric diets in the treatment of obesity: effects on appetite and mood. Am J Clin Nutr

(1982) 36: 463-469.

15. Rosen JC et. al. Mood and appetite during minimal-carbohydrate and carbohydrate-supplemented hypocaloric diets. Am J Clin Nutr (1985) 42: 371-379.

16. Cham BE et. al. Effect of a high energy, low carbohydrate diet on serum levels of lipids and lipoproteins. Med J Austr (1981) 1:237-240.

17. Rickman F. et. al. Change in serum cholesterol during the Stillman diet. JAMA (1974) 228: 54.

18. Hoffer LJ et. al. Metabolic effects of very low calorie weight reduction diets. J Clin Invest (1984) 73: 750-758.

19. Lewis SB et. al. Effect of diet composition on metabolic adaptations to hypocaloric nutrition: comparison of high carbohydrate and high fat isocaloric diets. Am J Clin Nutr (1977) 30: 160-170.

20. Alford BB et. al. The effects of variations in carbohydrate, protein and fat content of the diet upon weight loss, blood values, and nutrient intake of adult women. J Am Diet Assoc (1990) 90: 534-540.

21. Dekaban A. Plasma lipids in epileptic children treated with the high fat diet. Arch Neurol (1966) 15: 177-184.

22. Swink TD. et. al. The ketogenic diet: 1997. Adv Pediatr (1997) 44: 297-329.

23. Ho JJ et. al. Alaskan arctic Eskimo: responses to a customary high fat diet. Am J Clin Nutr (1972) 25: 737-745.

24. Krehl WA et. al. Some metabolic changes induced by low carbohydrate diets. Am J Clin Nutr (1967) 20: 139-148.

25. Golay A et al. Weight-loss with low or high carbohydrate diet? Int J Obes Relat Metab Disord. (1996) 20: 1067-1072.

26. Phinney SD et. al. The human metabolic response to chronic ketosis without caloric restriction: physical and biochemical adaptations. Metabolism (1983) 32: 757-768.

27. Phinney SD et. al. The transient hypercholesterolemia of major weight loss. Am J Clin Nutr (1991) 53: 1404-1410.

28. Larosa JC et. al. Effects of high-protein, low-carbohydrate dieting on plasma lipoproteins and body weight. J Am Diet Assoc (1980) 77: 264-270.

29. Owen OE et. al. Brain metabolism during fasting. J Clin Invest (1967) 10: 1589-1595.

30. Wheless JW. The ketogenic diet: Fa(c)t or fiction. J Child Neurol (1995) 10: 419-423 .

31. Withrow CD. The ketogenic diet: mechanism of anticonvulsant action. Adv Neurol (1980) 27: 635-642.

32. Patel MS. et. al. The metabolism of ketone bodies in developing human brain: development of ketone-body-utilizing enzymes and ketone bodies as precursors for lipid synthesis. J Neurochem (1975) 25: 905-908.

33. Wing RR et. al. Cognitive effects of ketogenic weight-reducing diets. Int J Obes (1995) 19:811-816.

34. Palgi A et. al. Multidisciplinary treatment of obesity with a protein-sparing modified fast: Results in 668 outpatients. Am Journal Pub Health (1985) 75: 1190-1194.

35. Worthington BS and Taylor LE. Balanced low-calorie vs. low-protein-low carbohydrate reducing diets. II: Biochemical changes. J Am Diet Assoc (1974) 64: 52-55.

36. Herzberg GZ et. al. Urolithiasis associated with the ketogenic diet. J Pediatr (1990) 117:743-745

37. Lemon P. Is increased dietary protein necessary or beneficial for individuals with a physically active lifestyle? Nutrition Reviews (1996) 54: S169-S175.

38. Fisher MC and Lachance PA Nutrition evaluation of published weight reducing diets. J Amer Dietetic Assoc (1985) 85: 450-454.

39. Stock A and Yudkin J. Nutrient intake of subjects on low carbohydrate diet used in treatment of obesity. Am J Clin Nutr (1970) 23: 948-952

40. Sigler MH. The mechanism of the natiuresis of fasting. J Clin Invest (1975) 55: 377-387.

41. Sours HE et. al. Sudden death associated with very low calorie weight reduction regimens. Am J Clin Nutr (1981) 34: 453-461.

42. Lantigua RA et. al Cardiac arrhythmias associated with a liquid protein diet for the treatment of obesity. N Engl J Med (1980) 303: 735-738.

43. Isner JM et. al. Sudden unexpected death in avid dieters using the liquid-protein-modified-fast diet: Observations in 17 patients and the role of the prolonged QT interval. Circulation (1979) 60: 1401-1412.

44. Phinney SD et. al. Normal cardiac rhythm during hypocalorie diets of varying carbohydrate content. Arch Intern Med (1982) 143: 2258-2261.

45. DeHaven JR at. al. Nitrogen and sodium balance and sympathetic-nervous-system activity in obese subjects treated with a very low calories protein or mixed diet. N Engl J Med (1980) 302: 302-477.

46. Bistrian B. Recent developments in the treatment of obesity with particular reference to semistarvation ketogenic regimens. Diabetes Care (1978) 1: 379-384.

47. Heaney RP. Excess dietary protein may not adversely affect bone. J Nutr (1998) 128:1054-1057.

48. Barzel US and Massey LK Excess dietary protein can adversely affect bone. J Nutr (1998) 128:1051-1053.

49. Hahn TJ et. al. Disordered mineral metabolism produced by ketogenic diet therapy. Calcif Tissue Int (1979) 28:17-22.

50. Woody RC et. al. Impaired neutrophil function in children with seizures treated with the ketogenic diet. J Pediatr (1989) 115: 427-430

51. McMurray RW et. al. Effect of prolonged modified fasting in obese persons on in vitro markers of immunity: lymphocyte function and serum effects on normal neutrophils. Am J Med Sci (1990) 299: 379-385.

52. Hoyt CS and Billson FA. Optic neuropathy in ketogenic diet. Br J Ophthalmol (1979) 63: 191-194

53. Hoyt CS and Billson FA. Low-carbohydrate diet optic neuropathy. Med J Austr (1977) 1: 65-66.

Part III:
The Diets

Chapter 8: General dieting principles
Chapter 9: The standard ketogenic diet (SKD)
Chapter 10: Carbs and the ketogenic diet
Chapter 11: The targeted ketogenic diet (TKD)
Chapter 12: The cyclical ketogenic diet (CKD)

Having discussed the physiology behind and adaptations to a ketogenic diet, we can now go about setting up the diet. Before addressing the specifics of the diet, a few general dieting concepts need to be discussed. The first is to differentiate between bodyweight and bodyfat. Most dieters use the scale as the only measure of a diet's effectiveness but this does not give any information as to what (i.e. muscle, fat, water) is being lost.

The second general dieting topic deals with metabolic rate, and setting calories for fat loss or weight gain. Most individuals desiring fat loss tend to restrict calories excessively, causing problems with metabolic slowdown. In this chapter, estimations are made to determine optimal calorie levels for different goals.

Chapter 9 details how to set up the standard ketogenic diet (SKD) which forms the template for the other two diets. Specifics regarding carbohydrate, protein and fat are discussed. As well, the effects of other nutritional substances such as caffeine and citric acid are discussed. Finally, two sample SKDs are set up.

Although the details of exercise physiology are discussed in chapter 18 through 20, it is a fact that a ketogenic diet can not sustain high intensity exercise for very long. This mandates that carbohydrates be introduced into the SKD. Chapters 10 through 12 include discussions of muscle glycogen and depletion as well as the modifications to the SKD which can be made to sustain exercise while maintaining ketosis.

Chapter 8:
General Dieting Principles

Before discussing the details of the ketogenic diet, it is necessary to first discuss some general concepts which relate to body composition, metabolic rate, dieting, and fat loss. Most dieters tend to focus on bodyweight as the only measure of a diet's effectiveness. This is an incomplete approach and may be partly responsible for the failure of many mainstream weight loss approaches. Simply put, changes in bodyweight do not tell the entire story during a diet. Rather the prospective dieter needs to change focus to look at body composition: the ratio of body fat to total body weight.

Experience has shown that most dieters tend to reduce calories excessively. While this causes rapid initial weight loss, a plateau occurs as metabolic rate slows. This drop in metabolic rate may increase the chance for weight regain when the diet is ended.

A discussion of the various components of metabolic rate is followed with equations to estimate maintenance calorie levels as well as how to estimate caloric intake for fat loss and muscle gain. Most dieters, especially those who are used to starving themselves to lose weight, are surprised to learn how much they should eat for optimal fat loss.

Section 1: Fat loss versus Weight loss

Most individuals starting a diet as well as most diet books tend to focus solely on one measure of progress: changes in bodyweight. The scale has been used for years as the only indicator of whether or not a diet is working. While this is a problem on any diet (for reasons discussed below), it can be of even greater importance when discussing low-carbohydrate diets and low-carbohydrate diet studies, due to shifts in water weight. To accurately know whether a diet is working or not, we have to be more specific in our measurements than simply bodyweight.

Bodyfat vs. Bodyweight

The primary distinction that dieters should consider is between **weight** loss and **fat** loss. Weight loss is easy: Don't drink any water for three days and you will lose three to five pounds by the scale. This obviously isn't 'real' weight loss since it returns when you drink water again. Whether they know it or not, most dieters want **fat loss** to occur.

Fat loss is a more specific type of weight loss. While this seems a trivial distinction, it is not. Without knowing where the lost weight is coming from (fat, muscle, or water), an individual cannot know whether their diet and exercise program is working optimally. Ideally, lean body mass (which includes muscle mass) will increase or stay the same while fat is reduced. In practice this rarely occurs. Any calorie restricted diet will cause the loss of some muscle through a variety of mechanisms (that are discussed in later chapters), more so if exercise is not included. In fact, if a person loses weight without exercising, over half of the total weight loss is muscle and water, not fat.

Body Composition

More than changes in scale weight, we need to focus on overall change in body composition. Body composition (or bodyfat percentage) represents the ratio of bodyfat to total body weight. The body is generally divided into two components (1):

1. Fat mass (FM): the sum of the body's fat stores
2. Lean body mass (LBM): everything else including bone, muscle, body water, minerals, the brain, internal organs, muscle glycogen, etc.

Total bodyweight (TB) = FM + LBM

Therefore,
Bodyfat percentage = FM/TB

The ultimate goal in dieting is to see a drop in bodyfat percentage primarily through a decrease in fat mass. Increases in lean body mass will also cause bodyfat percentage to decrease.

A sample body composition estimation

An individual is measured and found to have 15% bodyfat at a bodyweight of 180 lbs. He has:
180 lbs * 0.15 = 27 lbs of fat
180 lbs - 27 lbs = 153 lbs of lean body mass.

For an individual desiring a specific bodyfat percentage, there is an equation that will determine how much fat must be lost assuming 100% of the weight lost is fat and there is no change in lean body mass (2).

Desired bodyweight = lean body mass / (1-desired bodyfat).
Fat loss needed = current body weight - desired body weight.

So if our 180 lb., 15% bodyfat individual (with 153 lbs of lean body mass) wished to reach 10% bodyfat, he would have to lose the following:
Body weight needed = 153 / (1 - .10) = 153 / 0.90 = 170 lbs
Fat loss needed = 180 lbs -170 lbs = 10 lbs fat loss.

Problems with the scale

The primary problem with the scale is that it does not differentiate between what is being lost (or gained) on a diet. With regular exercise, especially weight training, there may be an increase in lean body mass as fat is being lost. Although body weight may not change, body composition is changing.

Let's say our 180 lb individual at 15% bodyfat begins a basic exercise program of weight training and aerobic exercise. Over the first eight weeks, he gains 4 lbs of lean body mass and loses 4 lbs of fat at the same time. Looking only at weight, nothing appears to have happened. But looking at changes in body composition (in table 1), it is obvious that the program is working.

Table 1: Changes in body composition

	Before	After	Change
Total weight (lbs)	180	180	No change
LBM (lbs)	153	157	+4
Fat (lbs)	27	23	-4
% bodyfat	15%	12.7%	-2.3%

Individuals beginning a weight training program often gain one or two pounds by the scale from increased water storage in the muscles. This weight gain is temporary and should not be confused with true fat gain. Similarly, consuming carbohydrates after a period of low carbohydrate dieting will cause a large, but transient, increase in bodyweight from increased body water. This weight gain also should not be confused with true fat gain.

Although the measurement of body composition may not be convenient for many individuals, as it requires special equipment, a similarly objective method exists: how clothes are fitting. Many individuals beginning an exercise program, especially if it includes weight training, will lose inches with no change on the scale. Since one pound of muscle takes up less space than one pound of fat, this reflects a gain in muscle that equals or exceeds the loss of fat. Keep in mind that a large gain in muscle may cause clothes to fit tighter and should not be misinterpreted as fat gain.

Subcutaneous vs. Essential fat

Before discussing how body composition is measured, it is necessary to know where the bodyfat is located. Total bodyfat is typically divided into subcutaneous fat (under the skin) and essential fat (in the spine, brain and around the internal organs). Average levels for these two types of fat appear in table 2 below along with the bodyfat levels recommended by health organizations (1). Bodybuilders are included as a reference point only for those individuals seeking extreme levels of leanness. In all likelihood, maintaining this level of leanness is unhealthy, especially for women.

Table 2: Comparison of bodyfat levels			
Group	Essential fat (%)	Average bodyfat (%)	Recommended
Men	3	11-18	10-15
Women	9-12	21-28	18-25
Male bodybuilder	3	3-4	N/A
Female bodybuilder	9-12	8-9	N/A

Measuring bodyfat (3)

Over the years, many methods have been used to measure bodyfat. The method currently considered the 'Gold Standard' is underwater weighing. Based on the fact that fat floats better than muscle (technically, fat is less dense than muscle), bodyfat percentage can be estimated by weighing an individual on ground and again when submerged underwater.

Many assumptions and estimations are made during underwater weighing. Although the subject is instructed to exhale all air from their lungs, there will always be a small amount left. A correction for this residual air must be made. Additional estimations are made on the density of bone, fat and muscle but these vary greatly depending on race, age, activity level, etc. Many of the assumptions which are being made for underwater weighing have been found to be incorrect (3).

The other methods of bodyfat measurement are generally based on underwater weighing. Descriptions of the most common methods of measuring body composition appear below.

Girth measures

Girth methods of bodyfat estimation typically use weight and several girth measures (i.e. circumference of the waist, wrist, or hips) to estimate bodyfat. While these measurements are fast and easy to perform, they are notoriously inaccurate as they cannot distinguish between an individual with excess fat, excess muscle, or simply a large bone structure.

For example, an equation which used hip circumference would vastly overestimate the bodyfat percentage of an individual with genetically wide hips, even if that person were very lean. Although girth measures can provide another measure of progress on a diet, they should not be used to estimate bodyfat percentage.

Bioelectrical impedance (BIA)

BIA estimates bodyfat by running a small electrical current through the body based on the fact that muscle, fat and water conduct electricity at different rates. With several other variables (height, age, weight), the BIA machine will estimate body fat percentage. BIA can be severely affected by hydration state. Due to changes in hydration during ketogenic diets (especially cyclical ketogenic diets), BIA is not recommended.

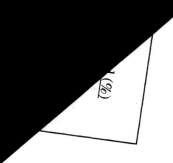

attempts to measure bodyfat thickness (and by extension estimate measuring the scatter of light through the tissue. Little research cy. IR is not recommended.

Because the majority of bodyfat is under the skin, an individual's total fat can be estimated with skinfold measurements taken with calipers (spring loaded pinchers). Three or more measurements are made at specific sites on the body which are entered into an equation with weight, age and gender to estimate bodyfat. The estimation equations are accurate to within plus or minus 5% (3) and tend to become less accurate at extremes of both leanness and fatness. Although current research is questioning the overall accuracy of skinfold equations (3,4), they are still considered the most accurate of the methods described above.

Due to the inherent inaccuracies involved in caliper estimations, it is suggested that regular skinfold measurements be used to track relative changes rather then to provide absolute measurements of bodyfat percentage (5). Table 3 compares the two skinfold measurements below.

Table 3: Comparison of skinfold measurements

	Skinfolds in millimeters	
Date	1/1/98	2/1/98
Pectoral	5	4
Abdominal	15	12
Thigh	10	8
Total	30	24

We can see that this person has lost bodyfat, irrespective of the estimated bodyfat percentages. Individuals using regular skinfold measurements should develop the habit of just comparing measurements rather than relying on estimations of bodyfat.

With regards to bodybuilders (arguably the athletes most concerned with bodyfat levels), a caliper measurement of 3-4 millimeters represents essentially zero subcutaneous fat. However experienced bodybuilders know not to rely only on the numbers, but rather on appearance. Striving for excessively low skinfold measurements may decrease muscle size, fullness and symmetry. Ultimately, bodybuilders aren't being judged on who has the lowest bodyfat level. Rather they are judged by who looks the best on stage.

Summary

Although most dieters rely solely on the scale to gauge the progress of their diet, this method leaves much to be desired unless coupled with another method of measurement. Ideally dieters should keep track of their body composition changes which give a better picture of what is being lost and gained during the diet (i.e. muscle or fat). Although no current method of measuring bodyfat is perfect, skinfold calipers seem to be the best choice, especially considering the fluid shifts which can occur on a ketogenic diet. With practice, most individuals should be able to keep track of their own skinfold measurements at home with a pair of inexpensive calipers.

Section 2:
Metabolic rate and calorie levels

Changes in bodyweight are ultimately tied into simple thermodynamics and the energy balance equation. The energy balance equations represents the difference between energy coming into the body (via diet) and energy going out (via metabolic rate). If intake exceeds expenditure, calories are stored in the body (i.e. weight gain). If expenditure exceeds intake, calories are taken from body stores (i.e. weight loss). The difference between caloric intake and caloric expenditure is referred to as the caloric deficit or excess as necessary. To better address the issue of setting calories, we must first look at the determinants of basal metabolic rate, which represents the number of calories needed to maintain bodyweight with no changes.

Metabolic Rate

Before discussing how to set calories for fat loss or muscle gain, maintenance calorie requirements should be determined. There are two ways to determine maintenance calorie levels: the food diary method and the calculation method.

Food diary method

This method requires an individual to record every food they consume over some period and then calculate the number of calories being consumed. Typically three days are used including at least one weekend day. If weight stays stable over this period, it is assumed that the caloric intake is the maintenance calorie level. Most individuals will not take the time to do this consistently and it has been shown that the simple act of recording one's food intake causes many people to change their eating patterns. Although only an estimate, a preferred method is to calculate caloric requirements, which is discussed next.

Calculation method

To estimate the number of calories needed to maintain bodyweight, we have to examine the three components of daily caloric requirements (1). They are:

1. Resting energy expenditure (REE)
2. Thermic effect of activity (TEA): which can be further subdivided into two
   components:
   A. Calories burned during exercise
   B. Calories burned after exercise
3. Thermic Effect of Feeding (TEF)

Total energy expenditure (also called basal metabolic rate) is equal to REE plus TEA plus TEF. Each component is discussed in detail below.

Resting energy expenditure (REE)

REE represents the number of calories needed by the body to sustain itself at rest. It typically comprises 60-75% of the total caloric expenditure per day. REE is determined by a number of factors including total body weight, lean body mass, thyroid hormones, and nervous system activity (6).

In general, REE correlates closely with total body weight as well as lean body mass. Total body weight is used to calculate REE due to the difficulty in obtaining accurate measures of lean body mass (see the previous section on body composition).

There are numerous equations to estimate REE. The simplest method is to multiply total bodyweight in pounds by 10-11 calories per pound (7). Women should generally use the lower value, men the higher. Again, this number represents how many calories the body will burn assuming zero activity.

Sample REE calculation

Female weighing 150 lbs * 10 calories/lb = ~1500 calories/day
Male weighing 180 lbs * 11 calories/lb = ~1980 calories/day

REE is adjusted upward by determining the number of calories expended during the day, called the thermic effect of activity.

Thermic Effect of Activity (TEA)

TEA includes general moving around, shivering, and exercise. Depending on the frequency, intensity and duration, exercise can increase total caloric expenditure by 15% (very sedentary) to 30% or more (very active) over baseline levels. Although it is possible to calculate the number of calories burned with varying types of exercise, it is generally sufficient to simply estimate the number of calories burned with activity.

The level of activity in a day will determine the increase in caloric requirements over REE. (7) Even someone who is totally sedentary will need to adjust REE upwards by at least 15%. See Table 4 below for REE multipliers:

Table 4: Multiplication modifiers for activity level

Description	Multiplier
Sedentary	1.15
Lightly active	1.3
Moderately active	1.5
Very active	1.7
Extremely active	2.0

For most people, assuming they exercise three to four times weekly at a moderate intensity, an activity modifier of 1.5-1.6 is sufficient. So, using our two dieters from above:

Female at 150 lbs = 1500 calories/day * 1.5 = 2250 calories per day
Male at 180 lbs = 1980 calories/day * 1.5 = 3000 calories per day

The final calculation necessary is to add the thermic effect of feeding (TEF).

The Thermic Effect of Feeding (TEF)

TEF represents the slight increase in metabolic rate which occurs when food is ingested. The term specific dynamic action (SDA) of food is also used. The three macronutrients: carbohydrate, protein and fat have different SDA values. Protein has the highest SDA, burning off 20-25% of its total calories during digestion. If 100 calories of protein are eaten, 20-25 calories are burned during digestion. Carbohydrate is slightly less, having a SDA of 15-20%. Fat has the lowest SDA, approximately 3%.

As an average, TEF will increase caloric requirements by roughly 10% per day.

Female at 150 lbs = 2250 calories/day + 10% (225 calories) = 2475 calories/day
Male at 180 lbs = 3000 calories/day + 10% (300 calories) = 3300 calories/day

These values represent the estimated caloric intake needed to maintain bodyweight and bodyfat at a stable level. It is modified based on whether an individual wishes to gain or lose weight/fat.

An alternative method

Another rough way to estimate daily maintenance calories is to simply multiply bodyweight in pounds by approximately 15-16 calories/pound. Women should use the lower value, men the higher.

Female at 150 lbs * 15 cal/lb = 2250 cal/day
Male at 180 lbs * 16 cal/lb = 2880 cal/day

Both values compare fairly closely to the those from the calculated method above.

Summary

The number of calories needed to maintain a stable bodyweight is determined by three factors: resting energy expenditure, thermic effect of activity, and the thermic effect of food. While estimations can be made for all three components of metabolic rate, a simpler and fairly accurate estimation of maintenance calorie needs can be made by multiplying bodyweight in pounds by 15-16 calories. Women should generally use the lower number, men the higher.

Section 3:
Setting calorie levels

Having determined maintenance calories levels, it is now time to discuss the concept of energy balance, fat loss and muscle gain. Energy balance refers to the difference in caloric intake via diet and caloric expenditure via metabolic rate and activity. It is given by:

Energy balance = calories in - calories out

When energy balance is positive (i.e. calories in exceeds calories out), energy is stored in the body as glycogen, protein and fat. When energy balance is negative (i.e. calories out exceeds calories in), energy is pulled from the body's stores. In the case of fat loss, stored energy in adipose tissue is converted to usable energy and burned by the body.

Thus to lose weight, one must burn more calories than they consume. Therefore any attempt to lose fat must center around decreasing caloric intake or increasing energy expenditure. By corollary, to gain weight one must consume more calories than they burn. Any attempt to gain weight must center around increasing caloric intake or decreasing energy expenditure.

A gain in muscle or fat tissue revolves around the creation of a caloric excess. For the most part, it is impossible to lose fat (requiring a caloric deficit) and gain muscle (requiring a caloric excess) at the same time. While it is attractive to think that the body will pull energy from fat stores to synthesize muscle tissue, this does not appear to occur in most cases. The only exception to this is beginning exercisers and those returning from a layoff from training, although the reasons for this are not known.

Calories and the Atkins diet: a misconception

A misconception, and commonly heard criticism, surrounding the Atkins diet is the (apparent) claim that fat can be lost with an 'unrestricted caloric intake', which contradicts basic thermodynamics (8). Strictly speaking, Atkins claimed that one could lose weight eating as much fat and protein 'as they liked' meaning they could eat until they were full without worrying about counting calories.

Atkins based this claim on the established fact that individuals on a diet restricted in carbohydrate but with 'unlimited' fat and protein will tend to automatically restrict calories. The mechanism behind the appetite suppressing effect of ketogenic diets is addressed in more detail in chapter 7.

Studies examining the ketogenic diet at maintenance calories show no weight loss other than the small water loss seen with carbohydrate restriction. Simply put, there is no magical effect of ketosis that allows one to lose weight without some type of shift in energy balance that leads to either an increased caloric expenditure or a decreased caloric intake. As with any diet, fat loss on a ketogenic diet will still require the creation of a caloric deficit.

Setting calories for fat Loss

Generally speaking, most dieters restrict calories too much when dieting for fat loss. The logic is that a greater caloric deficit will yield faster and greater fat loss, but this is not always the case. Excessively low caloric intakes are countered in the body by a reduction in metabolic rate which slows fat loss (9,10). This reduction can range from 5 to 36% of resting metabolic rate, depending on the severity of caloric restriction (9). While the exact cause of the decrease is unknown, possible causes are a decrease in thyroid hormones, loss of lean body mass, or a decrease in the activity of the sympathetic nervous system. A similar drop in metabolic rate can also occur with excessive amounts of exercise. When normal eating resumes, the decreased metabolic rate causes rapid weight regain, more so if exercise is not included in the fat loss efforts.

The loss of one pound of fat requires that 3,500 calories be burned in excess of what is being consumed. Therefore the typical advice to dieters is to restrict caloric intake by 500-1000 calories per day which should yield a 1-2 lb fat loss over the span of 7 days (500-1000 calories/day * 7 days = 3500-7000 caloric deficit per day = 1-2 lbs of fat loss). As discussed in chapter 22, the reduction of calories without the addition of exercise will cause muscle loss and metabolic slowdown. Therefore a restriction of calories should never be the only method of creating a caloric deficit.

A second approach to creating a caloric deficit is to eat at maintenance calories and add excessive amounts of exercise. As we will see in chapter 22, the expenditure of even 500 calories per day with exercise requires a larger amount of exercise (or exercise at a higher intensity) than most individuals are able to do. To expend 1000 calories per day with exercise generally requires 2 or more hours of exercise per day.

A third and preferable approach is to reduce caloric intake to some degree and increase activity at the same time. A decrease in caloric intake of 500 calories coupled with an increase in activity of 500 calories per day should also yield a 2 lb fat loss per week. It is unusual to see an exact fat loss of 2 pounds per week in most dieters.

How large of a deficit: two common methods

The primary question to be addressed is how large of a deficit to use when setting up a fat loss diet. As mentioned in the introduction, most dieters tend to drop calories extremely low based on the idea that the greater the deficit, the more weight that will be lost. Up to a point this appears to be true, in that greater caloric restriction yields greater fat loss. However this ignores the potential effects of extreme caloric restriction on metabolic rate, muscle loss, etc. A recent review of twenty-two studies found that extremely low calorie levels, below 1000 calories/day, caused a much greater drop in metabolic rate than even 1200 calories/day (10). So, there appears to be a threshold level of caloric intake where metabolic rate is more greatly affected.

There are two common methods of setting calories for a diet: at an absolute calorie level, or with an absolute caloric reduction. That is, consider two individuals, one weighing 120 pounds, the other weighing 240 pounds and assume both have a maintenance calorie intake of 15 cal/lb.

First let us examine what happens if both decide to diet at 1200 calories per day. Table 5 compares their caloric intake relative to their maintenance levels.

Table 5: Comparison of two individuals dieting at 1200 calories per day

Subject	Body weight (lbs)	Maintenance calories (cal/day)*	Intake (cal/day)	Intake (cal/lb)	Daily deficit (cal)
1	120	1800	1200	10	600
2	240	3600	1200	5	2400

* Estimated at 15 calories per pound of bodyweight

It would seem logical that the second person's body would perceive a greater deficit (relative to resting levels) and decrease metabolic rate more so than the first person. While anecdotal evidence suggests this to be the case, direct research looking at changes in metabolic rate at different caloric intakes relative to bodyweight is necessary.

In a second situation, assume both individuals decide to create a 1000 calorie deficit through some combination of diet and exercise. Table 6 compares them as above.

Table 6: Comparison of two individuals dieting at 1000 calories below maintenance

Subject	Body weight (lbs)	Maintenance calories (cal/day)*	Intake (cal/day)‡	Intake (cal/lb)	Daily deficit (cal)
1	120	1800	800	6.6	1000
2	240	3600	2600	10.8	1000

* Estimated at 15 calories per pound of bodyweight

‡ For all practical purposes, whether the deficit is created through calorie restriction alone, or a combination of calorie restriction and exercise, the body will only perceive that 800 or 2600 calories/day is being consumed.

In this case, the first dieter ends up with an extremely low calorie level, while the second does not. It would seem logical that the first dieter would see a much greater drop in metabolic rate under these conditions than the second.

A better method

The above example shows us that setting caloric intake relative to bodyweight (or by creating a deficit as some percentage of maintenance levels) would be more individualized than using an absolute deficit (such as 1000 calories below maintenance) or an absolute caloric intake (such as 1200 calories per day).

The method recommended in this book is to set caloric intake relative to either bodyweight or maintenance levels. It assumes that maintenance calories have either been determined with a food diary, or estimated from the equations in section 2. It also assumes that the total caloric deficit includes exercise. For a 500 calorie/day deficit, whether an individual reduces food intake by 250 cal/day and increases activity by 250 cal/day or eats at maintenance and increases activity by 500 cal/day, the deficit will be considered to be the same. Note that this only applies as long as some form of exercise is being done as numerous studies have found that reducing caloric intake without exercise causes muscle loss and a drop in metabolic rate.

When starting a fat loss diet, calorie levels should be restricted no more than 10-20% below maintenance levels. This caloric deficit can be generated by decreasing food intake or increasing activity with exercise. While the typical recommendation for increasing caloric expenditure is aerobic exercise, we shall see in chapter 22 that weight training coupled with either aerobic exercise OR a slight reduction in caloric intake yields the best fat loss. For all practical purposes, there is no difference between reducing calories by 300 per day and expending an additional 300 calories through aerobic exercise. The choice ultimately becomes the dieter's: whether to eat less or perform more aerobic exercise. It is the opinion of this author that weight training is NOT optional on any diet.

From a maintenance level of 15-16 calories per pound, reducing calorie levels by 20% yields a calorie intake of approximately 12-13 calories per pound of current bodyweight. Many diet books and dieters prefer to use a caloric goal based on goal bodyweight (i.e. 12-13 calories per pound of desired bodyweight). The problem with this method is that dieters, in their hurry to reach their goals, invariably set goal bodyweight or bodyfat far too low. Consequently, calories are set too low and metabolic rate slows down. Therefore, daily calorie levels should be based on current bodyweight.

Using the values for maintenance calories from the last section we have:
Female at 150 lbs * 15 cal/lb = 2250 cal/day
A 20% deficit yields 2250 * 0.20 = 450 calorie/day deficit
2250 calories - 450 calories = 1800 calories per day
1800 calories/day / 150 lbs = 12 calories/lb

Male at 180 lbs * 16 cal/lb = 2880 cal/day
A 20% deficit yields 2880 cal/day * 0.20 = 576 cal/day
2880 cal - 576 cal = 2304 cal/day
2304 cal/day / 180 lbs = ~13 calories/lb

These levels should be considered starting points only as they are based on averages and estimations for maintenance calorie levels. Some individuals may need to reduce calories further but this should be done cautiously to avoid muscle loss and metabolic slowdown.

Regular body composition measurements will indicate if the calorie level should be changed or not. Most individuals should be able to sustain a fat loss of 1-1.5 lbs of fat per week. If fat loss is occurring at less than 1 pound per week, calories can be reduced slightly (or aerobic exercise increased). It is rare to find anyone who can lose 2 lbs of fat per week consistently without losing muscle as well. Anyone losing more than 2 pounds of weight per week should increase calories or decrease aerobic activity to avoid muscle loss.

The maximum allowed deficit

The effects of exercise at different calorie levels on fat loss vary and are discussed in chapter 22. In general, the studies support the idea that there is a threshold deficit where maximum fat loss will occur with minimal changes in metabolic rate. This threshold occurs at approximately 1000 calories per day below maintenance and represents the maximum allowed deficit. As a general rule, the total daily deficit, created through caloric restriction and exercise, should be no greater than 1000 calories total per day. This should yield an average fat loss of 2 pounds per week. Some exceptions to this rule are discussed in chapter 13.

This 1000 calories per day deficit can be created through a variety of combinations of caloric restriction and exercise. If an individual prefers to eat more calories (such as eating at maintenance levels), they would need to do an extensive amount of exercise to generate a 1000 calorie/day deficit. By the same token, if an individual is involved in an activity (such as long distance running or cycling) that has them expending 1500 calories/day through exercise, they will need to increase calories by 500 calories above maintenance to avoid surpassing the 1000 calorie/day threshold.

For some individuals, even 1000 calories/day may be too great of a deficit. This is especially true for lighter individuals, for whom a 1000 calorie/day deficit may take their caloric excessively low. Arguably a better approach is to use a smaller caloric deficit with increased activity and aim for a sustainable and safe fat loss of 1-1.5 lbs of fat per week. While the ultimate bodyfat/bodyweight goal will take longer to achieve, it should be easier to sustain as there is less tendency for metabolic rate to decrease.

To summarize: dieters should initially create a net deficit (exercise plus caloric restriction) of approximately 10-20% below maintenance. For the average person, this means a caloric intake of 12-13 calories/lb of bodyweight with moderate activity levels. After 2 weeks, depending on total fat loss, the total deficit can be increased, to a maximum deficit of 1000 calories per day.

Weight Gain

For weight gain to occur, a calorie excess is needed to support muscle growth. There is little research into the number of calories needed to meet maintenance levels as well as allowing for muscle growth to occur.

A good starting point is to increase calories by 20% over maintenance. This gives an approximate calorie intake of 18-19 calories/day although many individuals may require much higher calorie levels (above 20 cal/day). Obviously muscle gain is predicated on performing weight training to stimulate muscle growth and protein synthesis. Other issues pertaining to the CKD and gaining muscle are discussed in chapter 29.

For example, using the values for maintenance calories from last chapter we have:

Female at 150 lbs * 15 cal/lb = 2250 cal/day

2250 * 0.20 = 450 cal/day

2250 + 450 = 2700 cal/day

2700 cal/day / 150 lbs = 18 cal/lb

Male at 180 lbs * 16 cal/lb = 2880 cal/day

2880 * 0.20 = 576 cal

2880 + 576 cal = 3,456 cal/day

3456 cal/day / 180 lbs = 19 cal/lb

Summary

Daily caloric requirements are comprised of resting energy expenditure, the thermic effect of activity and the thermic effect of food. While these can be calculated based on bodyweight and activity, an easy estimation for maintenance calories is to multiply bodyweight by 15-16 calories per pound.

As a rule of thumb, to avoid metabolic slowdown calories should be initially decreased 10-20% below maintenance for fat loss. This can be accomplished by either decreasing caloric intake, increasing activity, or some combination of the two. Repeated body composition measurements will indicate if less or greater caloric intakes are necessary to optimize fat loss. In general, a fat loss of 1 to 1.5 lbs per week should ensure that no muscle is being lost. A total weight loss of greater than 2 pounds per week (not counting water weight) indicates that some muscle is being lost and calories should be increased.

Those desiring to gain weight on a ketogenic diet will need to increase calories above maintenance. A good starting point is roughly 20% above maintenance levels which is approximately 18 cal/lb for most people. Depending on changes in body composition, calories can be adjusted upwards or downward in order to maximize gains in lean body mass, while minimizing gains in bodyfat.

References Cited

1. "Physiology of Sport and Exercise" Jack H. Wilmore and David L. Costill. Human Kinetics Publishers, 1994.
2. "Guidelines for Exercise Testing and Prescription, 5th ed." The American College of Sports Medicine. Lea & Febiger Publishers, 1995.
3. "Advances in Body Composition" Timothy G. Lohman Human Kinetics Publishers, 1992.
4. Heyward V. Evaluation of Body Composition. Sports Med (1996) 22: 146-156.
5. "Physiological Testing of the High-Performance Athlete" Ed. J Duncan McDougall, Howard A. Wenger, and Howard J. Green. Human Kinetics Publishers, 1982.

6. Astrup A. The sympathetic nervous system as a target for intervention in obesity. Int J Obes (1995) 19 (suppl 7): S24-S28.

7. "Advanced Fitness Assessment & Exercise Prescription" Vivian Heyward. Human Kinetics, 1998.

8. Council on Foods and Nutrition. A critique of low-carbohydrate ketogenic weight reducing regimes. JAMA (1973) 224: 1415-1419.

9. Saris WHM. Effects of energy restriction and exercise on the sympathetic nervous system. Int J Obes (1995) 19 (suppl 7): S17-S23.

10. Prentice AM et. al. Physiological responses to slimming. Proc Nutr Soc (1991) 50: 441-458.

Chapter 9:
The Standard Ketogenic Diet

The standard ketogenic diet (SKD) is what most think of as the ketogenic diet. It is a diet low in carbohydrate, and moderate-high in both protein and fat. Since the SKD forms the basis of the next two diets, it is discussed in detail. This includes a discussion of the effects of the macronutrients (carbohydrate, protein and fat) on ketosis, as well as discussions of how to determine optimal carbohydrate, protein and fat intake. Additionally, the effects of alcohol and other nutritional substances (such as caffeine and aspartame) on ketosis is discussed.

Section 1: Macronutrient intake on the ketogenic diet

Any diet which restricts calories will alter the intake of nutrients. This includes changes in caloric intake, the macronutrients (protein, carbohydrates, fat) and the micronutrients (vitamins and minerals). Micronutrients were discussed in the last chapter, and only caloric intake and macronutrients are discussed here.

Calories and weight loss

Although discussed in detail in Chapter 8, the basic idea of calories and weight loss (as well as fat loss) is mentioned again here. One of the prime selling points of many low-carbohydrate diets is a dieter can lose weight while 'eating as much protein and fat as they like'. While this is loosely true, this was misinterpreted by dieters and physicians alike to claim that dieters would lose weight eating unlimited amounts of foods.

This idea was criticized by the American Medical Association (AMA) as it seemed to suggest that a ketogenic diet could somehow break basic laws of thermodynamics (1). The AMA was correct that it is impossible for dieter's to lose weight while consuming unlimited calories. However, looking at the research on ketogenic diets, we see that most individuals will automatically reduce their caloric intake when they restrict carbohydrate to low levels. Therefore, in a sense individuals are losing weight eating 'as much as they like', it is simply that they are eating less than they think.

Studies of ketogenic diets have found that, when subjects are told to limit carbohydrate intake but to consume 'unlimited' quantities of protein and fat, they automatically limit caloric intake and consume between 1400-2100 calories (2-4). Any diet which automatically reduces caloric intake without inducing hunger is going to be attractive to dieters.

While early studies, discussed in detail in the previous chapter, were interpreted to show that ketogenic diets affected metabolism in some way to increase weight loss, other studies suggested that it was the decreased caloric intake that caused the weight loss (2).

Judging from the studies above, many ketogenic dieters may reduce calories too much. While this causes quick initial weight loss, as discussed in chapter 8, too severe a decrease in caloric intake can cause metabolic slowdown and a loss of muscle. Many ketogenic dieters will have to eat more than they feel necessary to keep fat loss from slowing down. This is especially important if exercise is part of the overall fat loss efforts. Recommendations for determining caloric intakes are discussed in chapter 8.

Macronutrients

The macronutrients are carbohydrate, protein and fat. Many individuals embarking upon a ketogenic diet will set protein and fat at certain levels based on their goals. This especially applies to athletes who will adjust protein and fat intake to vary calorie levels within the recommended range. While it is suggested that others pay attention to overall macronutrient intake, it is reasonable to assume that some will simply not go to the trouble to count every gram of food which they consume.

This raises the question of what type of macronutrient intake an unspecified ketogenic diet will produce, especially compared to a similar calorie 'balanced' diet. Several studies have examined this macronutrient intake, instructing subjects on a ketogenic diet to limit carbohydrate only but to consume unlimited quantities of fat and protein (2-4).

By its very definition, a ketogenic diet will reduce carbohydrate intake far below the levels of a 'balanced' diet. Typically any diet containing more than 100 grams of carbohydrate per day, which is enough to prevent ketosis, is referred to as a 'balanced' diet while any diet containing less than 100 grams of carbohydrate per day will be ketogenic to varying degrees (6). As discussed in chapter 5, the lower that carbohydrate intake falls, the greater the degree of ketosis that will occur.

It should be noted that diets are being compared on a gram to gram basis, rather than in terms of percentages. When dietary carbohydrate is restricted to low levels, the relative percentage of fat and protein will increase, even though the absolute intake in terms of grams of each may not change much. Saying that a ketogenic diet is a 'high-fat' diet because it is comprised of 70% fat by percentage of calories is misleading as the total number of fat grams being consumed per day may be no different than a diet with a lower percentage of fat but more carbohydrates.

These studies have found that protein intake stayed roughly the same, fat intake also stayed about the same or went down a bit, with carbohydrate intake the primary change (3,5). This led one researcher to suggest that the ketogenic diet should be described as a 'low-carbohydrate' diet rather than a 'high-fat' diet (7).

Another study examined the nutrient intake on a variety of popular diets, including the Atkins diet (4). They found that the average ketogenic dieter consumed approximately 2100 calories, 121 grams of protein, 172 grams of fat, and 24 grams of carbohydrate. A summary of these studies appears in Table 1.

Study	Balanced diet				Ketogenic diet			
	Calories	Protein	Carbs	Fat	Calories	Protein	Carbs	Fat
Larosa (3)	1995	96	171	113	1461	107	6	108
Fisher (4)		Not listed			2136	121	24	172
Yudkin (5)	2330	84	216	124	1560	83	67	105

Note: Protein, carbs, and fat are in grams per day.

Cholesterol intake

The high intake of animal source foods affects cholesterol intake as well. A typical balanced diet provides between 300 and 500 milligram (mg) per day of cholesterol (3). On a ketogenic diet, depending on total caloric intake, cholesterol intake was found to increase to 828 mg/day (484) on a 1400 calorie per day diet, and approximately 1500 mg/day on a 2100 calorie diet (4). This is far higher than the American Heart Association recommendation of no more than 300 mg/day of cholesterol, and concerns have been raised regarding the effect of ketogenic diets on blood cholesterol levels. The effects of the ketogenic diet on cholesterol levels are discussed in the chapter 7.

Summary

In general, individuals who begin a ketogenic diet without paying attention to calorie, protein, or fat levels will automatically lower their caloric intake below maintenance. The resulting caloric deficit will result in weight/fat loss. Typically, protein intake will stay about the same, fat intake may go up a little bit, and carbohydrate intake will drop compared to pre-ketogenic diet levels.

Section 2: Carbohydrates and the SKD

Carbohydrate intake is arguably the most significant aspect of a ketogenic diet as carbohydrates have the greatest effect on ketosis. As a general rule, carbohydrate intake must be reduced below 100 grams and most individuals find that a carbohydrate intake of 30 grams is the maximum that can be consumed. Irrespective of other other facets of the SKD, a carbohydrate intake which is too high will disrupt ketosis.

What are carbohydrates?

Carbohydrates are organic compounds made of carbon, hydrogen and oxygen (carbohydrate is frequently abbreviated as CHO for this reason). They are used by the body primarily as an energy source. Under normal dietary conditions, most tissues in the body use carbohydrates, in the form of glucose, for fuel. There are exceptions such as the heart which rely primarily on fatty acids for fuel.

Carbohydrates are generally subdivided into complex and simple carbohydrates. All carbohydrates are formed from the simple sugars glucose, fructose and galactose, called monosaccharides. Monosaccharides combine into chains of two, called disaccharides. As monosaccharides form into longer chains, they are called polysaccharides or simply starch, which is a chain of hundreds or thousands of glucose molecules attached to each other.

The term 'complex carbohydrates' refers to starches such as breads, pasta, potatoes, rice, and all grains. Simple carbohydrates refer to sugars such as table sugar (sucrose), fructose and fruit. Carbohydrates can be further delineated based on the Glycemic Index (GI) which is discussed below.

Digestion of carbohydrate

Despite dietary differences between carbohydrates, almost all ingested carbohydrate will enter the bloodstream as glucose, raising blood glucose levels. Each gram of dietary carbohydrate appears in the bloodstream as 1 gram of glucose. A very small amount of ingested carbohydrate (approximately one percent) will enter the bloodstream as fructose (fruit sugar).

Once in the bloodstream, glucose has a variety of fates. It can be burned immediately for energy by most tissues of the body or stored as glycogen (a long chain of glucose molecules attached to one another) in the muscle or in the liver for later use. If an excess of carbohydrates is consumed, glucose can be converted to fat in the liver (a process called de novo lipogenesis) or pushed directly into the fat cell as alpha-glycerophosphate.

How much carbohydrate can be eaten per day?

Chapter 5 established that the body can survive indefinitely on a diet completely devoid of dietary carbohydrate (assuming protein and vitamin/mineral intake is sufficient). However, from a practical standpoint, it is nearly impossible to avoid all sources of carbohydrate in the diet. Additionally, a diet completely devoid of carbohydrate foods may rapidly become monotonous. The question to be answered is how many grams of carbohydrate can be consumed without interrupting ketosis.

Although up to 100 grams of carbohydrate will allow ketosis to develop, it would be rare to see ketones excreted in the urine at this level of intake. Since the only measure of ketosis available to ketogenic dieters are Ketostix (tm) carbohydrates must be restricted below this level if ketosis is to be measured. As a general rule of thumb, dietary carbohydrates should be below 30 grams per day for ketosis to be rapidly established and for ketones to be lost in the urine.

However, this value varies from person to person and depends on other factors such as protein intake and activity, which allows individuals to consume relatively more carbohydrate without disrupting ketosis.

Assuming a non-excessive protein intake (see next section), a carbohydrate intake of 30 grams per day or less is advised during the first weeks of a SKD to allow for adaptations to take place. After adaptation to the diet, it appears that individuals can tolerate relatively greater carbohydrate intakes without disrupting ketosis. Although not completely accurate, Ketostix (tm) can provide a rough measure of how many carbohydrates can be consumed while still maintaining ketosis. As long as trace ketosis is maintained, carbohydrates can be gradually added to the diet. See chapter 15 for details on using Ketostix (tm).

An extremely low carbohydrate intake is relatively more important for those individuals following the CKD, who only have five or six days to establish ketosis. In this case, carbohydrate intake should be minimized as much as possible (meaning that protein intake must be adequate) during the first few days of each cycle so that ketosis will occur as quickly as possible. Individuals on a TKD follow a separate set of rules for daily carbohydrate intake which is discussed in chapter 11.

Types of carbohydrate consumed on a SKD

Carbohydrates are generally differentiated into complex and simple carbohydrates. This is a crude measure of the quality of carbohydrates. A more accurate measure of carbohydrate quality is the Glycemic Index (GI) which is a measure of how much insulin a given carbohydrate food will cause to be released (see appendix 1 for a partial GI).

The GI of a food is defined relative to white bread, which is arbitrarily given a value of 100. A food with a GI of 60 will cause glucose levels to rise in the blood 60% as quickly as white bread, causing the release of 60% as much insulin. Similarly, a food with a GI of 130 will raise blood glucose 30% more quickly than white bread, causing the body to release 30% more insulin. In general, starches and complex carbohydrates tend to have lower GI values than simple sugars like glucose and sucrose.

Since our wish is to minimize insulin release during a standard ketogenic diet, any dietary carbohydrates which are consumed on a SKD should come from low GI sources. This means that the majority of carbohydrates consumed will come from vegetable sources, as most starches have a GI that is too high.

One thing to note is that the GI of carbohydrates is affected by the ingestion of protein, fats and fiber at the same meal. The ingestion of other nutrients slows digestion of carbohydrates, lowering the effective GI (less insulin response) than eating that same carbohydrate by itself.

Timing of carbohydrate consumption on a SKD

Although there is little data on ideal timing of carbohydrates on a SKD, we can create a few guidelines. While the amount of insulin released from the ingestion of dietary carbohydrates is related to their quality (GI), it is also related somewhat to the quantity of carbs ingested. Ingestion of 30 grams of broccoli will cause a greater insulin release than the ingestion of 10 grams of broccoli although the GI is identical.

One approach is to spread carbohydrate intake throughout the day in small amounts. While this may minimize insulin response, it should be noted that 5-6 grams of carbohydrate per meal is not much carbohydrate. Some individuals may wish to have all of their daily carbohydrate at one main meal, such as a large salad with dinner or lunch. Although this will cause a slightly greater insulin release than spreading out the same amount of carbohydrate throughout the day, the low GI of vegetables coupled with the digestion slowing effect of protein, fat and fiber should prevent an excessive insulin response. Even if a large enough insulin response occurred to disrupt ketosis, it should be transient and ketosis should resume soon thereafter.

Summary

Although carbohydrate intake must be severely restricted on a SKD, a diet completely devoid of carbohydrate is impossible to achieve in practice and would be monotonous in any case. Depending on factors such as protein intake, a carbohydrate intake of 30 grams per day or less will generally allow the induction of ketosis although this varies from person to person. As a general rule, low GI carbohydrates such as vegetables are the best source as they have the least effect on insulin release. Fruits and starches should generally be avoided on a SKD. The daily carbohydrate amount can either be spread throughout the day or eaten all at once.

Section 3: Protein and the SKD

Having discussed the details of carbohydrate intake on a standard ketogenic diet (SKD) last chapter, we can now discuss issues pertaining to protein. Although carbohydrate intake is arguably the most important aspect of successfully inducing ketosis, protein intake is extremely important in order to prevent muscle loss. While an easy solution is to simply eat as much protein as possible, too much protein can prevent ketosis as well, disrupting the adaptations which ketogenic dieters seek. Therefore, protein intake must fall within a narrow range: high enough to prevent muscle loss but low enough that ketosis is not disrupted.

A common criticism of the ketogenic diet is that ketosis is catabolic. This is true in that any diet which is restricted in calories is catabolic . The question, addressed in chapters 5 and 6, is whether the ketogenic diet is inherently more catabolic than other dietary approaches.

As discussed in chapter 6, one of the problems with many diet studies comparing ketogenic to non-ketogenic diets was the provision of insufficient dietary protein to both groups, causing too much protein loss in both groups. The interpretation given was that the ketogenic diet had no benefit over a non-ketogenic diet when the proper interpretation was that both diets were ineffective in preventing muscle loss. With adequate protein intake, muscle loss should be minimal.

For any diet to minimize muscle loss, it must contain sufficient amounts of high quality protein. Due to the high intake of animal proteins, ketogenic diets will tend to contain high quality proteins by default.

What is a protein?

Proteins are organic compounds which provide the body with nitrogen for a variety of uses. Protein are used for tissue repair, as well as the synthesis of some hormones and enzymes. Proteins are made up of sub-units called amino acids (AAs). There are 20 AAs which occur in food, although more are present in the body. Of these, 8 are referred to as indispensable indicating that they must be obtained from the diet. The remaining 12 are considered dispensable in that they can be synthesized in the body.

With few exceptions (i.e. gelatin), every dietary protein contains all of the AAs in varying amounts. This means that that concept of 'complete' and 'incomplete' proteins is inaccurate. All proteins are complete, in that they contain all AA. It is more accurate to say that proteins have a limiting AA, which is the indispensable AA occurring in the lowest quantity relative to what is needed. Consuming a variety of protein sources should ensure adequate amounts of all amino acids.

The ratios of AAs determine, to a great degree, how well the human body can use these proteins. This is sometimes referred to as the biological value (BV) or protein efficiency ratio (PER).

Digestion of protein

As they are digested, proteins are broken down in the stomach into smaller chains of AAs. These chains include single AAs (peptides), chains of two AAs (dipeptides), and chains of three AAs (tripeptides). Once AAs enter the bloodstream, they are treated identically in the body. This means that, for all practical purposes, the protein from an egg is treated no differently than from an amino acid capsule. The only real difference in quality between proteins are in the relative ratios of AAs.

As described in the chapter 5, dietary protein is converted to glucose with 58% efficiency (8). This reflects the fact that over half of the AAs can be readily converted to glucose. While some AAs can be converted to ketones in the liver, this is not thought to contribute significantly to ketosis.

How much protein per day is needed to sustain the body?

Unlike carbohydrate and fat, the body does not have any way to store protein except as muscle tissue and a small pool of free AAs in the bloodstream, muscle and liver. The utilization of any body protein for uses other than tissue synthesis should be interpreted as a loss of skeletal muscle tissue. Additionally, periods of severe starvation can cause the loss of cardiac, smooth or organ protein. Although recent research differentiates between the loss of essential and non-essential lean body mass (LBM), any loss of LBM should generally be avoided as there is no way to ensure that only non-essential LBM is being lost (9).

Under all dietary conditions, the body has a certain minimum protein requirement needed for basic tissue repair, enzyme and hormone synthesis synthesis. This is represented by the

Recommended Dietary Allowance (RDA). For adults, the current RDA for protein is 0.8 grams of protein/ kilogram of bodyweight (0.36 grams of protein/ lb bodyweight). The RDA assumes a sedentary lifestyle and adequate caloric intake. Daily protein requirements are modified by at least two factors: carbohydrate intake and activity level.

Carbohydrate intake

As total carbohydrate goes down, protein requirements will go up (10). By corollary, as total carbohydrate intake goes up, protein requirements will go down. The reason for this is discussed in detail in chapter 5. To summarize, without factoring in activity, a protein intake of at least 1.75 grams of protein/kilogram lean body mass or a minimum of 150 grams per day are necessary to prevent nitrogen losses during the initial stages of a ketogenic diet.

Activity and protein intake

For years it has been assumed that protein intake at the level of the RDA was sufficient for all individuals including athletes. Much recent data suggests quite conclusively that athletes do in fact need more protein than the RDA, in some cases up to two to three times more (11). Bodybuilders and strength athletes have always consumed large amounts of protein as a matter of course. However, on a ketogenic diet, too much protein can be as much of a problem (by disrupting ketosis) as too little protein.

A review of the available research has determined that athletes have protein requirements as shown in Table 2 (11). While it is arguably more accurate to use lean body mass (LBM) to determine protein intakes, the difficulty in getting an accurate measure of LBM makes the use of total bodyweight a better choice. Obviously, if an individual is carrying an excessive amount of bodyfat, and has an accurate method of determining LBM, protein intake should be based on LBM.

Table 2: Protein requirements for athletes		
	Grams per pound	Grams per kilogram
Endurance athletes	0.54 - 0.63	1.2-1.4
Strength athletes	0.72 - 0.81	1.6-1.8

Source: Lemon P. Is increased dietary protein necessary or beneficial for individuals with a physically active lifestyle? Nutrition Reviews (1996) 54: S169-S175.

How much protein per day?

The most critical time to ensure sufficient protein intake is during the first few weeks of a ketogenic diet, when the need for protein breakdown to provide glucose is at its highest. After the first few weeks of ketosis, protein requirements will go down as the body reduces its need for glucose.

As established in chapter 5, the prevention of nitrogen losses requires a protein intake of at least 1.75 grams protein/kg LBM (0.8 grams/ lb of bodyweight) OR 150 grams of protein, whichever is higher.

For lighter individuals, 1.75 g/kg of protein may be less than 150 grams, in which case protein should be adjusted upwards to avoid nitrogen losses. After the third week of ketosis, when the major protein sparing adaptations have taken place, protein intake can be adjusted downwards as necessary. Please note that this value was determined for individuals who are not exercising and are consuming minimal carbohydrates.

If an individual is exercising, it is assumed that protein requirements are higher than the minimum of 1.75 grams/kg (~0.8 grams/lb). A protein intake of 0.9 grams of protein/lb of total bodyweight is an appropriate protein level to start at. Although this is slightly higher than the values suggested above, we can assume that extra protein is necessary during the initial phases of adaptation.

If an individual is consuming even marginal amounts of carbohydrates (30 grams), then less protein is necessary to achieve a positive nitrogen balance. Recall from the previous chapter that 1 gram of protein will produce 0.58 grams of glucose. So 2 grams of protein will produce a little more than 1 gram of glucose. Therefore, for every gram of carbohydrate consumed on a ketogenic diet, protein requirements should go down by 2 grams. Someone consuming the maximum of 30 grams of carbohydrate per day could reduce protein intake by approximately 15 grams per day.

It should be noted that women may not need as much protein as men, for reasons discussed in chapter 18, but research into gender differences is only starting to appear. Therefore, both male and female athletes should use the values in table 3 as a guide. If an individual has trouble establishing and maintaining ketosis, and all other aspects of the diet are in place, protein intake can be adjusted downward until ketosis is established.

Table 3: Protein requirements for various activity levels

	Protein intake	
Bodyweight	Sedentary (0.8 grams/lb)	Exercising (0.9 grams/lb)
130 lbs	104*	117*
150 lbs	120*	135*
180 lbs	144*	162
200 lbs	160	180
220 lbs	176	198
250 lbs	200	225

* During the first three weeks of the diet, these values should be raised to 150 grams for reasons already discussed. After three weeks have passed, protein intake can be lowered to the levels given above.

Protein and ketosis

Although there are no hard and fast rules for how much protein can inhibit ketosis, some individuals have reported trouble maintaining ketosis if they consume too much protein per day, or even excessive amounts of protein at a given meal. To the contrary, some individuals have eaten 1.2 grams protein/lb or higher and had no problems establishing and maintaining ketosis.

This may be related to the glycogen depletion caused by weight training. In a depleted state, incoming carbohydrate is used to refill muscle glycogen before it is used to refill liver glycogen. In essence, the depletion of muscle glycogen provides a 'sink' for excess glucose produced from dietary protein or carbohydrate intake.

Type of protein ingested

The amount of protein calculated in tables 2 and 3 is predicated on the consumption of high quality proteins such as animal flesh, eggs, and dairy products. The nature of the ketogenic diet almost ensures that protein intake is from high quality proteins. Many individuals choose to use commercial protein powders as a protein source and there are many different products available.

The only exception is certain liquid protein preparations which sometimes use low quality protein (such as collagen or gelatin) fortified with one or more AAs (generally tryptophan).

As detailed in chapter 7, the deaths associated with liquid very- low-calorie protein sparing modified fasts may have been related to the use of low quality collagen protein although insufficient vitamin and mineral intake has also been implicated. As long as high quality protein and adequate vitamins and minerals are ingested, there should not be problems of this sort on a ketogenic diet.

Timing of protein intake

For the most part, the timing of protein intake is not an issue on a SKD, except as it pertains to maintaining ketosis. The nature of the ketogenic diet ensures that protein is consumed at most meals with few exceptions. Consuming protein immediately after a workout may help with recovery, as protein synthesis is increased at this time. Typically 30-40 grams of protein are consumed immediately after training to provide the muscles with AAs for tissue synthesis.

Summary

Protein intake is a critical aspect of a ketogenic diet to prevent muscle loss. Approximately 150 grams per day of protein must be ingested to provide enough glucose to supply the brain and prevent the body from breaking down muscle protein. An individual's daily protein requirements are tied to activity level and bodyweight. Those individuals whose activity and bodyweight result in less than 150 grams of protein per day will need to either increase protein during the first 3 weeks of the diet or increase dietary carbohydrate to ensure adequate glucose for the brain.

The type of protein ingested should be of high quality from animal products such as red meat, chicken, fish, eggs and dairy. The nature of the ketogenic diet generally ensures that high quality protein is consumed unless some type of liquid protein fast is being performed. Some individuals also choose to use commercial protein powders as a protein source.

Section 4: Fat and the SKD

Having discussed the details of carbohydrate and protein amounts in the last two chapters, the only remaining macronutrient to be discussed is dietary fat. Although a ketogenic diet can be constructed with only protein and a small amount of carbohydrate, the caloric intake is so low that metabolic slowdown will occur. Fat is in essence a caloric ballast, a nutrient which has a relatively neutral effect on insulin levels or ketosis, and which is used to adjust calories.

What is a fat?

Fats are an organic compound, more accurately referred to as a triglyceride (TG), which is composed of a glycerol molecule with three free fatty acid (FFA) chains attached. Depending on the type of FFA chains, fats will vary in their types and effects on the human body. Generally, TG is subdivided into unsaturated fats, which occur in vegetable oils, and saturated fats, which occur in animal fats such as butter fat. A third type of TG, called a partially hydrogenated or trans-fat, is a man-made fat produced by bubbling hydrogen through vegetable oil to make a semi-solid fat, such as margarine.

Digestion of TG

Regardless of type, all TG is digested the same way: ultimately being broken down into glycerol and FFA. Depending on a variety of factors, the FFA can be burned for energy by the muscles or heart, resynthesized back to TG in fat cells, or converted to ketones in the liver. The glycerol portion of TG can be converted to glucose as discussed in chapter 5.

Cholesterol

Although cholesterol has no direct impact on ketone body formation, confusion about cholesterol warrants a brief discussion. While not strictly a fat, cholesterol is a compound most often associated with dietary fat intake.

Cholesterol is a steroid molecule which is used for a variety of functions in the body including the synthesis of some hormones such as testosterone and estrogen. Cholesterol only occurs in food of animal origin with an average of 100 milligrams of cholesterol present in 3 ounces of meat.

Digestion of cholesterol

The details of cholesterol digestion are extremely complex and unnecessary for the ensuing discussion. As dietary cholesterol has no direct affect on ketosis, it will not be discussed further in this chapter.

With regard to blood cholesterol levels, readers need to understand that the liver produces more cholesterol (up to 2000 milligrams per day) than most individuals would ever consume, even on a ketogenic diet. Additionally, when dietary cholesterol intake increases, the body's synthesis of cholesterol will typically go down. When dietary cholesterol intake goes down, the body's synthesis of cholesterol typically goes up. This supports the contention that dietary cholesterol generally has little impact on blood cholesterol levels. The effects of the ketogenic diet on blood cholesterol levels are discussed in chapter 7.

What tissues use fat?

As discussed in previous chapters, almost all tissues of the body can use FFA as a fuel under proper conditions. From a purely energy perspective, there is no difference between dietary fat and stored bodyfat. From that standpoint, there is no real requirement for dietary fat with the exception of two essential fatty acids which must be consumed through the diet. Given the same protein and carbohydrate intake, the more dietary fat which is ingested, the less bodyfat which will be lost and vice versa.

How much fat per day?

As opposed to carbohydrate and protein, the body is able to store an almost unlimited supply of calories as bodyfat. An average individual (150 lbs and 15% bodyfat or 22.5 lbs of fat) carries almost 80,000 calories worth of stored fat in their adipose tissue. This is enough stored energy to walk approximately 800 miles without exhausting fat stores. This, along with the fact that there is only a small essential fatty acid requirement, raises the question of why a dieter should eat any dietary fat on a ketogenic diet.

As discussed in the previous chapter, once ketosis is established, the majority of calories burned by the body will come from fat breakdown. The remainder comes from the small obligatory use of glucose by certain tissues, and the use of ketones. During total starvation, or the protein sparing modified fast, up to 1800 calories (200 grams) or more of FFA may be burned per day by an average sized person.

Although a high fat intake is necessary for epileptic children, this is because they must maintain deep ketosis and weight loss is not desirable for developing children in most cases. However, for epileptic children who are also obese, the ketogenic diet is used both as a treatment for the epilepsy as well as to cause weight loss (12).

All of this data suggests that dietary fat is not a necessary part of a ketogenic diet from a metabolic or adaptational standpoint as ketosis will readily develop without the consumption of dietary fat (assuming protein and carbohydrate intake are not too high). From a strictly metabolic standpoint, there appears to be no difference in a ketogenic diet which contains fat and one which does not contain fat.

The primary reason for the inclusion of dietary fat in the ketogenic diet is to keep caloric intake high enough to prevent a slowdown of metabolic rate. Recall from chapter 8 that a caloric deficit below 12 calories per pound of bodyweight can result in the loss of muscle and metabolic slowdown, both of which dieters want to avoid. Since protein and carbohydrate intake must be kept relatively constant on a ketogenic diet, the only way to modulate caloric intake is by changing the amount of dietary fat consumed.

From a practical standpoint, the inclusion of dietary fat tends to promote feelings of fullness as well as making food taste better, both important aspects of making a diet work for most people. Those who have tried an all-protein diet can attest to the monotony of consuming only lean protein at each meal for long periods of time.

In essence, after caloric requirements have been established and protein and carbohydrate intake set, the remaining calories will come from dietary fat. The details of calculating dietary fat requirements appear in section 6 where a complete SKD is set up.

An important observation with regards to fat intake is that some individuals have reported transient stomach upset (and occasionally nausea) when they begin a ketogenic diet, especially if they have been on a low-fat diet previously. Easing into the ketogenic diet more gradually, by slowly increasing fat intake and decreasing carb intake at the same time, seems to prevent some of these symptoms. Additionally, sufficient fiber intake may help.

Quality of fat consumed

Like carbohydrates and protein, fats can be rated in terms of their quality. Much of the stigma associated with dietary fat is related to fat quality as much as quantity . Almost all of the dietary fat which we eat on a daily basis is in the form of triglycerides (TG), which is a glycerol molecule bonded to three free fatty acid (FFA) chains. Depending on the types of FFA present, TG are typically delineated into unsaturated or saturated.

• Unsaturated fats: Typically speaking, unsaturated fats are found primarily in foods of vegetable origin such as vegetable oils, nuts and seeds. Unsaturated fats are liquid at room temperature. Two specific unsaturated fats, called essential fatty acids (EFAs), must be obtained from the diet as they can not be synthesized within the body. These are linoleic acid (LA) and alpha-linolenic acid (ALA). LA and ALA occur to some degree in all vegetable source fats, but the most concentrated sources are flax oil/flax meal, safflower oil, and sunflower oil.

• Saturated fats: With only two exceptions (coconut oil and palm kernel oil), saturated fats occur in foods of animal origin such as the fat in beef or chicken. Dairy fats such as butter and heavy cream are also sources of saturated fats. Saturated fats are solid at room temperature.

• Trans-fatty acids (TFAs): Trans-fatty acids, also called partially hydrogenated vegetable oil, occur only in processed foods. Food manufacturers bubble hydrogen through vegetable oils to make a semi-solid (i.e. margarine), which has a longer shelf life. TFAs are thought to have many negative health consequences and their intake should be minimized. An emphasis on unprocessed foods will minimize the intake of TFAs.

Little research has examined the effects of different types of TG on a ketogenic diet, although one study suggested a difference in weight loss and thermogenesis between olive and corn oil, with corn oil being the preferred choice (13). Anecdotally, many individuals find that increased intake of unsaturated fats, especially flax oil, tend to increase fat loss compared to a high intake of saturated fats. As well, many individuals who have found that their blood cholesterol levels increase on a ketogenic diet note that cholesterol decreases if more unsaturated fats are consumed.

To minimize potential health problems, consuming primarily unsaturated fats may be ideal. However, avoiding all saturated fats would be unrealistic since this will further limit the number of foods available to ketogenic dieters. In practice, most individuals will end up consuming a mix of both saturated and unsaturated fats during the day. A source of EFAs, such as flax or safflower oil, should be consumed. Alternately some individuals have consumed foods such as flax seeds or flax meal or consumed fatty nuts to fulfill their EFAs requirements.

Timing of fat intake

As with protein intake, there is no specific time to consume or not consume dietary fat on a SKD. Most individuals tend to spread dietary fat more or less evenly throughout the day, if for no other reason than to avoid stomach upset. The exception is immediately after a workout when dietary fat is not desirable, as it will slow digestion of post-workout protein intake.

Summary

With the exception of the small requirement for the EFAs, there is no essential reason to consume dietary fat as ketosis can readily be induced with a diet of all protein and a small amount of carbohydrate. However, to avoid metabolic slowdown from an excessively low caloric intake, dietary fat is necessary as a caloric ballast since protein and carbohydrates must be kept relatively static on a ketogenic diet. From a purely practical standpoint, dietary fat provides fullness and taste as a diet of pure protein is monotonously bland.

While little research has examined the optimal type of fats to consume on a SKD, when possible it is beneficial to consume more unsaturated vegetable fats over saturated animal fats to avoid any potential problems with blood lipid levels. To avoid all saturated fats is nearly impossible considering the generally high intake of animal products on a ketogenic diet.

Timing of fat intake is not critical to success of the diet. The exception is that dietary fat should be avoided post workout so that protein ingested at this time can enter the bloodstream quickly to help with post-workout recovery.

Section 5: Other dietary effects on ketosis

Other than protein, carbohydrate and fat, a number of other nutritional substances can affect the ability to establish and maintain ketosis. While not all have been studied with respect to their effects on ketosis, anecdotal evidence can help to determine which substances may or may not affect ketosis. The substances discussed in this chapter are water, alcohol, caffeine, and citric acid/aspartame.

Water

Strictly speaking, water intake should have no direct effect on ketogenesis (at least in terms of a direct effect at either the liver or the fat cell). However, water intake may affect the measurement of ketosis in more subtle ways.

As discussed in chapter 4, high concentrations of blood ketones tend to prevent further ketone body production by raising insulin and decreasing fat release from the fat cell. In theory, this might be seen to slow fat loss when ketone concentrations become high. By extension, a high water intake might dilute blood ketone levels and prevent this from occurring. Additionally, it seems possible that a high fluid intake might wash ketones out of the bloodstream into the kidneys (for excretion), causing more bodyfat to be used to synthesize more ketones.

Neither of these ideas have been studied directly. When the ketogenic diet is used to treat epilepsy, fluids of all types are restricted in an attempt to keep blood ketone concentrations very high, as high ketone body levels are thought to be part of the mechanism by which the diet works. This suggests that a high water intake might dilute blood ketone levels and prevent the rise in insulin which can occur.

However, a high water intake may also dilute urinary ketone levels, making it more difficult to determine if one actually is in ketosis or not. Anecdotally, individuals who consume very large amounts of water tend to show very light levels of urinary ketones on the Ketostix (tm) (which are discussed in detail in chapter 15).

From a purely health standpoint, a high water intake is necessary on a ketogenic diet due to the dehydrating effects of ketosis. Some of the side effects which occur in epileptic children (i.e. kidney stones) may be related to the dehydration which is imposed and individuals are suggested to keep water intake high as a general rule.

Alcohol

Although alcohol intake has been discussed briefly in previous sections, its effects on ketosis need to be discussed here, especially since many individuals want to know if alcohol is allowed on a ketogenic diet. In general, once ketosis is established alcohol tends to deepen the level of ketosis seen. Additionally, the pathological state of alcoholic ketoacidosis (which occurs when individuals consume nothing except alcohol for long periods) is known to result in potentially dangerous levels of ketones in the bloodstream. Alcohol may affect ketone body production in the liver and alcohol itself can be converted to ketones. As well, the production of ketones from alcohol tends to result in less fat loss since less FFA is converted to ketones.

Strictly speaking there is no reason that small amounts of alcohol cannot be consumed during a ketogenic diet although it should be realized that fat loss will be slowed. Additionally, anecdotal reports suggest that alcohol may affect individuals more (in terms of drunkenness, etc.) when they are in ketosis versus when they are not. Care should be taken by anyone consuming alcohol.

Caffeine

Although caffeine is discussed in more detail in the supplement chapter, its potential effects on ketosis are addressed here. A popular idea floating around states that caffeine raises insulin levels which might possibly disrupt ketosis. As well many individuals find that some caffeine containing drinks, such as diet soda, can interrupt ketosis.

However, this is contradictory to the known effects of caffeine ingestion, which are to raise levels of adrenaline and noradrenaline and raise FFA levels. The only way that caffeine could raise insulin would be indirectly. By raising adrenaline and noradrenaline levels, caffeine might cause liver glycogen to be broken down into glucose and released into the bloodstream, raising insulin. This would only occur prior to ketosis being established, such as after the carb-load phase of the CKD, and would help a dieter to establish ketosis.

Citric acid and aspartame

In all likelihood, problems with diet soda relate to one of these two compounds, both of which are used as artificial sweeteners in diet products. Citric acid may inhibit ketosis and diet sodas containing citric acid or aspartame are not allowed for epileptic children on the ketogenic diet (14). However, there is some debate over this point (15). Possibly, citric acid might affect ketosis by affecting liver metabolism, primarily the Krebs cycle. Some individuals report that citric acid prevents them from entering ketosis but does not affect ketosis once it has been established. One study, examining very-low-calorie diets, found that the consumption of citric acid inhibited ketosis and increased appetite in many individuals (16). Ultimately, individuals will have to determine for themselves whether citric acid or aspartame has any effect on ketosis, appetite or fat loss on a ketogenic diet.

Fiber

While fiber has already been discussed in terms of its effects on constipation in chapter 7, there is some concern that fiber may negatively impact ketosis. Strictly speaking fiber is a carbohydrate. However, humans do not have the enzymes necessary to digest fiber and derive any carbohydrate grams or calories from it. Therefore, fiber intake should not be counted as part of the total daily carbohydrate grams consumed on a ketogenic diet.

Similarly, there is some confusion regarding food labels and fiber content. By law, fiber has to be listed in the total carbohydrate grams part of the food label as well as being listed separately. However, it should not be counted as a carbohydrate in terms of ketosis and a ketogenic diet. Therefore, the total grams of fiber in a food should be subtracted from the total grams of carbohydrate in order to determine how many grams of carbohydrate that food will contribute to daily totals. If a food lists 20 grams of carbohydrates, but 7 grams of fiber, only 13 grams of carbohydrate should be counted towards the daily total.

Summary

A variety of nutritional substances may have an impact on ketosis including water, alcohol, caffeine, citric acid and aspartame, and fiber. Water has an indirect effect on ketosis, although large water intakes may dilute urinary ketone readings. In general, alcohol tends to deepen ketosis, and may increase an individual's susceptibility to becoming intoxicated. Despite popular belief, caffeine does not raise insulin except indirectly, and should not negatively affect ketosis. Citric acid and aspartame cause problems in some individuals and not others. Fiber has no direct impact on ketosis, but confusion exists as to how fiber should be treated in terms of carbohydrate intake. As humans lack the enzymes necessary to digest fiber, fiber should not be counted as part of the daily carbohydrate intake.

Section 6: Setting up an SKD

Having discussed the details behind carbohydrate, protein, and fat content several diet examples are presented here to demonstrate how the calculations are made.

General concepts

There are four steps to set up an optimal SKD.

Step 1: Set calorie levels as discussed in chapter 8.

Step 2: Set protein levels as discussed in section 2 of this chapter. Protein should be set at 0.9 gram/lb for individuals who are exercising and 0.8 grams/lb for those who are not. If daily protein intake is below 150 grams per day, it should be adjusted upwards for the first three weeks of the diet. Protein contains 4 calories per gram.

Step 3: Set carbohydrate levels. This will generally be below 30 grams per day, especially during the initial weeks of the diet. Carbohydrate contains 4 calories per gram.

Step 4: Set fat intake levels. Fat intake will represent the remainder of daily calories after protein and carbohydrate are determined. Fat has 9 calories per gram.

Two sample diets are set up below.

Example 1: 200 lb male who is weight training

Step 1: Set caloric intake: 200 lb * 12 cal/lb = 2400 calories per day

Step 2: Set protein intake: 200 lb * 0.8 g/lb = 160 grams of protein. Since protein has 4 calories/gram, this is 160 grams * 4 cal/gram = 640 calories from protein

Step 3: Set carbohydrate intake. For an SKD, we will assume 10 grams of carbohydrate per day. Since carbohydrate has 4 calories/gram, this is 10 grams * 4 cal/gram = 40 calories from carbohydrate.

Step 4: To determine fat intake, subtract calories from protein and carbohydrate from total calories.

2400 calories - 640 calories - 40 calories = 1720 calories from fat
Since fat has 9 calories/gram, this is 1720 calories / 9 cal/gram = 191 grams of fat

This person's overall diet is:
Calories: 2400
Protein intake: 160 grams/day
Carbohydrate intake: 10 grams/day
Fat intake: 191 grams/day

Example 2: 150 lb female who is sedentary

Step 1: Set calorie intake: 150 lbs * 12 cal/lb = 1800 cal/day

Step 2: Set protein intake: 150 lbs * 0.8 g/lb = 120 grams of protein. Since protein intake is below 150 grams per day, this should be adjusted to 150 grams/day for the first three weeks of the diet. At 4 cal/gram, this is 150 grams * 4 cal/gram = 600 calories from protein.

Step 3: Set carbohydrate intake: 10 grams per day * 4 cal/gram = 40 calories

Step 4: set fat intake
1800 cal/day - 600 calories - 40 calories = 1160 calories from fat
1160 calories from fat / 9 cal/gram = 128 grams of fat per day

After three weeks, dietary protein intake can be lowered to 120 grams per day or 480 calories/day. Thus fat intake must be adjusted upwards.
1800 cal/day - 480 calories - 40 calories = 1280 calories from fat
1280 calories from fat / 9 cal/gram = 142 grams of fat per day.

References Cited

1. Council on Foods and Nutrition. A critique of low-carbohydrate ketogenic weight reducing regimes. JAMA (1973) 224: 1415-1419.
2. Yudkin J and Carey M. The treatment of obesity by a 'high-fat' diet - the inevitably of calories. Lancet (1960) 939.
3. Larosa JC et. al. Effects of high-protein, low-carbohydrate dieting on plasma lipoproteins and body weight. J Am Diet Assoc (1980) 77: 264-270.

4. Fisher MC and Lachance PA. Nutrition evaluation of published weight reducing diets. J Amer Dietetic Assoc (1985) 85: 450-454.

5. Stock A and Yudkin J. Nutrient intake of subjects on low carbohydrate diet used in treatment of obesity. Am J Clin Nutr (1970) 23: 948-952

6. Phinney S. Exercise during and after very-low-calorie dieting. Am J Clin Nutr (1992) 56: 190S-194S.

7. Yudkin J. The low-carbohydrate diet in the treatment of obesity. Postgrad Med (1972) 51:151-154.

8. Jungas RL et. al. Quantitative analysis of amino acid oxidation and related gluconeogenesis in humans. Physiological Reviews (1992) 72: 419-448

9. Marks BL and Rippe J. The importance of fat free maintenance in weight loss programs. Sports Med (1996) 22: 273-281.

10. Richardson DP et. al. Quantitative effect of an isoenergetic exchange of fat for carbohydrate on dietary protein utilization in healthy young men. Am J Clin Nutr (1979) 32: 2217-2226.

11. Lemon P. Is increased dietary protein necessary or beneficial for individuals with a physically active lifestyle? Nutrition Reviews (1996) 54: S169-S175.

12. "The Epilepsy Diet Treatment: An introduction to the ketogenic diet" John M. Freeman, MD ; Millicent T. Kelly, RD, LD ; Jennifer B. Freeman. Demos Vermande, 1996.

13. Kasper H. et. al. Response of bodyweight to a low carbohydrate, high fat diet in normal and obese subjects. Am J Clin Nutr (1973) 26: 197-204.

14. Gasch AT. Use of the traditional ketogenic diet for treatment of intractable epilepsy. J Am Diet Assoc (1990) 90: 1433-1434.

15. Brunett A. Should diet soft drinks be restricted on a ketogenic diet [Letter]. J Am Diet Assoc (1991) 91: 776

16. Krietzman S. Factors influencing body composition during very-low-calorie diets. Am J Clin Nutr (1992) 56 (suppl): 217S-223S.

Chapter 10:
Carbohydrates and the ketogenic diet

In addition to the standard ketogenic diet (SKD), this book also details two modifications which have been made to the SKD. As discussed in forthcoming chapters on exercise, a SKD cannot sustain high-intensity exercise performance such as weight training or high-intensity aerobic training and carbohydrates must be integrated to the SKD in some fashion.

There are two primary types of 'modified ketogenic diets' which incorporate carbohydrate intake within the structure of a SKD. The first of these is the Targeted Ketogenic Diet (TKD) in which individuals consume carbohydrates around exercise only. This allows for a maintenance of exercise performance and glycogen resynthesis without interrupting ketosis for long periods of time.

The second type of 'modified ketogenic diet' is the Cyclical Ketogenic Diet or CKD. The CKD alternates periods of a ketogenic diet (generally 5-6 days) with periods of high carbohydrate intake (1-2 days).

Typically the TKD is used by those individuals who either can not or will not perform the longer carb-load of the cyclical ketogenic diet (CKD) or by individuals who are just starting exercise programs and are not ready to perform the amount of exercise needed to make the CKD work.

The CKD is typically aimed at individuals who are more advanced in terms of their exercise programs (i.e. bodybuilders) due to the high volume and intensity of training needed to optimize the diet. Before discussing the TKD and CKD in chapters 11 and 12, some general comments are made regarding glycogen levels and rates of glycogen depletion. This chapter discusses glycogen levels and depletion, topics which apply to both the TKD and CKD.

Section 1: Glycogen levels

To understand the basis of both the TKD and the CKD, a discussion of glycogen levels under a variety of conditions is necessary. To achieve optimal results from either the TKD or CKD requires that some estimations be made in terms of the amount of training which can and should be done as well as how much carbohydrate should be consumed at a given time.

Muscle glycogen is measured in millimoles per kilogram of muscle (mmol/kg). An individual following a normal mixed diet will maintain glycogen levels around 80-100 mmol/kg. Athletes following a mixed diet have higher levels, around 110-130 mmol/kg (1). On a standard ketogenic diet, with aerobic exercise only, muscle glycogen levels maintain around 70 mmol/kg with about 50 mmol/kg of that in the Type I muscle fibers (2,3).

As discussed in greater detail in upcoming chapters, fat oxidation increases, both at rest and during aerobic exercise around 70 mmol/kg. Below 40 mmol/kg, exercise performance is impaired. Total exhaustion during exercise occurs at 15-25 mmol/kg. Additionally, when glycogen levels fall too low (about 40 mmol/kg), protein can be used as a fuel source during exercise to a greater degree (4).

Following glycogen depletion, if an individual consumes enough carbohydrates over a sufficient amount of time (generally 24-48 hours), muscle glycogen can reach 175 mmol/kg or higher (1). The level of supercompensation which can be achieved depends on the amount of glycogen depleted (5,6). That is, the lower that muscle glycogen levels are taken, the greater compensation which is seen. If glycogen levels are depleted too far (below 25 mmol/kg), glycogen supercompensation is impaired as the enzymes involved in glycogen synthesis are impaired (7). A summary of glycogen levels under different conditions appears in table 1.

Table 1: Glycogen levels under different conditions

Condition	Diet	Glycogen level (mmol/kg)
Supercompensated	High carb	175
Athlete	Mixed diet	110-130
Normal individual	Mixed diet	80-100
Normal individual, - aerobic exercise only	Ketogenic diet	70
Fat burning increases		70
Exercise performance decreased		40
Exhaustion		15-25

Glycogen resynthesis without post exercise carb intake

Even without the consumption of carbohydrates there is some replenishment of muscle glycogen stores following exercise. This raises the question of whether carbohydrates are necessary while on a SKD. A few calculations will show that the small amount of glycogen resynthesized during exercise is insufficient to maintain glycogen stores for more than a few workouts.

When zero carbohydrates are consumed following training, there is a small amount of glycogen resynthesized. This glycogen comes from the conversion of lactate, a by-product of glycogen breakdown in the muscle, to glucose in the liver. This newly made glucose is released into the bloodstream and stored again in the muscle as glycogen. Two mmol of lactate are required to resynthesize 1 mmol of glycogen (8). Approximately 20% of the lactate generated during weight training can be used to resynthesize glycogen after training.

Lactate levels in the muscle during resistance training may only reach 10-15 mmol with a maximum of 21 mmol (seen only in highly trained bodybuilders). At 2 mmol of lactate/1 mmol glycogen and an efficiency of 20%, this would have the potential to resynthesize only 2 mmol/kg of glycogen, an insignificant amount.

Two studies have examined the phenomenon of post-workout glycogen resynthesis. One study using weight training with no carbohydrate given found a resynthesis rate of 1.9 mmol/kg/hour following resistance training with a total of 4 mmol/kg being resynthesized (8). As

40 mmol/kg of glycogen was depleted during the exercise, this small amount would not sustain exercise performance for long.

However, in a second study, 22 mmol/kg was synthesized after training (9). The major difference between these studies was that subjects in the second study (9) ate a small carbohydrate-containing meal the morning of the training session whereas the subjects in the first (8) did not. The elevation of blood glucose from the pre-workout meal allowed greater glycogen resynthesis to occur following training in the second study (8,10). This observation is the basis for the TKD which is discussed in chapter 11.

Summary

In the absence of dietary carbohydrates, the amount of glycogen resynthesis following weight training is insignificant and will not sustain high intensity performance for very long. This further stresses the importance of carbohydrate intake for individuals on a ketogenic diet wishing to perform weight or interval training.

If carbs are taken prior to a workout, there can be a significant amount of glycogen resynthesis following training depending on the quantity of carbohydrate consumed. This is the basis of the TKD, discussed in the next chapter.

Section 2: Glycogen depletion during weight training

Having looked at glycogen levels under various conditions, we can now examine the rates of glycogen depletion during weight training and use those values to make estimations of how much training can and should be done for both the TKD and CKD.

Very few studies have examined glycogen depletion rates during weight training. One early study found a very low rate of glycogen depletion of about 2 mmol/kg/set during 20 sets of leg exercise (11). In contrast, two later studies both found glycogen depletion levels of approximately 7-7.5 mmol/kg/set (8,9). As the difference between these studies cannot be adequately explained, we will assume a glycogen depletion rate of 7.5 mmol/kg/set.

Examining the data of these two studies further, we can estimate glycogen utilization relative to how long each set lasts. At 70% of maximum weight, both studies found a glycogen depletion rate of roughly 1.3 mmol/kg/repetition or 0.35 mmol/kg/second of work performed (8,9). This makes it possible to estimate the amount of glycogen which is depleted for a set of lasting a given amount of time (table 2).

Summary

Glycogen levels in muscle vary depending on a number of factors including diet and training status. While there is a small amount of glycogen resynthesized following exercise even if no carbohydrates are consumed, the amount is insignificant and will not be able to sustain exercise performance for more than a few workouts.

Since high-intensity activity such as weight training can only use carbohydrate as fuel, a SKD will not be able to sustain high-intensity exercise performance. This mandates that carbohydrate be introduced into the SKD without disrupting the effects of ketosis. The two primary ways to introduce carbohydrate to the SKD are the CKD, which allows a period of high carbohydrate consumption lasting from 24-48 hours every week, or the TKD where the dieter consumes carbohydrates around training.

Table 2: Amount of glycogen depleted for sets of differing lengths

Length of set (seconds)	Glycogen depleted (mmol/kg)
30	10
40	14
50	17
60	21
70	24
80	28
90	31

References Cited

1. Ivy J. Muscle glycogen synthesis before and after exercise. Sports Medicine (1991) 11: 6-19.
2. Phinney SD et. al. The human metabolic response to chronic ketosis without caloric restriction: physical and biochemical adaptations. Metabolism (1983) 32: 757-768.
3. Phinney SD et. al. The human metabolic response to chronic ketosis without caloric restriction: preservation of submaximal exercise capacity with reduced carbohydrate oxidation. Metabolism (1983) 32: 769-776.
4. Lemon PR and Mullin JP. Effect of initial muscle glycogen level on protein catabolism during exercise. J Appl Physiol (1980) 48: 624-629.
5. Zachweija JJ et. al. Influence of muscle glycogen depletion on the rate of resynthesis. Med Sci Sports Exerc (1991) 23: 44-48.
6. Price TB et. al. Human muscle glycogen resynthesis after exercise: insulin-dependent and -independent phases. J Appl Physiol (1994) 76: 104-111.
7. Yan Z et. al. Effect of low glycogen on glycogen synthase during and after exercise. Acta Physiol Scand (1992) 145: 345-352.
8. Pascoe DD and Gladden LB. Muscle glycogen resynthesis after short term, high intensity exercise and resistance exercise. Sports Med (1996) 21: 98-118.
9. Robergs RA et. al. Muscle glycogenolysis during different intensities of weight-resistance exercise. J Appl Physiol (1991) 70: 1700-1706.
10. Conley M and Stone M. Carbohydrate ingestion/supplementation for resistance exercise and training. Sports Med (1996) 21: 7-17.
11. Tesch PA et. al. Muscle metabolism during intense, heavy resistance exercise. Eur J Appl Physiol (1986) 55: 362-366.

Chapter 11:
The Targeted Ketogenic Diet (TKD)

Having examined glycogen levels and glycogen depletion in the last chapter, the details of the first 'modified ketogenic diet' can now be discussed. The targeted ketogenic diet (TKD) is nothing more than the standard ketogenic diet (SKD) with carbohydrates consumed at specific times around exercise. This means that the general guidelines for constructing a SKD in chapter 9 should be used with the exception that more carbohydrates are consumed on days when exercise is performed. If fat loss is the goal, the number of calories consumed as carbohydrates should be subtracted from total calories, meaning that less dietary fat is consumed on those days.

The TKD is based more on anecdotal experience than research. Invariably, individuals on a SKD are unable to maintain a high training intensity for reasons discussed in chapters 18 through 20. However, for a variety of reasons, some dieters choose not to do the full 1-2 day carb-up of the CKD (discussed in the next chapter). The TKD is a compromise approach between the SKD and the CKD. The TKD will allow individuals on a ketogenic diet to perform high intensity activity (or aerobic exercise for long periods of time) without having to interrupt ketosis for long periods of time.

Why pre-workout carbs?

Weight training is not generally limited by the availability of blood glucose. Studies giving carbs prior to resistance training have not found an increase in performance (1). However, almost without exception, individuals on a SKD who consume pre-workout carbs report improved strength and endurance and an ability to maintain a higher intensity of training during their workout. Anyone following a ketogenic diet who wishes to perform high intensity training can benefit from the TKD approach.

Very little research has examined the effects of a ketogenic diet on weight training performance and it is difficult to determine exactly why performance is improved with pre-workout carbs. It may be that raising blood glucose to normal levels, which only requires a minimal 5 grams of carbohydrate (2), allows better muscle fiber recruitment during training or prevent fatigue. Ultimately, the reason why carbohydrates improve performance is less critical than the fact that they do.

Additionally, individuals performing extensive amounts of aerobic training on a SKD typically report improved performance with carbs consumed before and during workouts. Even at low intensities, performance on a SKD is limited by glucose and muscle glycogen. For this reason, endurance athletes using a SKD are encouraged to experiment with carbohydrates around training.

Amounts, types and timing of carbs

The major goal with pre-workout carbs is not necessarily to improve performance, although that is a nice benefit. Primarily, the goal is to provide enough carbohydrate to promote post-workout glycogen synthesis without interrupting ketosis for very long. That is, the carbohydrate taken prior to one workout is really an attempt to 'set up' the body for better performance at the next workout by maintaining glycogen levels.

Although experimentation is encouraged, most individuals find that 25-50 grams of carbohydrates taken thirty minutes before a workout enhance performance. The type of carbohydrate consumed pre-workout is not critical and individuals are encouraged to experiment with different types of carbs. Most seem to prefer easily digestible carbohydrates, either liquids or high Glycemic Index (GI) candies to avoid problems with stomach upset during training. A wide variety of foods have been used prior to workouts: glucose polymers, Sweet Tarts, bagels, and food bars; all result in improved performance.

One concern of many SKDers (especially those who are using a ketogenic diet to control conditions such as hyperinsulinemia) is the potential insulin response from carbohydrate ingestion on a TKD. Generally speaking, insulin levels decrease during exercise. Exercise training itself improves insulin sensitivity as does glycogen depletion (3,4). So hyperinsulinemia should not be a problem during exercise for individuals consuming carbs pre-workout.

However, following training, if blood glucose is still elevated, there may be an increase in insulin (1). This has the potential to cause a hyperinsulinemic response in predisposed individuals. Sadly there is no direct research to say that this will happen and the only data points available are anecdotal. Most people appear to tolerate pre-workout carbohydrates quite well, and very few have reported problems with an insulin or blood glucose rebound with post-workout carbohydrates. Once again, for lack of any strict guidelines, experimentation is encouraged.

Effects on ketosis

Research suggests that carbohydrates consumed before or after exercise should not negatively affect ketosis (5). However, some individuals find that they drop out of ketosis transiently due to the ingestion of pre-workout carbohydrates. After workout, there will be a short period where insulin is elevated and free fatty acid availability for ketone production is decreased (5). However, as blood glucose is pushed into the muscles, insulin should drop again allowing ketogenesis to resume within several hours. Performing some low intensity cardio to lower insulin and increase blood levels of free fatty acids should help to more quickly reestablish ketosis (see chapter 21 for more detail).

Post-workout carbohydrates might be expected to have a greater effect on ketosis, in that insulin levels will most likely be higher than are seen with pre-workout carbohydrates (5,6). For this reason, individuals may want to experiment with pre-workout carbohydrates first, only adding post-workout carbohydrates if necessary.

Training and the TKD

While an intake of 25-50 grams of carbohydrates prior to training is a good rough guideline, some individuals have asked how to calculate the exact amounts of carbohydrate which they should consume around exercise.

For weight training, the amount of carbs needed will depend solely on the amount of training being done. Recall from the previous sections that a set of weight training lasting 45 seconds will use approximately 15.7 mmol/kg of glycogen. Individuals on an SKD typically maintain glycogen levels around 70 mmol/kg and performance will be extremely compromised if glycogen is lowered to 40 mmol/kg, allowing roughly 2 sets per bodypart to be performed.

Assuming ~30 mmol/kg used per bodypart in 2 sets, we can estimate how much carbohydrate is needed to replace that amount of glycogen. To convert mmol of glycogen to grams of carbohydrate, we simply divide mmol by 5.56.

30 mmol/kg divided by 5.56 = ~5 grams of carbohydrates to replace 30 mmol of glycogen.

So for every 2 sets performed during weight training, 5 grams of carbs should be consumed to replenish the glycogen used. If a large amount of training is being performed, necessitating a large amount of carbohydrate (greater than 100 grams) it may be beneficial to split the total amount of carbohydrate up, consuming half 30' prior to the workout and the other half when the workout begins. This should avoid problems with stomach upset during training. Some individuals have also experimented with consuming carbohydrates during training. All approaches seem to work effectively and experimentation is encouraged.

Post-workout nutrition

For individuals wishing to consume carbs post-training to help with recovery, an additional 25-50 grams of glucose or glucose polymers are recommended. In this situation, the type of carbohydrate ingested does matter and fructose and sucrose should ideally be avoided, since they may refill liver glycogen and risk interrupting ketone body formation. This limits post-workout carbohydrates to glucose or glucose-polymers, which are not used to refill liver glycogen (7).

With pre-workout carbs, there will be an increase in insulin after training ends. Even if individuals do not want to take in carbs after training, ingesting protein can help with recovery as the insulin from pre-workout carbs should push amino acids into the muscle cells. Consuming 25-50 grams of a high quality protein immediately after training may help with recovery.

Fat should generally be avoided in a post-workout meal. First and foremost, dietary fat will slow digestion of protein and/or carbohydrate. Second, the consumption of dietary fat when insulin levels are high may cause fat storage after training (1).

Summary of the guidelines for the TKD

1. Individuals following the SKD who want to perform high intensity activity will absolutely have to consume carbs at some point around exercise. The basic guidelines for setting up a SKD (from

chapter 9) should still be used to develop a TKD. The only difference is that calories must be adjusted to account for the carbohydrates being consumed around training.

2. The safest time to consume carbs, in terms of maintaining ketosis, is before a workout and ketosis should be reestablished soon after training. Depending on total training volume, 25-50 grams of carbohydrates taken 30-60' prior to training seems to be a good amount. The type of carbohydrate is less critical for pre-workout carbs but quickly digested, high GI carbs seem to work best to avoid stomach upset.

3. If more than 50 grams of carbohydrates must be consumed around training, it may be beneficial to split the total amount, consuming half 30' before training and the other half at the beginning (or during) of the workout.

4. If post-workout carbohydrates are consumed, an additional 25-50 grams of glucose or glucose polymers are recommended. Fructose and sucrose should be avoided as they can refill liver glycogen and interrupt ketosis. Additionally protein can be added to the post-workout meal to help with recovery. Dietary fat should be avoided since it will slow digestion and could lead to fat storage when insulin levels are high.

5. If post-workout carbohydrates are not consumed, taking in protein only can still enhance recovery as blood glucose and insulin should be slightly elevated from the consumption of pre-workout carbohydrates.

References Cited

1. Conley M and Stone M. Carbohydrate ingestion/supplementation for resistance exercise and training. Sports Med (1996) 21: 7-17.
2. Jacobs I. Lactate Muscle Glycogen and Exercise Performance in Man. Acta Physiol Scand Supplementum (1981) 495: 3-27.
3. Kelley DE. The regulation of glucose uptake and oxidation during exercise. Int J Obesity (1995) 19 (Suppl. 3): S14-S17.
4. Ivy JL. Effects of elevated and exercise-reduced muscle glycogen levels on insulin sensitivity. J Appl Physiol (1985) 59: 154-159.
5. Koeslag JH et al. Post-exercise ketosis in post-prandial exercise: effect of glucose and alanine ingestion in humans. J Physiol (Lond). (1985) 358: 395-403.
6. Carlin JI et al. The effects of post-exercise glucose and alanine ingestion on plasma carnitine and ketosis in humans. J Physiol (Lond). (1987) 390: 295-303.
7. McGarry JD et. al. From dietary glucose to liver glycogen: the full circle around. Ann Rev Nutr (1987) 7:51-73.

Chapter 12:
The Cyclical Ketogenic Diet (CKD)

As with the TKD, the CKD attempts to harness the effects of a ketogenic diet while maintaining exercise performance. However, rather than providing carbohydrates only around exercise, the CKD inserts a one- or two-day period of high carbohydrate eating to refill muscle glycogen. This means that for the CKD to work, muscle glycogen must be depleted fully each week. A few calculations which appear below show that full depletion of muscle glycogen requires a fairly large amount of training. This means that the CKD is not appropriate for beginning exercisers or those who are unable to perform the amount of training necessary.

Although some authors have suggested the use of CKD for mass gains, it is not optimal in that regard for a variety of reasons which are discussed in chapter 29. This chapter focuses primarily on optimizing the CKD for fat loss.

The standard format for a CKD is to alternate 5-6 days of ketogenic dieting with 1-2 days of high carbohydrate eating, although other variations can be developed. Individuals have experimented with longer cycles (10-12 days) as well as shorter cycles (3-4) days with good results. A 7 day cycle is more a choice of convenience than anything physiological, since it fits most people's work schedule and allows dieters to eat more or less 'normally' on the weekends.

The low-carb week of the CKD is identical to the SKD and all of the information discussed in chapter 9 applies. During the carb-loading phase of the CKD, the body's metabolism is temporarily switched out of ketosis, with the goal of refilling muscle glycogen levels to sustain exercise performance in the next cycle. One question, that unfortunately has no answer, is how the insertion of a carb-loading phase will affect the adaptations to ketosis, discussed in previous chapters.

This chapter focuses on the theory behind optimizing both the lowcarb week (in terms of weight training) as well as the carb-up. Additionally, it has been suggested that the weekend carb-load may be anabolic for a variety of reasons but this is poorly studied. Possible anabolic effects of the carb-load are discussed. Finally, specific guidelines for implementing the CKD appear at the end of this chapter.

Section 1: Muscle glycogen, training, and the CKD

Unlike the TKD, where the goal is to maintain muscle glycogen at an intermediate level, the goal of the CKD is to deplete muscle glycogen completely between carb-ups.

There are numerous workouts which can accomplish this goal. However, this section will show calculations based on a Monday, Tuesday, Friday format, for reasons discussed below. The particular nature of the CKD requires a slightly different workout schedule for optimal results.

For the CKD, the goal of the early week workouts (generally performed on Monday and

Tuesday) is to reduce muscle glycogen from initial levels to approximately 70 mmol/kg, but no lower. This should maximize fat utilization at rest and during aerobic exercise while avoiding problems with increased protein use during exercise. The total amount of training required to accomplish this will depend on the overall length of the carb-up and is discussed below.

Immediately prior to the carb-up, glycogen levels should be further lowered to between 25 and 40 mmol/kg. This will allow maximal glycogen compensation to occur during the carb-load. Calculations for the final workout are made in this chapter as well. Both the calculations made for the Monday and Tuesday workouts as well as the Friday workouts are used to develop the advanced CKD workout, which appears in chapter 28. The general format of the advanced CKD workout is:

Monday/Tuesday: split routine, such that the entire body is trained between these two days. For example, the lower body and abdominals might be trained on Monday, and the entire upper body trained on Tuesday

Friday: full body workout, either a high rep depletion workout or a low rep tension workout

Sample calculations for Monday and Tuesday workouts

To see how much weight training is necessary to achieve the above goals, let us look at a lifter who has just completed a carb-loading phase of 36 hours, achieving 150 mmol/kg of glycogen in all major muscle groups. In the first 2 workouts, this individual needs to lower glycogen to approximately 70 mmol/kg to maximize fat burning.

Therefore, this person needs to deplete:
150 mmol/kg - 70 mmol/kg = 80 mmol/kg of total glycogen.

Using the rate of glycogen depletion listed in chapter 10, we see that
80 mmol/kg divided by 1.3 mmol/kg/rep = 61 total reps.
or
80 mmol/kg divided by 0.35 mmol/kg/sec = 228 seconds of total set time.

Assuming an average set time of 45 seconds (10-12 reps at 4 seconds per repetition) this level of glycogen depletion would require approximately 5-6 sets per bodypart. This total amount of work can be divided up a number of ways. Simply performing 6 sets of 10 repetitions would be sufficient and a lifter might perform:
Squats: 4 sets of 10 reps (4 seconds per rep = 40 seconds per set)
Leg extension: 2 sets of 10 reps (4 seconds per rep = 40 seconds per set)

There are numerous other workout schemes to achieve the general goal of reducing glycogen levels and individuals are encouraged to experiment with their training. Regardless of what specific type of training is done, the important fact to remember is that the proper amount of total set time must be performed. Please note that the value of 15 mmol/kg/set was established at an intensity of 70% of 1 repetition maximum (the amount of weight which can be lifted only one time). There is unfortunately no way to know what the rate of glycogen depletion is at 50% or 90% of 1 rep maximum.

Someone starting at a lower or higher glycogen level would need less or more sets respectively. Table 1 shows the approximate amount of sets which would be necessary based on the approximate glycogen levels which would be reached for a given length of carbohydrate loading.

Table 1: Relationship between length of carb-up and sets needed for depletion

Carb-load (# hours)	Muscle glycogen (mmol/kg)	Glycogen depletion to reach 70 mmol/kg	Set time (sec.)	# of sets per bodypart *
12	~80	10	40	1
24	120	50	142	3
36	150	80	228	5
48	175-190	~120	342	8

* Assuming 45 seconds per set

If an individual did not want to perform as many heavy sets in training, the number of desired heavy sets could be performed and then several high rep sets performed at a lighter weight simply to deplete glycogen.

For example, an individual could perform:
Squats: 2 sets of 10 reps (4 seconds per rep)
Leg extensions: 2 sets of 10 reps (4 seconds per rep)
This would fulfill 160 seconds of the required work leaving 60 seconds.

The remaining 60 seconds of work could be fulfilled with three light sets of leg presses, each 20 seconds in length.

Alternately, the carb load could be shortened to compensate for a reduced training volume. That is, if a lifter only wished to perform three sets per bodypart during their Monday and Tuesday workouts, the carb-load would need to be shortened to 24 hours to adjust.

Sample calculations for the Friday workout

Having first depleted their muscles to 70 mmol/kg on Monday and Tuesday, our lifter now wants to deplete muscle glycogen to between 25-40 mmol/kg before starting the carb-up. This would require a further glycogen depletion of
70 mmol/kg - 25 mmol/kg = 45 mmol/kg
70 mmol/kg - 40 mmol/kg = 30 mmol/kg

30-45 mmol/kg.
This would require:

130

30-45 mmol/kg divided by 1.3 mmol/kg/rep = 20-30 reps
30-45 mmol/kg divided by 0.35 mmol/kg/second = 85-128 seconds.

Although discussed in greater detail in the exercise chapters, there are two options for the Friday workout which will determine how many sets are necessary to achieve full depletion. One option is to use heavy weights and low reps (8-10) in which case approximately two to three sets per bodypart are necessary. A second option is to use light weight and high reps (15-20) to deplete glycogen while minimizing muscle damage, in which case 5-6 sets may be necessary.

Keep in mind that there will is a great deal of overlap between bodyparts during both the Monday/Tuesday and Friday workouts. The glycogen depletion studies used to make these calculations used leg extensions, only working the quadriceps. Individuals depleting glycogen in the pectoral (chest) muscles with bench presses will also be working the deltoids and triceps to some degree. Unfortunately, it is impossible to know how much glycogen is depleted from the triceps from 4 sets of bench presses. The sample exercise routines will use a lower volume of exercise for bodyparts worked by previous movements in an attempt to compensate for overlap. That is to say, if chest has been worked for four sets (also working the shoulders and triceps), the shoulders and triceps will receive less total sets.

Summary

The amount of training needed to deplete muscle glycogen fully depends solely on the levels of glycogen reached on the weekend. Assuming an average carb-loading phase of 36 hours, approximately 4-6 sets will need to be performed during the Monday and Tuesday workouts. This will be adjusted upwards or downwards for different lengths of carb-ups. The number of sets done on the Friday workout will depend on what type of workout is done. If heavy weights/low reps are done, only 2-3 sets should be necessary. If light weights/high reps are used, 5-6 sets should be done. Please note that these values for number of sets are estimations only, and rough estimations at that. Individuals are encouraged to experiment with training structure and volume to determine what works best.

Section 2: The carb-load

The unique aspect of the CKD is the carb-loading phase which has its own set of implications and guidelines. Quite simply, the key to refilling muscle glycogen stores following depletion is the consumption of large amounts of carbohydrates (1). In fact many individuals find that the carb-load phase works just fine without much attention to the details of percentages and amounts. Simply eating a lot of carbohydrates for 24 to 36 hours works quite well for many people.

However many individuals want the details of how to optimize the amount of glycogen stored without gaining any fat. The amount of glycogen resynthesized depends on a number of factors including the degree of depletion, the amount and type of carbohydrates and the timing of carbohydrate consumption.

If sufficient amounts of carbohydrates are consumed for a long enough period of time, glycogen levels can reach greater than normal levels, a process called glycogen supercompensation. The process of glycogen depletion and supercompensation has been used for years by endurance athletes to improve performance (2). Only recently has it been applied to bodybuilders and other strength athletes. The carb-load can be classified by three distinct variables: duration and amount, type, and timing of carbohydrate intake. Each is discussed in detail below. Other factors which can affect the carb-load are also discussed in this chapter.

Duration and amount of the carb-load

The rate limiting step in glycogen resynthesis appears to be activity of the enzymes involved in glycogen synthesis (1). Regardless of carbohydrate intake, there is a maximal amount of glycogen which can be synthesized in a given amount of time, meaning that consuming all the necessary carbohydrates in a 4 hour time span, with the goal of returning to ketogenic eating that much sooner, will not work. Only when the proper amount of carbohydrates is consumed over a sufficient period of time, can glycogen compensation and/or supercompensation occur.

Following exhaustive exercise and full glycogen depletion, glycogen can be resynthesized to 100% of normal levels (roughly 100-110 mmol/kg) within 24 hours as long as sufficient amounts of carbohydrate are consumed (1,3). Assuming full depletion of the involved muscles, the amount of carbohydrate needed during this time period is 8-10 grams of carbohydrate per kilogram of lean body mass (LBM).

With 36 hours of carb-loading, roughly 150% compensation can occur, reaching levels of 150-160 mmol/kg of muscle glycogen. To achieve greater levels of muscle glycogen (175 mmol/kg or more) generally requires 3-4 days of high carbohydrate eating following exhaustive exercise (2).

The first 6 hours after training appear to be the most critical as enzyme activity and resynthesis rates are the highest, around 12 mmol/kg/hour (4). Following weight training, with a carbohydrate intake of 1.5 grams carbohydrate/kg LBM taken immediately after training and again 2 hours later, a total of 44 mmol/kg can be resynthesized (17).

Over the the first 24 hours, the average rate of glycogen resynthesis ranges from 5-12 mmol/kg/hour depending on the type of exercise performed (5). In general, aerobic exercise shows the lowest rate of glycogen resynthesis (2-8 mmol/kg/hour), weight training the second highest (1.3-11 mmol/kg/hour), and interval training the highest (15 to 33.6 mmol/kg/hour) (5,6). The reason that glycogen resynthesis is lower after weight training than after interval training may be related to the amount of lactic acid generated as well as the muscle damage that typically occurs during weight training (6).

At an average rate of 5 mmol/kg /hour, approximately 120 mmol/kg of glycogen can be synthesized over 24 hours. This can be achieved by the consumption of 50 grams or more of carbohydrate every 2 hours during the first 24 hours after training. Intake of greater than 50 grams of carbohydrate does not appear to increase the rate of glycogen synthesis.

Over 24 hours, at 50 grams every 2 hours, this yields 600 grams of carbohydrates total to maximize glycogen resynthesis. These values are for a 154 pound (70 kilogram) person.

Significantly heavier or lighter individuals will need proportionally more or less carbohydrate. Simply use the value of 8-10 grams of carbohydrate per kilogram of LBM as a guide.

In the second 24 hours, glycogen resynthesis rates decrease (1) and a carbohydrate intake of 5 grams/kg is recommended to further refill muscle glycogen stores while minimizing the chance of fat gain. For many individuals, the small amount of additional glycogen resynthesis which occurs during the second 24 hours of carbohydrate loading is not worth the risk of regaining some of the bodyfat which was lost during the preceding week.

Type of carbohydrates

The type of carbohydrate consumed during a carb-up can affect the rate at which glycogen is resynthesized. During the first 24 hours, when enzyme activity is at its highest, it appears that the consumption of high glycemic index (GI) foods promotes higher levels of glycogen resynthesis than lower GI carbs (5,7,8).

Glycogen resynthesis during the second 24 hours has not been studied as extensively. It appears that the consumption of lower GI carbs (starches, vegetables) promotes higher overall levels of glycogen resynthesis while avoiding fat gain by keeping insulin levels more stable (9). Most individuals find that their regain of bodyfat, as well as retention of water under the skin, is considerably less if they switch to lower GI carbohydrates during the second 24 hours of carbohydrate loading.

Fructose (fruit sugar, which preferentially refills liver glycogen) will not cause the same amount of glycogen resynthesis seen with glucose or sucrose (5,8). Whether liquids or solid carbohydrates are consumed also appears to have less impact on glycogen resynthesis as long as adequate amounts are consumed (10).

Anecdotally, many individuals have had success consuming liquid carbohydrates such as commercially available glucose polymers during their first few meals and then moving towards slightly more complex carbohydrates such as starches.

Timing of carbohydrates

While it would seem logical that consuming dietary carbohydrates in small amounts over the length of the carb-up would be ideal, at least one study suggests that glycogen resynthesis over 24 hours is related to the quantity of carbs consumed rather than how they are spaced out. In this study, subjects were glycogen depleted and then fed 525 grams of carbohydrate in either two or seven meals. Total glycogen resynthesis was the same in both groups (11). A similar study compared glycogen resynthesis with four large meals versus twelve smaller meals (12). Glycogen levels were the same in both groups.

Both of these studies suggest that the quantity of carbohydrates is more important than the timing of those carbohydrates. From a purely practical standpoint, smaller meals will generally make it easier to consume the necessary carbohydrate quantities and will keep blood sugar more stable.

Depending on when the carb-up is begun, some dieters may have to go long periods of time (i.e. during sleep) without eating, which may affect glycogen compensation. In this situation, a large amount of carbohydrates can be consumed at once, in order to maintain blood glucose and glycogen synthesis rates (5). For example, if an individual were going to sleep for 8 hours, they could consume 200 grams of carbohydrates (50 grams/2 hours for 8 hours) immediately before. Consuming these carbs with some protein, fat and fiber will slow digestion and give a more even blood glucose release, helping to promote glycogen resynthesis. Those wishing truly maximal glycogen resynthesis may wish to experiment with eating small carb meals throughout the night.

The carb-up should begin immediately following training. A delay of even 2 hours between the end of training and the start of the carb-up causes glycogen resynthesis to be 47% slower than if carbs are consumed immediately (13,14). Ideally trainees should consume a large amount of liquid carbs immediately after training. A good rule of thumb is to consume 1.5 grams of carbs/kg lean body mass, with approximately one half as much protein, immediately after training and then again two hours later.

Additionally, the consumption of carbohydrates prior to, or during, the workout prior to the carb-up will lead to higher rates of glycogen resynthesis, most likely as a result of higher insulin levels when the carb-up begins (1,13). Finally, the consumption of protein and carbohydrates immediately after training can raise insulin more than just carbohydrates by themselves, helping with glycogen synthesis (15).

Training and the carb-up

Another issue regarding the carb-up is the type of exercise that precedes the carb-up. Typical carb-ups have been studied in endurance athletes, but not weight trainers so extrapolations must be made with care. It has been long known that only the muscles worked immediately prior to the carb-up are supercompensated. Recall from above that a delay of even several hours slows glycogen resynthesis greatly.

Muscle groups which have been trained several days prior to the start of a carb-load will not be optimally supercompensated. This suggests that, for optimal results, the whole body should be worked during the workout prior to the carb-up (this is discussed in more detail in chapter 28). It should be noted that many individuals have achieved fine results not working the entire body prior to the carb-up, using a more traditional split routine workout.

Additionally, the type of training preceding the carb-up affects the rate and amount of glycogen resynthesized following training. Muscles that have been damaged with eccentric training show lower rates of glycogen resynthesis following training (16,17). However, this decrease in resynthesis does not show up immediately. In muscles which have undergone eccentric trauma, glycogen levels are typically 25% lower following a carb-up but this difference does not become apparent until three days after training (or when soreness sets in) (16,17). For individuals performing a 1 or 2 day carb-up, the type of training prior to the carb-up is probably not that critical. For bodybuilders performing a 3 day carb-up prior to a contest, eccentric muscle trauma should be avoided as much as possible.

Other macro-nutrients

Another issue regarding the carb-load is the amounts and types of other macronutrients (protein and fat) which should be consumed. The ingestion of protein and fat with carbohydrates do not affect the levels of glycogen storage during the carb-up as long as carbohydrate intake is sufficient (18). Some dieters find that too much dietary fat blunts their hunger and prevents them from consuming enough carbohydrates to refill glycogen stores.

Recall that carbohydrate level is 10 gram/kg LBM during the first 24 hours. This will make up 70% of the total calories consumed during the carb load. Protein and fat will make up 15% each.

Many bodybuilders may feel that this percentage of protein is too low but this is not the case. First and foremost, a high calorie intake reduces protein requirements and increases nitrogen retention (19). As a result, less dietary protein is needed when calorie/carbohydrate intake is high. Protein should be consumed with carbohydrates as this has been shown to increase glycogen resynthesis, especially after training (20)

Further the most protein lifters need is 1 gram per pound of bodyweight under extremely intensive training conditions (21). Even at 15% protein calories, most individuals will be consuming sufficient protein during the carb-up. Specific calculations for the carb-load phase appear in section 5.

Fat gain during the carb-up

During the first 24 hours of the carb-load, caloric intake will be approximately twice maintenance levels. This raises concerns regarding the potential for fat gain during this time period. We will see that fat gain during the carb-up should be minimal as long as a few guidelines are followed.

In a study which looked surprisingly like a CKD, subjects consumed a low-carb, high fat (but non-ketogenic) diet for 5 days and depleted muscle glycogen with exercise (22). Subjects were then given a total 500 grams of carbohydrate in three divided meals. During the first 24 hours, despite the high calorie (and carb) intake, there was a negative fat balance of 88 grams. This suggests that when muscle glycogen is depleted, incoming carbohydrates are used preferentially to refill glycogen stores, and fat continues to be used for energy production.

Additionally, the excess carbohydrates which were not stored as glycogen were used for energy (22). In general, the synthesis of fat from glycogen (referred to as de novo lipogenesis) in the short term is fairly small (23,24). During carbohydrate overfeeding, there is a decrease in fat use for energy. Most fat gain occurring during high carbohydrate overfeeding is from storage of excessive fat intake (25). Therefore, as long as fat intake is kept relatively low (below 88 grams) during the carb-up phase of the CKD, there should be minimal fat regain.

In a similar study, individuals consumed a low-carb, high fat diet for 5 days and then consumed very large amounts of carbohydrates (700 to 900 grams per day) over a five day period. During the first 24 hours, with a carbohydrate intake of 700 grams and a fat intake of 60 grams per day, there was a fat gain of only 7 grams. Collectively, these two studies suggest that the body continues to use bodyfat for fuel during the first 24 hours of carb-loading.

In the second 24 hours, with an intake of 800 grams of carbohydrate and a fat intake of 97 grams, there was a fat gain of 127 grams (26) indicating that the body had shifted out of 'fat burning' mode as muscle glycogen stores became full. This is unlike the suggestions being made for the CKD, where the carbohydrate intake during the second 24 hours should be lower than in the first 24 hours. A large fat gain, as seen in this study would not be expected to occur on a CKD.

As long as fat intake is kept low and carbohydrate intake is reduced to approximately 5 gram/kg lean body mass during the second 24 hours, fat regain should be minimal. Once again, individuals are encouraged to keep track of changes in body composition with different amounts and durations of carb-loading to determine what works for them. Those who desire to maximize fat loss may prefer only a 24 hour carb-up. This allows more potential days in ketosis for fat loss to occur as well as making it more difficult to regain significant amounts of body fat.

How long does glycogen compensation last?

Pre-contest bodybuilders (and other athletes) want to know how long they will maintain above normal glycogen levels following a carb-up so that they can time the carb-up around a specific event. With normal glycogen levels and no exercise, glycogen levels are maintained at least 3 days. (27,28) It appears that above-normal glycogen stores can be maintained at least 3 days as well. (29)

Section 3: The carb-load and adaptation to ketosis

In addition to the topics discussed in section 2, there are a number of other issues regarding the carb-load phase of the CKD. A question that currently has no answer is how the carb-load phase will affect the adaptations to ketosis. Additionally, the question of long-term effects of the CKD is discussed.

Effects of the carb-load on the adaptation to ketosis

As discussed in the previous chapters, there are a number of potentially beneficial adaptations which occur during ketosis in terms of decreased protein use and increased fat use. A question which arises is how the insertion of a 1-2 day carbohydrate loading phase will affect these adaptations.

To this author's knowledge, no research has examined the effects on ketosis to repeated carbohydrate loading. Recall that most of the adaptations to ketosis, especially maximum protein sparing, require at least three weeks to occur. A question without an answer is whether these adaptations will take longer, or whether they will occur at all, with repeated carbohydrate loading. Anecdotal experience suggests that they do in fact occur, but research is needed in this area.

Since no physiological measures of the adaptations to ketosis have been measured (except in the short term), it is impossible to make any conclusions regarding the long term adaptations to a CKD. Based on anecdotal reports, it seems that the adaptations do occur, but that they simply take longer.

For example, most people starting any type of ketogenic diet go through a period of low energy, where they are mentally 'fuzzy'. Those who stay on a SKD generally move past this stage by the second or third week of dieting. In contrast, those on a CKD seem to take slightly longer to overcome this feeling. For example, this author experienced a great deal of fatigue in the first week of being on a CKD, a smaller (but still above baseline) amount of fatigue during the second week, and essentially no fatigue by the third week.

This anecdotal data suggests that the adaptation of the brain to ketosis may take slightly longer due to the insertion of a carb-load phase. This also suggests that individuals may want to do two weeks of an SKD prior to their first carb-up, to allow the adaptations to occur more quickly. Of course, if this compromises training intensity, it is not a viable option.

Long term effects of a CKD

Although the myriad effects of ketogenic diets are discussed in detail in chapter 7, another concern is what long term metabolic effects a CKD will have. There is unfortunately no answer. It seems logical that any long-term adaptations to ketosis will be reversed when a non-ketogenic diet is followed for a sufficient period of time but this is mere speculation.

Anecdotally, it appears that some of the adaptations to ketogenic diets continue even after a non-ketogenic diet has been followed. The easiest one to examine is the aforementioned fatigue and 'mental fuzziness' during the first week. In general, individuals (including this author) returning to a CKD after a period of more 'balanced' dieting do not experience the same level of fatigue as when they first started the diet. This seems to suggest that some of the changes in the brain (especially with regards to ketone usage) may be longer lasting. Once again, the lack of long term data prevents any conclusions from being drawn.

However, and this is repeated throughout the book, the lack of long term data on the CKD (or any other ketogenic diet) is arguably the most compelling reason not to remain on it in the long term. Simply put, the lack of data means that no long term safety can or should be implied. The CKD, like any fat loss diet, should be used until the fat loss goal (whatever that may be) is achieved and then discontinued in favor of a more 'balanced' diet. Strategies for ending a CKD appear in chapter 14.

Section 4: Is the carb-load anabolic?

Several popular authors suggest that the carb-loading phase of a CKD is anabolic, stimulating muscle growth (30,31). However there is little direct research on this topic and only speculation can be offered. To understand the potential impact of the carb-load on muscle growth, it is necessary to discuss anabolic and catabolic processes, as well as some of the mechanisms regulating protein synthesis.

Anabolic and catabolic processes

The terms anabolic and catabolic tend to be misused and overgeneralized in popular media leading to misunderstandings. In a biological sense, 'anabolic' means the building of larger substances from smaller substances. Glucose is synthesized into glycogen, amino acids are built into larger proteins, and FFA are combined with glycerol and stored as triglycerides (TG). Anabolic processes occur as a result of overfeeding which raises anabolic hormones, such as insulin and testosterone, and lowers catabolic hormones such as cortisol and glucagon.

The term 'catabolic' refers to the breakdown of larger substances into smaller substances. Glycogen is broken down into glucose, large proteins are broken down into individual amino acids, and TG are broken down to FFAs and glycerol. Catabolic processes occur as a result of underfeeding, which lowers anabolic hormones and raises catabolic hormones. An overview of anabolic and catabolic processes appear in figure 1.

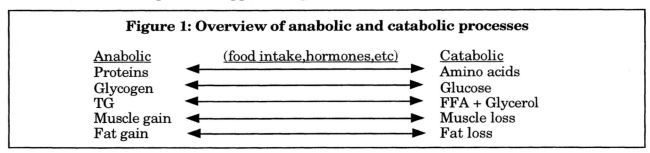

Figure 1: Overview of anabolic and catabolic processes

Anabolic	(food intake,hormones,etc)	Catabolic
Proteins	⟷	Amino acids
Glycogen	⟷	Glucose
TG	⟷	FFA + Glycerol
Muscle gain	⟷	Muscle loss
Fat gain	⟷	Fat loss

An often heard statement is that the ketogenic diet is catabolic. This is true in that all reduced calorie diets are catabolic. In general, without specific drugs, the body must be in either a systemically (whole body) anabolic state or a systematically catabolic state. It is quite rare to see anabolic processes occurring in one part of the body (i.e. muscle gain) while catabolic processes are occurring in another (i.e. fat loss).

In this respect, the CKD is somewhat unique in that it encompasses a phase which is catabolic (low carbs, below maintenance calories) and a phase which is anabolic (high carbs, above maintenance calories).

Anabolism and muscle growth

The catabolic effect of the ketogenic diet has been discussed in detail in chapter 5 and are not repeated here. Although anabolism is discussed in greater detail in chapter 20, a few general comments about anabolism and muscle growth are necessary. The exact mechanisms behind muscle growth are not well understood at this time. In general, it can be said that net muscle growth requires that protein synthesis be greater than protein breakdown. This assumes that a stimulus to synthesize new proteins (such as weight training) has been applied to the body.

Therefore, the carb-up could potentially affect muscle growth in two ways. The first would be by decreasing protein breakdown. The second by increasing protein synthesis. There are numerous factors affecting both protein synthesis and breakdown. These include the hormones insulin, testosterone, thyroid, glucagon, growth hormone and cortisol (32). Insulin plays an especially important role as high levels of insulin appear to decrease protein synthesis (33,34). The availability of sufficient amino acids is paramount for growth, and high levels of amino acids increase protein synthesis (33,34).

A recap of the lowcarb week

Recall from previous chapters that the ketogenic part of the CKD lowers insulin and thyroid levels, while raising glucagon. The data on GH is less clear, with some studies showing an increase, others a decrease. The effects of the ketogenic diet on testosterone and cortisol are less established. Thus, the overall effect of the ketogenic phase is a catabolic one, although ketosis appears to be selectively catabolic (i.e. the protein sparing effect of ketosis).

Also recall from chapter 5 that the status of the liver is one of the key regulatory processes in determining the anabolic or catabolic state of the body. Therefore, the first step in maximizing any anabolic processes is to reverse liver metabolism from catabolic to anabolic.

Reversing the liver's metabolic state

To optimize any anabolic processes following the training session immediately prior to the carb-up, it is necessary to start before the workout itself. Changing the metabolism of the liver from catabolic to anabolic requires two things: that the enzyme levels for glucose utilization are returned to normal and that liver glycogen is refilled.

During long-term carbohydrate restriction, the liver enzymes responsible for metabolizing carbohydrate decrease as discussed in chapter 7. During refeeding, it takes approximately 5 hours for liver enzymes to return to normal levels (35). Therefore, the start of the carb-up should begin 5 hours prior to the final workout. It is unclear whether glucose, fructose, or some combination of foods is ideal at the time. A good place to begin experimenting might be with 25 to 50 grams of total carbohydrate and 25 grams of protein. Dieter's may wish to add a small amount of unsaturated fats to this meal, to avoid an insulin spike.

Refilling of liver glycogen will shut down ketone body formation and shift the liver back towards anabolism. For reasons discussed in Chapter 10 (the TKD), dietary glucose is not used efficiently to resynthesize liver glycogen (36). Although no data on humans exists, due to difficulty in performing the studies, the effect of various nutrients on liver glycogen metabolism has been studied in rat livers which were removed from the animal (37).

This study found that glucose by itself refilled liver glycogen poorly, as expected. However, the combination of glucose and fructose was much more effective. The highest level of liver glycogen was found when glucose, fructose and glutamine (discussed in detail in chapter 33) were provided. It took approximately 2 hours to reverse liver metabolism (37). Therefore, 2 hours prior to the final carb-up, a combination of glucose and fructose (such as fruit) should be consumed. Individuals may wish to add glutamine as well to see if it has an added effect. It should be noted that some individuals find it more difficult to reestablish ketosis during the next weekly cycle if they use glutamine during the carb-load.

Insulin and amino acids

As mentioned above, both insulin and amino acids have profound effects on protein synthesis and breakdown. Insulin appears to primarily act by decreasing protein breakdown while excess amino acids directly stimulate protein synthesis (33,34). Therefore, it might be expected that increasing both insulin and amino acid levels would increase net muscle gain.

When carbohydrates are refed after even a few days of a ketogenic diet, the insulin response is higher than it would be under normal dietary conditions (38). This is probably due to the slight insulin resistance which occurs during a ketogenic diet, discussed in chapter 7. Hyperinsulinemia also increases the transport of some amino acids into muscle (39). These metabolic effects might contribute to muscle growth during the carb-up.

To maximize insulin levels during the carb-up, high glycemic index (GI) carbohydrates are preferred. Additionally, one study examining carb-loading after depletion found that insulin levels were higher with 4 large meals, versus smaller smaller hourly meals although the total amount of carbohydrates given was the same, as was the glycogen compensation (12).

Cellular hydration

A final way that the carb-load could affect anabolism is by drawing water into the muscle cells. It has been hypothesized that cellular hydration may affect numerous processes including protein breakdown and synthesis (40). For example, the extreme protein losses which accompanies illness and injury is commonly accompanied by cellular dehydration, and increasing hydration helps to prevent protein losses (40).

As glycogen depletion causes a loss of water within the muscle, the increased hydration seen with glycogen compensation might affect protein synthesis similarly. However, while it seems that taking a cell from pathologically dehydrated to normal hydration improves protein synthesis, it has not been shown that increasing cellular hydration above normal levels will improve protein synthesis above normal. So this mechanism can be considered speculative at best, and irrelevant at worst.

A final question

Irrespective of the mechanisms by which the carb-load might cause muscle growth, a question which must be asked is just how much additional true contractile tissue (i.e. the part of muscle which is not glycogen, water and electrolytes) can be synthesized during a 24-36 hour period of carbohydrate overfeeding. In all likelihood, the answer is very little.

Section 5: Setting up a CKD

Having discussed the physiological basis of the carb-load in the previous sections, we can now examine the specifics of developing a CKD. The low-carbohydrate phase of the CKD is identical to that of the SKD so please refer to chapter 9 for guidelines for protein, carbohydrate and fat intake on an SKD.

The lowcarb week

Although the specifics of the SKD been discussed in great detail in previous chapters, they are summarized here.

Caloric intake:

Mass gains: 18 calories per pound or more
Maintenance calories/starting the diet: 15-16 calories per pound
Fat loss: starting at 12 calories per pound

Carbohydrate intake

30 grams or less per day. The fewer carbohydrates which are consumed, the faster ketosis can be established. The amount of carbohydrates consumed is more critical on a CKD than on either the SKD or TKD as there are only 5-6 days to establish ketosis.

Protein intake

During the first 3 weeks of the CKD, protein intake should be set at either 0.9 grams of protein per pound of bodyweight or 150 grams per day, whichever is greater.

After three weeks of dieting, protein should be set at 0.9 grams of protein/pound of bodyweight.

Fat intake

Fat intake will make up the remainder of the calories in the diet

Getting out of ketosis: beginning the carb-load

To shift the body out of ketosis and toward a more anabolic state, dieters will need to begin consuming carbohydrates approximately 5 hours prior to the final workout. At this time, a small amount of carbohydrates, perhaps 25 to 50 grams, can be consumed along with some protein and unsaturated fats, to begin the upregulation of liver enzymes. The type of carbohydrate needed has not been studied and individuals are encouraged to experiment with different types and amounts of foods.

Approximately 2 hours before the final workout, a combination of glucose and fructose (with optional glutamine) should be consumed, to refill liver glycogen. Once again, specific amounts have not been determined but 25 to 50 grams total carbohydrate would seem a good place to start.

The carb-load: Two methods

There are essentially two methods for carb-loading on the CKD. The first is to ignore specific macronutrient ratios and simply consume a large amount of carbohydrates for the time period chosen. This approach, while more haphazard than paying attention to specific ratios, works well for many individuals. In fact, it is this aspect of the CKD that draws many individuals to the diet: you can essentially eat whatever you want during your carb-load phase. Having a 24 to 36 hour time period where you can consume whatever foods you want, without paying attention to calories or nutrient percentages, makes dieting psychologically easier. For those individuals who find that haphazard carb-loading leads to a lack of results in terms of fat loss, a more exacting approach can be used. Guidelines for optimizing the carb-load period appear below.

Nutrient intake

During the first 24 hours of carb-loading, carbohydrate intake should be 10 grams per kilogram of lean body mass or 4.5 grams of carbs per pound of lean body mass . This will represent 70% of the total calories consumed. The remaining calories are divided evenly between fat (15% of total calories) and protein (15% of total calories). Table 2 gives estimated amounts of carbohydrate, protein and fat for various amounts of lean body mass.

Table 2: Nutrient intake during first 24 hours of carb-loading				
LBM (lbs)	Carb (g)	Fat (g)	Protein (g)	Total calories*
100	450	43	98	2600
120	540	51	115	3100
140	630	60	135	3600
160	720	68	153	4100
180	810	76	172	4600
200	900	85	193	5100

* The total calories consumed during the first 24 hours of the carb-load should be approximately twice what was consumed during the lowcarb week.

During the second 24 hours of carb-loading, carbohydrates will make up 60% of the total calories, protein 25% and fat 15% as shown in table 3.

Table 3: Nutrient intake during second 24 hours of carb-loading				
LBM (lbs)	Carb (g)	Fat (g)	Protein (g)	Total calories
100	227	20	90	1448
120	270	25	108	1737
140	310	30	126	2014
160	360	35	144	2331
180	405	40	162	2628
200	450	45	180	2925

Once again, the above amounts should be considered guidelines only. Experimentation coupled with good record keeping will help an individual determine the optimal amounts of nutrients to consume during their carb-up.

Summary of guidelines for glycogen supercompensation on the CKD

1. 5 hours prior to your final workout before the carb-up, consume 25-50 grams of carbohydrate with some protein to begin the shift out of ketosis. Small amounts of protein and fat may be added to this meal.

2. 2 hours prior to the final workout, consume 25-50 grams of glucose and fructose (such as fruit) to refill liver glycogen.

3. The level of glycogen resynthesis depends on the duration of the carb-up and the amount of carbohydrates consumed. In 24 hours, glycogen levels of 100-110 mmol/kg can be achieved as long as 10 grams carb/kg lean body mass are consumed. During the second 24 hours of carbing, an intake of 5 grams/kg lean body mass is recommended.

4. During the first 24 hours, the macronutrient ratios should be 70% carbs, 15% protein and 15% fat. During the second 24 hours, the ratios are roughly 60% carbs, 25% protein and 15% fat.

5. As long as sufficient amounts of carbohydrate are consumed, the type and timing of intake is relatively less important. However, some data suggests the higher glycogen levels can be attained over 24 hours, if higher Glycemic Index (GI) carbs are consumed. If carbing is continued past 24 hours, lower GI foods should be consumed.

Summary

Assuming full depletion, which requires a variable amount of training depending on the length of the carb-up, glycogen levels can be refilled to normal within 24 hours, assuming that carbohydrate consumption is sufficient. With longer or shorter carb-loading periods, muscle glycogen levels can reach higher or lower levels respectively.

During the initial 24 hours of carb-loading, a carbohydrate intake of 8-10 grams of carbs per kilogram of lean body mass will refill muscle glycogen to normal levels. Although less well researched, it appears that a carbohydrate intake of roughly 5 grams/kg lean body mass is appropriate. While the type of carbohydrate ingested during the first 24 hours of carb-loading is less critical, it is recommended that lower GI carbs be consumed during the second 24 hours to avoid fat regain. The addition of other nutrients to the carb-load phase does not appear to affect glycogen resynthesis rates. However fat intake must be limited somewhat to avoid fat gain.

It is currently unknown how the insertion of a carb-loading phase will affect the adaptations to ketosis. As well, no long term data exists on the metabolic effects which are seen.

Therefore it can not be recommended that the CKD be followed indefinitely and a more 'balanced' diet should be undertaken as soon as one's goals are achieved.

A question which is asked is whether the carb-load is anabolic, stimulating muscle growth while dieting. As muscle growth requires an overall anabolic metabolism, the body must be shifted out of ketosis (which is catabolic) during the carb-load. This requires that liver metabolism be shifted away from ketone production, which necessitates both an increase in certain enzymes as well as a refilling of liver glycogen. Therefore the carb-load really begins about 5 hours prior to the final workout when a small amount of carbohydrates should be consumed to begin upregulating liver enzymes. Approximately 2 hours prior to the workout, a combination of glucose and fructose should be consumed to refill liver glycogen. Glutamine is an optional addition that may increase liver glycogen levels.

There are a number of ways that the carb-load might affect muscle growth. The primary mechanism is by increasing insulin and amino acid availability. The second is by increasing cellular hydration levels. Both have the potential to increase protein synthesis while decreasing protein breakdown.

Ultimately the question must be asked as to just how much new muscle can be synthesized during a carb-up of 24 to 48 hours. Even assuming zero muscle breakdown during the ketogenic week, the amount of new muscle synthesized is likely to be small. So while individuals may gain a small amount of muscle during a CKD, it should not be expected or counted on.

References Cited

1. Ivy J. Muscle glycogen synthesis before and after exercise. Sports Medicine (1991) 11: 6-19.
2. "Physiology of Sport and Exercise" Jack H. Wilmore and David L. Costill. Human Kinetics Publishers 1994.
3. Sherman W. Metabolism of sugars and physical performance. Am J Clin Nutr (1995) 62(suppl): 228S-41S.
4. Pascoe DD et. al. Glycogen resynthesis in skeletal muscle following resistive exercise. Med Sci Sports Exerc (1993) 25: 349-354.
5. Coyle EF. Substrate utilization during exercise in active people. Am J Clin Nutr (1995) 61 (suppl): 968S-979S.
6. Pascoe DD and Gladden LB. Muscle glycogen resynthesis after short term, high intensity exercise and resistance exercise. Sports Med (1996) 21: 98-118.
7. Burke LM et. al. Muscle glycogen storage after prolonged exercise: effects of the glycemic index of carbohydrate feedings. J Appl Physiol (1993) 75: 1019-1023.
8. Rankin J. Glycemic Index and Exercise Metabolism. in Gatorade Sports Science Exchange Volume 10(1).
9. Costill DL et. al. Muscle glycogen utilization during prolonged exercise on successive days. J Appl Physiol (1971) 31: 834-838.
10. Reed MJ et. al. Muscle glycogen storage postexercise: effect of mode of carbohydrate administration. Med Sci Sports Exerc (1989) 66: 720-726.
11. Costill DL et. al. The role of dietary carbohydrate in muscle glycogen resynthesis after running. Am J Clin Nutr (1981) 34: 1831-1836.

12. Burke LM et. al. Muscle glycogen storage after prolonged exercise: effect of the frequency of carbohydrate feedings. Am J Clin Nutr (1996) 64: 115-119.

13. Conley M and Stone M. Carbohydrate ingestion/supplementation for resistance exercise and training. Sports Med (1996) 21: 7-17.

14. Ivy JL et. al. Muscle glycogen synthesis after exercise: effect of time of carbohydrate ingestion. J Appl Physiol (1988) 64: 1480-1485.

15. Chandler RM et. al. Dietary supplements affect the anabolic hormones after weight-training exercise. J App Phys (1994) 76: 839-45.

16. Doyle J.A. et. al. Effects of eccentric and concentric exercise on muscle glycogen replenishment. J Appl Physiol (1993) 74: 1848-1855.

17. Widrick JJ et. al. Time course of glycogen accumulation after eccentric exercise. J Appl Physiol (1992): 1999-2004.

18. Burke LM et. al. Effect of coingestion of fat and protein with carbohydrate feeding on muscle glycogen storage. J Appl Physiol (1995) 78: 2187-2192.

19. Chiang An-Na and Huang P. Excess nitrogen balance at protein intakes above the requirement level in young men. Am J Clin Nutr (1988) 48: 1015-1022.

20. Zawadzki et al. Carbohydrate-protein complex increases the rate of muscle glycogen storage after exercise. J Appl Physiol (1992) 72: 1854-1859.

21. Lemon P. Is increased dietary protein necessary or beneficial for individuals with a physically active lifestyle? Nutrition Reviews (1996) 54: S169-S175.

22. Acheson KJ. Nutritional influences on lipogenesis and thermogenesis after a carbohydrate meal. Am J Physiol (1984) 246: E62-E70.

23. Shah M and Garg A. High-fat and high-carbohydrate diets and energy balance. Diabetes Care (1996) 19: 1142-1152.

24. Hellerstein M. Synthesis of fat in response to alterations in diet: insights from new stable isotope methodologies. Lipids (1996) 31 (suppl) S117-S125.

25. Jebb SA et. al. Changes in macronutrient balance during over- and underfeeding assessed by 12-d continuous whole body calorimetry. Am J Clin Nutr (1996) 64: 259-266.

26. Acheson KJ et. al. Glycogen storage capacity and de novo lipogenesis during massive carbohydrate overfeeding in man. Am J Clin Nutr (1988) 48: 240-247.

27. Knapik JJ et. al. Influence of fasting on carbohydrate and fat metabolism during rest and exercise in men. J Appl. Physiol (1988) 64: 1923-1929.

28. Loy S. et. al. Effects of 24-hour fast on cycling during endurance time at two different intensities. J Appl Physiol (1986) 61: 654-659.

29. Goldforth HW et. al. Persistence of supercompensated muscle glycogen in trained subjects after carbohydrate loading. J Appl Physiol (1997) 82: 324-347.

30. "The Anabolic Diet" Mauro DiPasquale, MD. Optimum Training Systems, 1995.

31. "BODYOPUS: Militant fat loss and body recomposition" Dan Duchaine. Xipe Press, 1996.

32. Borer K. Neurohumoral mediation of exercise-induced growth. Med Sci Sports Exerc (1994) 26:741-754.

33. Tessari P et. al. Differential effects of hyperinsulinemia and hyperaminoacidemia on leucine-carbon metabolism in vivo. J Clin Invest (1987) 79: 1062-1069.

34. Heslin MJ et. al. Effect of hyperinsulinemia on whole body and skeletal muscle leucine carbon kinetics in humans. Am J Physiol (1992) 262: E911-E918.

35. Randle PJ et. al. Glucose fatty acid interactions and the regulation of glucose disposal. J Cell Biochem (1994) 55 (suppl): 1-11.

36. McGarry JD et. al. From dietary glucose to liver glycogen: the full circle around. Ann Rev Nutr

(1987) 7:51-73.

37. Boyd ME et. al. In vitro reversal of the fasting state of liver metabolism in the rat. J Clin Invest (1981) 68: 142-152.

38. Sidery MB et. al. The initial physiological responses to glucose ingestion in normal subjects are modified with a 3 d high fat-diet. Br J Nutr (1990) 64: 705-713.

38. Biolo G et. al. Physiologic hyperinsulinemia stimulates protein synthesis and enhances transport of selected amino acids in human skeletal muscle. J Clin Investigation (1995) 95: 811-9.

39. Haussinger D et. al. Cellular hydration state: an important determinant of protein catabolism in health and disease. Lancet (1993) 341: 1330-1332.

Part IV:
Other dieting issues

Chapter 13: Breaking fat loss plateaus
Chapter 14: Ending a ketogenic diet
Chapter 15: Tools for the ketogenic diet
Chapter 16: Final considerations

Outside of the physiology and specifics of setting up the ketogenic diet, there are a number of other issues which need to be discussed. Chapter 13 addresses the reality of the fat-loss plateau, offering several strategies to overcome those plateaus. Chapter 14 addresses the issue of ending a ketogenic diet. Chapter 15 discusses the various tools, such as skinfold calipers and Ketostix (tm), which can be of use on a ketogenic diet to track results and optimize the diet. Finally, chapter 16 addresses the considerations which individuals must take into account before they decide to do the ketogenic diet.

Chapter 13:
Breaking fat loss plateaus

A reality of all fat loss diets is the dreaded plateau. Although the exact reasons are unknown, the body eventually adapts to the diet and fat loss slows or stops completely. The typical approach to breaking plateaus is to either decrease calories further or increase activity. Since calories can only be taken so low and only so much exercise can be performed each week, other strategies to break fat loss plateaus are necessary. Due to the differential nature of the SKD/TKD and the CKD, they are discussed separately.

Section 1: Tips for individuals on a SKD, TKD or CKD

Improve the nutrient quality of the lowcarb week.

The nature of the ketogenic diet is such that most individuals tend to consume a lot of saturated fats while on the diet. Substituting some of the saturated fat intake inherent to the ketogenic diet with unsaturated fats such as fish oils and vegetable oils, may increase thermogenesis (the burning of calories to produce heat) and increase fat loss. Many individuals report a significant amount of bodily warmth following a meal high in unsaturated fats, probably due to increased thermogenesis. Note that this further limits the food choices available on a ketogenic diet.

Eat the day's calories across fewer meals.

Although this strategy is purely conjectural, some people have reported better fat loss by eating the same daily calories across fewer meals. In theory, this could allow greater fat loss as the body may be required to draw more energy from body fat stores in between meals.

Take a week off the diet.

Although this goes against everything most dieters have been conditioned to believe, sometimes the best strategy to break a fat loss plateau is to take a week off of the diet and eat at maintenance calories. Some individuals choose to remain ketogenic, simply increasing their caloric intake, while others prefer to return to a carbohydrate based diet.

The body ultimately adapts to anything including diet and calorie levels. Taking a week off of the diet can help raise metabolic rate as well as rebuild any muscle which may have been lost. However, fat gain during a one week break is generally minimal as long as individuals do not overdo caloric intake. Keep in mind that adding carbohydrates back into the diet can cause a rapid but transient weight regain for individuals on an SKD or TKD.

Individuals on a CKD typically lengthen their carb-up to 5-7 days as their break from dieting. Obviously, carbohydrate intake during the first 24 hours should be lowered since a longer carb-load period is being performed. A one to two-week break from the diet every four to six weeks of dieting seems to work well for most people.

Cycle calories throughout the week.

Many individuals have found success by cycling caloric intake while on a ketogenic diet. If we use a rough guideline of 12 cal/lb as an average caloric intake during the lowcarb week, an individual might alternate a day at slightly lower calorie levels (for example one day at 11 calories/pound) with days at slightly higher calorie levels (14 calories per pound) to get fat loss going again.

Under these conditions, individuals can cautiously take calories below the 11-12 calorie/pound limit set in chapter 3 but only for a day or two at a time after which calories should be raised above 12 calories per pound. Although calorie cycling can restart fat loss, dieters must watch for signs of muscle loss. An example 7-day span where calories are cycled appears below.

Monday: 12 cal/lb
Tuesday: 10 cal/lb
Wednesday: 15 cal/lb
Thursday: 13 cal/lb
Friday: 12 cal/lb
Average caloric intake: 12.4 cal/lb

Note that the highest daily caloric intake (15 cal/lb) occurs immediately after the lowest daily caloric intake (10 cal/lb). In theory, this might help to prevent any metabolic slowdown from the low calorie day.

Section 2: Tips only for individuals on a CKD

Reduce the length of the carb-up period to 24 hours.

By allowing more time in ketosis, it should be possible to achieve greater fat loss. Carbohydrates should be consumed for 24 hours after the Friday workout, ending on Saturday evening. As usual, 10 g of carbs per kg of lean body mass should be consumed. As discussed in chapter 12, due to lower glycogen resynthesis, training volume will have to be decreased during the Mon and Tue workouts by about 2 sets per bodypart.

Some dieters consider cutting out the carb-up period completely but this is generally a mistake as inadequate glycogen will sap training intensity. With the exception of the week before a contest where no carb-up is done, and unless a longer cycle (such as the 10 day cycle discussed below) is being used, trainees should not reduce the carb-up to less than 24 hours in most cases.

Improve the quality of the carb-load phase.

A great number of individuals are drawn to the CKD by the idea that any and all carbohydrates can be consumed during the carb-loading period. While this is loosely true, it comes with the price of slowing fat loss. Some individuals have consumed as much as 10,000 calories during a carb-load. Dieters consuming lots of junk food (especially with a high sugar and fat content) oftentimes regain some of the bodyfat which was lost during the lowcarb week. Thus, the CKD becomes a two-steps forward, one-step backwards ordeal.

Making better food choices, limiting carbohydrate intake to 10 grams/kilogram lean body mass, emphasizing carbohydrates with a lower glycemic index, and eating less dietary fat can minimize any fat regain during the carb-load. Additionally, certain supplements (discussed in chapter 31) may help to prevent fat regain during the carb-load. Refer back to chapter 12 for details on optimizing the carb-load phase of the CKD.

Establish ketosis more quickly.

In theory, if ketosis can be established faster, more fat might be lost. Applying strategies #1 and #2 above is the first step. If individuals still having trouble establishing ketosis quickly, they may need to increase the amount of cardio done the morning after the carb-up. Alternately, the carb-up can be ended earlier in the previous day to allow liver glycogen to empty more quickly. Finally, fructose and sucrose can be avoided during the carb-load to avoid refilling liver glycogen. However, this may compromise potential muscle growth during the carb-up, due to the liver remaining in a catabolic state (see chapter 12).

Perform longer periods in ketosis before carbing

This ties into strategy #1 above. Some individuals have found that a 10 day cycle (one carb-load period every 10 days) significantly increases fat loss compared to a 7 day cycle. In this case, the weekly training should be spread out over 10 days. An example workout cycle appears below.

day 1: upper body (tension workout as per advanced CKD workout), cardio optional
day 2: lower body (tension workout as per advanced CKD workout), cardio optional

Note: The goal of these two workouts, as with the advanced CKD workout is to send an anabolic stimulus to the muscle to maintain muscle mass while dieting.

day 3: off to allow recovery from previous day's workouts
day 4: cardio or reduce calories 10% more
day 5: cardio or reduce calories 10% more
day 6: short depletion workout

Note: During this workout, high reps should be used with light weights, not training to failure. The goal is only to deplete glycogen more to enhance fat use by the muscle. Few sets, approximately 2-3 per bodypart should be done but no more.

day 7: cardio or reduce calories 10% more
day 8: cardio or reduce calories 10% more
day 9: cardio or reduce calories 10% more
day 10: depletion in morning; begin carb-up immediately after training.

The final depletion should be a repeat of the day 6 depletion, being comprised of an additional 2-3 sets per bodypart. This should completely deplete muscle glycogen, prior the starting the carb-up, which would last 24 hours before starting the cycle over again.

The problem with this cycle is that it does not fit neatly into a 7 day work-week and requires that different days of the week be trained on each cycle. However if a dieter has the flexibility in their schedule, and wants to pursue maximal fat loss from each cycle, it may be a worthwhile experiment.

Summary

A reality of fat loss diets is the inevitable plateau which occurs. There are a variety of strategies available to overcome a fat loss plateau. These range from making better choices in food quality, to taking a week off from the diet, to a variety of different workout schedules which can be tried. In general, only one strategy should be tried at any one time so that an individual can gauge how the change is or is not working.

Chapter 14:
Ending a ketogenic diet

One important aspect of any fat loss diet is how it should be ended. Realistically, one can not, and should not, be on a fat loss diet forever. At some point, an individual will have reached their goal and the focus will change to maintenance. Bodybuilders will frequently move from fat loss phases back into mass gaining phases, where some regain of bodyfat is accepted as an end result of gaining muscle mass.

A sad reality of fat/weight loss is the dismal statistics for long-term weight maintenance. Individuals who use caloric restriction as the only way to achieve their fat loss have a much lower chance of keeping that fat/weight off than those who use exercise or a combination of exercise and dietary changes (1). Simply put, dieters can not restrict their caloric intake and be hungry forever.

This is the primary reason that exercise has been emphasized in this book as an integral part of any diet. It is not realistic to subsist on low calories forever. Far more realistic is to maintain good exercise habits for a lifetime. This is also the reason that neither an excessive caloric deficit or an excessive amount of exercise is advocated. While it may take longer to reach one's personal fat loss goals with a more moderate approach, the chances of maintaining that fat loss are much higher if good habits have been developed.

If an individual tries to lose fat quickly by exercising ten hours per week, they will eventually run into problems with scheduling. As soon as they cut back to a few hours of exercise per week, the weight/fat will start to come back. Instead, if this individual develops a regular schedule of three to four hours per week of exercise, and couples that with a slight caloric deficit until they reach their fat loss goals, they will be more likely to maintain this amount of exercise on a consistent basis. This should make maintaining the fat loss easier.

Some individuals may choose to remain on some form of a ketogenic (or low carbohydrate) diet indefinitely while others will not. For those who remain on a ketogenic diet, there are fewer issues involved in moving from fat loss maintenance. Either calories can be increased (in the form of dietary fat or carbohydrate) or activity levels can be decreased until fat loss stops. Since the long term health implications of ketogenic diets are not known, this book cannot recommend that a ketogenic diet be sustained indefinitely.

For individuals who do move away from the ketogenic diet, there are more issues which need to be discussed including the physiological ramifications of adding carbohydrates back to the diet, maintaining bodyfat levels, etc. Each is discussed in this chapter. Most of the information presented here applies to individuals on a SKD or TKD. Due to the structure of the CKD, it has its own set of implications and consequences.

Section 1: General issues for ending a ketogenic diet

Weight regain

Although this topic has been discussed several times already, it bears repeating. Individuals who have been on a low-carbohydrate diet (of any type) will show a rapid increase in bodyweight when carbohydrates are added to the diet (2,3). This weight gain, similar to what occurs during the carb load phase of a CKD, can be anywhere from 5 to 11 pounds (2,3).

For dieters who focus only on the scale, this rapid weight gain can be disheartening, pushing them straight back into a low-carbohydrate eating style. The inability to differentiate between weight gain and fat gain tends to promote the belief in dieters that excess carbohydrates (rather than excess calories) are the cause of their problems. This may make it difficult for these individuals to ever wean themselves away from the ketogenic diet.

Once again, a distinction must be made between weight gain and true fat gain. Weight gains of 3-5 pounds or more are not uncommon for individuals who eat even small amounts of carbohydrates after being on a ketogenic diet for long periods of time. From an energy balance standpoint, we can easily see that it is impossible to gain this much true fat in a short time period.

To gain one pound of fat requires that 3,500 calories be consumed above the number of calories burned. To gain a true three pounds of fat would require that 10,500 calories be consumed above the number of calories burned that day. A five pound fat gain would require the consumption of 17,500 calories above the number of calories burned per day. It should be obvious that the weight gain from initial carbohydrate consumption reflects shifts in water weight only.

To fully discuss proper nutritional strategies for either bodyfat maintenance or mass gains would require another book. Simply keep in mind that maintenance of new bodyfat levels requires that caloric expenditure match caloric intake, regardless of diet. By the same token, gains in body mass (for bodybuilders or other strength athletes who wish to gain muscle mass) require that more calories be consumed than are expended. This will come with the consequence of some fat gain while lean body mass is being added.

Insulin resistance

As discussed in chapter 7, one effect of long term low-carbohydrate diets is an increase in insulin resistance, sometimes called 'starvation diabetes', when carbohydrates are refed (4). This effect is briefly discussed again here.

In brief, the initial physiological response to carbohydrate refeeding looks similar to what is seen in Type II diabetics, including blood sugar swings and hyperinsulinemia. Several possible hypotheses for this effect have been considered including a direct effect of ketones, but this is not the case (5,6) and ketones may improve insulin binding (4). The change in insulin sensitivity is caused by changes in enzyme levels, especially in those enzymes involved in both fat and carbohydrate burning (7). High levels of free fatty acid levels also affect glucose transport and utilization (8).

Long periods of time without carbohydrate consumption leads to a down regulation in the enzymes responsible for carbohydrate burning. Additionally, high levels of free fatty acids in the bloodstream may impair glucose transport (8). This change occurs both in the liver (7) and in the muscle (7,9). With carbohydrate refeeding, these changes are gone within 5 hours in the liver and 24-48 hours in muscle tissue (10,11).

In practice, many individuals report what appears to be rebound hypoglycemia (low blood sugar) either during the carb-up or during the first few days of eating carbohydrates when ketogenic eating is ended, for the reasons discussed above.

Ketones themselves do not appear to alter how cells respond to insulin (6) which goes against the popular belief that ketogenic diets somehow alter fat cells, making them more likely to store fat when the ketogenic diet is resumed. Practical experience shows this to be true, as many individuals have little trouble maintaining their bodyfat levels when the ketogenic diet is stopped, especially if their activity patterns are maintained.

To reiterate, the key to maintenance of a new bodyweight/bodyfat level is to balance energy consumption with energy expenditure. This makes exercise an absolute requirement for weight/fat maintenance when a diet is abandoned.

Section 2: Recommendations for ending a SKD or TKD

There are few practical recommendations for ending a ketogenic diet in the literature. In research studies of the protein sparing modified fast (PSMF), carbohydrates are typically reintroduced slowly to minimize weight gain and gastric upset, which occurs in some people. Ending a SKD or TKD can be done in one of two fashions. If an individual no longer wishes fat loss, but chooses to stay on the SKD/TKD, fat intake can be increased (to raise calories to a maintenance level of approximately 15-16 calories/pound) until fat loss stops.

If an individual wishes to stop the SKD/TKD altogether and de-establish ketosis, obviously carbohydrates will have to be added to the daily diet. This has several important consequences. First and foremost, as dietary carbohydrates are added to the diet, dietary fat must be reduced to avoid the consumption of excess calories. Since fat contains approximately twice as many calories per gram as carbohydrate (9 calories/gram vs. 4 calories/gram), for every 2 grams of carbohydrate which are added to the diet, 1 gram of fat must be removed.

Individuals concerned with rapid weight regain when they end a ketogenic diet should simply introduce carbohydrates slowly, perhaps adding twenty to thirty grams per day at most. To avoid possible problems with rebound hypoglycemia, primarily vegetables should be consumed with starches (pasta, rice, breads) remaining limited.

Many individuals who turn to ketogenic diets to lose bodyfat tend to have problems with excessive carbohydrate consumption in the first place, finding that high- carbohydrate, very-low-fat diets increase their hunger. By the same token, individuals coming off of a ketogenic diet frequently find that their taste for starchy foods, especially high glycemic index carbs, has diminished and caloric intake can be more easily controlled.

Obviously activity patterns should be maintained while calories/carbohydrates are being reintroduced to the diet. If individuals find themselves consuming too many calories (especially during the first few days of carbohydrate refeeding), an increase in activity may be useful during that time period.

Section 3: Recommendations for ending a CKD

Generally speaking, individuals who utilize the CKD for fat loss tend to be bodybuilders or athletes who need a way to reduce bodyfat without compromising high-intensity exercise performance. However, this is not universally the case. In this group of individuals it is not uncommon to move from a fat loss phase (which may be done by bodybuilders for a contest or simply to avoid gaining too much bodyfat during the off season) directly into a weight/muscle gaining phase where an excess of calories are consumed. As with ending the SKD/TKD there are two primary options for individuals who wish to end a fat loss CKD.

Option 1: Stay on the CKD

It is this author's opinion that the CKD is not the optimal diet for gaining lean body mass for bodybuilders or athletes. Ultimately, insulin is one of the most anabolic hormones in the body, stimulating protein synthesis and inhibiting protein breakdown. A high calorie CKD, by limiting insulin levels, will not allow optimal gains in LBM. However, athletes may be able to slow bodyfat gains by using CKD for mass gains, but this comes with the price of slower gains in lean body mass.

The major changes which must be made for those who want to stay on a CKD are in calorie levels, length of the carb-up, and training strategies. As discussed in chapter 3, gains in lean body mass may require a caloric intake of 18 calories per pound of bodyweight or more. Some individuals find consuming this many calories on a low-carbohydrate diet to be difficult. As well, since protein must still be somewhat limited to maintain ketosis, this means that fat intake must be raised to high levels. The potential health consequences of such a dietary strategy are unknown. To reiterate, without long term data on the health consequences of a SKD or CKD, it is not recommended that the CKD be followed indefinitely.

In practice, most lifters tend to reduce their carb-loading phase to 30 hours or less for maximal fat loss. For optimal mass gains, the carb-up should be increased in duration to a full 48 hours. While fat gain tends to be higher with this strategy, gains in lean body mass are typically greater as well. An alternate strategy, and one that will most likely help to prevent some of the fat gain which would otherwise occur, is to have two carb-loading phases of 24 hours performed in a 7 day span. That is, an individual might perform a 24 hour carb-load phase on Wednesday and again on Saturday. As discussed in chapter 12, the carb-up should optimally follow a workout.

Finally, training structure can be altered to fit the individuals preference for mass gain training. Training for mass gains on a CKD are discussed in chapter 29.

Option 2: Come off the CKD

This is the strategy advocated by this author. As discussed above, lean body mass gains will most likely be higher with a carbohydrate based diet although fat gain may be higher as well, especially if calories are excessive. A full discussion of nutritional strategies for mass gains or bodyfat maintenance are beyond the scope of this book.

As mentioned above, calories should be increased above maintenance if mass gains are the goal. As a general rule, protein intake should remain fairly stable, approximately 0.9 grams of protein/pound of bodyweight. Fat intake should be controlled, but 15-25% seems to work well for most lifters. The remainder of the diet should be carbohydrate, typically comprising 50-60% of the total daily calories. Once non-ketogenic eating has been resumed, the day's total calories should be consumed in five to six smaller meals to keep blood sugar stable. As well, a post-workout drink of carbohydrates and protein may help with recovery and gains.

By coming off of the CKD, trainees will have much greater flexibility in the types of training programs which can be used for mass gains, because they do not have to plan their training around the carb-loading phase. This is yet another reason that a carbohydrate based diet will most likely be superior to a CKD for mass gains. The format of the CKD mandates that training structure follow certain guidelines geared to the peculiarities of the diet. With a more balanced diet, training structure does not have to be as rigid.

For those individuals who are using a CKD but who simply want to maintain their current bodyfat without attempting to add lean body mass, the same options discussed above still apply. It would be somewhat unusual for someone to remain on the CKD indefinitely for bodyfat maintenance. Generally speaking most individuals will tend to come off the CKD and only use it when bodyfat levels start to increase again. Using the CKD in short stints, to bring bodyfat levels down again, should minimize any potential health problems.

As with the SKD/TKD, the long term health consequences of a CKD are unknown and its long term use cannot be recommended at this time. The biggest difference between those who simply want to maintain their fat loss versus those who want to gain mass are in calorie levels, which should be raised to maintenance.

Summary

Equally as important as losing fat initially is the maintenance of that new bodyfat level. Depending on an individual's goal (maintenance or muscle gain) and the diet which they were on to begin with, a variety of options exist for ending a ketogenic diet. Due to a lack of long term health data, it is not recommended that extreme carbohydrate restricted diets be followed in the long term.

References Cited

1. Miller WC et. al. A meta-analysis of the past 25 years of weight loss research using diet, exercise or diet plus exercise intervention. Int J Obes (1997) 21: 941-947.
2. Phinney SD et. al. The human metabolic response to chronic ketosis without caloric restriction:

physical and biochemical adaptations. Metabolism (1983) 32: 757-768.

3. Kreitzman SN et. al. Glycogen storage: illusions of easy weight loss, excessive weight regain, and distortions in estimates of body composition. Am J Clin Nutr (1992) 56: 292S-293S.

4. Robinson AM and Williamson DH Physiological roles of ketone bodies as substrates and signals in mammalian tissues. Physiol Rev (1980) 60: 143-187.

5. Kissebah AH. et. al. Interrelationship between glucose and acetoacetate metabolism in human adipose tissue. Diabetologia (1974) 10: 69-75.

6. Misbin RI et. al. Ketoacids and the insulin receptor. Diabetes (1978) 27: 539-542.

7. "Textbook of Biochemistry with Clinical Correlations 4th ed." Ed. Thomas M. Devlin. Wiley-Liss 1997.

8. Roden M et al. Mechanism of free fatty acid-induced insulin resistance in humans. J Clin Invest. (1996) 97: 2859-2865.

9. Cutler DL Low-carbohydrate diet alters intracellular glucose metabolism but not overall glucose disposal in exercise-trained subjects. Metabolism: Clinical and Experimental (1995) 44: 1364-70.

10. Randle PJ. Metabolic fuel selection: general integration at the whole-body level. Proc Nutr Soc (1995) 54: 317-327.

11. Randle PJ et. al. Glucose fatty acid interactions and the regulation of glucose disposal. J Cell Biochem (1994) 55 (suppl): 1-11.

Chapter 15:
Tools for ketogenic diets

There are a number of tools which can and should be used by ketogenic dieters to maximize results. These include the scale, skin fold calipers, glucometers, Ketostix (tm) and various tools to measure food amounts with. Some of the most frequently questions and issues which are raised about each are discussed.

Section 1: Measuring body composition

Measurements serve two purposes. First and foremost, measurements give dieters a way to gauge progress towards their ultimate goals. Second, to set up the diet, dieters need to know at least their body weight since calories and protein intake is determined relative to weight.

The three major types of measurement methods that most individuals will have access to are the scale, body fat measurement, and the tape measure. No method of measurement is perfectly accurate and all have built in errors that can make it difficult to gauge progress. The solution is to simply use them for comparative measures, rather than focusing on absolute numbers. By taking measurements at the same time each week, under identical conditions, dieters can get a rough idea of overall changes in body weight and body composition.

The Scale

The scale is overused by most dieters and is typically the only method used to chart progress. As discussed in chapter 8, the scale used by itself can be misleading on any diet but even moreso on a ketogenic diet.

The main problem with the scale is that it does not differentiate between what is being gained or lost (i.e. muscle, fat, water). Recall that glycogen depletion on a ketogenic diet results in a drop in body water causing immediate weight loss (5-10 lbs depending on bodyweight). Carbohydrate consumption following a period of carbohydrate restriction causes a similar increase in body weight. Individuals who tend to fixate on short-term weight changes will become frustrated by the changes in scale weight on a ketogenic diet, especially the CKD.

It is recommended that individuals use the scale only to make comparative measurements, described below. Recall that weight training may cause the scale to misrepresent actual fat loss due to increases in muscle mass.

Ideally the scale should always be used along with skin fold measurements or the tape measure for more accurate measures of changes in body composition. Even when body weight is stable, if body fat percentage or tape measure readings are decreasing, a loss of body fat has occurred. For best results, scale measurements should be taken first thing in the morning after going to the bathroom but before food is eaten. This will give the greatest consistency. More detailed suggestions for the best use of the scale on each of the three diets appears below.

Please note that very few individuals will make constant linear changes in body weight and plateaus are frequent. Women will frequently gain or lose water weight during different phases of their menstrual cycle. For these reasons, regular weighing is NOT recommended for most individuals. While weekly weighing may give some indication of changes, weighing every two to four weeks may give a better indication of long term changes.

The scale on the SKD/TKD

On a SKD, there is an initial drop in body weight due to a loss of glycogen and water, especially if an individual is exercising. After the initial weight loss, individuals can use the scale as a rough guide of overall changes by measuring at a consistent time each week, such as every Monday morning after awakening. Keep in mind that the consumption of even moderate amounts of carbs can cause a rapid jump in scale weight. This increase is temporary only and will disappear once ketogenic dieting is resumed.

Individuals on a TKD will only see shifts in scale weight if they weigh themselves around their workouts, when carbohydrates are being consumed. As long as scale measurements are taken at the same time each week, there should be no large scale changes in body weight from the consumption of pre- and/or post-workout carbs.

The scale on the CKD

Use of the scale is the most problematic on the CKD. Over the course of a one to two day carbohydrate loading phase, individuals have reported weight gains from one pound to fifteen pounds. In general, women seem to gain less overall weight (most likely due to lower amounts of lean body mass) during the carb-load than men but this is highly variable.

The scale can be used on the CKD as long as the measurement is made at consistent times of the week. Initial measurements should be taken the morning before the carb-up, when the dieter is the most depleted/lightest, and again after the carb-up when they are the heaviest. This should give a rough idea of overall changes in body composition. If weight increases by 7 lbs from the morning of the carb-load to the morning after the carb-load, the dieter know that they need to lose more than 7 lbs prior to the next carb-load for 'true' fat loss to have occurred. Most of the weight gained will disappear quickly as glycogen levels are depleted early in the week and trainees typically experience a large weight drop by the third day following the carb-load. A typical pattern of weight gain/loss on a CKD appears below.

Monday: 150 lbs
Friday: 143 lbs
Monday: 149 lbs
Friday: 142 lbs
Monday: 148 lbs
Friday: 141 lbs

Despite the large fluctuations from Monday to Friday, repeat measurements show a trend downwards, indicating true long term weight/fat loss.

Selecting a scale

In general, most scales seem to be fairly accurate. However some low cost scales seem to be affected significantly by where you stand on the scale, giving inaccurate results. A relatively inexpensive digital scale should yield consistent and accurate results. Some individuals choose to use the scale at their gym. If this results in inconsistent weighing (either different days of the week or different times of day when body weight can be affected by prior meals), using a gym scale is not the best choice. However, if consistency can be guaranteed, the scales at gyms should be sufficient to track progress.

Body fat measurements

As discussed in chapter 8, there are numerous methods of measuring body fat percentage including skin folds, infrared inductance, bioelectrical impedance, and underwater weighing. All make assumptions about body composition that appear to be inaccurate.

In general, the best method for most individuals is skin fold measurements taken with calipers, primarily because it can be done easily and yields consistent results. With practice it is possible for dieters to take their own skinfolds. In many cases, this is preferred since many gyms have a high turnover of employees. More critical than how accurate the skin fold measurements are is how consistent the measurements are. Everyone differs slightly in their measurement technique and comparing the skinfold measures taken by one person to those taken by another person will not be accurate. If dieters always take their own skinfolds, they can at least be sure of consistency in measuring.

In general, it is recommended that individuals measure skinfolds every two to four weeks to track changes in body composition. Beginners starting a diet or exercise program will generally not see changes in body composition for the first six to eight weeks. While it is recommended that measurements be taken prior to starting the diet/exercise program, remeasuring too frequently can cause frustration and drop-out from a lack of changes.

For this reason, beginners should not repeat body composition measurements any sooner than eight weeks into their diet/exercise programs. This is about how long it takes for the initial changes to occur. After the initial changes occur, more frequent measures can be made if desired. However it is rare to find an individual who makes linear, constant changes in body composition and it is very easy to become pathological about the lack of changes.

Skin folds on the SKD or TKD

Individuals using the SKD or TKD should try to have body composition measured at consistent times whenever it is done. As large changes in body weight and water are not occurring (as with the CKD), it is not that critical when skin folds are taken.

Skin folds on the CKD

As with the scale on the CKD (see above), to get the most out of caliper measurements, it is recommended that they be taken at consistent times during the week. Although fat cells contain very little water, changes in hydration level (especially water under the skin) does seem to affect skinfold readings. Comparing a set of measurements taken on Monday to another set taken on Friday may give inaccurate results. Rather, measurements taken on Monday should be compared to measurements taken on the following Monday, measurements taken on Friday to measurements taken the following Friday. Some tips for getting the most out of skinfolds on the CKD appear below (guidelines for pre-contest bodybuilders appear in chapter 30).

1. Weigh and take skin folds the morning of the last low-carbohydrate day of the week. This will show a dieter at their leanest and give the lowest bodyfat percentage and body weight (if they use the equations).

2. Measure skinfolds and weight the morning after the end of the carb-loading phase. Due to shifts in water weight, and depending on the changes in water under the skin, this will give the highest skinfold measurements and body weight.

Selecting calipers

Calipers vary greatly in price, quality and accuracy. The inexpensive one-site click-type calipers (which click to indicate when the measurement is made) have proven to be inaccurate. Oftentimes they show no change in skinfolds when other, more accurate sets of calipers show obvious changes. They are not recommended.

The most expensive, and most accurate caliper is the Lange caliper. However, it is cost prohibitive for most people. A good choice for a home caliper is the Slimguide caliper available from many different sources (see appendix 2 for resources). Its measurements agree quite closely with Lange calipers but at about one fourth the cost (approx. $30-40).

The Tape Measure

Many individuals will not have access to the equipment necessary to get accurate body composition measurements. In this case, a very rough estimate of changes in body composition can be made by using a measuring tape.

As with the scale and skin fold measurements, the tape measure should be used at a consistent time of the week, generally when weight is measured. Typical sites to measure are:

Chest: taken at nipple level
Arms: taken in the middle of the arm
Abdomen: taken at the level of the belly button
Hips: taken at the largest diameter of the buttocks
Thigh: taken halfway between the knee and where the thigh joins the hip
Calf: taken at the largest diameter of the calf

The biggest problem with the tape measure is obtaining consistent tension as it is quite easy to pull the tape tighter to get a smaller measurement. Ideally, the tape should be pulled just tight enough that it slightly depresses the skin. Another option is to have someone else take the measurements.

Also as discussed in chapter 8, keep in mind that changes in the tape measure are affected by changes in muscle mass. Those starting an exercise program often gain muscle more quickly than they lose bodyfat. This can show up as a temporary increase in tape measurements.

Section 2: Measuring ketosis

Whether correct or not, many ketogenic diets tend to live or die by the presence of ketones in their urine. The presence of ketosis, which is indicative of lipolysis can be psychologically reassuring to ketogenic dieters. However it should be noted that one can be in ketosis, defined as ketones in the bloodstream, without showing urinary ketones. Since dieters will not be able to determine blood ketones, other methods are necessary. The two measurement tools which most individuals will have access to are Ketostix (tm) and glucometers, which are small machines used by diabetics to measure blood glucose level. Both are discussed below.

Ketostix (tm)

Probably the most common tools used by ketogenic dieters are Ketostix (tm) or Diastix (tm), which measure the urinary concentrations of either ketones or ketones and glucose respectively. Typically, they are used by Type I diabetics for whom the presence of high urinary ketones/glucose can indicate the start of a diabetic emergency. Since a non-diabetic individual shouldn't show glucose in the bloodstream, there is no reason for most ketogenic dieters to use the Diastix (tm). Only Ketostix (tm) are discussed here.

Ketostix (tm) use the nitroprusside reaction, which reacts to the presence of acetoacetate, to indicate the concentration of urinary ketones. Depending on the concentrations of acetoacetate, the Ketostix (tm) react by turning various shades of purple with darker colors indicating greater concentrations.

Since Ketostix (tm) only register relative concentrations, rather than absolute amounts, changes in hydration state can affect the concentration of ketones which appear. A high water intake tends to dilute urinary ketone concentrations giving lighter readings.

Ketostix (tm) are typically used to indicate that one's diet is truly inducing a state of ketosis. The problem is that Ketostix (tm) are a only an indirect way of measuring ketosis. Recall from chapter 4 that ketosis is technically defined by the presence of ketones in the bloodstream (ketonemia). Ketones in the urine simply indicate an overproduction of ketones such that excess spill into the urine. So it is conceivable for someone to be in ketosis without showing urinary ketones.

Some individuals can never get past trace ketosis, while others always seem to show darker readings. There seems to be little rhyme or reason as to why some individuals will always show deep concentrations of urinary ketones while others will not. Some will show higher urinary ketones after a high fat meal, suggesting that dietary fat is being converted to ketones which are then excreted. Consuming medium chain triglycerides (MCT's) has the same effect. Other individuals seem to only register ketones on the stick after extensive aerobic exercise. Finally, there appear to be daily changes in ketone concentrations, caused by fluctuations in hormone levels. Generally ketone concentrations are smaller in the morning and larger in the evening, reaching a peak at midnight. Many individuals report high ketones at night but show no urinary ketones the next morning while others report the opposite.

No hard and fast rules can be given for the use of Ketostix (tm) except not to be obsessive about them. In the same way that the presence of ketones can be psychologically reassuring, the absence of ketones can be just as psychologically harmful. It is easy to mentally short-circuit by checking the Ketostix (tm) all the time.

A popular idea is that the deeper the level of ketosis as measured by Ketostix (tm), the greater the weight/fat loss. However there is no data to support or refute this claim. While some popular diet authors have commented that urinary ketone excretion means that bodyfat is being excreted causing fat loss, this is only loosely true in that ketones are made from the breakdown of fat in the liver. The number of calories lost in the urine as ketones amounts to 100 calories per day at most.

Anecdotally, higher levels of urinary ketones seem to be indicative of slower fat loss. Individuals who maintain trace ketosis seem to lose fat more efficiently although there is no research examining this phenomenon. A possible reason is this: high levels of ketones in the bloodstream raise insulin slightly and block the release of free fatty acids from fat cells. This seems to imply that higher levels of ketones will slow fat mobilization.

The ideal situation would seem to be one where trace ketosis (as measured by Ketostix (tm)) is maintained, since this is the lowest level of ketosis which can be measured while still ensuring that one is truly in ketosis. This should be indicative of relatively lower blood ketone concentrations, meaning that bodyfat can be mobilized more efficiently.

How to use Ketostix (tm)

To measure the level of urinary ketones, the Ketostick should be removed from the package and then the package closed. The reagent end of the stick should not be touched. The Ketostick should be passed through the stream of urine, wetting the reactive end of the stick. After 15 seconds have passed, the stick is compared to the chart on the side of the bottle of Ketostix (tm) giving a rough indication of the concentration of urinary ketones.

Again, please note that the lack of urinary ketones does not automatically mean that one does not have ketones in the bloodstream, simply that no excess are being excreted. Some individuals will show urinary ketones initially but show negative ketones at later tests. Assuming that something has not been done that would disrupt ketosis, such as eating carbohydrates, dieters should not assume that the lack of a reaction on the Ketostix (tm) means that they are out of ketosis.

Ketostix (tm) seem to have their greatest use for individuals just starting the diet. After a period of time on a ketogenic diet, most individuals can 'feel' when they are in ketosis. Many individuals get a metallic taste in their mouth, or report a certain smell to their breath or urine, making Ketostix (tm) unnecessary.

Glucometers

Due to the somewhat indirect method of measuring ketosis with Ketostix (tm), some individuals have tried to use glucometers, small handheld devices which measure the amount of glucose in the bloodstream, to check the progress of their diet. Glucometers are most typically used by diabetics who must ensure that their blood glucose does not rise too high which can cause a host of health complications. Non-diabetic individuals will maintain normal blood glucose levels between 80-120 mg/dl under most conditions.

Contrary to popular belief, blood glucose never drops that low on a ketogenic diet. Even during total fasting, blood glucose maintains a level of roughly 65-70 mmol/dl. Depending on the protein intake of a ketogenic diet, blood glucose will be higher, close to the low normal levels of 75-85 mmol/dl. Many individuals have measured blood glucose at a relatively normal value of 80 mmol/dl while showing urinary ketones and wondered if they were truly in ketosis. The answer is yes. With the exception noted previously for N-acetyl-cysteine, the presence of urinary ketones is indicative that a dieter is in ketosis, regardless of their blood glucose levels.

Additionally, glucometers can have an accuracy range of plus or minus 30 mmol/dl. For a diabetic individual trying to determine how much insulin is necessary to bring blood glucose down from 300 (or higher) to a normal level, an inaccuracy of 30 points is not a problem. For non-diabetics, the inaccuracies inherent in most glucometers make them a useless addition to a ketogenic diet. They are not recommended.

Section 3: Tools For measuring your diet

There are only two items which are truly necessary for measuring the diet. The first and arguably the most important is some sort of calorie/nutrient counter book. Many individuals are confused as to which foods have carbs in them and which foods do not. And while most foods are labeled with the proportions of carbohydrate, protein and fat many foods are not, especially meats and cheeses. In this case a food count book can be invaluable to ensure that carbohydrate intake stays low during a ketogenic diet. Although there are carbohydrate counter books available which only provide information on carbohydrate content, it is recommended that dieters obtain a book providing protein and fat gram information as well.

For those wishing to be meticulous about their diet, a full set of measuring spoons, cups, as well as a food scale is necessary. These can be bought at a variety of places from specific kitchen shops to grocery stores. With time, most individuals should be able to estimate their daily food intake but it is recommended that foods be measured initially. The generally calorically dense nature of many ketogenic foods makes it easy to exceed daily caloric requirements.

As a final option, there are computer programs that generally contain food databases which can be used to develop diet plans. As well, many individuals have used spreadsheet programs to track their intake of calories, protein, carbohydrate and fat.

Summary

A variety of tools can be used by ketogenic dieters to gauge progress and measure the effects of changes in the diet. These include a variety of ways to measure body composition, including the scale, skinfold calipers and the tape measure. The presence of ketosis can be measured with Ketostix (tm), which indicate the concentration of urinary ketones. While some have tried to use a glucometer, which measures blood glucose concentrations, they have proven inaccurate and are not recommended. Tools to measure food intake, as well as nutrient levels of foods, are recommended especially in the beginning stages of the diet.

Chapter 16:
Final considerations

As stated previously, this book is not meant to argue for or against the ketogenic diet as the ideal diet for weight/fat loss or any other application. Rather it is an attempt to present a comprehensive account of what occurs during a ketogenic diet, and to dispel the many misconceptions surrounding the state of dietary ketosis. Additionally, specific guidelines have been offered for those individuals who have decided to do a ketogenic diet.

As discussed in chapter 6, it is impossible to state unequivocally whether a ketogenic diet is better or worse in terms of fat loss and protein sparing than a carbohydrate-based diet with a similar calorie level. This is largely due to the paucity of applicable studies done with reasonable calorie levels and adequate protein. In essence, the definitive studies, which would apply to the calorie and protein recommendations being made in this book, have not been done.

It is this author's opinion that a variety of dietary approaches can be effective and that no single dietary approach is optimal for every goal. For example, a bodybuilder dieting for a contest has different dietary needs than an endurance athlete preparing for an event or the average person trying to lose a few pounds. As with any approach to fat loss, the ketogenic diet has various benefits and drawbacks. Although most of these have been mentioned within a specific context in previous chapters, they are briefly discussed again. Additionally, certain medical conditions preclude the use of a ketogenic diet, which are discussed in the next section.

Section 1: Comparison of ketogenic to balanced dieting

For any diet to be effective, it must match not only the individual's physiology but also their psychology. The best diet in the world will not work if an individual does not adhere to it. Like any dietary approach, ketogenic diets have benefits and drawbacks in this regard, which are discussed here. Note that this section is derived from mostly anecdotal sources rather than from research.

Food issues

The limited food choices on a ketogenic diet can be considered either good or bad. On the one hand, some individuals seem to do better with diets that are very restrictive, as it simplifies meal planning. The limited food choices on a ketogenic diet make it easier for some individuals to adhere to the diet. By the same token, this limitation in food choices can make the diet monotonous. With some creativity, low-carbohydrate food can be made more interesting, especially with the increased availability of low-carbohydrate cookbooks.

Similarly, the limited food choices of a ketogenic diet may mean that certain nutrients, namely those found in fruits and vegetables, are not consumed. As discussed in chapter 7, recent research has focused on the potential health benefits of phytonutrients, which are only found in vegetables and fruits. Since some carbohydrates are allowed during any ketogenic diet, limited intake of these nutrients is possible, but will be less than could be consumed on a balanced diet.

Finally, some individuals may find it difficult to resume balanced dieting after long periods on a ketogenic diet. Since many individuals gravitate towards a ketogenic diet out of a difficulty, whether real or perceived, in handling dietary carbohydrates (i.e. hypoglycemia, hyperinsulinemia), reintroducing carbohydrates in controlled amounts may be difficult. By the same token, some individuals find it easier to control a previously excessive carbohydrate intake after a ketogenic diet. For example, many individuals have reported a decreased taste for refined carbohydrates. This is discussed in greater detail in chapter 14.

The CKD: The ultimate solution?

To a great degree, the CKD avoids most of the problems discussed above. By allowing one or more days of essentially ad-libitum eating, many of the above issues are eliminated. Monotony is avoided since all food choices are allowed during the carb-up. Additionally, there can be some consumption of fruits and vegetables during the carb-up. However, the CKD carries its own particular problem for some people.

Many individuals see the carb-up as an 'eat-anything day' of their diet. Some individuals have reported consuming upwards of 10,000 calories in a 24 hour time span during the carb-up, a practice which is most likely unhealthy. In a sense, this makes the CKD look very much like a binge-purge cycle with alternations of strict dieting with free-for-all eating. This may have the potential to engender poor eating habits when the diet is ended. Ultimately, this is not different from many fat-loss diets, especially those which are very restrictive.

Body composition issues

The primary selling point of the ketogenic diet is that it causes greater fat loss while sparing protein losses. As discussed previously, this stance cannot be unequivocally defended based on the data available. Anecdotally, many individuals find that fat loss is more effective and that less muscle is lost with a ketogenic diet compared to more traditional dieting. This especially applies to bodybuilders, who may be starting with far more muscle and less bodyfat, than the average dieter. However this is not reported universally and most likely reflects differences in individual physiology, insulin sensitivity, and other factors.

Additionally, many dieters are drawn to the ketogenic diet due to the rapid initial weight loss which occurs from water loss. This is a double-edged sword. On the one hand, a rapid initial drop in bodyweight can be psychologically very encouraging for individuals who have battled with weight loss. By the same token, the rapid weight gain which can occur with even a small carbohydrate intake can be just as psychologically devastating. Understanding the distinction between weight loss and fat loss, as discussed in chapter 8, should help to avoid this problem.

Section 2: Choosing a diet

Three related but distinct dietary approaches are described in previous chapters. These are the standard ketogenic diet (SKD), the targeted ketogenic diet (TKD), and the cyclical ketogenic diet (CKD). Although it is not this book's goal to suggest that dieters choose a ketogenic diet over another dietary approach, a question which does arise is which of the three ketogenic diets is appropriate for a given individual. The major determinants of which diet is the best choice for any given individual are the amount and type of exercise being done, as well as some certain health related issues.

The SKD

The SKD described in this book is no different than a myriad of other dietary approaches which are currently in vogue, although greater specifics regarding calorie and protein intake have been given. The SKD is most appropriate for individuals who are either not exercising, or who are only doing low- or moderate-intensity aerobic exercise. As discussed in chapter 18, a diet devoid of carbohydrates can sustain this type of exercise. However those individuals who are performing any form of high-intensity exercise such as weight training will not be able to use the SKD for any extended periods of time as exercise performance will suffer. Additionally, many individuals involved in long-duration endurance activities tend to find that performance is enhanced by adding carbohydrates to their diet.

The CKD

The CKD alternates periods of ketosis with periods of high carbohydrate eating. Due to the structure of the CKD, it is critical to fully deplete muscle glycogen between carb-up periods. For individuals wishing to use a 7 day cycle (5-6 days of ketosis, 1-2 days of carbohydrates), this necessitates a fairly high volume and intensity of training. This makes the 7-day CKD most appropriate for fairly advanced exercisers and weight trainers. Beginning exercisers may not be able to do the amount of exercise necessary, at a sufficient intensity, to fully deplete glycogen.

Individuals who are using the ketogenic diet for various health reasons (such as hyperinsulinemia or hypertension) may find the CKD unworkable as the hormonal response to high-carbohydrate consumption can trigger the exact health consequences which are being treated with the ketogenic diet. Additionally, some individuals find that their food intake is uncontrollable during a full carb-load, for either psychological or physiological reasons. In this case, a CKD is not an appropriate dietary choice.

The TKD

Within certain limits, the TKD can sustain high intensity exercise performance, although perhaps not as well as the CKD. The TKD is generally most appropriate for beginning and intermediate weight-trainers, as it will allow them to sustain exercise intensity without disrupting ketosis for long periods of time. Additionally those individuals who cannot use the CKD for health reasons, but who are also involved in high-intensity exercise, may find the TKD appropriate.

Other options

The three approaches described in this book are by no means the only ways to implement a ketogenic diet and individuals may need to experiment to determine what works best for them. Anecdotally, some individuals have found a 10-day CKD cycle to be the most effective. Additionally, individuals who cannot do a full carb-load every 7 days have done a 14 day cycle with a carb-load every other week. This allows some of the freedom of the carb-up, without requiring the large amount of exercise needed.

Which diet gives the best fat loss?

A question which is often asked is whether the SKD, TKD, or CKD yields the best fat loss. This is not really a question with a single answer. Ultimately, fat loss is going to be determined primarily by caloric considerations. In the long run, a SKD, TKD or CKD at the same calorie level will probably yield fairly similar fat loss.

Section 3: Contraindications to the ketogenic diet

Like any dietary approach, the ketogenic diet is not universally applicable. Individuals with certain preexisting medical conditions should seriously consider whether an extreme approach such as the ketogenic diet is appropriate. Although little data is available on this topic, some major conditions which might preclude the use of a ketogenic diet are discussed below.

Kidney problems

Although no data exists to suggest that the 'high protein' nature of a ketogenic diet is problematic for individuals with normal kidney functioning, high protein intake may cause problems for individuals with preexisting conditions. Therefore, individuals who are prone to kidney stones should seriously consider whether the ketogenic diet is appropriate for them. The slight dehydration which occurs coupled with a high protein intake may increase the risk of stones. For individuals on the ketogenic diet, it is imperative to drink sufficient water and to be aware of the potential for problems.

Diabetes

As previously discussed, Type I (insulin dependent) diabetics may have problems with ketoacidosis if insulin levels drop too low. Since these individuals rely on injections to normalize insulin, a ketogenic diet conceivably poses no problems. However, the lack of carbohydrates, as well as changes in insulin sensitivity, on a ketogenic diet will affect insulin requirements (1). Any Type I diabetic who wishes to try a lowered carbohydrate diet must consult with their physician or health provider to determine changes in their insulin regimen.

Type II (non-insulin dependent) diabetics are frequently drawn to low carbohydrate or ketogenic diets as they may help to control blood glucose and insulin levels (2). Individuals with severe hyperinsulinemia and/or hypoglycemia will need to be careful when implementing a ketogenic diet to avoid problems with blood sugar crashes and related difficulties.

Individuals with Type II diabetes may have greater difficulty establishing ketosis, as some data suggests that liver glycogen is more difficult to deplete (3,4). Additionally, it has been found that obese individuals, who typically suffer from insulin resistance, have greater difficulty establishing ketosis (5). This points even more to the importance of exercise to help deplete liver glycogen and establish ketosis.

Coronary artery disease/high cholesterol

The impact of a ketogenic diet on blood cholesterol is discussed in detail in chapter 7. For many individuals, the ketogenic diet causes an improvement in blood lipid levels, especially in cases where bodyfat is lost. However, this is not a universal finding. Individuals with diagnosed coronary artery disease or high blood cholesterol must monitor their blood lipid levels for negative changes. Individuals who show negative changes can try decreasing saturated fat intake, while increasing unsaturated fat. Additionally, a fiber supplement may be helpful. If blood cholesterol levels continue to respond negatively, the ketogenic diet should be abandoned.

Gout

Individuals with a past history or genetic propensity for gout should seriously consider whether or not a ketogenic diet is appropriate. As discussed previously, a rise in uric acid levels occurs when the ketogenic diet is started and this may trigger gout in predisposed individuals. Since even small amounts of dietary carbohydrates (5% of total calories) appear to alleviate problems with uric acid buildup, a less restrictive ketogenic diet may be possible for individuals who are prone to gout.

Pregnancy

This author is unaware of any research looking specifically at the effects of the ketogenic diet in pregnant humans. However, malformations of the neural tube occur with increased frequency in diabetic mothers and exposure of pregnant female rats to high ketone levels can increase the risk of these same neural tube defects, suggesting that ketones may be a cause (6). Additionally, it appears that glucose is the primary fuel for the developing fetus (7).

Considering the above data, as well as the potential harm which might occur to an unborn child, a ketogenic diet is not considered appropriate during pregnancy. In fact, any diet whose aim is weight or fat loss is inappropriate during pregnancy as diet should be optimal to support the developing fetus and the mother.

Epilepsy

Although the ketogenic diet has shown great impact in the treatment of childhood epilepsy, the diet used for epilepsy is significantly different than the diet described in this book. Additionally, implementation of the ketogenic diet for therapeutic purposes requires medical supervision. Under no circumstances should individuals attempt to implement the ketogenic diet for the treatment of epilepsy without medical supervision.

Adolescents

Although the epileptic diet is used in children under the age of 10, its use in adolescents is less well studied. From the standpoint of fat loss, the pediatric epilepsy diet is used for weight loss if necessary, by adjusting calories (8). Additionally, the protein sparing modified fast has shown some benefits in treating morbid childhood obesity (9). Although adolescent obesity is increasing, parents should be careful in self-administering diets, due to the possibility of stunted or altered growth. Due to the lack of data on the CKD, and due to the hormonal fluctuations which occur, its use is not recommended in adolescents.

Summary

There are certain medical conditions which either directly preclude the use of the ketogenic diet, or that warrant serious consideration prior to beginning such a diet. While there is no data for a majority of disease states, individuals should exercise caution prior to making any large scale changes in diet. When in doubt, the proper medical authorities should be consulted and no self-diagnosis should be made.

References Cited

1. Bistrian B. et. al. Nitrogen metabolism and insulin requirements in obese diabetic adults on a protein-sparing modified fast. Diabetes (1976) 25: 494-504.
2. Grey NJ and Kipnis DM. Effect of diet composition on the hyperinsulinism of obesity. New Engl J Med (1971) 285: 827
3. Clore JN et. al. Evidence for increased liver glycogen in patients with noninsulin-dependent diabetes-melliture after a 3-day fast. J Clin Endocrinol Metab (1992) 74: 660-666.

4. Clore J and Blackard W. Suppression of gluconeogenesis after a 3-day fast does not deplete liver glycogen in patients with NIDDM. Diabetes (1994) 43: 256-262.

5. Mohammadiha H. Resistance to ketonuria and ketosis in obese subjects. Am J Clin Nutr (1974) 27: 1213-1213.

6. Mitchell GA et al. Medical aspects of ketone body metabolism. Clinical & Investigative Medicine (1995) 18: 193-216.

7. Robinson AM and Williamson DH. Physiological roles of ketone bodies as substrates and signals in mammalian tissues. Physiol Rev (1980) 60: 143-187.

8. "The Epilepsy Diet Treatment: An introduction to the ketogenic diet" John M. Freeman, MD; Millicent T. Kelly, RD, LD ; Jennifer B. Freeman. Demos Vermande, 1996

9. Willi SM et. al. The effects of a high-protein, low-fat, ketogenic diet on adolescents with morbid obesity: Body composition, blood chemistries, and sleep abnormalities. Pediatrics (1998) 101: 61-67.

Part V:
Exercise Physiology

Chapter 17: Muscular physiology and energy production
Chapter 18: The physiology of aerobic exercise
Chapter 19: The physiology of interval training
Chapter 20: The physiology of strength training
Chapter 21: The effects of exercise on ketosis
Chapter 22: Exercise and fat loss

As more and more research is performed, the conclusion is fairly unequivocal: if there is one thing that improves overall health, it is regular exercise. The best diet and all of the supplements in the world cannot make up for a lack of regular activity.

Exercise has the potential to impact numerous facets of daily life. Some of the benefits of regular exercise are an increase in overall health, stronger bones, a stronger heart and lungs, improved cholesterol levels, etc. This book is not going to spend time trying to convince individuals that they should exercise. As discussed in chapter 14, beyond the health-related reasons to exercise, dieting without exercise has an extremely low rate of long-term success. Unless there is some specific reason that exercise can not be performed, such as an injury, exercise should be considered a mandatory part of any attempt to lose bodyfat.

There are three general categories of exercise which are discussed in this book. They are aerobic exercise (such as walking, swimming or bicycling), interval training (sprinting), and resistance training (weight training). The next 6 chapters focus on the underlying physiology of exercise, especially as it pertains to the ketogenic diet. The impact of exercise on ketosis and fat loss is also addressed.

Chapter 17:
Basic muscular physiology and energy production

The human body contains roughly 600 muscles, ranging from the large muscles of the quadriceps (front thigh) to the small muscles that control the movement of the eyes. All force production depends on the ability of these muscles to contract and cause movement within our body. All forms of exercise ultimately depend on force production by muscles so it is necessary to briefly discuss some basic muscular physiology and detail about force production. Additionally, basic concepts regarding energy production is discussed.

Section 1: Muscle Fiber Types

There are three different types of muscle fibers. Each possesses its own specific characteristics. The distinction between different fiber types is important from the standpoint of understanding the adaptations which occur during exercise as well as what fuels are used.

Types of muscle fibers

Human skeletal muscle contains three distinct types of fibers (1): Type I or slow oxidative (SO), Type IIa or fast oxidative glycolytic (FOG), and Type IIb or fast glycolytic (FG).

Each fiber type has distinct physical and physiological characteristics (such as preferred fuel) which determine the type of activity they are best suited for. Depending on the type of exercise done, fibers will adapt accordingly (adaptations to specific types of exercise are addressed in separate chapters). A summary of the fiber types and their primary metabolic characteristics appears in table 1.

Table 1: Comparison of various characteristics of fiber types			
	Type I	Type IIa	Type IIb
Metabolic Characteristic			
Oxidative capacity (a)	High	Medium	Low
Glycolytic capacity (b)	Low	High	Highest
Mitochondrial density	High	Medium	Low
Capillary density	High	Medium	Low
Speed of contraction	Slow	Fast	Fast
Resistance to fatigue	high	moderate	low
Time to fatigue	4'+	about 4'	about 2'
Force production capacity	low	moderate	high
Growth capacity	low	moderate	high

a. Oxidative capacity refers to a muscle's ability to generate energy through the aerobic metabolism of fats and glycogen (see fuel metabolism section).
b. Glycolytic capacity refers to a muscle's ability to generate energy through the anaerobic metabolism of glycogen and ATP and CP.

Source: "Physiology of Sport and Exercise" Jack H. Wilmore and David L. Costill. Human Kinetics Publishers 1994. ; "Exercise Physiology: Human Bioenergetics and it's applications" George A Brooks, Thomas D. Fahey, and Timothy P. White. Mayfield Publishing Company 1996. ; Eric Hultman "Fuel selection, muscle fibre" Proceedings of the Nutrition Society (1995) 54: 107-121.

Overview of fiber types

Type I muscle fibers are endurance fibers. They utilize primarily free fatty acids (FFA) for fuel, fatigue slowly but can't generate much force. They are used primarily during low-intensity, long-duration activity such as walking. Type I fibers have the least capacity for muscle growth of the fiber types. Type I fibers are sometimes called red fibers because of their reddish color under a microscope.

Type IIb muscle fibers are high force fibers. They generate more force but fatigue quickly. Type IIb fibers use glycogen as their primary fuel, generating lactic acid as a byproduct. Type IIb fibers are primarily used for high-intensity, high-force, short-duration activities such as weight training and sprinting. They have the greatest capacity for growth and appear white under a microscope.

Type IIa fibers are intermediate fibers. They have medium-force capacity and fatigue characteristics. They can derive energy either from glycogen or fat depending on the type of activity that is being done. They have a growth capacity between Type I and IIb fibers and appear pinkish under a microscope.

Most people have roughly equal numbers of Type I and Type II fibers although elite athletes may have extreme distributions of fibers (2). Typically, endurance athletes have a preponderance of Type I fibers while elite strength athletes are Type II fiber dominant.

Generally speaking, fibers do not change from one type to another but the overall characteristics of the fibers can shift towards more aerobic or anaerobic (1,5). The effects of different types of training on fiber characteristics appears in figure 1.

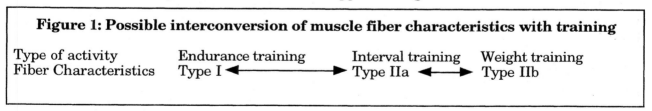

Figure 1: Possible interconversion of muscle fiber characteristics with training

Type of activity   Endurance training   Interval training   Weight training
Fiber Characteristics   Type I ←————————→ Type IIa ←——→ Type IIb

Section 2: Muscle Fiber Recruitment

The concept of muscle fiber recruitment is important to understand for this reason: different types of exercise rely on each muscle fiber type to a greater or lesser degree. The utilization of different fiber types (due to differences in physical characteristic) greatly affects the fuel used, the adaptations seen to training, and the effects of a ketogenic diet. All of the information which follows regarding exercise types and the necessity of carbohydrates or not is ultimately tied into the issue of recruitment.

Recruitment and rate coding

The body generates force through one of two different mechanisms. It can either recruit more fibers (called recruitment) or send more signals so that the fibers contract more strongly (called rate coding). For large muscles, the body uses recruitment up to roughly 80-85% of maximal force production at which point all fibers available have been recruited (6). Above this point, force production is accomplished solely through rate coding. Untrained individuals may not be able to recruit all of their Type IIb muscle fibers. With regular training, complete recruitment can be developed (7,8,9).

Muscle fiber recruitment and the Size principle (2)

Fibers recruit from smallest (Type I) to largest (Type IIb) according to the Size Principle. At low intensities (i.e. slow walking or about 20% of maximal force), only Type I fibers are recruited. As intensity increases (i.e. jogging), more Type I fibers are recruited until they can no longer provide sufficient force. At this point, some Type IIa fibers are recruited. As force production requirements continue to increase towards maximal levels, Type IIb fibers are recruited. Please note that recruitment is determined by force, not velocity. Near maximal slow movements will recruit Type IIb fibers as long as force requirement are high enough (see below).

With regards to specific fiber types, Type I fibers are recruited from zero to about 60% of maximum force production capacities. Around 20% of maximal force, some Type IIa fibers are recruited and are maximally recruited around 75-80% of maximal force. Type IIb fibers do not begin to recruit until about 60-65% of maximal force production and continue to be recruited up to about 85% of max. as stated before. An overview of recruitment of different fiber types appears in figure 2.

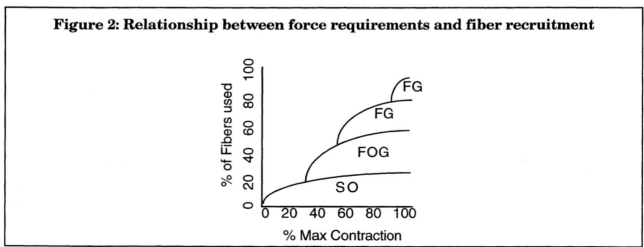

Figure 2: Relationship between force requirements and fiber recruitment

With few exceptions (most of which would never occur during normal training), it is impossible to recruit Type II fibers before Type I fibers. The only case where Type II fibers are recruited without Type I fibers being recruited is during eccentric muscle actions (see chapter 20).

In summary:

At low intensities of exercise (i.e. walking), only Type I fibers are recruited.

At moderate intensities (i.e. jogging, weight training), Type I and IIa fibers are recruited.

At maximal intensities (i.e. sprinting, weight training), all fiber types are recruited.

Section 3: An overview of exercise and energy production

Exercise is classified into two main categories: aerobic or anaerobic. These categories differ in intensity, duration and the way that energy is produced by the body. Generally speaking, aerobic exercise relies on energy pathways that require oxygen (oxidative metabolism). Anaerobic exercise relies on energy pathways that do not require oxygen (glycolytic metabolism).

Energy production during exercise

The only fuel source that can be used directly by muscles is a compound called adenosine-tri phosphate (ATP). During exercise, ATP is broken down to adenosine-diphosphate (ADP) in the muscles and must be regenerated. However, there is only enough ATP stored in the muscle for roughly 6 seconds of effort. There are four different energy systems which regenerate ATP during exercise (2), and each of the energy systems is examined in more detail in subsequent chapters. The contribution of each energy system during exercise depends primarily on the intensity and duration of the activity, but other factors such as gender, diet and training status also play a role.

1. ATP-CP system: From one to twenty seconds of activity, the body relies on stored ATP and creatine phosphate (CP) to provide fuel. This energy pathway is used primarily during maximal intensity exercise such as sprinting and low rep weight training. This reaction does not require the presence of oxygen (i.e. it is anaerobic).

2. Anaerobic glycolysis: From twenty to sixty seconds, the body breaks down carbohydrate stored in the muscle (called glycogen) for energy resulting in the production of lactic acid. Lactic acid causes a burning sensation and may be one cause of fatigue during exercise. Anaerobic glycolysis will predominate during near maximal intensity exercise such as a 400 meter sprint or medium rep weight training (6-20 reps). Anaerobic glycolysis does not require oxygen to proceed.

3. Aerobic glycolysis: During exercise of about 20' maximal duration, the muscle primarily breaks down stored muscle glycogen as well as blood glucose to provide energy. This produces pyruvate as an end product which is used to make more energy. This energy system is used during activities such as a 2 mile run.

4. Aerobic lipolysis: During exercise of longer than 20', the body will break down free fatty acids to produce energy. This energy system is used during low intensity aerobic activities.

The body may also use other fuel sources (ketones, protein, and intramuscular triglyceride) during exercise to varying degrees. The involvement of each fuel is discussed in specific situations. A brief overview of the four energy systems and their duration appears in table 2.

Summary

Muscle fibers are typically delineated into three different types, depending on their characteristics. During exercise, depending on the intensity, the various muscle fibers are recruited as necessary to produce force. As muscles produce force, they utilize the fuel adenosine-triphosphate (ATP). Since there is limited ATP stored in the muscle itself, a variety of energy systems exist to produce more ATP. The energy system which is used will depend on the duration and intensity of exercise.

Table 2: Overview of energy systems for different activities

Energy System	Time	Exercise Intensity	Example Activity
ATP-CP	1-20"	Maximal	Shot putting, low rep weight training (1-5 reps)
Anaerobic glycolysis	20-60"	Near maximal	400 meter sprint, medium rep weight training (6 reps+)
Aerobic glycolysis	1-10'	High	2 mile run
FFA Oxidation	10' and up	Low	slow walking, jogging

Source: Hawley JA and Hopkins WG. Aerobic glycolytic and aerobic lipolytic power systems: A new paradigm with implications for endurance and ultraendurance events. Sports Med (1995) 19: 240-250.

References Cited
1. "Designing Resistance Training Programs, 2nd edition" W. Kraemer and S. Fleck, Human Kinetics 1996.
2. "Physiology of Sport and Exercise" Jack H. Wilmore and David L. Costill. Human Kinetics Publishers 1994.
3. "Exercise Physiology: Human Bioenergetics and it's applications" George A Brooks, Thomas D. Fahey, and Timothy P. White. Mayfield Publishing Company 1996.

4. Hultman E. Fuel selection, muscle fibre. Proc of the Nutrition Society (1995) 54: 107-121.

5. Baumann H et. al. Exercise training induces transitions of myosin isoform subunits within histochemically typed human muscle fibers. Pflugers Archiv (1987) 409: 349-360.

6. "Strength and Power in Sport" Ed. P.V. Komi Blackwell Scientific Publications 1992.

7. Behm DG. Neuromuscular implications and adaptations of resistance training. J Strength and Cond Res (1995) 9: 264-274.

8. Stone WJ and Coulter SP. Strength/endurance effects from three resistance training protocols with women. J Strength Cond Res (1994) 8: 231-234.

9. "Neuromechanical basis of kinesiology" Roger M. Enoka. Human Kinetics Publishers 1994.

10. Hawley JA and Hopkins WG. Aerobic glycolytic and aerobic lipolytic power systems: A new paradigm with implications for endurance and ultraendurance events. Sports Medicine (1995) 19: 240-250.

Chapter 18:
The Physiology of Aerobic Exercise

The word 'aerobic' literally means 'with oxygen' and aerobic exercise is fueled by reactions which require oxygen to proceed. Typical aerobic activities are walking, running, cycling and swimming. While activities like basketball and soccer could be considered aerobic (as they rely on aerobic energy systems), their stop and start nature would cause them to be more typically referred to as interval training discussed in the next chapter.

We will define aerobic exercise as any activity that is fueled by aerobic energy sources and only consider exercise such as walking, cycling, etc in this chapter. Aerobic energy pathways include the breakdown of glycogen, blood glucose, free fatty acids, intramuscular triglyceride, ketones and protein. The intensity and duration of exercise will determine which of these fuels is the primary energy source.

Aerobic exercise typically causes heart rate to reach 50% to 80-85% of maximum heart rate (or about the lactate threshold, defined below). In general, the adaptations to aerobic exercise are for the body to become more efficient at producing energy aerobically. These adaptations occur in the enzymes necessary for aerobic energy production as well as in the muscle and heart. As a general rule, maximal strength and muscle size do not increase with aerobic exercise.

Section 1: Adaptations to aerobic exercise

Aerobic exercise affects two major tissues in the body: the heart and the muscles. With regular aerobic training, the heart becomes stronger and more efficient, pumping more blood with every beat. Heart rate at rest and during exercise decreases indicating a greater efficiency. Normal resting heart rate is around 70 to 80 beats per minute (bpm), but elite endurance athletes may have resting heart rates of 40 bpm. (1)

The primary change in the muscle is an increase in the capacity to utilize fats for fuel during exercise and at rest (2,3), and this adaptation only occurs in the muscles which are trained (4). For example, when subjects trained the quadriceps of only one leg, that leg's ability to use free fatty acids (FFA) increased while the untrained leg did not. (4) This is why running (which primarily uses the hamstrings and gluteal muscles) does not improve cycling (which primarily uses the quadriceps) and vice versa.

The main site of aerobic energy production in the muscle is the mitochondria. Regular training increases the number and activity of mitochondria. (2,5) Training also increases the number of capillaries in the muscle which deliver blood, oxygen and nutrients to the muscles. (2,4,6) Finally, the enzymes required for the oxidation (burning) of FFA all increase with regular aerobic training (2,4,6). These adaptations in the mitochondria and capillaries may also occur as a result of weight training, especially if high reps and short rest periods are used (see chapter 20 for more information).

During aerobic exercise, levels of adrenaline increase, raising heart rate and mobilizing fuel for energy. However, regular aerobic training decreases the amount of adrenaline released during exercise (7). This is accompanied by greater oxidation of FFA and a larger proportion of the FFA oxidized comes from intramuscular triglycerides (3,7). Thus, despite lower levels of adrenaline, there are higher rates of fat breakdown indicating an increase in tissue sensitivity to adrenaline (8). These adaptations in adrenaline sensitivity are completed after three weeks of regular training (3) and last as long as training is performed at least once every four days (9). Individuals performing aerobic exercise should exercise at least once every four days or these adaptations begin to disappear. Older individuals typically show a decrease in tissue sensitivity to adrenaline which may be partially corrected with regular aerobic training.

Finally, chronic aerobic training causes a shift in muscle fiber type from Type IIb towards Type IIa and I characteristics (10). That is, Type IIb and IIa fibers (which are typically strength and power oriented), take on the characteristics of Type I fibers (endurance oriented) (2).

Regular aerobic exercise also causes a decrease in fiber size and loss of muscle (6,11). Individuals in strength/power sports (powerlifting, etc) as well as bodybuilders should incorporate aerobic training sparingly to avoid a loss of muscle size and strength.

Section 2: Aerobic Fuel Metabolism

Aerobic exercise can rely on multiple fuel sources for energy. These include glycogen (a storage form of carbohydrate) in the muscle and liver, free fatty acids (FFA) from adipose tissue, intramuscular triglyceride (droplets of fat stored within the muscle fibers), ketones and protein. The use of protein during aerobic exercise has implications for protein requirements, as discussed in chapter 9. The body's total stores of each appear in table 1 (reprinted from page 19).

Table 1: Comparison of bodily fuels in a 150 lb man with 22% bodyfat

Tissue	Average weight (lbs)	Caloric worth (kcal)
Adipose tissue triglyceride	~33	135,000
Carbohydrate stores		
Muscle glycogen (normal)	~ .25	480
Liver glycogen	~ .5	280
Blood glucose	0.04	80
Total carbohydrate stores	0.8	840
Intramuscular TG	0.35	1465
Ketones (a)	Varies	Varies
Muscle protein (b)	~13	24,000

(a) Ketones rarely provide more than 7-8% of total energy yield even in highly ketotic individuals
(b) Protein only provides 5-10% of total energy yield (up to 13 grams of protein per hour).

Source: "Textbook of Biochemistry with Clinical Correlations 4th ed." Ed. Thomas M. Devlin. Wiley-Liss, 1997.

An overview of fat and carbohydrate regulation

As at rest, the primary fuels during aerobic exercise are carbohydrate (muscle glycogen and blood glucose) and FFA (from adipose tissue as well as intramuscular triglyceride) (13,14). At low intensities, fat is the primary fuel source during exercise. As exercise intensity increases, glycogen is used to a greater degree. This fact has been misinterpreted by some to suggest that low-intensity activity is the best choice for fat loss. However, the absolute amount of fat used during exercise is greater at higher exercise intensities. This topic is discussed in detail in chapter 22.

As exercise intensity increases, less fat and more glycogen is used as fuel. Eventually, as exercise intensity increases, there is a crossover point where glycogen becomes the primary fuel during exercise (15). This point corresponds roughly with the lactate threshold, described below.

The increase in glycogen utilization at higher intensities is related to a number of factors including greater adrenaline release (1,15), decreased availability of FFA (16), and greater recruitment of Type II muscle fibers (15,17,18). The ketogenic diet shifts the crossover (i.e. lactate threshold) point to higher training intensities (15) as does regular endurance training (1,5). As discussed further below, this means that endurance athletes are able to maintain higher exercise intensities while relying on FFA for energy.

The interactions between fat and carbohydrate utilization during exercise has been studied extensively. The determining factor of fat versus carbohydrate utilization appears to be related to glucose availability rather than FFA availability (14,19). When carbohydrates are abundant, they are the primary fuel for exercise.

As discussed in detail in chapter 3, depleting muscle glycogen and lowering glucose availability in the muscle and bloodstream increases utilization of FFA while increasing muscle glycogen stores increases carbohydrate use (and decreases fat utilization) during exercise (20). Additionally, protein use increases with glycogen depletion.

The proposed reason that high glucose availability may impair fat burning is similar to the processes which occur in the liver (see chapter 4). High levels of glucose and glycogen raise levels of malonyl-Coa which inhibits enzymes necessary for the oxidation (burning) of fat for fuel. The end result is an inhibition of fat oxidation when glucose availability is high and an increase in fat oxidation when glucose is low (19).

Having discussed some of the general determinants for carbohydrate and fat metabolism during exercise, we can examine the details of energy production from each fuel source.

Glycolysis

Glycolysis refers generally to the breakdown of carbohydrates for energy. Carbohydrates are stored in the muscle and liver (in long chains called glycogen) and also circulate in the blood as glucose. During exercise, glycogen or glucose is broken down to provide ATP as shown in figure 1.

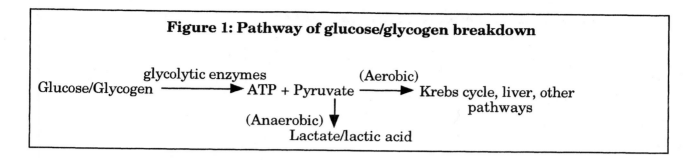

Figure 1: Pathway of glucose/glycogen breakdown

During exercise below the lactate threshold (discussed below), glycolysis results primarily in the production of pyruvate which can be reused in the mitochondria to produce more ATP. Alternately pyruvate is released into the bloodstream where it travels to the liver and is converted to glucose (to be released back into the bloodstream) through a process called gluconeogenesis. Regardless of the ultimate fate of pyruvate, it is reused to produce ATP. The overall energy yield of aerobic glycolysis is 36-39 ATP molecules per molecule of glycogen or glucose broken down (5). This is sometimes called slow glycolysis.

At higher exercise intensities, pyruvate is converted to lactic acid, which lowers pH inside the muscle and causes a burning sensation. Lactic acid separates in the muscle to lactate (a salt) and H+ (a proton). The accumulation of H+ lowers the pH of muscle, inhibiting further energy production. High levels of lactic acid/lactate are likely involved in fatigue during high-intensity aerobic exercise. The production of lactate from the breakdown of glycogen or glucose is referred to as fast glycolysis (5).

It should be noted that lactate is always being produced by the muscle to a small degree. Lactate levels are low at rest and increase gradually as exercise intensity increases (21). In the past, lactate was thought of as only a waste product of glycolysis that caused fatigue. It is now recognized that lactate is another useful fuel during and after exercise. Lactate can be used for energy by slow twitch muscle fibers (Type I) as well as by the heart. Alternately, lactate can diffuse into the bloodstream, travel to the liver, and be converted to glucose or glycogen through the process of gluconeogenesis.

Following exercise, lactate can be regenerated to muscle glycogen which may have implications for individuals following a standard ketogenic diet as glycogen availability is the limiting factor in many types of exercise. Post-workout glycogen resynthesis from lactate is discussed in chapter 10.

Exercise and the lactate threshold

The body has a limited capacity to buffer the lactate produced during glycolysis. As exercise intensity increases, the body's ability to buffer and/or reuse lactate is surpassed and lactate accumulates in the bloodstream. Although there is still debate in the literature over proper terminology, this is generally referred to as the lactate threshold (LT). (21)

The LT represents the maximum exercise intensity which can be sustained for long periods of time. Above this level lactate levels increase quickly (see figure 3) causing fatigue. In untrained individuals, LT may occur at exercise intensities as low as 50% of maximum heart rate but this can be raised to 85-90% of maximum heart rate in elite athletes. Exercise above LT is generally considered anaerobic and is discussed in the following chapter. With training at and above LT, there is a shift to the right in LT. This allows higher intensities of exercise to be performed before fatigue sets in. The changes which occur in LT are shown in figure 3

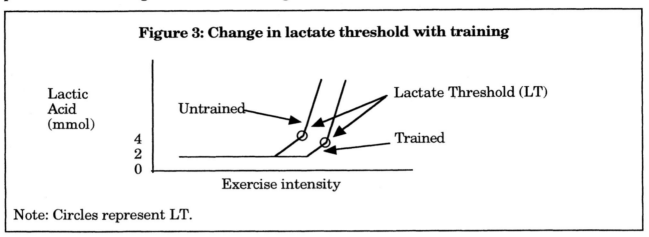

Figure 3: Change in lactate threshold with training

Note: Circles represent LT.

Liver glycogen

In addition to muscle glycogen and freely circulating blood glucose, liver glycogen plays a role in energy production during exercise. The liver stores about 110 grams of glycogen under normal conditions and this can be almost doubled to approximately 200 grams with a high carbohydrate diet. A ketogenic diet will reduce liver glycogen to approximately 13 grams (22).

Liver glycogen breakdown accelerates in response to the increase in adrenaline and noradrenaline during exercise (see section 3 of this chapter). Glycogen depletion will occur 15-24 hours after carbohydrates have been removed from the diet depending on initial liver glycogen levels (23).

Approximately 2 hours of low-intensity aerobics are necessary to totally deplete liver glycogen following an overnight fast (22). High-intensity exercise will cause greater liver glycogen output (1) although it is difficult to estimate exactly how much exercise would be needed to totally deplete liver glycogen. As discussed in detail in chapter 4, the depletion of liver glycogen is critical for the rapid establishment of ketosis, especially for individuals on a CKD. The effects of exercise on the establishment of ketosis is discussed in chapter 22.

Additionally, glucagon and cortisol levels (which increase with exercise) further influence liver glycogen release into the bloodstream. When liver glycogen is depleted, blood glucose drops and the resulting hypoglycemia (low blood sugar) may be one cause of fatigue during aerobic exercise.

It should be noted that total bodily glycogen and glucose stores can only provide approximately 1500 calories of energy (this can be doubled with carbohydrate loading), enough to run approximately 15 miles. As this is still fairly limiting energy wise, the body has several other sources of fuel that it can utilize during exercise. The other major fuel for energy during aerobic exercise is fat, in the form of free fatty acids or intramuscular triglyceride.

Metabolism of free fatty acids (FFA) and intramuscular triglyceride (TG)

The body has two major stores of fats which can be used during exercise to provide energy: adipose tissue and intramuscular triglycerides. One pound of fat contains 3,500 calories worth of usable energy. A 154 lb (70kg) male with 12% bodyfat and 18 lbs (8.4 kg) of total fat has approximately 70,000 calories stored in bodyfat and an additional 1,500 calories stored as intramuscular triglyceride. Running one mile requires about 100 calories so this individual could run 720 miles if he could use 100% fat for fuel.

Even the leanest athlete with only 5 lbs. of bodyfat (containing approximately 17,500 calories worth of usable energy) could run 17 miles if they were able to use just fat for fuel. This has led most researchers to the conclusion that diets higher in fat are not necessary since the body has more than enough stored (24). Others have suggested that adaptation to a higher fat diet may be beneficial for the endurance athlete by sparing glycogen during exercise (20).

Why humans are unable to utilize 100% fat for fuel during activity is a question that many researchers have asked and is a topic that is discussed in greater detail below (25).

Adipose tissue triglyceride metabolism

Bodily stores of adipose tissue may contain 70,000 calories or more of usable energy stored in the form of triglyceride (TG). TG is composed of a glycerol backbone with three FFA attached to it. While intramuscular TG are contained within the muscle and can be used directly, FFA from adipose tissue must be carried through the bloodstream to the muscles to be used for energy.

The process of burning adipose tissue TG involves four steps. First the TG must be mobilized, which refers to the breakdown of TG to three FFAs and a glycerol molecule. Glycerol is released into the bloodstream and regenerated into glucose in the liver (8). The breakdown of TG occurs due to the enzyme hormone sensitive lipase (HSL) which is regulated by insulin and the catecholamines, adrenaline and noradrenaline (8,26,27).

Adrenaline and noradrenaline (which increase during exercise) bind to beta-adrenergic receptors in the fat cell stimulating HSL to release FFA into the bloodstream (8). Insulin (which decreases during exercise but increases in response to increases in blood glucose) inhibits HSL activity and blocks the release of FFA for energy production.

Once broken down within the fat cell, FFAs enter the bloodstream and travel to the muscle or liver. Consequently, changes in blood flow during exercise affect FFA transport (8). FFA is taken up into the muscle and transported into the mitochondria for burning via the enzyme carnitine palmityl transferase 1 (CPT-1). FFA are also broken down in the liver and may be used to make ketones if liver glycogen is depleted.

Finally, FFA is burned in the mitochondria to produce ATP and acetyl-CoA. The acetyl-Coa is used to produce more energy in muscle. In the liver, excess acetyl-CoA is condensed into ketones as discussed in chapter 4. Alternately, incoming FFA may be stored as intramuscular triglyceride .

One molecule of FFA will yield 129 to 300 ATP or more depending on the length of the FFA that is burned. Compared to aerobic glycolysis (which produces 36-39 ATP per molecule of glucose), fats provide far more energy. However, more oxygen is required to burn one molecule of FFA compared to burning one molecule of carbohydrate. This means that the body has to work harder to oxidize fats than glycogen during exercise. Although FFA produces more energy per molecule, carbohydrate is still a more efficient fuel.

Questions about fat metabolism

One question that arises is why fats cannot be used as the sole source of energy during exercise, especially considering their abundance compared to carbohydrate stores. (25) The limiting factor in fat oxidation is related to the muscle's oxidative capacity (i.e. mitochondrial density, enzyme activity). Recall that the major adaptation to aerobic training is an increase in the amount and activity of mitochondria and the enzymes needed for fat oxidation. At high exercise intensities the inhibition of FFA release may also limit fat oxidation.

The rate of FFA oxidation during exercise is generally related to its concentration in the bloodstream (28). During low-intensity exercise (below 65% of maximum heart rate), fats can provide nearly 100% of the energy required (14,28). The rest comes from blood glucose.

As exercise intensity increases to about 75% of maximum heart rate, the rate of FFA appearance into the bloodstream decreases, but the rates of fat oxidation increase (16). This indicates an increased reliance on intramuscular TG use at higher intensities.

However, at this intensity, higher levels of FFA do not further increase fat burning indicating that the muscle is not able to use fat quickly enough (16,29). The limiting factor appears to be the muscle's oxidative capacity (28). During high-intensity activity, more fast twitch muscle fibers are called into play but the ability of fast twitch muscle fibers to derive energy from fat is low (13). Recall that the primary adaptation to regular aerobic training is an increased capacity to use fat for fuel at any intensity.

As exercise intensity increases to 85% of maximum heart rate (or roughly the lactate threshold), blood FFA levels do not increase during exercise and FFA utilization decreases (28). The decrease in FFA release during high-intensity exercise may be related to one of several factors. The first is a decrease in blood flow through adipose tissue at high exercise intensities. Additionally, FFA appears to become trapped in the adipose cells due to high levels of lactic acid (13,16,25).

This 'trapping' effect of lactic acid is indirectly supported by a large post-exercise FFA release following exercise at 85% VO2 max. (16). Also, when the blood is made alkaline (with sodium bicarbonate), higher rates of FFA release are seen during exercise further supporting the effects of blood lactic acid levels and pH on FFA release (30).

Summary of adipose tissue metabolism

The amount of fat utilized during exercise depends on the intensity and duration of exercise. At low intensities, there is abundant FFA in the bloodstream and the rate of oxidation appears to be limited by the muscle's capacity to oxidize them for energy. As exercise intensity increases to high levels, FFA release from the adipose cell is inhibited by lactic acid and the decrease in fat oxidation (and subsequent increase in glycogen utilization) is related primarily to decreased availability.

Additionally, during high-intensity activity, even with sufficient FFA present, fat oxidation is still impaired. This indicates that other factors, such as oxygen availability, also play a role. Oxygen availability during exercise is determined both by the amount of blood being pumped (by the heart) as well as the muscle's capacity to use oxygen in the bloodstream.

Intramuscular triglyceride (TG) metabolism

As an additional source of energy, there are droplets of fat, called intramuscular triglyceride (IM TG), stored within the muscle fiber (1,5,31). IM TG is oxidized in the same manner as blood borne FFA and play a large role in energy production (32). As this type of TG is stored within the muscle, they are thought to be a more rapidly accessible form of fat energy during exercise. The utilization of IM TG is highest in Type I fibers due to higher levels of oxidative enzymes (3,31). Type II muscle fibers do not readily use IM TG for fuel, relying almost solely on glycogen for energy (31).

Utilization of IM TG ranges from 10% during low-intensity exercise to 50% at high intensities. (3,31) This is related to changes in hormone levels and blood flow (32). As adrenaline levels go up at higher intensities, IM TG use is stimulated. Well trained individuals use more IM TG during exercise than untrained (14, 31). Following exercise which depletes IM TG, there is a rapid uptake of FFA into the muscle to replenish the TG stores (31).

Ketones

The oxidation of ketones for fuel is similar to that of FFA and intramuscular triglyceride. Under normal (non-ketotic) conditions, ketones may provide 1% of the total energy yield during exercise (33). During the initial stage of a ketogenic diet, ketones may provide up to 20% of the total energy yield during exercise (34). After adaptation, even under conditions of heavy ketosis, ketones rarely provide more than 7-8% of the total energy produced, a relatively insignificant amount (35-37).

The reason that more ketones are not used during exercise is to ensure that the brain has adequate amounts of ketones. Therefore, during aerobic exercise, the muscle will primarily use FFA and glucose for fuel and ketones can generally be ignored as a fuel source. As we will see in a later section, blood glucose availability does not appear to limit aerobic exercise on a ketogenic diet.

Protein

In each muscle there is a pool of amino acids (AAs), that can be used to provide energy under specific circumstances. Generally, the oxidation of AAs during exercise is small, accounting for perhaps 5% of the total energy yield in men and less in women (see section on gender differences below). With glycogen depletion, this may increase to 10% of the total energy yield, amounting to the oxidation of about 10-13 grams of protein per hour of continuous exercise (38). The primary type of AAs oxidized are the branch-chain amino acids (BCAAs): valine, leucine, and isoleucine.

BCAA oxidation has been studied extensively in individuals with a metabolic defect called McArdle's disease. Due to an enzyme insufficiency, these patients are unable to utilize glycogen for fuel during exercise. This makes them a good (although extreme) group to study in terms of glycogen depletion as would be seen during prolonged exercise or a ketogenic diet (39).

During prolonged exercise, McArdle's patients show increased levels of ammonia which comes from the breakdown of ATP shown in figure 3.

Figure 3: Breakdown of ATP to ammonia when glycogen is unavailable

ATP $\longrightarrow$ ADP $\longrightarrow$ AMP $\longrightarrow$ IMP + ammonia

---

To buffer the increased ammonia, glutamate is converted to glutamine, which carries the ammonia to the liver to be excreted as urea. The BCAA's (especially leucine) are used to generate glutamine which is then released into the bloodstream (39). The increased ammonia load seen in this situation may be one cause of fatigue during exercise. During prolonged exercise, the increase in ammonia is caused by AA oxidation due to muscle glycogen depletion (39).

The protein oxidized in this fashion appears to comes from the intramuscular AA pool and not from actual contractile tissue. However several studies have shown an increase in protein requirements for endurance athletes in heavy training (40,41) indicating that depletion of the intramuscular AA pool is ultimately damaging to the body. Therefore, excessive aerobic activity should be avoided to prevent muscle loss. Specific recommendations for aerobic exercise appear in chapter 24.

As the contribution of protein and ketone bodies to energy generation during exercise is generally small, they will both be ignored in further discussion of exercise metabolism.

Summary of IM TG, ketone and protein oxidation

As an alternative source of fat derived fuel, the body has a store of triglyceride within the muscle which can be used to provide energy during higher intensity aerobic exercise. As well, ketones and protein can provide small amounts of energy during aerobic exercise . In general ketones do not provide significant amounts of energy during aerobic exercise and protein will only be broken down to a great degree when glycogen is depleted.

Gender Differences in fuel metabolism

There are differences between men and women in terms of the physiological response to aerobic exercise. While the exact implication of these differences are unclear, they have one major consequence with regards to the ketogenic diet, especially the CKD.

At any aerobic intensity, women use more fat and less carbohydrate and protein during exercise (42-45). Studies also show that women do not respond to carb loading the same as men do, most likely because they deplete less muscle glycogen less during aerobic exercise (42). This has two important ramifications for women wishing to follow a ketogenic diet. First and foremost, less dietary protein is required during the week as less protein is used during exercise and at rest (43). As discussed in chapter 9, if ketosis can not be established and all other facets of the diet are in order, protein should be reduced gradually until trace ketosis is established. Additionally, since less glycogen is depleted during aerobic exercise (42,44) carbohydrate requirements for women on a ketogenic diet are affected.

Anecdotally, some women report excessive fat regain during the carb-load portion of a CKD, especially if they are not weight training during the week. This may be related to the physiological differences outlined above. Since glycogen levels are depleted less in women than in men, the chance for extra carbohydrate calories to 'spill over' during the carb-up and be stored as fat is more likely.

If a woman is only performing aerobic exercise, a CKD will not be appropriate and the TKD is the better choice. If a woman is weight training and following the CKD, but finds that fat regain is occurring during the carb-up, the carb-up can be shortened or only performed once every two weeks.

The exact cause of these gender differences is unknown but is probably related to one or more of the following factors. Women have higher growth hormone levels than men at rest and have a greater increase in GH during exercise (46). Additionally, women show a higher adrenaline release to exercise than men as well as having lower baseline insulin levels (42,44,45). Finally, women have a greater capacity for beta-oxidation (fat burning) than do men (47).

These differences only appear to occur during the luteal phase of the menstrual cycle, which is the time period between ovulation and menstruation (42). Higher levels of estradiol (one of the estrogens) also appear to be involved (44). Interestingly, this difference in substrate utilization occurs only in untrained women and well trained women show roughly the same fuel utilization pattern as men (48).

Section 3: The hormonal response to aerobic exercise

Several hormones are affected by aerobic exercise depending on exercise intensity and duration. Overall, the hormonal response to aerobic exercise is very similar to what is seen during a ketogenic diet. Levels of anabolic hormones, such as insulin, go down while levels of catabolic hormones, such as the catecholamines, cortisol and growth hormone, go up. The major hormones which are affected by aerobic exercise are discussed below.

The catecholamines are adrenaline and noradrenaline and both are involved in energy production. The catecholamines raise heart rate and blood pressure, stimulate fat breakdown, increase liver and muscle glycogen breakdown, and inhibit insulin release from the pancreas (49). Both adrenaline and noradrenaline increase during exercise although in differing amounts depending on intensity of exercise. Noradrenaline levels rise at relatively low exercise intensities. This stimulates FFA utilization in the muscles but has little effect on the breakdown of liver and muscle glycogen.

Adrenaline levels increase more slowly with increasing exercise intensity until the lactate threshold (LT) is reached at which time levels increase quickly (3). This point is sometimes called the adrenaline threshold and corresponds very well with the lactate threshold (50). As adrenaline is one of the primary hormones responsible for stimulating the liver to release glycogen, raising adrenaline levels by training at or above the LT is one way to quickly empty liver glycogen to establish ketosis (this topic is further discussed in chapter 21).

After exercise, adrenaline levels decrease quickly but noradrenaline levels may stay elevated for several hours depending on the intensity and duration of exercise. Noradrenaline stimulates calorie burning in muscle cells and the elevations in NA following exercise may explain part of the post-exercise calorie burn (see chapter 22 for more details on this topic).

During aerobic exercise, insulin levels drop quickly due to an inhibitory effect of adrenaline on its release from the pancreas (3,49). The drop in insulin allows FFA release to occur from the fat cells during exercise. Lowering insulin is also important for establishing ketosis. Despite a decrease in insulin levels during exercise, there is an increased uptake of blood glucose by the muscle. An increase in glucose uptake with a decrease in insulin indicates improved insulin sensitivity at the muscle cells during exercise.

Increased insulin sensitivity occurs because muscular contraction causes a specialized receptor called the glucose transporter-4 (GLUT-4) receptor to move to the cell membrane. For individuals suffering from hyperinsulinemia (overproduction of insulin), the increase in insulin sensitivity means that carbohydrates can be consumed during exercise with a minimal increase in insulin.

Insulin levels can not go up during exercise when glucose is consumed due to the inhibitory effect of adrenaline on insulin secretion. As soon as exercise ceases, insulin returns to baseline depending on blood glucose levels. So the amounts of carbs consumed will have to be determined through trial and error to avoid a insulin reaction after exercise. This topic is discussed in greater detail in chapter 11.

As the mirror hormone of insulin, glucagon levels increase during aerobic exercise (49). Thus the overall response to aerobic exercise is pro-ketogenic in that it causes the necessary shift in the I/G ratio to occur.

As duration and intensity of aerobic exercise increases, the body releases cortisol to further stimulate liver glycolysis (to maintain blood sugar) and stimulate FFA release. Growth hormone is also released to help stimulate FFA release (49).

Summary

The overall hormonal response to aerobic exercise is geared towards fuel mobilization and the maintenance of blood glucose. The primary storage hormone of the body, insulin, decreases while the major fuel mobilization hormones (adrenaline, noradrenaline, cortisol, glucagon, and GH) all increase. This mimics the hormonal response to a ketogenic diet and aerobic exercise is inherently ketogenic in nature.

Section 4: Fatigue during aerobic exercise

The cause of fatigue during aerobic exercise depends on the intensity and duration of activity. This has implications for the effects of a ketogenic diet and each intensity of exercise is discussed.

During low-intensity exercise (65% maximum heart rate and below), only Type I muscle fibers are recruited (51). Type I fibers have a high oxidative capacity and use mainly fat for fuel (13). Additionally, Type I fibers do not generate much lactic acid. The majority of energy during exercise at this intensity comes from the oxidation of FFA with a small contribution from blood glucose. As there is essentially an unlimited amount of bodyfat to provide energy, fatigue during this type of exercise is caused by dehydration, boredom and hypoglycemia (22,52). A ketogenic diet would not be expected to affect exercise of this intensity.

As exercise intensity increases towards the lactate threshold, more Type II muscle fibers are recruited (13). Recall that Type II fibers rely more heavily on glycogen for fuel and there is a greater reliance on stored muscle glycogen as intensity of exercise increases. Fatigue at this intensity generally correlates with muscle glycogen depletion (22,35). Increasing glycogen levels with diet invariably improves performance time (52,53).

Interestingly, the exact reason that glycogen depletion causes fatigue is not known (54). It does not appear to be related to a lack of ATP so it is not simply a matter of a lack of energy. It may be that some glycogen breakdown is necessary to provide Krebs cycle intermediates for FFA breakdown (54). Alternately, changes in potassium levels or an impairment of muscle contraction may occur with glycogen depletion (54).

Another possible source of fatigue during exercise of this type of the buildup of ammonia in the bloodstream (55). As shown in figure 2 above, ammonia is generated from the breakdown of ATP and tends to occur when carbohydrates are unavailable. Ammonia production can also occur from the oxidation of amino acids (56,57). Studies of the ketogenic diet have shown no change in ammonia levels at rest (57) but inreased levels during aerobic exercise. (56,57).

A ketogenic diet will have a negative impact on performance during moderate- intensity aerobic exercise (between 75% of maximum heart rate up to the lactate threshold) as this type of exercise due to the lack of dietary carbohydrates.

Section 5: Effects of short-term carbohydrate depletion on endurance exercise

As early as 1967, it was established that overall endurance performance was dependent on the availability of glycogen in the muscle, finding that exhaustion during aerobic exercise occurred when muscle glycogen decreased below a certain level (35). At exhaustion, glycogen levels in the working muscle were almost entirely emptied.

At the same time, it was found that the rate of glycogen used during exercise was related to the amount of glycogen present in the muscle. When glycogen levels were the highest, glycogen breakdown was also the highest. As muscle glycogen levels dropped, the rate of glycogen utilization decreased as well. Since that time, glycogen stores have been assumed to be the ultimate determinant of endurance exercise performance, but that viewpoint has recently been challenged (58). Additionally, it is currently unclear why depleted muscle glycogen would necessitate a reduction in exercise intensity when FFA are so readily available (54).

As discussed in chapter 10, normal glycogen levels are roughly 100-110 mmol/kg. One interesting observation in the afforementioned study (35) was that glycogen utilization was severely impaired below a level of 40 mmol/kg of muscle suggesting an impairment in the glycolytic pathway. Additionally, below 10 mmol/kg, a further decrease in glycogen utilization was observed suggesting that there may be some critical level below which exercise performance is severely impaired. This is remarkably consistent with the observation that performance during a 30 kilometer run was severely impaired when glycogen fell to level of 15-25 mmol/kg (53). Numerous studies have examined the effects of short-term glycogen depletion during endurance exercise of various intensities and duration. In general all support the early study described above: that performance is impaired with glycogen depletion

Endurance exercise below 85% of maximum heart rate

At low exercise intensities, fat is the main fuel for exercise. As intensity increases, muscle glycogen plays a greater role in energy production. This has led researchers to examine the effects of both short-term and long-term carbohydrate depletion on endurance performance.

Typically, subjects are tested during exercise at normal glycogen levels and then perform glycogen depleting exercise followed by 1-5 days of a high fat, carbohydrate restricted diet at which point they are retested. Following the second test, the subjects are frequently given a diet high in carbohydrates (causing glycogen super compensation) to examine the effects of above normal glycogen levels on various parameters of exercise performance. A schematic of this study design appears in figure 4 on the next page.

Almost without exception, the studies of short-term glycogen depletion on endurance exercise below 85% of maximum heart rate find similar results. The primary result is a decrease in glycogen use during exercise (35,59-64). This simply reflects a lack of availability of glucose, prompting the body to find an alternative fuel source (i.e. FFA). The initial decrease in glycogen utilization (and increase in fat utilization) during exercise occurs around 70 mmol/kg (65). Other studies suggest that muscle glycogen breakdown does not decrease until very low glycogen levels (around 40 mmol/kg) are reached (66).

Figure 4: Schematic of study design for short-term glycogen depletion studies

Day	1	2	5	5-8	8
Exercise	Baseline Exercise test	Deplete glycogen with exhaustive exercise	Repeat exercise test	No exercise	Repeat exercise test
Diet	Normal	Low carb, high fat	Low carb, high fat	Carb load	

With decreased glycogen levels, there is a decrease in blood lactate levels both at rest (61-65,67) and during exercise (35, 59-68). This reflects the decreased use of carbohydrate and greater use of FFA for fuel.

The increased use of FFA for fuel occurs both at rest (35,60-62,69) and during exercise (35,59,60,62,64,67,69), as indicated by a decreased respiratory quotient (RQ). RQ is a measure of the proportion of fat and carbohydrate being burned. Lower RQ values indicate greater fat utilization and higher RQ values greater carbohydrate utilization.

Blood levels of FFA acids increase at rest (60,61-63) and during exercise (60,62). This occurs due to the drop in insulin and blood glucose (60,62,63) as well as the increase in levels of adrenaline and noradrenaline (70). The increase in FFA levels provides ample substrate for ketogenesis in the liver. In the short-term there is no change in blood glucose uptake during exercise (60,61,64).

Despite the increased use of fat for fuel and the 'glycogen sparing' effect, exercise performance still suffers. Time to exhaustion decreases significantly with short-term carbohydrate depletion at both low and moderate aerobic intensities (59,60,65,71).

Additionally, there is higher oxygen uptake at rest (61) and during exercise (29,60,62 67,69) as well as a higher heart rate at rest (61,69) and during exercise (60,62,67,69). The oxidation of fat requires more oxygen than the oxidation of the same amount of carbohydrate so this is to be expected. From a practical standpoint this means that, at any given workload, exercise will feel subjectively harder under conditions of glycogen depletion. It should be noted that not all studies have shown a change in heart rate or oxygen uptake during exercise (64) when carbohydrates are restricted. Finally, there is increased activity of the enzyme lipoprotein lipase, an enzyme involved in fat utilization in the muscle (66).

Effects of glycogen super compensation on aerobic exercise

In general, studies that compare glycogen loading to normal or depleted glycogen levels find the opposite of the above results. In a glycogen compensated state, some studies find increased levels of lactate during exercise (35,68) while others have found no change (66). There is also a higher RQ during exercise indicating greater use of glycogen (35). Despite increased reliance on carbohydrate, there is still a greater time to exhaustion (65) and higher peak power output (67) in a carb-loaded state. Overall performance capacity increases.

193

Summary

With short-term glycogen depletion, there is a progressive decrease in glycogen breakdown during exercise accompanied by an increase in fat utilization. While this 'glycogen sparing' effect might be expected to increase endurance performance, this does not appear to be the case for short-term (1-5 days) carbohydrate restriction as endurance time invariably decreases and effort level increases in the glycogen depleted subjects. This is remarkably consistent with data from fasted subjects (72) which find that, despite drastically increased utilization of fats for fuel, performance is still hindered by the lack of muscle glycogen. The effects of long-term adaptation to carbohydrate restriction are addressed in the next section.

Additionally, there are breakpoints where glycogen utilization during exercise changes. The first appears to occur around 70 mmol/kg where an initial drop in glycogen utilization (and an increase in fat use) occurs. The second occurs at 40 mmol/kg which is near the glycogen levels where exhaustion occurs during continuous exercise. Below 40 mmol/kg, glycolysis appears to be impaired although the exact mechanism is unknown.

With carbohydrate supercompensation the opposite results are seen. Glycogen utilization during exercise and at rest increases with a decrease in fat utilization. Exercise heart rate and oxygen uptake during exercise and an increased in time to exhaustion. Whether this adaptation would occur following longer term adaptation to a ketogenic diet followed by carb-loading is discussed in the next section.

Thus, from a purely performance standpoint, at least in the short-term, it appears that carbohydrates are still the body's preferred fuel. Fat is simply unable to sustain optimal performance at high intensities.

Section 6: Long-term ketogenic diet and endurance activity

Although many studies have examined the effects of short-term glycogen depletion with a high fat diet, only a few have examined the long-term effects of a ketogenic diet on endurance performance. As we shall see, there appears to be a difference between short-term glycogen depletion and long-term ketogenic adaptation. Please note that these studies generally did not examine the effects of exercise on fat loss on a ketogenic diet. Rather, they simply examined what types of exercise could be sustained on a diet devoid of carbohydrates.

Studies on longer term ketogenic (2 to 6 weeks) diets find either a maintenance (73,74) or increase (75,76) in endurance at low-intensity exercise (75% of maximum heart rate and below). At higher intensities (around 85% of maximum heart rate which is likely above the lactate threshold) performance decreases (77). As higher intensity exercise relies proportionally more on carbohydrate for fuel, this would be expected to occur. A recent review of the ketogenic diet and exercise literature (78) has criticized the one study showing a performance decrement (77) on the basis that high-intensity exercise (85% of maximum) was inappropriate for untrained individuals.

Despite increases in the muscle's ability to utilize fat for fuel, exhaustion during exercise is still related to a depletion of glycogen in Type I muscle fibers (73). As discussed previously, the exact cause of fatigue is unknown in this case but may relate to a decrease in Krebs cycle intermediates such as citrate which are necessary for oxidation of FFA (79). This means that endurance athletes following a ketogenic diet will still require carbohydrates for optimal performance.

As with short-term carbohydrate depletion, there is a drop in RQ both at rest and during exercise indicating greater reliance on fat for fuel (73-76). At least part of the long-term adaptation to a ketogenic diet is an increase in the carnitine palmityl transferase 1 (CPT-1) system allowing for greater utilization of fats during exercise (79). This may in part explain the difference between short-term glycogen depletion and long-term adaptation and it has been suggested that "These adaptations to a chronic exposure to high-fat or low CHO feeding may 'retool' the working muscle mitochondria and increase their capacity for fat oxidation." and that adaptation to a ketogenic diet are similar to that seen with endurance training (58)

Why the discrepancy between short and long-term studies?

As noted, there is a discrepancy in the capacity for endurance performance between studies of short-term (1-5 day) glycogen depletion compared to longer term (2-6 weeks) adaptation to a ketogenic diet. It appears, as with many aspects of human adaptation, the impact on skeletal muscle metabolism of a ketogenic diet may take several weeks or more to occur (58). Thus during the first few 3-4 weeks of a ketogenic or CKD, aerobic exercise performance will most likely decrease. With chronic carbohydrate depletion, the muscles adapt by improving their ability to use fat for fuel and performance may improve again.

Summary

Long-term adaptation to a ketogenic diet appears to improve the ability of the muscle to use fat for fuel, although the exact mechanisms are not known. Endurance during low-intensity exercise (below 75% of maximum heart rate) can be maintained or improved with a total lack of dietary carbohydrates.

As exercise intensity increases, glycogen plays a much greater role in performance. And the limited studies available suggest that performance at moderate-intensity (75-85% of maximum heart rate) is decreased with a ketogenic diet. At higher intensities (90% VO2 max. and above), fatigue is generally caused by factors other than glycogen availability and is discussed in a later section.

The primary point of this section is this: individuals on a long-term ketogenic diet are limited in the types of activity that they may comfortably perform. It appears that either low-intensity activity or high-intensity activity is tolerated and only moderate-intensity activity (near the lactate threshold where glycogen availability is the primary determinant of performance) is compromised and should be avoided.

Additionally, even with the adaptations to a high fat diet, it appears that submaximal exercise endurance is still ultimately limited by muscle glycogen stores. Individuals wishing to perform high-intensity aerobic exercise will need to consume carbohydrates at some point. So, while the ketogenic diet may be more effective for fat loss, it simply is not the ideal endurance performance diet.

References Cited

1. "Physiology of Sport and Exercise" Jack H. Wilmore and David L. Costill. Human Kinetics Publishers 1994.
2. Simoneau JA. Adaptations of human skeletal muscle to exercise-training. Int J Obesity (1995) 19 (Suppl 3): S9-S13.
3. Martin WH. Effects of acute and chronic exercise on fat metabolism. Exercise and Sports Science Reviews (1994) Vol 24: 203-231.
4. Kiens B et. al. Skeletal muscle substrate utilization during submaximal exercise in man: effect of endurance training. J Physiology (93) 469: 459-478.
5. "Exercise Physiology: Human Bioenergetics and it's applications" George A Brooks, Thomas D. Fahey, and Timothy P. White. Mayfield Publishing Company 1996.
6. Klausen K et. al. Adaptive changes in work capacity, skeletal muscle capillarization and enzyme levels during training and detraining. Acta Physiol Scand (1981) 113:9-16.
7. Martin WH et. al. Effect of endurance training on plasma free fatty acid turnover and oxidation during exercise. Am J Physiol (1993) 265: E708-714.
8. Arner P. Impact of exercise on adipose tissue metabolism during exercise" Int J Obesity (1995) 19 Suppl 3: S18-S21.
9. Martin WH et. al. Effects of stopping exercise training on epinephrine-induced lipolysis in humans. J Appl Physiol (1984) 56: 845-848.
10. Baumann H et. al. Exercise training induces transitions of myosin isoform subunits within histochemically typed human muscle fibers. Pflugers Archiv (1987) 409: 349-360.
11. Terados NJM et. al. Decrease in skeletal muscle myoglobin with intensive training in man. Acta Physiol Scand (1986) 651-652.
12. "Textbook of Biochemistry with Clinical Correlations 4th ed." Ed. Thomas M. Devlin. Wiley-Liss, 1997.
13. Hultman E. Fuel selection, muscle fibre. Proceedings of the Nutrition Society (1995) 54: 107-121.
14. Coyle EF. Substrate Utilization during exercise in active people. Am J Clin Nutr (1995) 61 (suppl): 968S-979S.
15. Brooks G and Mercier J. Balance of carbohydrate and lipid utilization during exercise: the "crossover" concept. J Appl Physiol (1994) 76: 2253-2261.
16. Romijn JA et. al. Regulation of endogenous fat and carbohydrate metabolism in relation to exercise intensity and duration. Am J Physiol (1993) 265: E380-391.
17. Vollestad NK et al. Muscle glycogen depletion patterns in type I and subgroups of Type II fibers during prolonged severe exercise in man. Acta Physiol Scand (1984) 122: 433-441.
18. Gollnick PD et. al. Selective glycogen depletion in skeletal muscle fibres of man following sustained contractions. J Physiol (1974) 241: 59-67.
19. Sidossis LS and Wolfe RR. Glucose and insulin-induced inhibition of fatty acid oxidation: the glucose-fatty acid cycle reversed. Am J Physiol (1996) 270: E733-E738.

20. Hawley JA and Hopkins WG. Aerobic glycolytic and aerobic lipolytic power systems: A new paradigm with implications for endurance and ultraendurance events. Sports Medicine (1995) 19: 240-250.
21. "The Blood lactate response to exercise" Arthur Weltman Human Kinetics Publishers 1995.
22. Sherman W Metabolism of sugars and physical performance. Am J Clin Nutr (1995) 62(suppl): 228S-41S.
23. Lavoie JM et. al. Effects of dietary manipulations on blood glucose and hormonal responses following supramaximal exercise. Eur J Appl Physiol (1987) 56: 109-114.
24. Clarkson PM. Nutrition for improved sports performance: Current issues on ergogenic aids. Sports Med (1996) 21: 393-401.
25. Guezennec CY. Role of lipids on endurance capacity in man. Int J Sports Med (1992) 13: S114-S118.
26. Wahrenberg H et. al. Adrenergic regulation of lipolysis in human fat cells during exercise. Eur J Clin Invest (1991) 21: 534-541.
27. Wahrenberg H et. al. Mechanisms underlying regional differences in lipolysis in human adipose tissue. J Clin Invest (1989) 84: 458-467.
28. Romijn JA et. al. Relationship between fatty acid delivery and fatty acid oxidation during strenuous exercise. J Appl Physiol (1995) 79: 1939-1945.
29. Hargreaves M et. al. Effect of increased plasma FFA concentrations on muscle metabolism in exercising man. J Appl Physiol (1995) 78: 288-292.
30. Hood VL. Systemic pH modifies ketone body production rates and lipolysis in humans. Am J Physiol 259 (1990) 22: E327-E334.
31. Gorski J. Muscle Triglyceride metabolism during exercise. Can J Physiol Pharmacol (1993) 70: 123-131.
32. Maggs DG et. al. Interstitial fluid concentrations of glycerol, glucose, and amino acids in human quadricep muscle and adipose tissue. J Clin. Invest (1995) 96: 370-377.
33. "Exercise Metabolism" Ed. Mark Hargreaves. Human Kinetics Publishers 1995.
34. Elia M et. al. Ketone body metabolism in lean male adults during short-term starvation, with particular reference to forearm muscle metabolism. Clinical Science (1990) 78: 579-584.
35. Bergstrom J et. al. Diet, muscle glycogen and physical performance. Acta Physiol Scand (1967) 71: 140-150.
36. Balasse EO and Fery F. Ketone body production and disposal: Effects of fasting, diabetes and exercise. Diabetes/Metabolism Reviews (1989) 5: 247-270.
37. Wahren J et. al. Turnover and splanchnic metabolism of free fatty acids and ketones in insulin-dependent diabetics at rest and in response to exercise. J Clin Invest (1984) 73: 1367-1376.
38. Lemon PR and Mullin JP. Effect of initial muscle glycogen level on protein catabolism during exercise. J Appl Physiol (1980) 48: 624-629.
39. Wagenmakers AJM et. al. Metabolism of Branched-Chain Amino Acids and Ammonia During Exercise: Clues from McArdle's Disease. Int J Sports Med (1990) 11: S101-113.
40. Lemon P. Is increased dietary protein necessary or beneficial for individuals with a physically active lifestyle? Nutrition Reviews (1996) 54: S169-S175.
41. Friedman JE and Lemon P. Effect of chronic endurance exercise on retention of dietary protein. Int J Sports Med (1989) 10: 118-123.
42. Tarnopolsky MS et. al. Carbohydrate loading and metabolism during exercise in men and women. J Appl Physiology (1995) 78: 1360-1368.
43. Phillips SM et al. Gender differences in leucine kinetics and nitrogen balance in endurance

athletes. J Appl Physiol (1993) 75: 2134-2141.

44. Ruby BC and Robergs R. Gender differences in substrate utilisation during exercise. Sports Med (1994) 17: 393-410.

45. Tarnopolsky LJ et. al. Gender differences in substrate for endurance exercise. J Appl Physiol (1990) 68: 302-308.

46. Bunt JC et. al. Sex and training differences in human growth hormone levels during prolonged exercise. J Appl Physiol (1986) 61: 1796-1801.

47. Green HJ et. al. Male and female differences in enzyme activities of energy metabolism in vastus lateralis muscle. J Neurol Sci (1984) 65: 323-331.

48. Friedmann B and Kindermann W. Energy metabolism and regulatory hormones in women and men during endurance exercise. Eur J Appl Phys (1989) 59: 1-9.

49. "Exercise Physiology: Human Bioenergetics and it's applications" George A Brooks, Thomas D. Fahey, and Timothy P. White. Mayfield Publishing Company 1996.

50. "The Blood lactate response to exercise" Arthur Weltman Human Kinetics Publishers 1995.

51. Vollestad NK. Metabolic correlates of fatigue from different types of exercise in man. Advances in Experimental Medicine and Biology 384: Fatigue Ed: Simon C Gandevia et al. Plenum Press 1995.

52. Sahlin K. Metabolic factors in fatigue. Sports Medicine (1992) 13: 99-107.

53. Karlsson J and Saltin B. Diet, muscle glycogen, and endurance performance. J Appl Physiol (1971) 31: 203-206.

54. Green HJ. How Important is endogenous muscle glycogen to fatigue in prolonged exercise. Can J Physiol Pharmacol (1991) 69: 290-297.

55. Sewell DA et. al. Hyperammonaemia in relation to high-intensity exercise duration in man. Eur J Appl Physiol (1994) 69: 350-354.

56. Greenhaff PL et. al. The influence of dietary manipulation on plasma ammonia accumulation during incremental exercise in man. Eur J Apply Physiol (1991) 63: 338-344.

57. Czarnowski D et. al. Effect of a low-carbohydrate diet on plasma and sweat ammonia concentrations during prolonged nonexhausting exercise. Eur J Appl Physiol (1995) 70:70-74.

58. Conlee RE. Muscle glycogen and exercise endurance: a twenty year perspective. Exercise and Sports Science Reviews (1987) 15: 1-28.

59. Galbo H et. al. The effect of different diets and of insulin on the hormonal response to prolonged exercise. Acta Physiol Scand (1979) 107: 19-32.

60. Jansson E and Kaijser L. Effect of diet on the utilization of blood-borne and intramuscular substrates during exercise in man. Acta Physiol Scand (1982) 115: 19-30.

61. Jannson J and Kaijser L. Effect of diet on muscle glycogen and blood glucose during a short-term exercise in man. Acta Physiol Scand (1982) 115:341-347.

62. Spencer MK et. al. Effect of low glycogen on carbohydrate and energy metabolism in human muscle during exercise. Am J Physiol (1992) 262: C975-C979.

63. Yan Z et. al. Effect of low glycogen on glycogen synthase during and after exercise. Acta Physiol Scand (1992) 145: 345-352.

64. Hargreaves M et. al. Influence of muscle glycogen on glycogenolysis and glucose uptake during exercise in humans. J Appl Physiol (1995) 78: 288-292.

65. Bosch AN et. al. Influence of carbohydrate loading on fuel substrate turnover and oxidation during prolonged exercise. J Appl Physiol (1993) 74: 1921-1927.

66. Jacobs I. Lactate Muscle Glycogen and Exercise Performance in Man. Acta Physiol Scand Supplementum (1981) 495: 3-27.

67. Heigenhauser GJF et. al. Effect of glycogen depletion on the ventilatory response to exercise. J Appl Physiol (1983) 54: 470-474.

68. Asmussen E et. al. Lactate Production and anaerobic work capacity after prolonged exercise. Acta Physiol Scand (1974) 90:731-742.

69. Jannson E and Kaijser L. Leg citrate metabolism at rest and during exercise in relation to diet and substrate utilization in man. Acta Physiol Scand (1984) 122: 145-153

70. Jansson E et. al. Diet induced changes in sympatho-adrenal activity during submaximal exercise in relation to substrate utilization in man. Acta Physiol Scand (1982) 114: 171-178.

71. Johannessen A et. al. Prolactin, growth hormone, thyrotropin, 3,4,3'-trioiodothyronine, and thyroxine responses to exercise after fat- and carbohydrate-enriched diet. J Clin Endocrinology and Metabolism (1981) 52: 56-61.

72. Aragon-Vargas LF. Effects of fasting on endurance exercise. Sports Medicine (1993) 16: 255-265.

73. Phinney SD et. al. The human metabolic response to chronic ketosis without caloric restriction: preservation of submaximal exercise capacity with reduced carbohydrate oxidation. Metabolism (1983) 32: 769-776.

74. Phinney SD et. al. Effects of aerobic exercise on energy expenditure and nitrogen balance during very low calorie dieting. Metabolism (1988) 37: 758-765.

75. Phinney SD et. al. Capacity for moderate exercise in obese subjects after adaptation to a hypocaloric, ketogenic diet. J Clin Invest (1980) 66: 1152-1161.

76. Lambert EV et. al. Enhanced endurance in trained cyclists during moderate intensity exercise following 2 weeks adaptation to a high fat diet. Eur J Apply Physiol (1994) 69: 387-293.

77. Bogardus C et. al. Comparison of Carbohydrate-containing and carbohydrate-restricted hypocaloric diets in the treatment of obesity. J Clin Invest (1981) 68: 399-404.

78. Phinney S. Exercise during and after very-low-calorie dieting" Am J Clin Nutr (1992) 56: 190S-194S.

79. Spencer M and Katz A. Role of glycogen in control of glycolysis and IMP formation in human muscle metabolism. Am J Physiol (1991) 260: E859-E864.

80. Fisher EC et. al. Changes in skeletal muscle metabolism induced by a eucaloric ketogenic diet. In Knuttgen, H.G. et. al. (eds) "Biochemistry of exercise" Champaign, Ill.: Human Kinetics, 1983.

Chapter 19:
Physiology of interval training

Interval training refers generally to any activity which alternates periods of high intensity exercise with periods of lower intensity exercise. While interval training is most commonly thought of as sprint training, activities such as basketball and football, which are of a stop and start nature, should be classified as interval training as well. Although weight training is interval in nature, it is discussed separately in the next chapter.

As was discussed in the previous chapter, the breakdown of glycogen during exercise can yield either pyruvate or lactate. At low exercise intensities, glycogen breakdown produces pyruvate which is used to generate more ATP. At higher intensities of exercise, lactate is produced in greater and greater amounts and begins to accumulate in the muscle and bloodstream.

Up to a certain point, the body can deal with the increased lactate by reusing it for fuel or buffering it with bicarbonate to producing water and carbon dioxide. The point at which production of lactic acid exceeds the body's ability to cope with increasing amounts is referred to as the lactate threshold (LT) and, in essence, reflects the body's switch from primarily aerobic to primarily anaerobic energy production.

Lactic acid causes fatigue by inhibiting muscular contraction and preventing further energy production from glycogen breakdown. Thus, the duration of exercise above LT is limited. Depending on the intensity of activity, the duration of activity will vary from twenty minutes or more at LT to thirty seconds or less at maximal intensities.

The primary adaptation to interval training is to shift the LT to the right allowing higher intensities of exercise to be performed before lactic acid buildup causes fatigue. This allows endurance athletes to perform at higher intensities without fatigue.

Section 1: Adaptations to interval training

At intensities around LT, both Type I and Type IIa muscle fibers are recruited (1). As exercise intensity approaches maximum, Type IIb fibers are also recruited (2,3,4). Similar to aerobic exercise, the primary adaptation to interval training is an increase in the oxidative capacity of the recruited muscle fibers (i.e. Type IIa and IIb fibers) (5). Additionally, with regular exercise above LT, there is a gradual shift in LT to the right during exercise (5). That is, higher exercise intensities can be sustained with less lactic acid buildup.

For endurance athletes looking to maximize performance, this is an important adaptation as the majority of endurance events are performed close to or at the LT. Performance in endurance events has improved greatly in the past 15 years despite little or no increase in maximal aerobic capacity. This is explained by the greater amount of training time spent at or above LT by modern endurance athletes (5).

For bodybuilders and other strength/power athletes, the adaptations to interval training may be detrimental to performance. Several studies have reported a shift of Type IIb muscle fibers towards Type IIa characteristics with intensive interval training (6,7,8). Therefore, individuals wishing to maximize muscle size or strength are advised to stick with low intensity aerobic activity (below LT) under most circumstances (9). Specific guidelines for frequency of interval training is discussed in chapter 25.

Section 2: Hormonal response to interval training

The hormonal response to interval training is very similar to aerobic exercise. The higher intensity nature of interval training simply causes a greater hormonal response to be seen as compared to lower intensity aerobic training.

Adrenaline and noradrenaline both cause an increase in glycogen breakdown in the liver and muscles and increases in blood glucose and free fatty acids (2). Exercise above the LT causes a significant increase in both hormones. Blood glucose increases during interval training due to increased output of liver glycogen. This is further discussed in chapter 21.

Despite the increase in blood glucose during interval training, insulin levels still go down. However, if blood glucose is elevated following exercise, insulin levels will increase to drive blood glucose into the muscles. The increase in blood glucose and insulin may de-establish ketosis for a brief period after exercise.

As mentioned previously, growth hormone (GH) helps to control fuel mobilization by increasing fat breakdown and decreasing glycogen and protein use. Interval training significantly increases GH levels most likely by raising lactic acid levels (10,11).

Section 3: Energy Metabolism

By its very nature, interval training will rely on anaerobic energy metabolism, namely anaerobic glycolysis and the phosphagen energy system. Both are described below.

The Phosphagen System

Recall that ATP is the only fuel that muscles can use directly and all other energy systems have as their ultimate goal ATP production. When muscle contracts, ATP provides energy by being broken down to adenosine diphosphate (ADP) in the following reaction with the help of an enzyme called an ATPase as shown in figure 1.

Figure 1: Breakdown of ATP

$$ATP \xrightarrow{\text{ATPase}} ADP + Pi + energy$$

Note: Pi represents an inorganic phosphate molecule

Within a muscle, there is about 6 seconds worth of ATP stored which can be used for immediate energy. For activity to continue past 6 seconds, ATP must be generated through various other reactions. The first of these of these is through the creatine phosphate (CP) system.

The creatine phosphate system

Also stored in the muscle is a substance called creatine phosphate (CP). This provides a phosphate molecule to ADP to regenerate ATP so that muscular activity can continue. CP donates its high energy phosphate molecule to ADP to regenerate ATP via an enzyme called creatine kinase as shown in figure 2.

Figure 2: Breakdown of CP to regenerate ATP

$$ADP + CP \xrightarrow{\text{Creatine kinase}} ATP + Creatine$$

There is enough stored CP in a normal muscle to provide energy for approximately the first 20 seconds of muscular activity at which time intramuscular CP is depleted. The CP system operates in the absence of oxygen (it is anaerobic) and can provide energy very quickly during exercise. Collectively stored ATP and CP are known as the ATP-CP or phosphagen system. The total energy yield from the ATP-CP system is low due to the small amount of ATP and CP available in the muscle. The ATP-CP system is used to fuel maximal intensity activities of a duration of 20 seconds or less such as low rep weight training and sprinting. At exhaustion during these types of exercise, fatigue is most likely caused by CP depletion. It should be noted that, even at complete exhaustion, muscle ATP stores do not decrease very much during any type of exercise. After depletion, CP is resynthesized fully in approximately 3-4 minutes (12).

For activity to continue past 20 seconds, the body must rely on other fuel sources to generate ATP. One of these is the breakdown of blood glucose or glycogen (the storage form of glucose found in the muscles and liver), which is called glycolysis.

Aerobic glycolysis is discussed in the previous chapter and is not repeated here. The major difference between aerobic glycolysis (during exercise below LT) and anaerobic glycolysis is the ultimate fate of pyruvate. Whereas in aerobic glycolysis, pyruvate goes into the Krebs cycle to provide more energy, in anaerobic glycolysis pyruvate is converted to lactate. The fate of lactate is discussed in the previous chapter and will not be reproduced here. To briefly recap, the increased rate of lactate production during interval training overwhelms the body's ability to buffer or reuse the lactate and there will be a build-up of lactate in the bloodstream.

Section 4: Fatigue during interval training and the effects of a ketogenic diet

As stated, during exercise above lactate threshold, anaerobic glycolysis leads to a generation of lactic acid. During high intensity exercise of 20-60 seconds duration, lactic acid accumulation is the most likely cause of fatigue (13,14). At fatigue, glycogen levels in the muscle fibers typically remain high (15,16) further suggesting that fatigue is occurring from the buildup of waste products. Thus, it would not appear that a ketogenic diet would directly impair performance during this type of exercise as glycogen availability is not the limiting factor. During repeated bouts of high intensity exercise (i.e. sprint training), depletion of glycogen will become an important factor in fatigue (17).

The effects of glycogen depletion during interval sprint exercise has been thoroughly studied. Most studies (18-24) have reported a decrease in exercise performance during sprint training (at various intensities above LT). The reason for the drop in performance is not immediately apparent.

While on a ketogenic diet, although pH is rapidly normalized, there is a decrease in the body's buffering capacity due to lower bicarbonate levels (19,20,21,25). Since bicarbonate is used to buffer the lactic acid produced from anaerobic glycolysis, fatigue during a single interval may occur faster due to greater lactic acid buildup in the muscle.

This link between blood pH and sprint performance is not supported by at least two studies. Following 5 days of a ketogenic diet, lactate levels do not differ during sprint exercise (20) which indicates no impairment in glycolysis. Additionally, reversal of the acidosis by bicarbonate ingestion (23) did not improve performance in the ketogenic diet group.

Another possible cause of fatigue is a decrease in the muscle's capacity to generate energy through anaerobic glycolysis. The major regulating enzyme of glycolysis (called phosphorylase) breaks stored glycogen down to glucose for the cell to use. Phosphorylase activity decreases when glycogen levels fall below a certain level (about 40 mmol/kg) and this may be a cause of muscular fatigue (24, 26,27).

Indirectly supporting this idea are studies examining the effects of higher than normal glycogen levels on performance and glucose use. It appears that glycogen supercompensation above normal does not increase glycolysis (27-29) compared to normal glycogen levels. Thus, as long as glycogen is above a certain level (40 mmol/kg), glycolysis is not affected. Only when glycogen falls below a certain critical level does performance suffer.

Summary

Interval training refers to any type of activity which alternates periods of high intensity activity with periods of low intensity activity. The adaptations to interval training are similar to what is seen with aerobic exercise but occur in Type II muscle fibers. As glycogen plays a much larger role in energy production during high intensity activity it would be expected that a ketogenic diet will affect performance. Although the exact reason why fatigue occurs more quickly while on a ketogenic diet is unknown, it is well established that performance will decrease.

References Cited

1. Vollestad NK et al. Muscle glycogen depletion patterns in type I and subgroups of Type II fibers during prolonged severe exercise in man. Acta Physiol Scand (1984) 122: 433-441.
2. "Physiology of Sport and Exercise" Jack H. Wilmore and David L. Costill. Human Kinetics Publishers 1994.
3. "Endurance in Sport" Ed. R.J. Shephard & P.-O. Astrand. Blackwell Scientific Publishers 1992.
4. "Exercise Physiology: Human Bioenergetics and it's applications" George A Brooks, Thomas D. Fahey, and Timothy P. White. Mayfield Publishing Company 1996.
5. "The Blood lactate response to exercise" Arthur Weltman Human Kinetics Publishers 1995.
6. Simoneau JA. Adaptations of human skeletal muscle to exercise-training. Int J Obesity (1995) 19 (Suppl 3): S9-S13.
7. Simoneau JA et. al. Human skeletal muscle fiber alteration with high-intensity intermittent training. Eur J Appl Physiol (1985) 54: 250-253.
8. Simoneau JA et. al. Inheritance of human skeletal muscle and anaerobic capacity to adaptation to high-intensity intermittent training. Int J Sports Med (1986) 7:167-171.
9. "Max O2: The Complete Guide to Synergistic Aerobic Training" Jerry Robinson and Frank Carrino, Health for Life 1993.
10. Chwalbinska-Monet J et. al. Threshold increases in plasma growth hormone in relationship to plasma catecholamine and blood lactate concentrations during progressive exercise in endurance-trained athletes. Eur J Appl Physiol (1996) 73: 117-120.
11. Nevill ME et. al. Growth hormone responses to treadmill sprinting in sprint- and endurance-trained athletes. Eur J Appl Physiol (1996) 72: 460-467.
12. "Exercise Metabolism" Ed. Mark Hargreaves. Human Kinetics Publishers 1995.
13. Yu-Yahiro H. Electrolytes and their relationship to normal and abnormal muscle function. Orthopaedic Nursing (1994) 13: 38-40.
14. Allen DG et. al. The role of intracellular acidosis in muscle fatigue. in Advances in Experimental Medicine and Biology 384: Fatigue Ed: Simon C Gandevia et al. Plenum Press 1995.
15. Karlsson J and Saltin B. Diet, muscle glycogen, and endurance performance. J Appl Physiol (1971) 31: 203-206.
16. Sahlin K. Metabolic factors in fatigue. Sports Medicine 13(2): 99-107, 1992.
17. Abernathy PH et. al. Acute and chronic response of skeletal muscle to resistance exercise. Sports Med (1994) 17: 22-38
18. Maughan RJ and Poole DC. The effects of a glycogen-loading regimen on the capacity to perform anaerobic exercise. Eur J Appl Physiol (1981) 46: 211-219.

19. Greenhaff PL et. al. The effects of dietary manipulation on blood acid-base status and the performance of high intensity exercise. Eur J Appl Physiol (1987) 56: 331-337.
20. Greenhaff PL et. al. The effects of a glycogen loading regime on acid-base status and blood lactate concentration before and after a fixed period of high intensity exercise in man. Eur J Appl Physiol (1988) 57: 254-259.
21. Greenhaff PL et. al. The effects of diet on muscle pH and metabolism during high intensity exercise. Eur J Appl Phys (1988) 57: 531- 539.
22. Jenkins DG et. al. The influence of dietary carbohydrate on performance of supramaximal intermittent exercise. Eur J Appl Phys (1993) 67: 309-314.
23. Ball D et. al. The acute reversal of a diet-induced metabolic acidosis does not restore endurance capacity during high-intensity exercise in man. Eur J Appl Phys (1996) 73: 105-112.
24. Casey A et. al. The effect of glycogen availability on power output and the metabolic response to repeated bouts of maximal, isokinetic exercise in man. Eur J Apply Physiol (1996) 72: 249-255.
25. Greenhaff PL et. al. The influence of dietary manipulation on plasma ammonia accumulation during incremental exercise in man. Eur J Apply Physiol (1991) 63: 338-344.
26. Jacobs I. Lactate concentrations after short maximal exercise at various glycogen levels. Acta Physiol Scand (1981) 111: 465-469.
27. Bangsbo J et. al. Elevated muscle glycogen and anaerobic energy production during exhaustive exercise in man. J Physiol (1992) 451: 205-227.
28. Vandenberghe K et. al. No effect of glycogen level on glycogen metabolism during high intensity exercise. Med Sci Sports Exerc (1995) 27: 1278-1283.
29. Hargreaves M Effect of muscle glycogen availability on maximal exercise performance. Eur J Appl Phys (1997) 75: 188-192.

Chapter 20:
Physiology of weight training

Weight training refers generally to any activity where muscles must produce high forces against an external resistance (such as a dumbbell, weight machine, or rubber tubing). Due to the high forces involved, weight training can recruit all muscle fiber types similar to interval training. However the adaptations seen with weight training are significantly different than with interval training and are discussed separately.

Section 1: Adaptations to weight training

In general, the adaptations to resistance training improve the body's ability to generate force. In the laboratory, strength is defined as the amount of force an individual can produce during an isometric contraction (where the muscle contracts but the limbs do not move). This measurement of strength is referred to as maximal voluntary isometric contraction (MVIC). Many lifters are familiar with the term 1 Repetition Maximum (1RM) which is the weight which can be lifted only once in perfect form. For all practical purposes MVIC is equal to 1RM.

As a general rule, MVIC is proportional to a muscle's cross sectional area (CSA, essentially its size). However, there is also a neural component of strength and some have suggested that size and strength can be developed preferentially. Schematically, maximal strength can be represented as (1)

MVIC/1RM = muscle CSA * neural factors

An individual with well-developed neural factors but small muscle CSA would have overall lower maximal force capacity than an individual with the same neural factors but larger muscles. By the same token, an individual with a large muscle CSA but poorly developed neural factors would not achieve his or her strength potential.

Adaptations from strength training occur both centrally, in the nervous system, and peripherally, in the muscle itself (2,3). The major nervous system adaptations to strength training include increased Type IIb fiber recruitment, increased rate coding (the number of signals sent to the muscle), a decrease in activity of non-involved or opposing muscles during activity (called disinhibition), better motor unit synchronization within a single muscle, better synchronization between several muscles involved in the same movement (i.e. pectorals, deltoids and triceps in the bench press), and changes in muscle fiber recruitment as exercises are learned (1, 3-10)

Peripherally, the primary adaptation is an increase in muscle CSA with preferential growth occurring in the Type II fibers (11,12). Growth also occurs in the Type I fibers, simply to a smaller degree. Muscle growth can potentially occur in one of two ways: hypertrophy or hyperplasia. Hypertrophy is an increase in the actual size of the individual muscle fibers while hyperplasia refers to an increase in the total number of muscle fibers (1). While hyperplasia has been repeatedly documented in animals, it is not believed to contribute to human muscle growth to a significant degree (13-15). If hyperplasia were to occur in humans, it would be most likely to occur with heavy eccentric loading and slow movement speeds (13).

Timing for central versus peripheral adaptations

The time course for the different adaptations to strength training has been studied using a variety of testing protocols. During the first four to eight weeks of training, there typically is an increase in MVIC without an increase muscle size. This implies that the majority of changes during this time period are occurring due to the neural adaptations outlined above (6,11,16-18).

In beginning trainees, increases in muscle size do not begin to occur during the first 4-5 week (12,19) and may contribute to further increases in strength for several years. Eventually the muscles reach a genetic upper limit in terms of strength and size which can only be surpassed with the use of growth enhancing drugs (20). Once muscle size has reached this limit, further increases in strength can occur due to improved technique and further neural adaptation (1).

Beginning weight trainers should not expect to see increases in muscle size until the fourth or fifth week of training. Although strength is increasing, the improvements are mainly in the nervous system and simply reflect 'learning' how to lift weights (6,21). Some beginners are unable to recruit the largest Type II muscle fibers which may explain the delay in growth. (1,6,22).

Differences between bodybuilders vs. powerlifters

As stated above, some training authorities have suggested that neural factors and muscle CSA can be developed differentially (23-25). Although little research appears to have directly examined this assumption, we may be able to gain insight from comparisons of the adaptations seen in elite powerlifters and bodybuilders. Powerlifters typically train with low reps often considered the 'neural' training zone ; while bodybuilders typically train with higher reps, often considered the 'growth' zone. Please note that it is impossible to know for certain if the following adaptations are a result of the type of training done or individual genetics. The major differences between powerlifters and bodybuilders appears in table 1. With the exception of total number of muscle fibers, all of the characteristics listed have been shown to change with training.

Overall, it appears that bodybuilding training has the effect of increasing muscular endurance (i.e. capillary density and mitochondrial density) probably due to the higher levels of lactic acid produced with a program of high volume and short rest periods. In essence, typical bodybuilding programs are similar to interval training in terms of the adaptations seen. It has been suggested that bodybuilding training preferentially cause sarcoplasmic hypertrophy, which is growth of non-contractile components such as mitochondria and capillaries, while powerlifting training causes the actual muscle fiber growth (3,23,24,33).

Table 1: A comparison of bodybuilders and powerlifters		
Characteristic	Bodybuilders	Powerlifters
Type IIb fiber size (3,15,26)	Smaller	Larger
Type II fiber number (13,26,27)	Lower	Higher
Capillary density (3,11,15,27,28)	Higher	Lower
Tolerance to lactic acid (29)	Higher	Lower
Sarcoplasmic volume (30)	Higher	Lower
Mitochondrial density (3,15,30,32)	Higher?	Lower
Activate lipolysis during training (13)	Yes	No
Total number of muscle fibers (30)	Same?	Same?

Adaptations in capillary density and mitochondrial volume are affected by the specifics of the training program and are linked to lactic acid levels. Generating high amounts of lactic acid (using long set times, around 60 seconds) may stimulate capillary growth and increases in mitochondria similar to what is seen with aerobic training.

Several authors have suggested 20 to 60 seconds as the ideal time range for muscle growth (23-25) and we might tentatively subdivide that time period into the adaptations listed in table 2.

Table 2: Set time and the possible adaptations seen		
Time/set	#Reps *	Primary Adaptation seen
5-20 seconds	1-5	Neural improvement
20-30 seconds	4-6	Growth of Type IIb fibers
30-45 seconds	12-15	Growth of Type IIa fibers
45-60 seconds	25+	Increased sarcoplasmic volume (glycogen, mitochondria, capillaries, etc).

* assumes 3-5 seconds per repetition.

Section 2: What Causes Muscle Growth?

Weight training results in an alteration in the rate of protein synthesis and degradation (34,35). Following resistance training, levels of 3-methylhistidine (a marker of protein breakdown) increase (34) and protein synthesis increases over the next 24-36 hours (36-38).

Although the exact stimulus for growth is not known, research supports one or more of the following factors as critical to stimulate growth: high tension, metabolic work, eccentric muscle actions and the hormonal response to training (33,39-41). Additionally, sufficient nutrients and protein must be available to support the synthesis of new muscle proteins. Each factor is discussed in further detail.

Tension

For a fiber to adapt, it must be used during an activity (24). Recall from chapter 17 that muscle fiber recruitment is primarily determined by the load which must be lifted. The minimum tension considered to stimulate growth and strength gains is roughly 60% of 1RM. Recall also that muscle fibers continue to be recruited up to about 80-85% of 1RM at which time further force production occurs through rate coding. Therefore optimal Type II muscle fiber involvement will occur with loads between 60-85% of 1RM (approximately 6-20 reps). However, simply recruiting a fiber is not sufficient to make it adapt.

Metabolic work

Once a muscle fiber is recruited, it must do more work than normal for adaptations to occur (40). Recent research has found that muscle growth is greater with longer sets and that the metabolic changes (increased blood metabolites such as lactic acid, phosphate, etc) seen with longer set times may be part of the growth stimulus (42-44). It has also been suggested that increased levels of lactic acid may play a role in the growth stimulus possibly explaining why sets of 20-60 seconds (in the anaerobic glycolysis range) seem to give better growth than shorter sets (45).

Tension plus metabolic work: the time under tension hypothesis

Factors 1 and 2 combined make up the time under tension (TUT) hypothesis of growth (39,46). TUT simply says that fibers must develop sufficient tension for a sufficient time period to adapt. While the exact amount of time necessary to stimulate growth is not known and will most likely vary from muscle fiber to muscle fiber, it has been suggested that set times between 20-60 seconds (corresponding with anaerobic glycolysis) be used for one or more sets (23,24,46). Even within the context of high tension for sufficient time, growth is not guaranteed. We also need to consider how the time under tension is spent. Although muscles only contract, depending on the relationship between the force generated, and the load which must be lifted, one of three types of muscle actions can occur.

The first is referred to as a concentric muscle action, where the muscle shortens while contracting, lifting the weight. The second is isometric muscle action, where the muscle does not change length while contracting, and the weight does not move. The third is eccentric muscle action, where the muscle lengthens while contracting, and the weight is lowered.

Performing 40 seconds of pure concentric work is not the same as performing 40 seconds of isometric work is not the same as performing 40 seconds of pure eccentric work. The third part of the growth stimulus is thought to be the eccentric muscle action, which has different characteristics than concentric or isometric actions.

An eccentric muscle action

Numerous studies have have compared concentric only training to eccentric only training. Most find that the eccentric training groups experiences more growth even when the total number of repetitions (time under tension) performed by both groups is identical (2,47-51) .

There are a number of physiological differences between the performance of concentric and eccentric muscle actions, summarized below. In general, force capacity during an eccentric muscle action is approximately 30-40% greater than that during a concentric muscle action (8,9). That is, if 100 pounds can be lifted by a muscle, typically 130 to 140 pounds can be lowered.

Additionally, Type II muscle fibers (which show the greatest amount of growth) are preferentially recruited during eccentric actions (8,9). As Type II fibers have a greater force production capacity than Type I, this may partly explain the greater strength seen during eccentric training.

During eccentric muscle actions, fewer muscle fibers are recruited (8,9). This means that the fibers recruited receive more overload per fiber (54) which may explain the preferential growth seen. Finally, eccentric but not concentric lifting stimulates protein synthesis (9).

If eccentric actions are the primary stimulus for growth, the question arises of why perform concentric (lifting) muscle actions at all? First and foremost, concentric actions are responsible for most of the metabolic work during training contributing 84% of the total metabolic work (49). Additionally, concentric strength limits eccentric strength (55). That is, you can only lower as much weight as you can lift unless you have partners lift the weight for you, so that it can be lowered. This implies that periods of concentric only training (to improve concentric strength capacity) may be useful so that more weight may be used during the eccentric portion of the lift.

A final observation about eccentric training is that heavy eccentric loading is associated with most of the muscle soreness from training (56). Twenty-four to thirty-six hours after training, soreness occurs and is called delayed onset muscle soreness (DOMS). DOMS is thought to reflect direct mechanical damage (small tears) in the muscle fibers (57). Following eccentric induced trauma, the muscle undergoes an adaptation to prevent further damage and DOMS from the same overload (58).

It has also been suggested that tears to the cell membrane allow calcium to flow into the cell, activating enzymes which break down protein (59,60). Full recovery from this type of eccentric trauma is completed with 4-7 days suggesting that the same muscle should not be worked any more frequently than that, at least not with heavy eccentric contractions.

Another possible mechanism by which eccentric muscle actions may be involved in muscle growth is through satellite cell proliferation (61). Satellite cells are a type of cell located on the surface of muscle fibers involved in muscle cell regrowth.

In response to both hormonal and mechanical stimuli (such as muscle damage), satellite cells become active to help with tissue repair. In animal models, satellite cell activity is involved in muscle hyperplasia (generation of new muscle fibers). Although hyperplasia does not appear to play a role in human growth (14), heavy eccentric muscle actions may have the capacity to stimulate satellite cell proliferation by damaging the cell and causing a local release of insulin-like growth factor 1 (IGF-1) (61-63).

All of the above information (tension, metabolic work, and eccentric induced damage) has led to the development of the following schema, which requires further validation, for muscle damage and growth. (59)

1. Depending on the force requirements, a given number of muscle fibers are recruited.

2. The recruited muscle fibers fatigue from performing metabolic work.

3. Upon reaching fatigue, individual fibers reach a point, termed ischemic rigor, where they physically 'lock up' due to insufficient ATP. This 'locking up' occurs during the concentric part of the movement

4. The subsequent eccentric muscle action causes small tears to occur in the muscle, stimulating remodeling and growth.

The schema presented above fits well with the TUT hypothesis. To stimulate the maximum number of fibers requires performing a high set time with a high tension (within a range of 20-60 seconds). As each fiber has a different fatigue time (based on its physiological characteristics), each will require a relatively shorter or longer set time to lock up and be damaged. As only the fibers which are fatigued and damaged will adapt by the subsequent eccentric contraction, varying set times may be necessary for optimal growth (24).

The hormonal response to weight training

Weight training affects levels of many hormones in the human body depending on factors such as order of exercise, loads, number of sets, number of repetitions, etc. The primary hormones which are affected by weight training are growth hormone (GH), testosterone, the catecholamines, and cortisol.

The hormonal response to exercise is thought to be of secondary importance to the factors listed above in terms of muscle growth. With the exception of testosterone, the hormonal response to weight training primarily affects fuel availability and utilization (64).

GH is a peptide hormone released from the hypothalamus in response to many different stimuli including sleep and breath-holding (65). At the levels seen in humans, its main role is to mobilize fat and decrease carbohydrate and protein utilization (66). The primary role of GH on muscle growth is most likely indirect by increasing release of IGF-1 from the liver (66).

GH release during weight training appears to be related to lactic acid levels and the highest GH response is seen with moderate weights (~75% of 1RM), multiple long sets (3-4 sets of 10-12 repetitions, about 40-60 seconds per set) with short rest periods (60-90 seconds). Studies using this type of protocol (generally 3X10 RM with a 1' rest period) have repeatedly shown increases in GH levels in men (67,68) and women (69,70) and may be useful for fat loss due to the lipolytic (fat mobilizing) actions of GH. Multiple sets of the same exercise are required for GH release (70).

Testosterone is frequently described as the 'male' hormone although women possess testosterone as well (at about 1/10th the level of men or less) (1). Testosterone's main role in muscle growth is by directly stimulating protein synthesis (65,71). Increases in testosterone occur in response to the use of basic exercises (squats, deadlifts, bench presses), heavy weights (85% of 1RM and higher), multiple short sets (3 sets of 5 repetitions, about 20-30 seconds per set) and long rest periods (3-5 minutes). Studies have found a regimen of 3X5RM with 3' rest to increase testosterone significantly in men (67,68,72) but not in women (69). It is unknown whether the transient increase in testosterone following training has an impact on muscle growth.

IGF-1 is a hormone released from the liver, most likely in response to increases in GH levels (62). However, the small increases in GH seen with training do not appear to affect IGF-1 levels (73). More likely, IGF-1 is released from damaged muscle cells (due to eccentric muscle actions) and acts locally to stimulate growth (42,63).

Cortisol is a catabolic hormone meaning that it breaks down larger substances to smaller (i.e. triglycerides to fatty acids and glycerol, and proteins to amino acids). It is released from the adrenal cortex in response to stress such as exercise or starvation. Cortisol may have a role in the tissue remodeling seen with heavy resistance training as it increases protein breakdown at high levels (1). Increases in cortisol tend to mirror the increases seen in growth hormone (74) and it has been suggested that the increase in cortisol is a necessary part of the muscle remodeling stimulus. (65,70) The basis for this is that the breakdown of tissue is necessary to stimulate a rebuilding of that same tissue.

The major role of catecholamines (adrenaline and noradrenaline) is fuel utilization. As described previously, increases in levels of adrenaline and noradrenaline increase liver output of glucose, mobilize fat from adipose tissue, and stimulate glycogen breakdown in muscles. High intensity weight training with multiple exercises increases catecholamine levels similar to that seen in sprint training (65,75). The overall effect of the rise in catecholamine levels is an increase in blood glucose and stimulation of fat breakdown.

Adequate nutrients and energy

Once muscle growth is stimulated, the final requirement for growth to actually occur is an excess of nutrients and energy (63). Reduced calorie diets put the body in a systemically catabolic (tissue breakdown) condition due to changes in hormone levels. Low-calorie diets cause a decrease in growth promoting hormones such as insulin and thyroid while increasing growth inhibiting hormones such as adrenaline, glucagon, and cortisol (63). Similarly, overfeeding causes and increase in those same hormones and an increase in lean body mass as well as fat (76). It is generally impossible, except for beginners or those returning from a layoff, for most individuals to gain muscle while losing fat at the same time.

Simply put, the body must either be systemically catabolic (for fat loss) or systemically anabolic (for muscle gain). Attempting to gain significant amounts of muscle while losing fat at the same time or vice versa tends to minimize the results of either goal. Most individuals find that focusing on either fat loss or muscle growth yields the best results. The CKD is somewhat unique among diets in that it couples a catabolic phase (at below maintenance calories) with an anabolic phase (at above maintenance calories), meaning that the potential to gain muscle and lose fat simultaneously exists. This topic is discussed in greater detail in chapter 12.

Progressive overload: the ultimate determinant of growth

Irrespective of the above factors, the ultimate key to larger and stronger muscles is progressive overload. Individuals have achieved growth using from 1 rep to 50 reps with a number of different protocols, so it is impossible to say unequivocally that there is a 'best' program for stimulating growth. As long as stress continues to be applied to the body and muscles are forced to work against progressively greater loads, assuming adequate recovery and nutrients are provided, growth should occur in the long run. The above discussion is an attempt to optimize the nature of the growth stimulus. A summary of the requirements for growth appear in table 3.

Table 3: Summary of training requirements for growth
1. Use weights between 60-85% of maximum (roughly 6-20 reps) 2. Use a controlled eccentric (lowering) movement. 3. Apply proper progressive overload. 4. Supply adequate nutrients and allow adequate recovery 5. Train a muscle once every 4-7 days.

Section 3: Energy Metabolism during weight training

During muscular contraction above 20% of 1RM, blood flow to the muscle is blocked (90) and energy production comes solely from anaerobic sources such as the breakdown of ATP-CP and glycogen depending on the length of the set (see chapter 19 for more details). Weight training cannot use fat for fuel during a set. However, fat breakdown increases during heavy weight training (91,92) indicating that fat may be used during recovery between sets to replenish ATP. Increases in fat breakdown during weight training are most likely stimulated by the hormonal response to training, especially increases in levels of adrenaline and noradrenaline.

Fatigue during weight training is addressed in section 4 based on energy systems. Sets of 1-5 repetitions, as typically used by powerlifters and lasting 20 seconds or less, are discussed separately from sets of 20-60 seconds, typically used by bodybuilders. The metabolism of both energy systems are discussed in the previous chapter and are not be repeated here.

Section 4: Fatigue and weight training

As discussed in chapter 18, the impact of a total lack of carbohydrates on endurance training is very consistent: performance is maintained or improved at low intensities (below 75% of maximum heart rate) but decreased at higher intensities (75-85% of maximum heart rate or approximately the lactate threshold). However, the effects of a ketogenic diet on weight training are not as well established.

Weight lifting recruits all three fiber types. Although Type I fibers have little anaerobic potential for energy production, all fiber types will produce energy anaerobically (through the degradation of ATP-CP and glycogen) during weight training. Thus, a carbohydrate-free diet should negatively effect performance.

Fatigue during weight training can have one of three potential causes: metabolic (related to depletion of fuel or accumulation of waste products), neural (due to impairment in nervous system activation of the muscle), and non-metabolic (everything else).

Metabolic causes of fatigue

The potential metabolic causes of fatigue during weight training depend on the length of the set being performed and the energy system which is being primarily used. During very short weight training sets (less than 20 seconds), the metabolic cause of fatigue is most likely depletion of creatine phosphate (CP). Although ATP never drops more than 20% below resting values even at exhaustion (93), CP may be fully depleted after 20 seconds of maximal intensity exercise. Although CP may be 96% resynthesized within 3 minutes (55), force production capacity frequently takes longer to recover to normal, as much as 4-5 minutes (8). This suggests an additional component of fatigue during this type of exercise (see neural fatigue below).

Lactic acid is not generated to any great degree during exercise of this short duration and is unlikely to be a cause of fatigue. However, in general, lactic acid impairs muscle fiber recruitment (8) which has implications for warm-ups and workout design. Raising lactic acid with high repetition sets or high intensity aerobics will impair performance during short rep sets. To the contrary, moving to your heaviest weights (and lowest rep sets) first and then performing high reps sets afterwards will prevent high lactic acid levels from causing early fatigue. This is further discussed in the section on proper warm-ups and weight training systems.

For longer weight training sets of 20-60 seconds, anaerobic glycolysis is activated relying primarily on glycogen breakdown for ATP production. Intramuscular triglycerides may also play a role in energy production, especially when short rest periods are used (91). However, fatigue can occur even when glycogen stores are still fairly high. This indicates that, in general, there is another cause of fatigue during weight training, most likely the buildup of metabolites that affect force production (90).

During weight training of 20-60 seconds duration, the exact cause of fatigue is not known (53). It is most likely related to buildup of lactic acid, H+ and other metabolites within the cell that directly affect force production. However, individuals suffering from McArdle's disease (a total inability to use glycogen for fuel) show fatigue during high intensity exercise with no change in lactic acid levels suggesting other causes of fatigue (94).

Increases in H+ lowers muscle and blood pH both of which inhibit force production in the muscle (95,96). During exercise, lactate and H+ is removed from the muscle cell where it can be buffered in the bloodstream by bicarbonate and myoglobin (97). Lowering blood pH decreases performance (98), while increasing the buffering capacity of the blood by ingesting sodium bicarbonate improves performance (95,99,100).

Neural fatigue

In addition to the metabolic causes of fatigue discussed above, there is also a neural component of fatigue. When, a 'diverting' activity (such as light activity of another limb) is performed in-between bouts of high intensity activity , force output is maintained at a higher level than if the diverting activity is not performed (101,102). This has been attributed to 'distracting' the nervous system, allowing faster recovery.

During a weight training session, alternating exercises with different bodyparts (i.e. one set for legs, one set for chest) allows for greater recovery because of this diverting activity (as well as giving more rest time between sets). Physical therapists have long known that the contraction of one muscle (for example the biceps) causes the antagonist muscle (in this case, the triceps) to relax. So alternating sets for opposing muscle groups (i.e. one set for biceps, rest, one set for triceps) may allow greater force production and decrease fatigue (103).

Other causes of fatigue

Finally, there are possible non-metabolic causes of fatigue. During muscular contraction, signals are sent from the brain to the muscle, eventually reaching the muscle fibers through a structure called the sarcoplasmic reticulum (SR). Normal SR function may be impaired during exercise and this impairment may be related to a loss of intracellular potassium (71,104,105). Muscle potassium levels are decreased on a ketogenic diet as a result of glycogen depletion (104) further implicating glycogen depletion as one source of fatigue on a ketogenic diet.

Additionally a glycogen-SR complex has been proposed (106) such that depletion of glycogen may physically impair conduction of signals to the muscle. Finally, the intracellular dehydration seen with a ketogenic diet may also affect strength levels (52,104,107,108).

Summary

Regardless of the ultimate cause of fatigue during weight training, glycogen depletion has the potential to decrease performance through one of several mechanisms. Until more research is done, we can only speculate as to the exact cause of fatigue. For the purpose of the ketogenic diet, the exact cause of fatigue is more an academic question than a practical one. It is a basic physiological fact that Type II fibers require glycogen to function optimally. Therefore, a SKD will eventually decrease performance as well as inhibit muscle growth. Individuals who wish to weight train on a ketogenic diet will have to consume carbohydrates at some point.

Section 5: Effects of the Ketogenic Diet on Weight Training

Relatively few studies have examined the effects of carbohydrate depletion on resistance training. Typically, researchers measure maximal force production during a single isometric contraction or muscular endurance during multiple rep sets during isokinetic exercise. Isokinetic exercise machines are special types of weight training equipment that control speed of movement. They are typically not found outside the laboratory and may not be an applicable model to normal strength training.

As a general rule, the maximum amount of force generated ultimately depends on Type II muscle fibers while muscular endurance depends more on Type I fibers. The effects of glycogen depletion on force production is fiber type specific. Glycogen depletion of only Type I fibers does not impair maximum force but decreases muscular endurance as would be expected (109,110). Glycogen depletion in both Type I and Type II fibers causes a decrease in both maximal force production and muscular endurance (109). In contrast, one study found that depleting both muscle fiber types of glycogen to approximately 40 mmol/kg did not cause a decrease in force production or muscular endurance (111).

It is difficult to draw conclusions with regards to strength training from these studies as performance was only measured during a single set. Multiple sets of weight training are much more likely to be affected by glycogen availability. As discussed in the section on interval training, glycolysis may be impaired when glycogen levels fall below a critical level (40 mmol/kg). Although data on strength training is lacking to verify or deny this concept, many individuals report fatigue during weight training sessions performed later in the week, so something is occurring.

Not all lifters report this occurrence though so it may simply be individual, related to the total amount of training done during the week. Individuals who perform a high volume of training (number of sets) during the early part of the week tend to report a drop in performance compared to those who do not. This suggests that the fatigue is local (i.e. glycogen depletion, dehydration, potassium loss) rather than systemic (i.e. changes in blood pH) as discussed in section 4.

Long term ketogenic diet and high intensity activity

At this time, only one study (112) has examined high intensity exercise performance after long term adaptation to a ketogenic diet, finding no decrease in performance. As performance at higher intensities are generally determined by non-oxidative metabolism, it seems unlikely that long term adaptation to a ketogenic diet would have an effect on exercise of this type. Since no research on this topic exists, any long term effects on performance are purely speculative at this time. The main determinant in performance in weight training is probably muscle glycogen levels. Thus, the amount of work that can be performed in a given workout will depend on starting muscle glycogen levels.

Summary

When muscle glycogen falls to extremely low levels (about 40 mmol/kg), anaerobic exercise performance may be negatively affected. Individuals following a ketogenic diet who wish to lift weights or perform sprint training must make modifications by consuming carbohydrates for optimal performance as discussed in chapter 10 through 12.

During long term ketogenic diets, muscle glycogen maintains at about 70 mmol/kg (113-115) leaving a 'safety factor' of about 30 mmol/kg at which time glycolysis will most likely be impaired.

Section 6: Other Topics

Beyond the adaptations and effects of the ketogenic diet discussed above, there are several other topics regarding weight training that need to be discussed. This includes the effects of combining strength and endurance training, gender differences, and the effect of detraining.

Combining strength and endurance training

Many individuals wish to combine strength and endurance training in their exercise program. Whether it's a pre-contest bodybuilder looking to shed fat or an individual looking for basic fitness, the combination of weight and aerobic training is a topic of interest. Keep in mind that the general adaptations to aerobic/interval training are to make muscle fibers more aerobic and enduring while the adaptations to weight training are to make the fibers larger and stronger. These two adaptations are somewhat at odds with one another (77). Therefore, we might expect the combination of both types of training to impair overall adaptations.

Several studies have examined the physiological effects of various combinations of aerobic exercise with resistance training. With one exception, these studies find a decrease in the strength gains seen in individuals performing both resistance training and high intensity aerobics (78-80). The decrease in strength typically occurs after 8 weeks. However, these studies have problems that need to be addressed.

First, the combined training groups (endurance and strength) typically train their legs more total days than either the strength or endurance only groups. So, the interference effects may simply reflect local overtraining (78). One recent study examined this possibility, having subjects perform strength and aerobic training a total of three days per week so that all groups only trained three days per week total (81). No decrease in strength improvements were seen which further suggests local overtraining of the legs as the cause of the strength impairments.

Second, the studies cited used heavy resistance training in combination with interval training (as a football player or rugby player might be expected to train) (78-80). High intensity aerobic training recruits Type II muscle fibers, causing them to become smaller and more aerobic. The body can generally only adapt maximally in one direction or another so it may simply be that combining heavy strength training with HIGH intensity aerobic training is the problem.

In direct contrast to the data presented above, when endurance athletes (cyclists and runners) perform heavy resistance training, endurance performance improves (82,83). This further supports that the studies above were simply measuring overtraining rather than true interference effects of strength and aerobic training.

No one has examined the effects of combining weight training with low intensity aerobic training only. Anecdotally, many individuals find that a small amount of aerobic training, perhaps 20 minutes, two to three times per week at a low intensity (heart rate at least 15 beats/minute below lactate threshold) may aid in recovery by improving blood flow and general conditioning (23). As well, individuals trying to gain weight find that a small amount of aerobics can stimulate hunger.

Individuals wishing to maximize performance in the weight room are discouraged from performing extensive amounts of aerobic training, especially at high intensities (77). However, small amounts of aerobic training should not be detrimental, and may even aid in recovery and overall performance.

Gender Differences

Under a microscope, there is no physiological difference between women's muscle and men's. By the same token, men and women's muscle respond similarly to training. When placed on the same training program, women respond as well if not better than men do (84-86). Women can gain muscle in the same fashion as male trainees do, just not to the same levels typically seen in males (12,19).

The largest difference between male and female trainees is in the ultimate level of muscular development which can occur. The majority of this difference in trainability is due to differences in testosterone levels. Women have lower levels of testosterone at rest (65,86) and do not show the same increase from training as men (1,69).

There is preliminary data that women should be trained differently during the different phases of the menstrual cycle. However, this requires more research (87). For the time being, there is no evidence that men and women should follow different training programs (84).

Detraining

For various reasons, athletes frequently have to take time away from training and a discussion of detraining is necessary. The deadaptations from stopping weight workouts are essentially the opposite of the initial adaptations. Recall that the initial adaptations to strength training are neural with adaptations in the muscle occurring later. Detraining occurs in the reverse order. Maximal strength begins to drop within a week but muscle size does not begin to decrease for at least 2 weeks (18,88) reflecting a decrease in the neural aspects of strength (13,18).

This has implications for any individual who must cease training, including pre-contest bodybuilders. Individuals who must stop training for some time simply need to realize that the initial drop in strength is neural and not related to a loss of muscle mass. As little as one heavy weight training session has been shown to maintain strength and size for 8 weeks (89).

For pre-contest bodybuilders, as the contest gets closer and dieting begins to take its toll, many individuals will have to reduce their training weights. As long as training is maintained at high loads until 2 weeks before the contest, no muscle mass should be lost. In fact, many individuals find that they increase muscle size during the last two weeks of the contest as muscles fully repair.

Finally, during detraining, growth hormone and testosterone increase while cortisol decreases possibly explaining the maintenance of muscle size with no training (88). Also, strength gains during detraining are better maintained if eccentric contractions have been performed during training (48). Therefore, individuals who must take time off may want to slightly overtrain themselves (with an emphasis on eccentric muscle actions) prior to their layoff. The hormonal response during detraining should help to maintain and perhaps even increase size and strength.

References Cited

1. "Strength and Power in Sport" Ed. P.V. Komi Blackwell Scientific Publications 1992.
2. Hortobagyi T et. al. Greater initial adaptations to submaximal muscle lengthening than maximal shortening. J Appl Physiol (1996) 81: 1677-1682.
3. Kraemer WJ et. al. Physiological adaptations to resistance exercise: Implications for athletic conditioning. Sports Med (1988) 6:246-256.
4. Ploutz L et. al. Effect of resistance exercise on muscle use during exercise. J Appl Physiol (1994) 76: 1675-1681.
5. Fleck S and Kraemer W. Resistance Training: basic Principles (Part 3 of 4). Physician and Sportsmedicine (1988) 16 May: 63-72.
6. Sale D. Neural adaptations to resistance training. Med Sci Sports Exerc (1988) 20 (Suppl) 20: S135-S145.
7. Behm DG. Neuromuscular implications and adaptations of resistance training. J Strength and Cond Res (1995) 9: 264-274.
8. "Neuromechanical basis of kinesiology" Roger M. Enoka. Human Kinetics Publishers 1994.
9. "Skeletal muscle: Form and Function" Alan J. McComas. Human Kinetics Publishers 1996.
10. Bernardi M et. al. Motor unit recruitment strategy changes with skill acquisition. Eur J Appl Physiol (1996) 74: 52-59.
11. Kraemer WJ et. al. Strength and Power training: Physiological mechanisms of adaptation. Exercise and Sports Science Reviews (1997) 363-397.
12. Staron RS et. al. Skeletal muscle adaptations during early phase of heavy-resistance training in men and women. J Appl Physiol (1994) 76: 1247-1255.
13. Abernathy PH et. al. Acute and chronic response of skeletal muscle to resistance exercise. Sports Med (1994) 17: 22-38
14. Antonio J and Gonyea WJ. Skeletal muscle fiber hyperplasia. Med Sci Sports Exerc (1993) 25: 1333-1345.
15. Fleck S and Kraemer W. Resistance Training: basic Principles (Part 2 of 4). Physician and

Sportsmedicine (1988) 16 April: 108-117.

16. Sale DG et. al. Hypertrophy without increased isometric strength after weight training. Eur J Appl Physiol (1992) 64: 51-55.

17. Komi PV. Training of muscle strength and power: interactions of neuromotoric, hypertrophic, and mechanical factors. Int J Sports Med (1986) 7 (suppl): 10-15.

18. Houston ME et. al. Muscle performance, morphology, and metabolic capacity during strength training and detraining: a one leg model. Eur J Appl Physiol (1983) 51: 25-35.

19. Staron RS et. al. Muscle hypertrophy and fast fiber type conversions in heavy resistance-trained women. Eur J Appl Physiol (1990) 60: 71-79.

20. Alway SE et. al. Effects of resistance training on elbow flexors of highly competitive bodybuilders. J Appl Physiol (1992) 72: 1512-1521.

21. Hakkinen K and Komi P. Training-induced changes in neuromuscular performance under voluntary and reflex conditions. Eur J Appl Physiol (1986) 55: 147-155.

22. Ruther CL et. al. Hypertrophy, resistance training, and the nature of skeletal muscle activation. J Strength and Cond Res (1995) 9: 155-159.

23. "Supertraining: Special Training for Sporting Excellence" Mel Siff and Yuri Verkoshanksy, School of Mechanical Engineering Press 1993.

24. "Science and practice of strength training" Vladimir Zatsiorsky, Human Kinetics 1995.

25. "Program Design: Choosing sets, reps, loads, tempo and rest periods" Paul Chek, Paul Chek Seminars 1996.

26. Tesch PA and Larson L. Muscle hypertrophy in bodybuilders. Eur J Appl Physiol (1982) 49: 301-306.

27. Tesch P. Skeletal adaptations consequent to long-term heavy resistance exercise. Med Sci Sports Exerc (1988) 20 (Suppl): S132-S134.

28. Tesch PA et. al. Muscle capillary supply and fiber type characteristics in weight and power lifters".J Appl Physiol (1984) 56: 35-38.

29. Kraemer WJ et. al. Physiologic response to heavy-resistance exercise with very short rest periods. Int J Sports Med (1987) 8: 247-252.

30. MacDougall KD et. al. Muscle ultrastructural characteristics of elite powerlifters and bodybuilders. Eur J Appl Physiol (1982) 48: 117-126.

31. Kuipers H and Keizer HA. Overtraining in elite athletes: Review and directions for the future. Sports Med (1988) 6: 79-92.

32. Alway SE et. al. Functional and structural adaptations in skeletal muscle of trained athletes. J Appl Physiol (1988) 64: 1114-1120.

33. Jones DA. Strength of skeletal muscle and the effects of training. British Med Bulletin (1992) 48: 592-604.

34. Viru A. Mobilisation of structural proteins during exercise. Sports Medicine (1987) 4: 95-128.

35. Yarasheski KE et. al. Acute effects of resistance exercise on muscle protein synthesis rate in young and elderly men and women. Am J Physiol (1993) 265:E210-E214.

36. Chesley A et al. Changes in human muscle protein synthesis after resistance exercise. J Appl Physiol (1992) 73:1383-8.

37. Phillips SM et al. Mixed muscle protein synthesis and breakdown after resistance exercise in humans. Am J Physiol (1997) 273:E99-107.

38. MacDougall JD et. al. The time course of elevated muscle protein synthesis following heavy resistance exercise. Can J Appl Physiol (1995) 20: 480-6.

39. Jones DA and Rutherford OM. Human muscle strength training: the effects of three different regimes and the nature of the resultant changes. J Physiol Lond (1987) 391: 1-11.

40. Goldberg AL et. al. Mechanism of work-induced hypertrophy of skeletal muscle. Med Sci Sports Exerc (1975) 7: 185-198.

41. Booth FW. Perspectives on molecular and cellular exercise physiology. J Appl Physiol (1988) 65: 1461-1471.

42. Smith R and Rutherford OM. The role of metabolites in strength training I. A comparison of eccentric and concentric contractions. Eur J apply Physiol (1995) 71: 332-336.

43. Smith R and Rutherford OM. The role of metabolites in strength training II. Short versus long isometric contractions. Eur J Appl Physiol (1995) 71: 337-347.

44. Rooney KJ et. al. Fatigue contributes to the strength training stimulus. Med Sci Sports Exerc (1994) 26: 1160-1164.

45. Hunt T. Can wound healing be a paradigm for tissue repair? Med Sci Sports Exerc (1994) 26: 755-758.

46. "Current trends in strength training" Charles Poliquin Dayton Publishing Group 1997.

47. Hortobagyi T et. al. Adaptive responses to muscle lengthening and shortening in humans. J Apply Physiol (1996) 80: 765-772.

48. Colliander EB and Tesch PA. Effects of detraining following short term resistance training on eccentric and concentric muscle strength. Acta Physiol Scand (1992) 144: 23-29.

49. Dudley GA et. al. Influence of eccentric actions on the metabolic cost of resistance exercise. Aviat Space Environ Med (1991) 62: 678-682.

50. Hather BM et. al. Influence of eccentric contractions on skeletal muscle adaptations to resistance training. Acta Physiol Scand (1991) 143: 177-185.

51. Armstrong RB Mechanisms of exercise-induced muscle fibre injury. Sports Med (1991) 12: 184-207.

52. Physiology of Sport and Exercise" Jack H. Wilmore and David L. Costill. Human Kinetics Publishers 1994.

53. "Exercise Physiology: Human Bioenergetics and it's applications" George A Brooks, Thomas D. Fahey, and Timothy P. White. Mayfield Publishing Company 1996.

54. Teague BN and Schwane JA. Effect of intermittent eccentric contractions on symptoms of muscle microinjury. Med Sci Sports Exerc (1995) 27: 1378-1384.

55. Hortobagyi T and Katch FI. Role of concentric force in limiting improvements in muscular strength and hypertrophy. J Appl Physiol (1990) 68: 650-658.

56. Kuipers H. Exercise-induced muscle damage. Int J Sports Med (1994) 15: 132-135.

57. Clarkson PM and Newham DH. Associations between muscle soreness, damage and fatigue. Advances in Experimental Medicine and Biology 384: Fatigue Ed: Simon C Gandevia et al. Plenum Press 1995.

58. Clarkson P and Tremblay I. Exercise-induced muscle damage, repair, and adaptation in humans. J Appl Physiol (1988) 65: 1-6.

59. Friden J and Lieber RL. Structural and mechanical basis of exercise-induced muscle injury. Med Sci Sports Exerc (1992) 24: 521-530.

60. Colliander EB and Tesch PA. Effects of eccentric and concentric muscle actions in resistance training. Acta Physiol Scand (1990) 140: 31-39.

61. White T and Esser K. Satellite cell and growth factor involvement in skeletal muscle growth. Med Sci Sports Exerc (1989) 21 (Suppl): S158-S163.

62. Cooper D. Evidence for and mechanisms of exercise modulation of growth - an overview. Med Sci Sports Exerc (1994) 26: 733-740.

63. DeVol DL et. al. Activation of insulin-like work-induced skeletal muscle growth. Am J Physiol (1990) 259: E89-E95.

64. Borer K. Neurohumoral mediation of exercise-induced growth. Med Sci Sports Exerc (1994) 26:741-754.
65. Kraemer W. Endocrine responses to resistance exercise. Med Sci Sports Exerc (1989) 20 (suppl): S152-S157.
66. Rogol AD. Growth hormone: physiology, therapeutic use, and potential for abuse. Exercise and Sports Science Reviews (1989) 17: 353-377.
67. Hakkinen K and Pakarinen A. Acute hormonal responses to two different fatiguing heavy-resistance protocols in male athletes. J Appl Physiol (1993) 74: 882-887.
68. Kraemer WJ et. al. Hormonal and growth factor responses to heavy resistance exercise protocols. J Appl Physiol (1990) 69: 1442-1450.
69. Kraemer WJ et. al. Changes in hormonal concentrations following different heavy resistance exercise protocols in women. J Appl Physiol (1993) 75: 594-604.
70. Mulligan SE et. al. Influence of resistance exercise volume on serum growth hormone and cortisol concentrations in women. J Strength Cond Res (1996) 10: 256-262.
71. Griggs RC et. al. Effect of testosterone on muscle mass and protein synthesis. J Appl Physiol (1989) 66: 498-503.
72. Schwab R et. al. Acute effects of different intensities of weight lifting on serum testosterone. Med Sci Sports Exerc (1993) 25: 1381-1385.
73. Kraemer WJ et. al. Responses of IGF-1 to endogenous increases in growth hormone after heavy-resistance exercise. J Appl Physiol (1995) 79:1310-1315.
74. Kraemer WJ et. al. Effects of different heavy-resistance exercise protocols on plasma b-endorphin concentrations. J Appl Physiol (1993) 74: 450-459.
75. Guezennec Y et. al. Hormone and metabolite response to weight-lifting training sessions. Int J Sports Med (1986) 7: 100-105.
76. Jebb SA et. al. Changes in macronutrient balance during over- and underfeeding assessed by 12-d continuous whole body calorimetry. Am J Clin Nutr (1996) 64: 259-266.
77. Jacksin CGR et. al. Skeletal muscle fiber area alterations in two opposing modes of resistance-exercise training in the same individual. Eur J Appl Physiol (1990) 61: 37-41.
78. Kraemer WJ et. al. Compatibility of high intensity strength and endurance training on hormonal and skeletal adaptations. J Appl Physiol (1995) 78: 976-989.
79. Hennessy LC et. al. The interference effects of training for strength and endurance simultaneously. J Strength Cond Res (1994) 8: 12-19.
80. Hickson RC Interference of strength development by simultaneously training for strength and endurance. Eur J Appl Physiol (1980) 45: 255-269.
81. McCarthy JP. Compatability of adaptive responses with combining strength and endurance training. Med Sci Sports Exerc (1995) 27: 429-436.
82. Hickson RC Strength training effects on aerobic power and short-term endurance. Med Sci Sports Exerc (1980) 12: 336-339.
83. Hickson RC Potential for strength and endurance training to amplify endurance performance. J Appl Phys (1988) 65: 2285-2290.
84. Holloway JB and Baechle TR. Strength training for female athletes: A review of selected aspects. Sports Medicine (1990) 9: 216-228.
85. O'Hagen FT et. al. Response to resistance training in young women and men. Int J Sports Med (1995) 16: 314-321.
86. Hakkinen K et. al. Neuromuscular adaptations and serum hormones in women during short term intensive strength training. Eur J Appl Physiol (1992) 64: 106-11.
87. Reis E et. al. Frequency variations of strength training sessions triggered by the phases of

the menstrual cycle. Int J Sports Med (1995) 16: 545-550.

98. Hortobaygi T et. al. The effects of detraining on power athletes. Med Sci Sports Exerc (1993) 25: 929-935.

89. "Designing Resistance Training Programs, 2nd edition" W. Kraemer and S. Fleck, Human Kinetics 1996.

90. Sahlin K. Metabolic factors in fatigue. Sports Medicine (1992) 13: 99-107.

91. Tesch PA et. al. Muscle metabolism during intense, heavy resistance exercise. Eur J Appl Physiol (1986) 55: 362-366.

92. Essen-Gustavsson B and Tesch P. Glycogen and triglyceride utilization in relation to muscle metabolic characteristics in men performing heavy-resistance exercise. Eur J Appl Physiol (1990) 61: 5-10.

93. "Exercise Metabolism" Ed. Mark Hargreaves. Human Kinetics Publishers 1995.

94. Wagenmakers AJM et. al. Metabolism of Branched-Chain Amino Acids and Ammonia During Exercise: Clues from McArdle's Disease. Int J Sports Med (1990) 11: S101-113.

95. Jon L and Fahey TD. Sodium Bicarbonate Ingestion and Exercise Performance: An Update. Sports Medicine (1991) 11: 71-77.

96. Vollestad NK and Sejersted OM. Biochemical correlates of fatigue. Eur J Appl Physiol (1988) 57: 336-347.

97. Juel C. Lactate/proton co-transport in skeletal muscle: regulation and importance for pH homeostasis. Acta Physiologica Scand (1996) 156: 369-74.

98. Galloway SDR and Maughan R. The effects of induced alkalosis on the metabolic response to prolonged exercise in humans. Eur J Appl Physiol (1996) 74: 384-389.

99. Hood VL et. al. Effect of systemic pH on pH_i and lactic acid generation in exhaustive forearm exercise, Am J Physiol (1988) 255: F479-F485.

100. Allen DG et. al. The role of intracellular acidosis in muscle fatigue. in Advanced in Experimental Medicine and Biology 384: Fatigue Ed: Simon C Gandevia et al. Plenum Press 1995.

101. Asmussen E and Mazin B. A central nervous system component in local muscular fatigue. Eur J Appl Physiol (1978) 38: 9-15.

102. Asmussen E and Mazin B. A central nervous system component in local muscular fatigue. Eur J Appl Physiol (1978) 38: 1-8.

103. Caiozzo VJ et. al. The effect of precontractions on the slow-velocity-high-force region of the in vivo force-velocity relationship. (abstract) Med Sci Sports Exerc (1981) 13: 128.

104. Green HJ. How Important is endogenous muscle glycogen to fatigue in prolonged exercise. Can J Physiol Pharmacol (1991) 69: 290-297.

105. Yu-Yahiro H. Electrolytes and their relationship to normal and abnormal muscle function. Orthopaedic Nursing (1994) 13: 38-40.

106. Enteman M et. al. The sarcoplasmic reticulum glcyogenolytic complex in mammalian fast twitch skeletal muscles. J Biol Chem (1980) 255: 6245-6252.

107. Viitasalo JT. Effects of Rapid Weight Reduction on Force Production and Vertical Jumping Height. Int J Sports Med (1987) 8: 281-285.

108. Fogelholm M. Effects of Bodyweight reduction on sports performance. Sports Med (1994) 18: 249-267.

109. Jacobs I. Lactate concentrations after short maximal exercise at various glycogen levels. Acta Physiol Scand (1981) 111: 465-469.

110. Young K and Davies CTM. Effect of diet on human muscle weakness following prolonged exercise. Eur J Apply Physiol (1984) 53: 81-85.

111. Symons JD and Jacobs I. High-intensity exercise performance is not impaired by low intramuscular glycogen. Med Sci Sports Exerc (1989) 21: 550-557.
112. Lambert EV et. al. Enhanced endurance in trained cyclists during moderate intensity exercise following 2 weeks adaptation to a high fat diet. Eur J Apply Physiol (1994) 69: 387-293.
113. Phinney SD et. al. Capacity for moderate exercise in obese subjects after adaptation to a hypocaloric, ketogenic diet. J Clin Invest (1980) 66: 1152-1161.
114. Phinney SD et. al. The human metabolic response to chronic ketosis without caloric restriction: physical and biochemical adaptations. Metabolism (1983) 32: 757-768.
115. Phinney SD et. al. The human metabolic response to chronic ketosis without caloric restriction: preservation of submaximal exercise capacity with reduced carbohydrate oxidation. Metabolism (1983) 32: 769-776.

Chapter 21:
Effects of exercise on ketosis

Simply restricting carbohydrates will establish ketonuria (presence of ketones in the urine) given enough time (typically 3-4 days). The requirements for the establishment of ketosis are discussed in detail in chapter 4 but are briefly reviewed here. Additionally, exercise interacts with carbohydrate restriction and affects ketosis. This chapter discusses the role of exercise, both in helping to establish ketosis, as well as its impact on ketosis once established.

A recap of ketogenesis

Ketosis requires a shift in the liver away from triglyceride synthesis and towards free fatty acid (FFA) oxidation and ketone body formation. Blood glucose must also drop, lowering insulin and increasing glucagon and decreasing the I/G ratio. Along with this hormonal shift, there must be adequate FFA present for the liver to produce ketones.

Exercise is inherently ketogenic and all forms of exercise will increase the rate at which the liver releases its glycogen, helping to establish ketosis. As the rapid establishment of ketosis is important for individuals using the CKD approach (who only have 5-6 days to maximize their time in ketosis), strategies for entering ketosis are discussed. The overall effects of exercise on ketone concentrations is also discussed.

Section 1: Aerobic exercise

It has been known for almost a century that ketones appear in higher concentrations in the blood following aerobic exercise (1). During aerobic exercise, liver glycogen decreases, insulin decreases, glucagon increases and there is an increase in FFA levels in the bloodstream. During aerobic exercise, there is a slight increase in blood glucose uptake which peaks around ten minutes. To maintain blood glucose, the liver will increase liver glycogen breakdown, keeping blood glucose stable for several hours.

Thus, the overall effect of aerobic exercise is to increase the production of ketone bodies (2,3). The increase in ketone bodies during exercise is smaller in trained versus untrained individuals, due to decreased FFA mobilization during exercise (2).

Aerobic exercise can quickly induce ketosis following an overnight fast. One hour at 65% of maximum heart rate causes a large increase in ketone body levels. However, ketones do not contribute to energy production to any significant degree (4). Two hours of exercise at 65% of maximum heart rate will raise ketone levels to 3mM after three hours. High levels of ketonemia (similar to those seen in prolonged fasting) can be achieved five hours post-exercise (4). This increase in ketone bodies post exercise allows for glycogen replenishment in the muscle. Since the brain will not be using glucose for energy, any incoming carbohydrates can be diverted to the muscles (4). Obviously, if no dietary carbohydrates are consumed following training, ketosis should be maintained.

Aerobic exercise decreases blood flow to the liver which should decrease the availability of FFA for ketogenesis (4-6). However, this is offset by an increase in FFA availability and extraction by the liver (3-7).

If ketone body levels are low at the onset of exercise, there is an increase in ketone concentrations during exercise. If ketone body levels are high during exercise (above 2-3 mmol), exercise has little effect on overall ketone body levels simply because they are already high (i.e. levels of ketosis will not deepen). This reflects one of the many feedback loops to prevent ketoacidosis during exercise and afterwards (4). High levels of ketones inhibit further fat breakdown during exercise although insulin levels still decrease. The primary fuel for exercise is FFA and the body will simply use the FFA already present in the blood for fuel.

Section 2: High-intensity exercise

Very little research has looked at the effects of high-intensity exercise on establishing ketosis or post-exercise ketosis. However, we can make some educated guesses based on what is known to occur during high-intensity exercise.

During high-intensity exercise, the same overall hormonal picture described above occurs, just to a greater degree. Adrenaline and noradrenaline increase during high-intensity activities (both interval and weight training). The large increase in adrenaline causes the liver to release liver glycogen faster than it is being used, raising blood glucose (8,9). While this may impair ketogenesis in the short term, it is ultimately helpful in establishing ketosis. Insulin goes down during exercise but may increase after training due to increases in blood glucose. Glucagon goes up also helping to establish ketosis. Probably the biggest difference between high and low-intensity exercise is that FFA release is inhibited during high-intensity activity, due to increases in lactic acid (10).

Many individuals report finding a decrease in urinary ketones (or a complete absence) following the performance of high-intensity exercise. Most likely, this reflects a temporary decrease in blood FFA concentrations and increase in blood glucose and insulin. Additionally, the large increase in adrenaline and noradrenaline decreases blood flow to the liver further decreasing FFA availability for ketone production.

So while high-intensity exercise is arguably the quickest way to establish ketosis (due to its effects on liver glycogen breakdown), the overall effect of this type of exercise could be described as temporarily anti-ketogenic. The solution to this dilemma is simple: follow high-intensity activity (to empty liver glycogen) with low-intensity activity (to provide FFA for ketone formation). Ten to fifteen minutes of low-intensity aerobics (below lactate threshold) following intervals or a weight workout should help to reestablish ketosis by lowering blood glucose and providing FFA for the liver.The impact of different forms of exercise on ketosis appears in table 1.

Table 1: Impact of exercise on ketosis			
Type of exercise	Blood glucose	Insulin	Depth of Ketosis
Aerobic, below LT	No change or decrease	decrease	increase
Aerobic, above LT	increase	decrease during may increase after	decrease during increase after
Anaerobic training (weights or intervals)	increase	decrease during may increase after	decrease during increase after

Summary

Low-intensity aerobic exercise, below the lactate threshold, is useful for both establishing ketosis following an overnight fast as well as deepening ketosis. High-intensity exercise will more quickly establish ketosis by forcing the liver to release glycogen into the bloodstream. However it can decrease the depth of ketosis by decreasing the availability of FFA. Performing ten minutes or more of low-intensity aerobics following high-intensity activity will help reestablish ketosis after high-intensity activity.

Guidelines for Establishing and Maintaining Ketosis

1. After a carb-up, if not weight training the following day, perform 45'+ of low-intensity aerobic exercise (~65% of maximum heart rate) to deplete liver glycogen and establish ketosis without depleting muscle glycogen. Interval training will establish ketosis more quickly by depleting liver glycogen but will negatively affect your leg workout.

OR

2. Perform a high-intensity workout (weight training or intervals) followed by 10-20' of low-intensity aerobics to provide adequate FFA for the liver to produce ketones.

3. Perform 10-15' of low-intensity aerobics after high-intensity training to provide FFA for the liver for ketone body formation.

References Cited

1. Koeslag JH. Post-exercise ketosis and the hormone response to exercise: a review. Med Sci Sports Exerc (1982) 14: 327-334
2. Gorski J et. al. Hepatic lipid metabolism in exercise training. Med Sci Sports Exerc (1990) 22(2): 213-221.
3. Wasserman DH et. al. Role of the endocrine pancreas in control of fuel metabolism by the liver during exercise. Int J Obesity (1995) 19 (Suppl 4): S22-30.
4. Balasse EO and Fery F. Ketone body production and disposal: Effects of fasting, diabetes and exercise. Diabetes/Metabolism Reviews (1989) 5: 247-270.
5. Keller U et. al. Human ketone body production and utilization studied using tracer techniques: regulation by free fatty acids, insulin, catecholamines, and thyroid hormones.

Diabetes/Metabolism Reviews (1989) 5: 285-298.

6. Wahren J et. al. Turnover and splanchnic metabolism of free fatty acids and ketones in insulin-dependent diabetics at rest and in response to exercise. J Clin Invest (1984) 73: 1367-1376.

7. Fery F and Balasse EO. Response of ketone body metabolism to exercise during transition from postabsorptive to fasted state. Am J Physiol (1986) 250: E495-E501.

8. "Physiology of Sport and Exercise" Jack H. Wilmore and David L. Costill. Human Kinetics Publishers 1994.

9. "Exercise Physiology: Human Bioenergetics and it's applications" George A Brooks, Thomas D. Fahey, and Timothy P. White. Mayfield Publishing Company 1996.

10. Romijn JA et. al. Regulation of endogenous fat and carbohydrate metabolism in relation to exercise intensity and duration. Am J Physiol (1993) 265: E380-391.

Chapter 22:
Exercise and fat loss

Having examined the physiology behind the different types of exercise, it is time to examine the effects of exercise on fat loss. There are a number of misconceptions regarding the role of exercise in fat loss. One of the many misconceptions about is the overestimation of calories burned during and after exercise.

As well, there is great debate about the 'best' form of exercise when fat loss is the goal. In general, people tend to over-emphasize aerobic exercise for fat loss while downplaying other forms of exercise, such as interval or weight training. Recent research highlights the benefits of weight and interval training for fat loss.

In addition to the type of exercise done, total caloric intake has an impact on fat loss when combined with exercise. At moderate caloric deficits, both weight training and endurance exercise can increase fat loss. However, if caloric intake is too low, exercise can have a negative effect on fat loss.

Section 1: Caloric expenditure during and after exercise

Calorie burned during exercise

Most exercisers tend to overestimate the number of calories expended during exercise (1). During aerobic exercise, caloric expenditure averages about 5 calories/minute at low intensities increasing to 10+ calories/minute as intensity increases. As a point of reference, a threshold calorie expenditure of 300 calories three times per week or 200 calories four times per week has been established as the minimum amount of aerobic exercise that will cause fat loss (2).

Additionally, exercising two days per week does not result in significant fat loss, even if more calories are expended. Burning 500 calories twice per week (a total of 1000 calories expended) does not cause the same fat loss as burning 300 calories three times per week (only 900 calories). The body must receive an exercise stimulus at least three days per week. How this stimulus is divided between weights, aerobic exercise and/or interval training will depend on an individual's goals. Generally speaking, for fat loss, weight training should be performed 2-3 times per week minimum and aerobic exercise of some sort 3 or more times per week.

The loss of one pound of fat requires a calorie deficit of 3500 calories. At five to ten calories per minute, 300 calories would require 30-60 minutes of aerobic exercise at least three times per week. This bare minimum expenditure would only be expected to yield 800-900 calories/week deficit and fat loss would only occur at about 1 lb per month (assuming no other changes in diet or activity). Some authors have used this to argue **against** regular exercise, claiming that this small amount of caloric expenditure cannot possibly have any effect on body weight.

However, an individual who walked briskly 2 miles daily (expending approximately 200 calories or so in 30 minutes) would expend 1400 calories per week (a little less than 1/2 of a pound of fat). Assuming no change in caloric intake, this should yield a fat loss of about 2 lb per month,

24 lbs per year. Table 1 provides a comparison of estimated fat loss with different amounts of aerobic exercise.

Table 1: Estimated fat loss with no change in calorie intake					
Intensity	Cal/min	Time	Frequency	Total cal/wk	Est. fat loss/month*
Low	5	60'	3/week	900	1 lb
Low	5	60'	5/week	1500	1.7 lb
High	10	60'	3/week	1800	2 lb
High	10	60'	5/week	3000	3.5 lb

* Assuming no other changes in diet or activity

Simply adding aerobic exercise with no change in diet causes weight loss to occur for men but not always women (3,4). The reasons for this gender discrepancy are not fully understood. Simply put, when women add aerobic exercise without performing resistance training or making changes to their diet, the rate of fat loss is extremely slow.

The caloric burn from interval training is harder to pinpoint since it depends highly on the intensity and duration of the activity. The impact of interval training on fat loss is discussed further below.

Weight training uses approximately seven to nine calories per minute, including the rest between sets. As with aerobic exercise, weight training per se has a fairly minimal direct effect on caloric expenditure. However, weight training has several indirect effects on the energy balance equation which are arguably more important.

Muscle is one of the body's most active tissues and adding muscle can permanently raise metabolic rate. This is especially important for older individuals who may have lost muscle mass due to inactivity. The amount of calories burned from increased muscle mass is discussed in the next section.

Calories burned after exercise

In addition to the calories burned during exercise, there is an additional calorie expenditure after exercise referred to as Excess Post-exercise Oxygen Consumption (EPOC) (5). EPOC is caused by increases in circulating hormones such as adrenaline and noradrenaline, as well as other factors, which causes the body to continue to expend calories after exercise (5). These calories come primarily from fat stores (6). Another common exercise misconception is that the EPOC following aerobic exercise lasts for 24 hours and contributes significantly to the overall calorie balance equation (1).

The magnitude of EPOC is related to both the intensity and duration of activity (7,8,9). Following low-intensity aerobic activity (65% of maximum heart rate for less than one hour), approximately 5 total calories are burned after exercise. Moderate-intensity activity (65% of maximum heart rate for more than an hour), may raise EPOC to 35 total calories. Following exhaustive exercise (above 85% maximum heart rate), a post-exercise calorie expenditure of 180 calories may occur (7). Most individuals will not be able to sustain exercise intensities high enough to generate a large EPOC with aerobic exercise. With few exceptions, primarily elite endurance athletes, the EPOC from aerobic exercise is unlikely to be significant in the overall energy balance equation (1).

Following resistance training (and perhaps interval training), the magnitude of EPOC is much higher. Increases in metabolic rate of 4-7% over 24 hours have been seen following extensive resistance training (10). For an individual with a 2000 calorie per day metabolic rate, this could amount to 80-140 calories burned following every resistance training session, the equivalent of walking an extra mile.

Part of this increase reflects increased protein synthesis which rises for 24-36 hours and which is energetically costly. The energy used for protein synthesis will come primarily from fat stores (11).

Section 2: The effect of exercise on fat loss

Dieting without exercise

The most common approach to fat loss for most people is to simply restrict calories without exercise. The biggest problem with weight loss by caloric restriction alone is an inevitable loss in lean body mass (LBM), with a large part of the LBM drop from muscle stores, and a drop in metabolic rate. The more that calories are restricted, the more the body lowers metabolic rate to compensate. This reflects the body going into starvation mode to prevent further weight loss. Depending on the amount of caloric restriction, the addition of exercise may or may not have benefits in alleviating or preventing this drop in metabolic rate.

When food intake invariably increases again, the lowered metabolic rate makes the change of fat regain very likely. As many individuals have found out, dieting by itself is not effective for long term weight loss. In fact a recent analysis of studies shows that weight maintenance is much better when individuals include exercise as part of their weight loss efforts than when it is not. Other issues dealing with weight regain are discussed in more detail in chapter 14.

Exercise at different caloric levels

Although the exact reasons are unknown, the impact of exercise with caloric restriction on fat loss is not as simple as eating less and exercising more. Many individuals have found that eating too little and exercising too much can put the body into a starvation mode, and fat loss slows or stops completely. The reason for this starvation response is not known at this time. It is sufficient to say that moderate approaches to both exercise and caloric restriction tend to yield the best long term results. Additionally, exercise appears to have its greatest effect with moderate, not excessive, caloric deficits (12).

The key is to find the optimal combination of dietary modification and exercise to generate maximum fat loss without any muscle loss. Of course, the right type of exercise is also important. In an attempt to develop guidelines for calorie intake and exercise we will examine the impact of exercise on three different dietary conditions: maintenance calories, low-calorie dieting (10% below maintenance levels to 1200 calories per day), and very-low-calorie dieting (below 800 calories per day).

Exercise at Maintenance calories

The most basic approach to create a caloric deficit is through the addition of exercise to a maintenance calorie diet. As stated previously, while the addition of aerobic exercise with no change in diet causes fat loss in men, it does not reliably do so in women (3,14).

At maintenance calories, in both men and women, the performance of resistance training causes a loss of bodyfat with no changes in dietary habits. (14-18) At this calorie level, weight training alone generally causes a greater fat loss and muscle gain than endurance exercise alone (14,15). In 8 weeks, beginning trainees can expect to gain 2-4 pounds of lean body mass and lose 2-4 lbs of fat with weight training alone as little as 30 minutes three times per week (17-19).

In a longer study of 20 weeks, women performed three sets of eight repetitions in four lower body exercises (12 total sets) twice per week. At the end of the study, they had gained 10 lbs of muscle and lost 10 lbs of fat (20). The overall changes may have been even more significant had the subjects trained their upper body as well. This occurred without dieting or aerobic exercise, although fat loss would have probably been greater and/or faster with the addition of either.

Considering the low caloric expenditure of weight training, it is difficult to understand how weight training can cause fat loss at maintenance calories. The reason is the indirect effect of weight training on metabolic rate. Every pound of muscle added through weight training burns an additional 30-40 calories per day in both men (17,18) and women (18).

A beginning exerciser can gain 3-4 pounds of muscle in the first 8 weeks of training with even the most basic of programs. This gain may increase metabolic rate by 120-150 calories per day, the equivalent of walking 1.5 miles every day. At maintenance calories, the addition of aerobic training to weight training will yield even better fat loss results. However, weight training is critical for long term fat loss and weight maintenance.

Beginners can gain 3-4 lbs of muscle and to lose of 5-10 lbs of bodyfat over 8 weeks following a very basic program of resistance training (1 set of 8-12 repetitions of 8-10 basic exercises) and aerobic exercise (30' at 65% of maximum heart rate), which is described in more detail in chapter 27 (21).

Exercise with low-calorie dieting (10% below maintenance to 1200 calories/day)

With a moderate calorie restriction (from 10% below maintenance to approximately 1000 calories below maintenance) without exercise, there is inevitably a decline in resting energy expenditure and a loss of muscle. When exercise is added fat loss increases and the loss of muscle decreases. The drop in metabolic rate is also decreased. (22-25).

Resistance training alone, combined with a slight calorie restriction causes greater bodyfat loss and a maintenance/increase in lean body mass than just restricting calories alone (24,26). Essentially, the caloric deficit causes the fat loss and the weight training signals the body to keep the muscle so that only fat is lost. This is an important consideration. From a calorie burning perspective, aerobic exercise and caloric restriction are essentially identical.

Aerobic training alone, while increasing fat loss in some studies, does not generally increase muscle except in very inactive individuals (24) . Remember that adding muscle **raises** metabolic rate in the long term. Any caloric restriction should be accompanied by resistance training to prevent the loss of LBM and possibly to even increase it.

Aerobic exercise can increase fat loss and may be added if desired and if time allows. However, too much aerobic exercise can have the same effect as too few calories: lowering metabolic rate and slowing fat loss. A total caloric deficit of more than 1000 cal/day seems to be the threshold for slowing the metabolism (14).

Exercise with very-low-calorie diets: less than 800 calories per day

In a very low-calorie diet situation (VLCD, 800 calories per day or less), there are significant changes compared to higher calorie levels. VLCD without exercise causes a large drop in LBM and metabolic rate. The addition of aerobic exercise alone does not improve fat loss or prevent the drop in LBM and metabolic rate (27-30).

In severe dieting situations, aerobic exercise may actually be worse than just dieting (health benefits excepted). In one study, the addition of aerobic exercise (27 hours total over 5 weeks) to a very-low-calorie ketogenic diet (500 cal/day) caused a greater drop in metabolic rate than dieting alone and caused no additional weight or fat loss (29). It appeared that the body compensated for the aerobic exercise by slowing metabolic rate at other times of the day.

When resistance training only is added to an 800 calorie diet, muscle size increases despite a similar loss in LBM in both the diet only and diet plus exercise groups (31). This implies that the loss in LBM is due to loss of water, glycogen and other non-muscle tissues (32). Metabolic rate still goes down.

The conclusion from this data is this: on a VLCD, weight training but not aerobic exercise will slow the drop in metabolic rate but not stop it. The inclusion of aerobic exercise may do more harm than good at this calorie level.

Summary

There is a caloric threshold for exercise to improve the rate of fat loss. A calorie deficit more than 1000 cal/day will slow metabolism. Further increases in energy expenditure past that level does not increase fat loss (14). In some cases, excess exercise will increase the drop in metabolic rate seen with very large calorie deficits.

This value of 1000 calories per day includes any caloric deficit AND exercise. Meaning that if 500 calories per day are removed from the diet, no more than 500 calories per day of exercise should be performed. If someone chose to remove 1000 calories per day from their diet, no aerobic exercise should be done to avoid metabolic slowdown.

The decrease in metabolic rate seen with very low-calorie diets makes weight regain likely. Eventually, a dieter will have to eat. And when normal eating habits are resumed after a period of starvation dieting, weight and bodyfat regain will be the result.

Therefore the best fat loss solution, in terms of both fat loss as well as maintenance of that fat loss, is to eat at maintenance (or a slight deficit, no more than 10-20% below maintenance) in combination with resistance training (33). Aerobic training can be added as required and will increase fat loss as long as it is not overdone. For most, 20-40' of aerobic exercise several times per week should be sufficient. In this case, more is NOT better. However, if an individual has significant amounts of fat to lose, a greater frequency of aerobic exercise may be beneficial.

The ultimate point of the above discussion is this: resistance training coupled with a slight decrease in energy balance is the key to fat loss. The inclusion of aerobic training can increase fat loss as long as total calories are not taken too low.

Section 3: The fat burning myth

A commonly held idea in the field of exercise is that one must burn fat during exercise in order to lose bodyfat. This has led to the development of charts which indicate a certain 'fat burning zone' during aerobic exercise. However, recent research as well as anecdotal experience draws into question the idea of the fat burning zone, a topic discussed in greater detail below.

The fat burning myth

A very prevalent misconception about aerobic exercise is the so-called 'fat burning zone' which is supposed to optimize fat loss. It is true that a greater **percentage** of fat is used during low-intensity exercise (see chapter 18 for details). This suggests that low-intensity exercise is the best form of exercise to lose fat (6). However, due to the low total caloric expenditure, the **total** amount of fat used is small. As exercise intensity increases (up to about 75% of maximum heart rate), while the **percentage** of total calories derived from fat is smaller, the **total** amount of fat used is greater (34).

The physiology of fuel utilization described above ultimately ignores the following fact: the utilization of fat during exercise has little bearing on fat loss (1). Numerous studies have compared the effect of different intensities of aerobic exercise on fat loss. As long as the caloric expenditure is the same, total fat loss is identical whether the exercise is done at low or high-intensity (35-37). That is, the fuel used during exercise is of secondary importance compared to the amount of calories expended. As long as more calories are burned than eaten, the body will reduce fat stores.

One thing to note is that as the intensity of exercise increases, the duration of activity decreases (see chapter 24). This means that some individuals will burn more calories by using lower intensities but increasing duration, while others will burn more calories exercising at higher intensities for a shorter period of time. Ultimately dieters must find the optimal combination of intensity and duration which maximizes caloric expenditure.

This partly explains why simply restricting calories while weight training causes fat loss. Fat loss is primarily a function of calories in versus calories out. Weight training 'signals' the body to keep muscle and the caloric deficit signals the body to lose fat. Whether a calorie deficit is generated with a slight restriction in calories or through aerobic exercise, the end result is basically the same. Additionally, the caloric cost of weight training, both during and after the workout, will contribute to the overall calorie deficit. As long as weight training is being performed and calories are not restricted too much, the majority of weight lost should be fat.

High-intensity aerobics and interval training

Interval training is an advanced exercise technique alternating short periods (15-90 seconds) of near maximal intensity activity with periods (1-2 minutes) of very low-intensity activity. Several recent studies have found that either high-intensity endurance activity (38) or interval training (39) yields greater fat loss than lower intensity continuous activity when diet is not controlled. This is probably due to an appetite blunting mechanism or a greater EPOC from higher intensity exercise.

Tremblay compared the effects of a high-intensity interval program to continuous exercise (39). The interval group used a progressive program working up to 5 ninety-second intervals near their maximum heart rate three times per week. The continuous exercise group worked up to 45 minutes of exercise five times per week. Although the interval training group only exercised one hour per week, compared to 3.75 hours in the aerobic group, and expended only half as many calories during the interval workouts, fat loss as measured by skinfolds was **nine times** greater. Although fat loss per se was not measured, total bodyweight was. As both groups maintained their overall weight, this suggests that the interval group gained more muscle as their fat loss was greater.

For most individuals (excepting pre-contest bodybuilders who are addressed separately in chapter 30), the primary goal of aerobic exercise should be on total caloric expenditure. For individuals with limited time, maximizing calorie expenditure by working at the highest intensity that can be maintained safely, and is compatible with a ketogenic diet, is the best choice. The inclusion of interval training from time to time can raise fitness level and increase fat loss. Specific guidelines for when and how to incorporate training techniques such as intervals are discussed in chapter 25.

Summary

Contrary to popular opinion, there is no 'fat burning zone', at least not in terms of an optimal intensity range which will maximize fat loss. The fat loss from aerobic exercise is tied intimately to caloric expenditure, not the particular fuel which is used during exercise. Some studies suggest that high-intensity aerobic exercise or interval training may actually cause greater fat loss than lower intensity activities. From a practical standpoint, this means that a ketogenic dieter wanting optimal fat loss should train at as high an intensity as they can which is compatible with a ketogenic diet. Individuals on an SKD are limited in terms of intensity while individuals on a TKD or CKD may wish to experiment with interval training to maximize fat loss.

References cited

1. Zelasko C. Exercise for weight loss: What are the facts? J Am Diet Assoc (1995) 95: 1414-1417.
2. American College of Sports Medicine Position Stand. The recommended quantity and quality of exercise for developing and maintaining cardiorespiratory and muscular fitness in healthy adults. Med Sci Sports Exerc (1990) 22: 265-274.
3. Gleim GW. Exercise is not an effective weight loss modality in women. J Am Coll Nutr (1993) 12: 363-367.
4. Despres JP et al. Effect of a 20 week endurance training program on adipose tissue morphology and lipolysis in men and women. Metabolism (1984) 33: 235-239.
5. "Physiology of Sport and Exercise" Jack H. Wilmore and David L. Costill. Human Kinetics Publishers 1994.
6. McCarty MF. Optimizing exercise for fat loss. Medical Hypotheses (1995) 44: 325-330.
7. Bahr R. Excess postexercise oxygen consumption - magnitude, mechanisms, and practical implications. Acta Physiol Scand (1992) (Suppl 605): 1-70.
8. Maehlum S et. al. Magnitude and duration of excess postexercise oxygen consumption in healthy young subjects. Metabolism (1986) 35(5): 425-429.
9. Quinn TJ Postexercise oxygen consumption in trained females: effects of exercise duration. Med Sci Sports Exerc (1994): 26: 908-913.
10. Melby C et. al. Effect of acute resistance exercise on postexercise energy expenditure and resting metabolic rate. J Appl Physiol (1993) 75: 1847-1853.
11. MacDougall JD et. al. The time course of elevated muscle protein synthesis following heavy resistance exercise. Can J Appl Physiol (1995) 20: 480-6.
12. Saris WHM. The role of exercise in the dietary treatment of obesity. Int J Obes (1993) 17 (suppl 1): S17-S21.
13. Ballor DL and Keesey RE. A meta-analysis of the factors affecting exercise-induced changes in body mass, fat mass, and fat-free mass in males and females. Int J Obes (1991) 15: 717-726.
14. Wilmore J. Increasing physical activity: alterations in body mass and composition. Am J Clin Nutr (1996) 63 (suppl): 456S-460S.
15. Broeder CE et. al. The effects of either high-intensity resistance or endurance training on resting metabolic rate. Am J Clin Nutr (1992) 55: 802-810.
16. Butts NK and Price S. Effects of a 12-week weight training program on the body composition of women over 30 years of age. J Strength Cond Res (1994) 8: 265-269.
17. Pratley R et. al. Strength training increases resting metabolic rate and norepinephrine levels in healthy 50- to 65-yr-old men. J Appl Physiol (1994) 76: 133-137.
18. Cambell WW et. al. Increased energy requirements and changes in body composition with resistance training in older adults. Am J Clin Nutr (1994) 60: 167-175.
19. Ludo ML et. al. Effect of weight-training on energy expenditure and substrate utilization during sleep. Med Sci Sports Exerc (1995) 27: 188-193.

20. Staron RS et. al. Muscle hypertrophy and fast fiber type conversions in heavy resistance-trained women. Eur J Appl Physiol (1990) 60: 71-79.

21. Westcott W. Transformation: How to take them from sedentary to active. Idea Today Magazine (1995) pp. 46-54.

22. Ross R et. al. Response of total and regional lean tissue and skeletal muscle to a program of energy restriction and resistance exercise. Int J Obes (1995) 19: 781-787.

23. Ross R et. al. Effects of energy restriction and exercise on skeletal muscle and adipose tissue in women as measured by magnetic resonancing imaging. Am J Clin Nutr (1995) 61: 1179-85.

24. Shinkai S et. al. Effects of 12 weeks of aerobic exercise plus dietary restriction on body composition, resting energy expenditure and aerobic fitness in mildly obese middle-aged women. Eur J Appl Physiol (1994) 68: 258-265

25. Belko AZ et. al. Diet, exercise, weight loss and energy expenditure in moderately overweight women. Int J Obes (1987) 11: 93-104.

26. Ballor DL et. al. Resistance weight training during caloric restriction enhances body weight maintenance. Am J Clin Nutr (1988) 47: 19-25.

27. Van Dale D et. al. Does exercise give an additional effect in weight reduction regimens. Int J Obes (1987) 11: 367-375.

28. Hill JO et. al. Effects of exercise and food restriction on body composition and metabolic rate in obese women. Am J Clin Nutr (1987) 46: 622-630.

29. Phinney SD et. al. Effects of aerobic exercise on energy expenditure and nitrogen balance during very low calorie dieting. Metabolism (1988) 37: 758-765.

30. Phinney SD. Exercise during and after very-low-calorie dieting. Am J Clin Nutr (1992) 56: 190S-194S.

31. Donnely JE. Muscle hypertrophy with large-scale weight loss and resistance training. Am J Clin Nutr (1993) 58: 561-565.

32. Marks BL and Rippe J. The importance of fat free maintenance in weight loss programs. Sports Med (1996) 22: 273-281.

33. Sweeny ME et. al. Severe vs. moderate energy restriction with and without exercise in the treatment of obesity: efficiency of weight loss. Am J Clin Nutr (1993) 57: 127-134.

34. Romijn JA et. al. Regulation of endogenous fat and carbohydrate metabolism in relation to exercise intensity and duration. Am J Physiol (1993) 265: E380-391.

35. Grediagin M et al. Exercise intensity does not effect body composition changes in untrained, moderately overfat women. J Am Diet Assoc (1995) 95: 661-665.

36. Ballor DL et. al. Exercise intensity does not affect the composition of diet- and exercise-induced body mass loss. Am J Clin Nutr (1990) 51: 142-146.

37. Duncan JJ et. al. Women walking for health and fitness: how much is enough? JAMA (1991) 266: 3295-3299.

38. Bryner RW The effects of exercise intensity on body composition, weight loss, and dietary composition in women. J Am College Nutrition (1997) 16: 68-73.

39. Tremblay A et. al. Impact of exercise intensity on body fatness and skeletal muscle metabolism. Metabolism (1994) 43: 818-818.

Part VI:
Exercise guidelines

Chapter 23: General exercise principles
Chapter 24: Aerobic exercise
Chapter 25: Interval training
Chapter 26: Weight training

Having discussed the underlying physiology behind aerobic, interval, and weight training exercise, we can now develop some general guidelines for each type of exercise. Chapter 23 discusses several general principles such as progressive overload and the FITT equation. Chapters 24 through 26 give general guidelines for implementing the different types of exercise, depending on goals. These general guidelines are applied in part 7, which provides sample exercise programs.

Chapter 23:
General Training Principles

There are a number of general exercise principles that apply to all forms of exercise. These include progressive overload and specificity. Both are discussed below. Additionally, the FITT equation, which is used to determine the various components of an exercise program is also discussed.

Section 1: Progressive overload and SAID

Progressive overload

The most basic principle of exercise training is progressive overload which means that the body must be overloaded for fitness to increase. The specific type of overload used will depend on the type of training being done. Aerobic fitness can be improved by performing longer duration exercise or covering the same distance in less time. Progressive overload can be applied to interval training by completing more intervals, or working at a higher intensity. Increases in strength and size can be attained by increasing the weight being lifted, lifting the same weight for more repetitions, performing more or different exercises,etc. Regardless of the specific nature of adaptation, the body tends to have a general mode of adaptation (1). This is sometimes referred to as the General Adaptation Syndrome or G.A.S.

The G.A.S. involves three steps:

1. Alarm: Following a stress to the body (i.e. a workout), there is a temporary decline in performance,

2. Resistance: the alarm stage is followed by super compensation in the system which was trained (muscle, nervous system, aerobic system),

3. Exhaustion: If inadequate rest or nutrients are given or the stress occurs too frequently, the body's performance capacity will decrease, called the exhaustion stage (more commonly called overtraining).

Specificity and the SAID Principle

The adaptations seen in training are specific to the type of training done. This is sometimes called Specific Adaptations to Imposed Demands or SAID by exercise physiologists. For example, aerobic training improves the body's ability to perform aerobically (by making muscle fibers smaller and more oxidative), but does not improve strength. Strength training improves the body's ability to generate strength (by making muscle fibers bigger and more glycolytic) but does not improve aerobic endurance (2,3).

Another example is the carryover between different exercises. Strength gains in one exercise (i.e. the squat) show little carryover to other exercises (i.e. leg extensions) due to differences in muscle fiber recruitment (4-6). Therefore, training must be specific to individual goals.

Prior to establishing the specifics of a training program, individuals must decide what they ultimately want to accomplish. In general, the body can only adapt maximally in one direction or another. Trying to gain muscle and lose fat at the same time is generally impossible, except for beginners. Maximizing both strength and aerobic performance is similarly impossible and one or the other will be compromised. The more specific an individual is about their goals, the more success they will have.

Section 2: The FITT equation

All types of exercise can generally be described by four variables. They are frequency, which is how often a given type of exercise is performed ; intensity, which is how hard a given exercise is ; time, which is how long a given type of exercise is performed for ; and type, which is the specific type of exercise done. These four variables are sometimes referred to as the FITT equation. In the following chapters, each major form of exercise is discussed within the context of these four variables.

References

1. Viru A. Mechanism of general adaptation. Medical Hypotheses (1992) 38: 296-300.
2. "Physiology of Sport and Exercise" Jack H. Wilmore and David L. Costill. Human Kinetics Publishers 1994.
3. Hawley JA and Hopkins WG. Aerobic glycolytic and aerobic lipolytic power systems: A new paradigm with implications for endurance and ultraendurance events. Sports Medicine (1995) 19: 240-250.
4. Morrisey MC et. al. Resistance training modes: specificity and effectiveness. Med Sci Sports Exerc (1995) 27: 648-660.
5. Pipes T. Variable resistance versus constant resistance strength training in adult males. Eur J Appl Physiol (1978) 39: 27-35.
6. Sale D And MacDougall D. Specificity in Strength Training: A Review for the Coach and Athlete. Can J Appl Sports Sci (1981) 6:87-92.

Chapter 24:
Aerobic exercise guidelines

Having discussed the physiology behind aerobic exercise as well as its effects on fat loss, we will now discuss the parameters for developing the aerobic portion of an exercise program.

Frequency

The frequency of aerobic exercise depends solely on one's goals. For general health, a minimum of three times per week is required. For fat loss, three times per week also appears to be the minimum. For individuals wishing greater fat loss, a frequency of four to five days per week is frequently recommended (1,2). However, too much aerobic exercise can be as detrimental as too little. Many individuals find that their fat loss can slow with too much aerobic exercise. As well, excessive aerobic exercise can cause muscle loss. In practice, three to five aerobic sessions per week seems to work for most individuals.

Endurance athletes looking to maximize performance typically perform three to seven aerobic exercise sessions per week. Generally, there is an alternation of high and low intensity workouts and varying duration. The specifics of developing an endurance program for competition are beyond the scope of this book.

Off-season bodybuilders should try to minimize aerobic training, performing perhaps 2-3 very short sessions of 20' each. This should maintain aerobic fitness without cutting severely into recovery. Bodybuilders who are preparing for a contest, or just embarking upon a fat loss cycle, typically add more aerobic exercise into their routine. However, most pre-contest bodybuilders tend to perform far too much aerobic exercise, frequently 7 days per week and often times twice per day. The specifics of aerobic exercise for pre-contest bodybuilders is discussed in chapter 30.

Intensity

The intensity of aerobic exercise is generally described as the percentage of maximum heart rate. To estimate maximum heart rate, use the following formulas (2):
Men: 220 -age = maximum heart rate
Women: 227 - age = maximum heart rate

The recommended intensity for aerobic exercise is between 60-85% of maximum heart rate although beginners will benefit from intensities as low as 50% of maximum (1,2). Multiplying maximum heart rate by .60 to .85 will yield the proper target heart range.

60% maximum = _____ * .60 = _____ beats/minute
      (max. HR)

85% maximum = _____ * .85 = _____ beats/minute
      (max. HR)

Endurance athletes may work anywhere in this range depending on their goals. Typically recovery workouts are done near the low end of the range, while higher intensities are used to improve aerobic fitness. Intensities above 85% of maximum should be done in an interval fashion and are discussed in the next chapter.

In general, bodybuilders should stay at low aerobic intensities to avoid losing muscle mass and strength. If lactate threshold (LT) has been determined (see below), 15 beats per minute below LT should be used as a guideline for aerobic intensity (3). If LT has not been established, a heart rate of 60% of maximum should be used.

Non-bodybuilders looking solely at maximum weight/fat loss will benefit most from exercising at the highest intensity they can safely maintain to maximize caloric burn. On a standard ketogenic diet, about the highest intensity which can be maintained is 75% of maximum heart rate. Higher intensities can be sustained following a carb-up for CKDers or pre-workout carbs on the TKD.

Determining the lactate threshold (LT)

Determining the LT is typically done in a lab using highly accurate and specific testing devices. However, the LT can be determined roughly in the gym as well. The LT is highly specific to a given activity. That is, determining LT on a bicycle tells you nothing about your LT on a treadmill or a Stairmaster. Therefore LT should be determined on the specific piece of equipment an individual will be using during their exercise session.

Recall from the previous chapter that lactic acid is the primary cause of the burning sensation felt in muscles during high-intensity exercise. Since LT is defined as the point where lactic acid begins to accumulate in the bloodstream, it can be roughly determined by noting when a burning sensation in your muscles is felt.

To most accurately determine LT, individuals need to be proficient at taking their heart rate or have access to a digital heart rate monitor. Many aerobic exercise machines have heart rate monitors built in. To determine LT, intensity should be gradually increased, while monitoring heart rate, until a significant burning sensation is felt. As a general rule, each increase in intensity level should be maintained for three minutes to allow for lactic acid to accumulate. When a significant burning sensation is felt in the muscles being used, heart rate should be taken, and assumed to roughly indicate the LT for that exercise.

Time

For health benefits, a minimum duration of twenty minutes per session is necessary (1). For fat loss, a duration sufficient to expend 300 calories three times per week or 200 calories four time per week is considered the minimum (1). Depending on the intensity of the exercise, 300 calories may require anywhere from thirty to forty five minutes of exercise. Unconditioned individuals can obtain similar results by performing several shorter workout sessions per day (i.e. ten minutes three or more times per day) as with performing the entire exercise session all at once (4). This strategy may be useful for busy individuals or those who are just beginning an exercise program.

Detrained individuals may not be able to exercise for 20' continuously when they start their exercise program. In this case, a modified type of interval training should be used. A total of 20-30' can be performed by alternating periods of exercise (of several minutes duration, whatever the individual is capable of) with periods of total rest (to allow for recovery). As fitness improves, longer periods of exercise will be possible and less rest required until a full 20' can be done without stopping.

At this point, exercise time can be increased at each workout by a minute or two until the final time goal is reached. Longer durations of exercise will burn more calories and may be more beneficial for fat loss. Total caloric expenditure can also be increased by keeping duration the same and exercising at higher intensities. For beginners, duration should be increased before increasing intensity to avoid injury and burnout.

Intensity and duration: an inverse relationship

There is an inverse relationship between intensity and time of aerobic activity. High exercise intensities (especially above LT) limit time. High workout times generally mandate lower exercise intensity. As discussed in chapter 22, individuals seeking fat loss should find the combination of intensity and duration which allows them to maximize caloric expenditure.

Type

In general, the type of activity done is less important than the previous three variables. Ultimately, the best aerobic activity is that which an individual enjoys and will do regularly. Bodybuilders should avoid high impact aerobic activities such as running as their higher body mass may increase the chance of joint injury.

Aerobics classes are generally not encouraged for bodybuilders because it is relatively more difficult to keep heart rate at low intensities. Endurance athletes should perform the majority of their training with the same type of activity they will compete in (i.e. cyclists should cycle, runners should run). The topic of cross-training is beyond the scope of this book.

The combination of the above principles will differ for different goals. The amount of training needed for general fitness differs from that needed for a pre-contest bodybuilder or an endurance athlete. Table 1 shows a sample aerobic progression for an untrained individual.

	Frequency	Intensity	Time	
Table 1: Sample aerobic progression for untrained individuals				
Week 1	3Xweek	60% of max.	20'	
Week 2	3Xweek	60% of max.	30'	
Week 3	3Xweek	60% of max.	40'	
Week 4	3-4Xweek	60-65% of max.	30-40'	
Week 5	4Xweek	65% of max.	40'	(or begin intervals)
Week 6	4Xweek	65-70% of max.	40'	
Week 7	4-5Xweek	65-70% of max.	40-45'	
Week 8	4-5Xweek	65%+ of max.	40-45'	

References

1. American College of Sports Medicine Position Stand. The recommended quantity and quality of exercise for developing and maintaining cardiorespiratory and muscular fitness in healthy adults. Med Sci Sports Exerc (1990) 22: 265-274.
2. "Guidelines for Exercise Testing and Prescription, 5th ed." The American College of Sports Medicine. Lea & Febiger Publishers 1995.
3. Max O2: The Complete Guide to Synergistic Aerobic Training. Jerry Robinson and Frank Carrino, Health for Life 1993.
4. Jakicic JM et. al. Prescribing exercise in multiple short bouts versus one continuous bout: effects on adherence, cardiorespiratory fitness, and weight loss in overweight women. Int J Obes (1995) 19: 893-901.

Chapter 25:
Interval training guidelines

Interval training is an advanced technique that can be used to improve fitness level and increase fat loss. Generally defined, interval training is any activity which alternates periods of high intensity activity (i.e. sprinting) with periods of lower intensity (i.e. walking or slow jogging). Weight training can be considered a special case of interval training but is discussed separately.

As with aerobic exercise, interval training is discussed relative to the FITT equation. Recall that interval training is limited without dietary carbohydrates and is not an appropriate form of exercise for individuals consuming zero carbohydrates on the SKD. Individuals on a CKD or TKD may use interval training.

Interval training requires a few special considerations. First and foremost, the risk of injury with interval training is higher than with aerobic exercise due to the increased intensity. Individuals beginning an exercise program are encouraged to develop a basic level of aerobic fitness (a minimum of four weeks, three times per week, 30 minutes per session at 60-65% of maximum heart rate) before incorporating higher intensity interval training.

Second, interval training should be gradually incorporated into training and the number and length of the intervals should be progressively increased as fitness level improves. Third, interval training may or may not be appropriate for bodybuilders. Done in excess, it may cause a loss of muscle size and strength by making Type II muscle fibers more Type I in nature. However, some individuals have found that interval training, performed judiciously, improves fat loss with no loss in muscle mass or strength. Finally, endurance athletes looking to maximize performance will need to perform interval training during specific periods of their training.

Frequency

As a very high intensity activity, interval training should be performed a maximum of three times per week and many individuals find that one or two interval sessions are plenty. During periods where interval training is incorporated, other forms of high intensity training may need to be reduced to maintenance levels (i.e. weight training for the legs may be reduced to once per week if intervals are being performed). Additionally, intervals should take the place of a normal aerobic training session. An individual performing 4 aerobic training sessions who wished to incorporate intervals once per week should reduce aerobic training frequency to 3 times weekly.

Intensity

Intensity of interval training may be anywhere from lactate threshold to maximum. To begin interval training, individuals should use intensities just above lactate threshold (generally around 75-85% of maximum heart rate). As fitness improves, higher intensities (up to 95% of maximum heart rate) can be used. Due to the short duration of most intervals, heart rate does not give an accurate measure of intensity and trainees will have to subjectively estimate intensity level.

In most cases, recovery in between intervals should be performed at low intensities, around 50-60% of maximum heart rate. The recovery should almost always be active. After a maximal sprint on a bike, recover with light spinning instead of stopping completely. This will help with recovery between intervals by allowing the body to remove lactic acid from the muscles.

Time

The duration of a given interval may be anywhere from fifteen seconds to five minutes or more. Generally, the shorter the interval the higher the intensity which is used and vice versa. Fifteen second intervals are done at maximal effort while a five minute interval may be done just above lactate threshold. The recovery time between intervals can be measured one of two ways:

1. Relative to the work interval: With this method, the duration of rest is expressed in some ratio of time to the work interval. A 90 second interval might have a rest interval of 2:1 meaning that twice as much rest (180 seconds or 3 minutes) would be given. A five minute interval would require a 1:1 rest interval (5').

2. When heart rate returns to 120 beats per minute: this method is more individual and takes fitness level into account. However it requires some method of measuring heart rate during exercise.

Total interval time

The total amount of intervals which should be done in any given workout ranges from 5 to 25 minutes of high intensity work not counting recovery. Obviously, this is affected by the length of the interval done. A cyclist doing 1 minute repeats would need to do from 5 to 25 total repeats. A sprinter might need to do 50 repeats of 15 second intervals.

In general, beginners should start with the low number of intervals and increase the number of intervals before increasing the intensity. Once the high number of intervals is reached, intensity can be further increased.

Type of activity

Intervals can be done on any type of equipment or outdoors. For individuals carrying extra bodyweight who wish to incorporate intervals to hasten fat loss, non-impact activities such as cycling or the stair climber are preferable to activities such as sprinting which may impose too much pounding on the joints. Athletes will need to perform intervals in their particular sport. Table 2 provides guidelines for interval training. Trainees should always warm-up and cool-down for at least 5 minutes at low intensities prior to interval training.

Table 2: General guidelines for interval training

Length of Interval	Number of Intervals	Work: Rest ratio
15"	20+	1: 5-10
30"	10-20	1: 2-3
60"	5-10	1:1.5
120"	3-5	1:1
5-10'	1-2	1: 0.5

Source: "Interval Training: Conditioning for sports and general fitness." Edward Fox and Donald Matthews. WB Saunders Company, 1974.

An alternative form of interval training is called Fartlek which is Scandinavian for speedplay. Fartlek training is a type of free-form interval training and is an excellent way for non-competitive athletes to incorporate interval training. Rather than performing a specific number of intervals for a specific amount of time, intensity is increased whenever a trainee wishes. This might be a sprint up a hill during a bike ride, or a several minute increase in intensity during a workout on the treadmill. The effort would be followed by several minutes of lower intensity activity to allow for recovery. Table 2 provides a sample interval training for untrained individuals seeking fat loss.

Table 2: Sample Interval Training Program

	Frequency (times/week)	# intervals	Interval length (seconds)	Rest time (second)	Intensity (% of max.)
Week 1	2	2-3	15-30	30-60	70
Week 2	2	3-5	15-30	30-60	70
Week 3	2	6-10	15-30	30-60	75
Week 4	2-3	2-3	30-60	60-90	75-80
Week 5	2-3	3-5	30-60	60-90	75-85
Week 6	2-3	6-8	30-60	60-90	85-90
Week 7	2-3	2-3	60-90	60-90	90-95
Week 8	2-3	3-5	60-90	60-90	90-95

Frequency: Additional aerobic workouts would consist of standard moderate intensity, longer duration activities (see guidelines for aerobic training)
Interval length: If a trainee is capable of performing the longer interval at the outset, they should go ahead and do so.
Rest time: If trainees perform the longer interval length, they should use the longer rest time.
Intensity: This is intensity of maximum capacity. Recovery intervals should be performed at 60% of max. or less.

After an 8 week interval training program had been completed, interval training would be discontinued for several weeks to allow for recovery.

Reference cited

1. "Interval Training: Conditioning for sports and general fitness." Edward Fox and Donald Matthews. WB Saunders Company, 1974.

Chapter 26:
Weight Training Guidelines

Relative to aerobic and interval training, weight training is far more complex. The number of workout permutations is literally infinite and there are few definitive guidelines which exist. Individuals are encouraged to experiment within the context of the following guidelines to find what works for them personally. The FITT equation, explained in chapter 23, does not apply as well to weight training although topics of frequency and intensity are discussed below.

Section 1: Definitions

To better understand the topics to be discussed later in this chapter, a number of basic weight training concepts need to be defined. They are muscle actions, muscular fatigue, repetitions, and repetition maximum.

Muscle actions (1)

Although muscles can only contract and pull against the bones that they are attached to, it is possible to define three different types of muscle actions depending on what happens while the muscle is contracting. These three actions are:

1. Concentric muscle action: This type of muscle action occurs when the muscle generates more force than the weight of the bar, causing the muscle to shorten. A concentric muscle action would represent lifting the weight.
2. Eccentric muscle action: This type of muscle action occurs when the force being produced is less than the force required to lift the weight. When this occurs, the weight is lowered.
3. Isometric muscle action: This type of muscle action occurs when the amount of force generated by the muscle equals the the amount of force needed. When this occurs, the weight is neither lifted nor lowered.

Fatigue and muscular failure

Fatigue during weight training is discussed in chapter 20 and refers to the loss of force production potential. Muscular failure is typically defined as the momentary inability to move a weight through a full range of motion in good form and will occur when force production capabilities have fallen below force requirements. If moving a barbell through the full range of motion (ROM) requires 100 pounds of force, failure will occur when the muscle can no longer generate that much force. In that there are three types of muscle actions, there are also three ways that muscular fatigue can occur.

Concentric failure: the momentary inability to lift a weight through the full range of motion
Isometric failure: the inability to hold the weight without movement
Eccentric failure: the inability to lower the weight under control

Concentric failure will occur before isometric failure which will occur before eccentric failure. On a calorically restricted diet, going past the point of positive failure is probably not a good idea and will most likely induce overtraining. Therefore, we will only consider positive failure in the exercise routines.

There is a great deal of debate both in research and popular literature about training to muscular failure. Some authors feel that training to muscular failure is the ONLY way to generate adaptations to strength training while others argue that failure is not a prerequisite. A full discussion of both sides is beyond the scope of this book. This author feels that as long as individuals are training within a repetition or two of failure (such that at least 10 repetitions are performed when 12 could have been done in good form) progress should occur.

Repetition (rep or reps)

One repetition of an exercise is the combination of a concentric muscle action and an eccentric muscle action (a lifting followed by a lowering). Some individuals will perform eccentric only training (where the weight is lifted by a partner and lowered by the trainee) in which case one lowering would count as a repetition.

Repetition Maximum (RM)

RM refers to a weight that can be performed X reps but not X+1 reps in perfect form. For example, if a trainee can do 8 reps in perfect form with 100 lbs but not 9, 100 lbs would be their 8RM weight. The relationship between RM loads and percentage of 1 repetition maximum (the amount you can lift for 1 rep and 1 rep only) appears in figure 1.

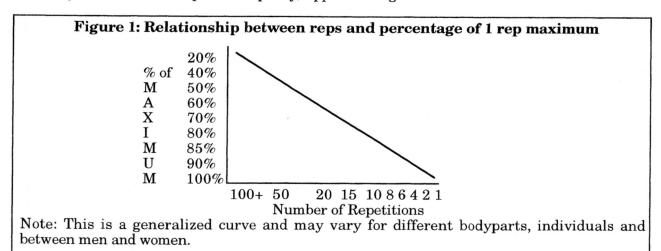

Figure 1: Relationship between reps and percentage of 1 rep maximum

Note: This is a generalized curve and may vary for different bodyparts, individuals and between men and women.

249

Set

One set of an exercise is a series of repetitions (typically with no rest between repetitions) terminated when the weight can no longer be moved or when some particular number (i.e. 10) is attained.

Compound versus isolation exercises

Weight training exercises are typically delineated into compound and isolation exercises. Compound exercises refer to any exercise where multiple muscles are worked, such as the bench press or squat. Isolation exercises refer to any exercise where only a single muscle is worked, such as the cable crossover or leg extension.

Section 2: Acute Program Variables

A number of program variables can be altered during strength training to achieve different goals. They are: choice of exercise, order of exercise, load used, number of sets/reps, training frequency, length of the rest interval, and lifting speed (3, 4,5).

Choice of Exercise

The choice of exercise depends on the goal of training. In general, beginners are advised to stick with compound exercises (i.e. bench press) over isolation exercises (i.e. pec deck) whenever possible. Compound exercises work more muscles during the same exercise, which burn more calories and allow more weight to be lifted. However, advanced lifters may wish to incorporate isolation exercises as necessary. Changing exercises changes motor unit recruitment (6) and may be necessary for more complete muscular and strength development. The exercise routines are based around common exercises but individuals are encouraged to substitute exercises as necessary.

Order of exercise

The typical order of exercise is from larger muscles groups (legs, back) to smaller muscles (arms, abdominals) as this allows heavier loads to be used during training (7). Larger muscles require more energy and are generally done earlier in the training session. However, individuals wishing to work on a specific weak point may choose to train that part first in a routine when energy levels are high. For example, a bodybuilder with poor hamstrings may train the hamstrings prior to quadriceps at every other leg workout. Exercise routines typically progress from larger to smaller muscle groups.

Intensity of loading

In research terms, intensity in weight training is defined as the percentage of maximal capacity that you are lifting (8). Beginners achieve strength gains using weights as low as 50% of their maximum strength (5). This may allow 20 repetitions or more to be performed.

Advanced lifters will need to use at least 60% of their maximum to obtain strength gains (5,9). This corresponds to 20 reps or less in most individuals. Maximal strength gains appear to occur between 4-6RM with lower gains in maximal strength at less than 2RM and greater than 10RM (9). For hypertrophy, it is recommended that lifters work between 60 and 85% of 1RM, as discussed in chapter 20. This generally falls within the range of 6 to 20 reps. For the greatest strength gains loads of 85-100% may be used (5). This corresponds to between one and five repetitions in most people.

In practice, the use of % of 1RM to determine intensity can be problematic since it varies from exercise to exercise, from individual to individual, and from day to day. In the gym setting, intensity is typically used as an indication of the overall effort of exercise. By this definition, higher rep sets (such as 12-15RM) taken to failure can actually be more intense than lower rep sets (such as a 2-3RM). More accurately, the higher rep set puts a much greater stress on metabolic factors (such as lactic acid accumulation) while the lower rep set puts less stress on these same factors (because the set is too short).

Number of reps

There is currently no data to suggest that any one rep range is better than another for the stimulus of growth. Anecdotally, many authorities suggest a range of 6-20 repetitions completed in 20-60 seconds as a growth stimulus (4,10-13). The reasons for this time period are discussed in chapter 20.

There is no need for beginners to use low rep sets early in their training. Recall that the initial adaptations to strength training are neural. In one study, whether beginners performed sets of 4-6RM of 15-20RM, they obtained the same adaptations (14). Higher repetitions (no lower than 8) are recommended for the first several months of training (5). After the first 8-12 weeks of training, beginners may begin working with heavier loads and lower repetitions if desired.

Training volume/number of sets

Volume of training can refer to the total poundage lifted, total number of sets done or total number of reps done (8). This book will use total sets and reps as as measure of volume, especially with regards to glycogen depletion and the ketogenic diet.

There is a great deal of debate over how many sets are necessary for optimal results. For hypertrophy, anywhere from 1 to 20 sets has been used by lifters (4) and 3-6 sets per bodypart has been suggested as optimal for growth (3,4). However, this depends greatly on individual recovery capacity and genetics. Some individuals, typically referred to as 'hardgainers', may have trouble recovering from even two or three maximal sets, while others can handle much higher training loads.

In general, the number of sets done is inversely proportional to the number of reps performed (5). If 20 rep sets are done, only 1-2 sets may be needed while 4 rep sets may require 4 or more sets.

Most research on the topic of sets has been done on beginners who are not representative of advanced lifters. In beginners, one set gives the same results as three in terms of strength and muscle size gains, at least over the first fourteen weeks of training (15). Most authorities agree that 1-2 sets per exercise are sufficient for beginning trainees during the first six to eight weeks of training (5,8,16). Whether advanced lifters need more sets is a matter of great debate. After this initial conditioning period where only 1-2 sets are done per exercise, more sets (3-6 per exercise) may be necessary to elicit further strength gains (5).

Reps, sets, loads and the repetition continuum

Although not all authorities agree, there is thought to be a continuum of adaptations which may occur with different repetition sets (17). That is, optimal strength gains appear to occur between 2 and 20RM loads (17) with strength gains becoming progressively lower as more than 20 reps per set are done. In a classic review paper, Atha determined that 4-6 sets of 4-6RM gave optimal improvements in maximal strength but that higher and lower loads were not as beneficial (18).

There is a dynamic interaction between the variables of reps, sets and loads. The load used (% of 1RM) ultimately determines how many reps per set are done. Reps per set (or set time) ultimately determines how many total sets must be done. The interaction between the three will affect what adaptation is seen.

The interplay between load and volume (sets and reps) can be looked at as an interplay between tension and fatigue. Tension is roughly equivalent to the weight being lifting (as a percentage of maximum). Fatigue refers to the total amount of metabolic work done. In general, the following appears to hold true.

High tension/low fatigue: 1-5 RM : develops 1RM strength primarily (18)
Low tension/high fatigue: 25+RM : develops muscular endurance
Moderate tension/moderate fatigue: 6-20RM : develops muscle size (19)

The above chart does not take set time into account. It is more accurate to say that low set times will develop primarily strength, medium set times hypertrophy, and long set times muscular endurance. However, this is highly variable and many individuals can develop hypertrophy with very low or very high reps.

Frequency of training

Beginners typically train every other day, three times per week. However, research has found that beginners may get similar strength gains (about 75-85%) lifting twice a week (20). As lifters advance, they will need to train a given bodypart less frequently as they will be training it more intensely. Recall from chapter 20 that a muscle may require four to seven days to recover from eccentric loading. This fact has led many individuals to train each bodypart once per week and train every day in the gym. This may be a mistake for natural lifters. On top of local fatigue, trainees also have to deal with systemic fatigue as daily high intensity training generally stresses the body. So while daily training may give each bodypart up to seven days of rest, the body as a whole is never allowed to recover.

For natural lifters, it is suggested that no more than two days of heavy training be performed without a day of rest to avoid negatively affecting hormone levels. In addition, three to four days per week in the gym is probably the maximum a natural lifter should perform (11). The exercise routines presented in chapters 27 and 28 reflect this philosophy.

Rest periods

The rest period between sets is inversely proportional to the number of reps done (5). For sets of 1-5 reps, a rest of three to five minutes may be required. For sets of 12-15 reps, only ninety seconds may be required for recovery to occur (5, 8). For sets of 25 and up, as little as 30" may be required between sets

Recall from chapter 20 that the interplay of reps, sets and rest periods can affect the hormonal response to weight training. To recap:

1. Multiple (3-4), longer sets (10-12RM, lasting 40-60 seconds), with short rest periods (60-90 seconds) raise growth hormone levels and may be helpful for fat loss.
2. Multiple (3-4), short sets (5RM, lasting 20-30 seconds), with long rest periods (3-5') raise testosterone levels in men and may be beneficial for strength and size gains.

Tempo

Very little research has examined the effects of lifting speed on strength and mass gains and no consensus exists on optimal lifting speed (21). Several studies compare high-speed to slow-speed lifting and find that slow speed lifting increases maximal strength while explosive training (plyometrics) increases rate of force development (22,23,24).

Most exercises in the weight room are not safely done at high speeds due to the possibility of injury. Controlled lifting speeds are recommended for strength and mass gains (5). While high-speed lifting may improve power, training for this type of event is beyond the scope of this book.

More importantly, rep speed should probably be varied in the same way that other program variables are. Within the context of 20-60 seconds of total set time, a large variety of rep tempos can be chosen, with the number of repetitions changing to accommodate. For example, a lifter could do 1 rep of 30 seconds up, 30 seconds down or 15 reps of 2 seconds up, 2 seconds down or 10 reps at 2 second up, 4 seconds down.

Simply keep in mind that the eccentric portion of the movement must be controlled for the growth stimulus to occur. Most studies use a 4 to 6 second repetition and we will assume a 4 second repetition from this point on. If trainees prefer a faster or slower tempo, simply change the rep count to keep set time the same.

Section 3: Other topics

Range of motion (ROM)

Range of motion refers to the total range a weight is moved through from the beginning to the end of the movement. Strength gains in response to training are very joint angle specific (25) meaning that strength gains will only be seen in the ROM trained. Thus for strength gains throughout the full ROM, exercises must be taken through a full ROM during training (8). Partial movements are sometimes used by advanced lifters to overcome sticking points in a movement (i.e. lockout of the bench press), but they are beyond the scope of this book.

Circuit Training

Circuit training refers to high rep, continuous weight training used in an attempt to elicit both strength and aerobic gains. While programs of this nature increase aerobic capacity slightly, on the order of 4-5%, this can not compare to the improvements in aerobic capacity of 20 to 30% seen with regular aerobic training (17,26). In most cases, circuit training is NOT recommended for optimal results. The only exception is the circuit depletion workout for individuals on the CKD which is discussed in the advanced CKD workout in chapter 28.

Aerobics or weight training first?

While trainees should always perform a short aerobic warm-up prior to weight training, the choice of whether to do weight training or aerobics first in the same workout session is debatable. Performing aerobics after weights will make the aerobic training harder (27). So if the primary goal is aerobic training, that should be done first. If the primary goal is weight training, that should be performed first when the trainee is fresh. While performing aerobics after training should in theory rely more on fat for fuel, recall that it does not appear that using fat during exercise has any bearing on fat loss. Bodybuilders, powerlifters and other strength athletes should always perform weight training first after a short warmup.

Warm ups

A warm muscle can produce more force than a cold muscle (28,29). Thus a proper warm-up prior to training will ensure maximal strength as well as help to prevent injuries. The warm-up can be broken into two components:

1. General warm-up: This is 5-10' of light aerobic activity to raise the core temperature of the body. The general warm-up need only be continued until a light sweat is broken, as this indicates that the body is as warm as it will get. This will also increase liver glycogen output to help establish ketosis for early week workouts.

2. Specific warm-up: In addition to the general warm-up, a specific warm-up should also be done to prepare the body for the specific activity which will be done. If a trainee was training chest with the bench press, they would perform several lighter sets of bench presses prior to their heavy sets. A common misconception among trainees is the performance of high rep warm-up sets. All this serves to do is use valuable energy that could be used for the work sets. Warm-up sets should generally use low reps unless there is an injury present requiring more warm-up (13).

Anywhere from 1-5 warm-up sets may be performed depending on a trainees strength level. Beginners may not need to do any warm-up sets for the first 6-8 weeks of training.

A comparison of warmups between two lifters appears in table 2. The first lifter will be lifting 135 lbs for 8 reps during their work sets. The second lifter will be lifting 315 lbs for 8 reps.

Table 2: Comparison of warmups for two different lifters	
Lifter 1 (135X8)	Lifter 2 (315X8)
barX5, rest 30"	135X5, rest 30"
95X3, rest 180"	185X3, rest 30"
135X8	225X1, rest 30"
	275X1, rest 180"
	315X8

Section 4: Weight training systems

The number of training systems in existence is immense, possibly infinite. Rather than try to describe them all, we will discuss only three: straight sets, ascending pyramids and descending pyramids.

1. Straight sets is a method where the weight is kept constant on all work sets. If sets are being taken to failure, most trainees will not be able to perform the same number of reps at each set. Table 3 on the next page shows an example of straight sets. When all three sets of 10 are accomplished during a given workout, the weight should be raised about 5% at the next workout.

2. Ascending pyramids are probably the most common type of workout. They are not the most effective (13). In an ascending pyramid, after warm-ups, the first work set is taken to failure. Then weight is added to the bar and another set to failure is done at lower reps. This is continued until all sets have been completed. In a descending pyramid, the first work set is done at the heaviest weight and the weight is reduced on subsequent sets. Compare the workouts in table 4 for a lifter who will use 275 for their heaviest set.

Table 3: Straight set workout for a lifter with a 10RM of 315 lbs	
WeightXreps	Rest (seconds)
135X5	30-60
185X3	30-60
225X1	30-60
275X1	180 (end of warm-ups)
315X10	120-180
315X8	120-180
315X6	move to next exercise

With the descending pyramid, many more reps are performed with the heaviest weight (275 lbs) which would simulate more growth. Then, to take fatigue into account, subsequent sets are done at a lower weight. With few exceptions, lifters should always use descending pyramids.

Table 4: Comparison of ascending and descending pyramids	
Ascending pyramid	Descending Pyramid
135X15	135X8
185X12	185X3
225X10	225X3
245X8	255X1 (End of warm-up sets)
255X8 (failure)	275 to failure (6+ reps)
265X7 (failure)	255 to failure (8+ reps)
275X6 (failure)	245 to failure (9+ reps)

Periodization

Periodization refers to the systematic variation in some aspect of training (such as sets, reps, rest periods, exercise selection, etc) throughout the training period (1,4,5). Periodization originally came from Eastern Europe for training weightlifters and there is much debate over its usefulness for the average trainee. Several research studies show that periodized routines do not give an advantage in strength gains in the short term (30,31).

However, the body can adapt to any stress and changing some aspect of training from time to time is one way to generate further adaptation. However, individuals vary in how frequently they need to vary their programming. Beginners may be able to perform the same routine for 6 weeks or more without any changes. Intermediate lifters may wish to alter one or more of the acute program variables ever 4 weeks and advanced lifters may vary some aspect of their training every 2 to 3 weeks (5). However, many individuals achieve excellent results making no changes to their program (other than weight lifted) for much longer periods of 12 to 18 weeks.

Although there are a number of different types of periodization which can be used, two of the most common are linear and undulating periodization (11). Sample programs to increase both muscle size and increase 1 RM strength appear in table 5.

Table 5: Comparison of linear and undulating periodization					
Weeks	1-3	4-6	7-9	10-12	13-15
Linear	3X10RM	4X6RM	5X3RM	6X2RM	8X1RM
Undulating	3X10RM	4X6RM	3X8RM	4X3RM	4X5RM

As discussed previously, it does not appear that lower repetitions stimulate muscle growth to the same degree as higher rep sets but may increase maximal strength more. Thus, a linear periodization routine may result in loss of muscle near the end of the cycle (4). Undulating periodization allows an individual to alternate between strength and growth training to maintain muscle mass while pushing up maximal strength.

References cited

1. "Essentials of strength and conditioning" Ed. T. Baechle, Human Kinetics Publishers 1994.
2. Sale D And MacDougall D. Specificity in Strength Training: A Review for the Coach and Athlete. Can J Appl Sports Sci (1981) 6:87-92.
3. Fleck S and Kraemer W. Resistance Training: basic Principles (Part 4 of 4). Physician and Sportsmedicine (1988) 16 June: 69-81.
4. "Designing Resistance Training Programs, 2nd edition" W. Kraemer and S. Fleck, Human Kinetics 1996.
5. "Program Design: Choosing sets, reps, loads, tempo and rest periods" Paul Chek, Paul Chek Seminars 1996.
6. "Neuromechanical basis of kinesiology" Roger M. Enoka. Human Kinetics Publishers 1994.
7. Sforzo GA and Touey PR. Manipulating exercise order affects muscular performance during a resistance exercise training session. J Strength Cond Res (1996) 10: 20-24.
8. Fleck S and Kraemer W. Resistance Training: basic Principles (Part 1 of 4). Physician and Sportsmedicine (1988) 16 March: 160-171.
9. McDonagh, MJN and Davies CTM. Adaptive response of mammalian skeletal muscle to exercise with high loads. Eur J Appl Physiol (1984) 52: 139-155.
10. "Fitness and Strength Training For All sports: Theory, Methods, Programs" J. Hartmann and H. Tunnemann. Sports Books Publishers 1995.
11. "Current trends in strength training" Charles Poliquin Dayton Publishing Group 1997.
12. "Supertraining: Special Training for Sporting Excellence" Mel Siff and Yuri Verkoshanksy, School of Mechanical Engineering Press 1993.
13. "Science and practice of strength training" Vladimir Zatsiorsky, Human Kinetics 1995.
14. Hisaeda H et. al. Influence of two different modes of resistance training in female subjects. Ergonomics (1996) 39: 842-852.
15. Starkey DB et al. Effect of resistance training volume on strength and muscle thickness. Med Sci Sports Exerc (1996) 28: 1311-1320.
16. Westcott W. Transformation: How to take them from sedentary to active. Idea Today Magazine (1995) pp. 46-54.
17. Kraemer WJ et. al. Physiological adaptations to resistance exercise: Implications for athletic conditioning. Sports Med (1988) 6:246-256.

18. Atha J. Strengthening muscle. Exercise and Sports Science Reviews (1981) 9: 1-73.

19. Stone WJ and Coulter SP. Strength/endurance effects from three resistance training protocols with women. J Strength Cond Res (1994) 8: 231-234.

20. American College of Sports Medicine Position Stand. The recommended quantity and quality of exercise for developing and maintaining cardiorespiratory and muscular fitness in healthy adults. Med Sci Sports Exerc (1990) 22: 265-274.

21. LaChance PF and Hortobagyi T. Influence of cadence on muscular performance during push-up and pull-up exercise. J Strength Cond Res (1994) 8: 76-79.

22. Hakkinen K et. al. Changes in isometric force and relaxation time, electromyographic and muscular fiber characteristics of human skeletal muscle during strength training and detraining. Acta Physiol Scand (1985) 125: 573-585.

23. Hakkinen K et. al. Effect of explosive type strength training on isometric force and relaxation time, electromyographic and muscle fibre characteristics of leg extensor muscles. Acta Physiol Scand (1985) 125: 587-600.

24. Hakkinen K and Komi P. Training-induced changes in neuromuscular performance under voluntary and reflex conditions. Eur J Appl Physiol (1986) 55: 147-155.

25. Graves JE Specificity of limited range of motion variable resistance training. Med Sci Sports Exerc (1989) 21: 84-89.

26. "Strength and Power in Sport" Ed. P.V. Komi Blackwell Scientific Publications 1992.

27. Bailey ML et. al. Effects of resistance exercise on selected physiological parameters during subsequent aerobic exercise. J Strength Cond Res (1996) 10: 101-104.

28. "Physiology of Sport and Exercise" Jack H. Wilmore and David L. Costill. Human Kinetics Publishers 1994.

29. "Exercise Physiology: Human Bioenergetics and it's applications" George A Brooks, Thomas D. Fahey, and Timothy P. White. Mayfield Publishing Company 1996.

30. Baker D et. al. Periodization: The effect on strength of manipulating volume and intensity. J Strength Cond Res (1994) 8: 235-242.

31. Herrick AB and Stone WJ. The effects of periodization versus progressive resistance exercise on upper and lower body strength in women. J Strength Cond Res (1996) 10: 72-76.

Part VII:
Exercise programs

Chapter 27: Beginner/intermediate programs
Chapter 28: The Advanced CKD workout
Chapter 29: Other applications for the ketogenic diet
Chapter 30: Fat loss for the pre-contest bodybuilder

Previous sections have laid the groundwork for the actual training programs to be presented in this chapter. Depending on the goals of the individual, differing amounts of each type of training (aerobic, interval, weight training) are necessary.

Chapter 27 presents programs for the beginning and intermediate trainee. Chapter 28 discusses the advanced CKD workout, based on the information presented in chapter 12. Chapter 29 presents possible ways to implement the ketogenic diet for other applications such as endurance training, power/strength sports, and mass gains. Finally, chapter 30 discusses fat loss for the pre-contest bodybuilder.

Chapter 27:
Beginner/Intermediate programs

Having discussed general guidelines for the three types of exercise in previous chapters, this chapter presents sample exercise programs for beginning and intermediate exercises. There is also a discussion of split routines.

Section 1: Beginner routine/General Fitness

The following routine is for individuals who have never lifted weights before or who may be starting a diet and exercise program after a long time of being inactive. It is appropriate to use with the TKD but not the CKD (as the total amount of training is not sufficient to deplete glycogen in all muscle groups within 5 days).

Aerobic training

A frequency of three days per week with a duration of 20-30' and a moderate intensity (~60-70% of maximum heart rate) is all that is necessary to build basic fitness. Aerobic exercise can be performed prior to the weight workout or afterwards. If fat loss is the goal, trainees may wish to perform more aerobic exercise than the bare minimum, up to 4-5 days per week. When beginning an exercise program, it is recommended that individuals start slowly and build up. Volume and intensity of exercise can be increased gradually as fitness improves. Doing too much too soon is an excellent way to get injured or burn-out on an exercise program. A sample aerobic progression appears in chapter 24.

Interval training

Interval training is an option for individuals wishing basic health and fitness but is not required. Individuals just starting an exercise program should not consider performing interval training until a base fitness level of at least four weeks with a minimum of 30' of aerobic exercise three times per week has been achieved. Beginners wishing to begin interval training should refer to chapter 25 for guidelines.

Weight training

For basic fitness, a weight routine of 25-30' two to three times per week is sufficient. A 5' warmup on the bike or treadmill (or full aerobic workout) should precede every weight training session. Beginners should generally start with the lightest weight possible, focusing on form and breathing during their first few workouts. Once form has been learned, progressive overload is applied by attempting to improve performance at each workout, by adding either repetitions or weight. When 12 repetitions can be completed in perfect form, the weight should be raised approximately 5% (or whatever the smallest weight increment available is), bringing the rep count back down to 8. The lifter would then attempt to perform more reps until 12 were performed at which point the weight would be raised again. Most beginners find they can raise weights consistently for the first 8 weeks of training. Beginners should be sure to use a controlled, slow lifting speed while they are learning the movements. Lifting the weight in 2-3 seconds and lowering it in 3-4 seconds is a general guideline. A sample beginner weight training workout appears in table 1.

Table 1: Beginning weight workout			
Exercise	Sets	Reps	Rest
Leg press(1*)	1	8-12	60"
Calf raise (2)	1	8-12	60"
Leg curl (3)	1	8-12	60"
Bench press(1*)	1	8-12	60"
Row (1*)	1	8-12	60"
Shoulder press (2)	1	8-12	60"
Pulldown (2)	1	8-12	60"
Triceps pushdown (3)	1	8-12	60"
Biceps curl (3)	1	8-12	60"
Crunch (1*)	1	8-12	60"
Low back extension (3)	1	8-12	60"

* Individuals with very limited time can obtain significant benefits from performing these four exercises (which should take approximately 5') with 20-25' of aerobic exercise. Alternately, if a trainee has 30' four times per week or more to exercise, they should perform weight training twice per week for 30' and aerobics 2-3 times per week for 30'.

Beginning trainees starting on the ketogenic diet should not need to consume pre-workout carbs for at least the first 2-3 weeks. This should allow the major adaptations to the ketogenic diet to occur as rapidly as possible. After 2-3 weeks of regular training, carbohydrates can be consumed around training as described in chapter 11.

Numbers after each exercise indicate what exercise session a given exercise should be introduced. The first workout would be one set of leg presses, one set of bench presses, one set of rows, and one set of crunches. At the second workout, the first four exercises would be done and the calf raise, shoulder press, and pulldown would be added. At the third workout, the previous seven exercises would be done with the addition of the leg curl, triceps pushdown, biceps curl, and back extension at which point no new exercises would be added. This progression allows beginners to ease into training without generating too much muscle soreness.

Section 2: Intermediate workout routines

After 8 weeks of the beginner training program, many individuals wish to move to a more advanced workout. Due to the higher number of sets, the CKD approach becomes possible at this time. We will assume an average set time of 45" this point in the exercise programs. This allows a lifting speed of 2-3 seconds up and 2-4 seconds down for an average of 10 reps per set. An intermediate workout appears in table 2.

Table 2: Intermediate 3 day full body workout			
Exercise	Sets	Reps	Rest
Leg press*	2	6-8	90"
Calf raise	1	8-10	60"
Leg curl	1	8-10	60"
Bench press*	2	6-8	90"
Row*	2	6-8	90"
Shoulder press	1	8-10	60"
Pulldown to front	1	8-10	60"
Triceps pushdown	1	12-15	60"
Arm curl	1	12-15	60"
Crunch	2	12-15	60"
Back extension	1	8-12	60"

* Perform 1-2 warmup sets prior to these exercises.

Section 3: Split routines

As trainees progress, they will frequently be unable to recover from working each bodypart three times weekly. At this time they must move to a split routine. Split routines allows a greater amount of recovery to occur between sessions as well as allowing more work to be done for each bodypart.

There are many different ways to split the body. The simplest split is the two day split. This way, instead of working the whole body in one workout, it is divided into two parts. The main types of two day splits are:

1. The Upper/Lower + abs split
2. The Push/Pull+leg split

The Upper/Lower + abs split

With the Upper/Lower split, the upper body is trained one day and lower body + abs the next training day. A sample upper/lower split routine appears in tables 3 and 4.

Table 3: Sample lower body+abs workout

Exercise	Sets	Reps	Rest
Leg press/squat*	3	8-10	90-120"
Leg curl*	3	8-10	90"
Leg extension	2	10-12	90"
Seated leg curl	2	12-15	90"
Standing calf raise*	3	8-10	90"
Seated calf raise	2	12-15	90"
Reverse crunch	2	15-20	60"
Crunch	2	15-20	60"

* Perform 1-3 warmup sets prior to these exercises.

Table 4: Sample upper body workout

Exercise	Sets	Reps	Rest
Bench press*	3	8-10	90"
Cable row*	3	8-10	60"
Shoulder press	2	10-12	60"
Pulldown to front	2	10-12	60"
Triceps pushdown	1-2	12-15	60"
Arm curl	1-2	12-15	60"
Back Extension	2	12-15	60"

* Perform 1-3 warmup sets prior to these exercises.

There are two ways to work the Upper/Lower split into a routine. One is to alternate workouts on a Monday, Wednesday, Friday workout schedule. A second is to train each bodypart twice a week. Both options appear in table 5.

Table 5: Comparison of two different ways to sequence the Upper/Lower Split

Option 1: every other day	Option 2: 4 days per week
Mon: Lower body	Mon: Lower body
Tue: off	Tue: Upper body
Wed: Upper body	Wed: off
Thu: off	Thu: Lower body
Fri: Lower body	Fri: Upper body
Sat: off	Sat: off
Sun: off	Sun: off
Mon: Upper body	Mon: Lower body
Tue: off	Tue: Upper body
Wed: Lower body	Wed: off
Thu: off	Thu: Lower body
Fri: Upper body	Fri: Upper body

The every other day routine gives a lot of recovery between workouts. If using the CKD approach, each workout will come before the carb-up every 2 weeks. The 4 day per week routine hits each bodypart more frequently but the same workout will precede the carb-load every week.

The Push/Pull + legs split

The second type of 2 day split is the Push/Pull + legs split. With this workout, the body is split into pushing muscles (chest, shoulders, triceps) and pulling muscles (back, biceps). Legs are trained with pulling muscles to keep the workouts approximately the same length. Sample workouts appear in tables 6 and 7.

Table 6: Sample pushing workout + abs

Exercise	Sets	Reps	Rest
Bench press*	4	6-8	90"
Incline bench press	2	10-12	60"
Shoulder press	3	10-12	90"
Triceps pushdown	2	12-15	60"
Reverse crunches	3	15-20	60"
Crunch	2	15-20	60"

* Perform 1-3 warmup sets prior to these exercises.

Table 7: Sample pulling workout + legs

Exercise	Sets	Reps	Rest
Leg press/squat*	4	6-8	120"
Leg curl	4	6-8	90"
Calf raise	2	15-20	90"
Cable row*	4	6-8	60"
Pulldown to front	2	8-10	60"
Barbell curl	2	10-12	60"
Back extension	2	12-15	60"

* Perform 1-3 warmup sets prior to these exercises.

The Upper/Lower split can be sequenced in the same way as the Push/Pull split, outlined in table 6 above.

The three way split

Some individuals prefer to train a three or four day split (or more), dividing the entire body into three or four separate sections. This is probably not ideal for the CKD approach since bodyparts will not be optimally compensated during the carb-up. However, this type of workout approach is usable with the TKD. Some sample three day splits appear in table 8.

Table 9: Possible three way splits

Option 1	Option 2	Option 3
Mon: Chest/back	Chest/shoulders/triceps	Chest/triceps
Tue: off	off	off
Wed: Legs/abs	Leg/abs	Back/biceps
Thu: off	off	off
Fri: delts/arms	back/biceps	Legs/shoulders
Sat/Sun: off	off	off

Summary

The amount of exercise needed by beginning trainees is small. A minimum of three hours per week, generally divided half into weight training and half into intervals is all that is necessary for basic health and fitness. Beginners can add interval training if desired.

As trainees become more advanced, they may be unable to weight train each bodypart three times per week. In this case the body can be split, such that different bodyparts are worked at each workout. A number of types of splits is possible.

Chapter 28:
The Advanced CKD for fat loss

Advanced trainees frequently want to know how to optimize the CKD for fat loss. This chapter presents a routine which incorporates all of the information presented in the previous chapters. The goal of this routine is to co-ordinate training to take maximal advantage of the peculiar format of the CKD. This goal incorporates the following factors:

1. Deplete muscle glycogen in all bodyparts to approximately 70 mmol/kg by Tuesday to maximize fat utilization by the muscles but not increase protein utilization.

2. Maximize growth hormone output (which is a lipolytic hormone) on Monday and Tuesday with the combination of multiple, long sets, and short rest periods.

3. Maintain muscle mass with tension work outs on Monday and Tuesday.

4. Deplete muscle glycogen to between 25 and 40 mmol/kg on Friday to stimulate optimal glycogen supercompensation.

5. Stimulate mass gains during the weekend of overfeeding with a tension workout or utilize a high rep depletion workout to deplete glycogen completely.

Three possible formats for this routine appear in table 1.

	Table 1: Possible variants for the 7 days CKD		
	Variant 1	Variant 2	Variant 3
Sun:	30-60 minutes of low intensity aerobics to reestablish ketosis		
Mon:	Legs	Legs/Chest/Back	Back/biceps/legs
Tue:	Upper body	Delts/arms/abs	Chest/delts/triceps/abs
Wed:	Aerobics or off	Aerobics or off	Aerobics or off
Thu:	Aerobics or off	Aerobics of off	Aerobics or off
Fri:	Full body	Full body	Full body
Sat:	No workout during the carb-up phase of the diet		

This format assumes that the carb-up ends Saturday at bedtime. If lifters choose to carb-up for longer than 36 hours, the Sunday cardio session would be moved to Monday morning or eliminated completely.

Aerobics are optional on Mon and Tue and should be done after lifting. Legs should generally be trained on Monday when the trainee is strongest. Alternately weak body parts can be trained on Monday to take advantage of glycogen compensation.

The Friday full body workout can either be a tension workout (i.e. high loads, low reps) or a high-rep, circuit-type depletion workout. The choice of one or the other will depend on the level of the lifter. Advanced lifters may not be able to train a bodypart heavily twice each week and fully recover. In that case, the high-rep depletion workout would be the best choice.

Others may choose to do a heavy workout prior to the carb-up to take advantage of any possible anabolism during the carb-load. For lifters wishing to use the advanced workout with the CKD, they must calculate how many sets per bodypart are needed to deplete muscle glycogen.

Keep in mind the goal to reach 70 mmol/kg by the end of Tuesday's workout and then between 25-40 mmol/kg before the carb-up. The example workout is based on a lifter carbing for 36 hours, achieving a glycogen level of ~150 mmol/kg in each major muscle group. Calculations were done in chapter 12 and sample workouts appear in table 2 and 3.

Table 2: Sample Monday workout: legs and abdominals

Exercise	Sets	Reps	Rest
Squats *	4	8-10	90"
Leg curl *	4	8-10	90"
Leg extension OR feet high leg press	2	10-12	60"
Seated leg curl	2	10-12	60"
Standing calf raise *	4	8-10	90"
Seated calf raise	2	10-12	60"
Reverse crunch	2	15-20	60"
Crunch	2	15-20	60"

* Perform 1-3 warmup sets for these exercises

Table 3: Sample Tuesday workout: upper body

Exercise	Sets	Reps	Rest
Incline bench press *	4	8-10	60"
Cable row *	4	8-10	60"
Flat bench press	2	10-12	60"
Pulldown to front	2	10-12	60"
Shoulder press	3	10-12	60"
Barbell curl	2	12-15	45"
Triceps pushdown	2	12-15	45"

* Perform 1-3 warmup sets for these exercises

The above workouts should deplete glycogen in all target muscle groups to roughly 70 mmol/kg. On Friday, the goal is to deplete the muscles to between 25-40 mmol/kg, requiring 85-128 seconds more work. Again, at 45" per set average, this requires 2-3 heavy sets per bodypart. Due to the significant overlap between body parts, only 1 set should be needed for small muscle groups. Arms receive sufficient work from benching, rows, presses and pulldowns. Additionally, different exercises are selected from the Mon/Tue workouts to target different muscle fibers. A sample Friday tension workout appears in table 4.

Table 4: Sample Friday tension workout			
Exercise	Sets	Reps	Rest
Leg press *	3	8-10	90"
or Deadlift *	2	10-15	2-3'
Leg curl	1	10-12	60"
Calf raise *	2	10-12	60"
Bench press *	2-3	8-10	90"
Wide grip row *	2-3	8-10	90"
Shoulder press	1-2	10-12	60"
Undergrip pulldown	1-2	10-12	60"

* Perform 1-3 warmup sets for these exercises

Note: Sets and reps differ for deadlifts due to decrease the chance of low-back strain.

The depletion workout

Another option for the Friday workout is a high-rep, circuit depletion workout. If a trainee chooses to do this workout, he or she should simply pick one exercise per bodypart and work the body in a giant loop. For best recovery between body parts, alternate a leg exercise, a pushing exercise, and a pulling exercise. A possible order would be legs, chest, back, hamstrings, shoulders, lats, calves, triceps, biceps, and finally abdominals.

Each set should consist of 10-20 quick reps per set (1 second up/1 second down) with a light weight. One minute of rest should be taken between exercises, and five minutes rest between each circuit. This will help to limit fatigue and nausea from lactic acid buildup. The sets should not be taken to failure as the goal is simply to deplete muscle glycogen. The depletion circuit is the workout that pre-contest bodybuilders will do the week of the contest before the final carb-up. Sample circuits appear below:

1. leg press, dumbbell (DB) bench press, cable row, leg curl, shoulder press, overgrip pulldown, calf raise, triceps pushdown, barbell curl, reverse crunch.
2. leg extension, incline DB bench press, narrow grip row, seated leg curl, lateral raise, undergrip pulldown, seated calf raise, close grip bench press, alternate DB curl, twisting crunch.
3. squat, flat flye, cable row, standing leg curl, upright row, overgrip pulldown, donkey calf raise, overhead triceps extension, hammer curl, crunch.

Since the intensity is lower (roughly 50-60% of maximum) glycogen depletion per set will also be lower. Additionally, 20 reps will only require about 20-40 seconds to complete. Assuming glycogen had started at 70 mmol/kg, it will likely take 4-6 circuits to fully deplete glycogen.

The Hardgainer CKD fat loss workout

A potential problem with CKD for fat loss is that a fairly high volume of weight training is required to deplete glycogen between carb-ups. Additionally, training bodyparts twice each week can cause overtraining in those with poor recovery ability. As discussed in chapter 12, one option is to perform less heavy tension sets on Monday and Tuesday and deplete muscle glycogen with light, high rep sets not taken to failure.

Another option is to make the CKD a 14 day cycle rather than a seven day cycle. Thus, the total volume of work needed to deplete muscle glycogen (roughly 4-6 sets per bodypart assuming a 36 hour carb-up) can be stretched across two weeks of training. This allows 2-3 sets per major bodypart (smaller bodyparts would require less sets) at each workout. Sample Hardgainer CKD schedules appear in tables 5 and 6.

Table 5: Hardgainer option

Mon:	Workout 1
Tue:	Off
Wed:	Workout 2
Thu:	Off
Fri:	Workout 1 ; no carb-up
Sat/Sun:	Off
Mon:	Workout 2
Tue:	Off
Wed:	Workout 1
Thu:	Off
Fri:	Workout 2 ; start carb-up

Table 6: Extreme Hardgainer option

Mon:	Workout 1
Tue-Thu:	Off
Fri:	Workout 2 ; no carb-up
Sat/Sun:	Off
Mon:	Workout 1
Tue-Thu:	Off
Fri:	Workout 2, start carb-up

Chapter 29:
The ketogenic diet for other goals

Many individuals want to know if the CKD or other ketogenic diets can be used for specific exercise goals. With the exception of long duration, low intensity aerobic exercise, ketogenic diets are not optimal performance diets in most cases. In certain situations, they can be used for individuals involved in high-intensity sports who need to lose bodyfat without sacrificing muscle mass. However, most individuals will find that their performance is better with a carbohydrate-based diet.

Section 1: The CKD and Mass gains

For reasons discussed in other chapters, the CKD is not optimal for mass or strength gains. The lowness of insulin and other anabolic hormones, coupled with depleted liver glycogen (which affects overall anabolic status) means that growth will be less compared to a carbohydrate based diet.

Although lifters vary in their individual nutritional requirements, a diet with a moderate carb intake (40-50%), moderate protein (20-30%, or 1 gram protein/lb of body weight), moderate fat (20-30%) and above maintenance calories (10-20% above maintenance) will be more beneficial for gaining mass and strength than a CKD. However, some lifters will choose to use a CKD for mass gains, usually in an attempt to minimize bodyfat gains. The following guidelines should be applied.

The lowcarb week

Gain in muscle require that calories be raised above maintenance. This also means that some fat gain will occur. A good starting point is to raise calories during the lowcarb week to 10-20% above maintenance. In practice, this yields 18 calories per pound of body weight or more per day (see chapter 8). Some lifters require even higher calorie intakes, 20+ cal/lb depending on their metabolic rate.

For some lifters, it can be problematic to consume this much food on a low-carbohydrate diet, especially if they find that their appetite is blunted. Dividing the day's total calories into smaller meals, and using calorically dense foods to raise calories may be useful in this regard.

The carb-up

For maximal anabolism, the carb-up period should be lengthened to a full 48 hours. While this may cause greater fat deposition, especially if lots of high glycemic index (GI) sugars are consumed, this strategy should also yield greater lean body mass gains. Switching to lower GI carbs during the second half of the carb-up should help maximize anabolism but limit fat gains. Additionally, using Citrimax (see chapter 31) may help limit fat gain on the weekends.

The Targeted CKD

One useful strategy for maximizing anabolism with the CKD is the inclusion of pre- and post-workout carbohydrates during the week, in addition to the weekend carb-up. In this case, the guidelines presented for the TKD (chapter 11) should be used. Post-workout carbohydrates may be especially useful to help keep cortisol levels down and help with recovery. Many lifters report decreased soreness and increased recovery when carbs are taken post-workout. As with the TKD, the choice of pre-workout carbohydrates is not critical and lifters should choose easily digested carbohydrates.

Up to 25-50 grams of carbs can be consumed 30-60 minutes before working out. Some lifters have also experimented with consuming carbs during training, but many report problems with stomach upset, especially on leg training days.

The choice of post-workout carbs is important so that muscle but not liver glycogen is refilled. The ideal carb source is glucose or glucose polymers. Fructose and sucrose should ideally be avoided as they may refill liver glycogen, possibly interrupting ketosis.

Lifters should consume 50-100 grams of liquid high GI carbs with 25-50 grams of protein (and supplements of choice) immediately after training. The carbs should preferentially go to the muscles to refill muscle glycogen and ketosis should resume within an hour or two. Ketone levels should be checked pre- and post-workout to ensure that ketosis is not being interrupted for long periods.

The mid-week carb spike

An alternative strategy to carbing around workouts is the use of a mid-week carb-spike. With this dietary strategy, up to 1000 calories of carbs (250 grams) with some protein (25-50 grams) but no fat is consumed as the first meal Wednesday morning. Ketogenic eating should be resumed a few hours later to give blood glucose and insulin time to return to normal. Weight training should take place at some point later in the day to reestablish ketosis.

Splitting up the carb-load

A final strategy which lifters may wish to try is to perform 2 shorter carb-load periods of 24 hours each at different times each week. For example, a lifter might carb-load for 24 hours on Tuesday (following a workout) and again for 24 hours on Saturday. In theory, this might generate more anabolism while limiting the potential for fat gain.

Body composition

During mass gaining phases, body composition should be measured every two to three weeks to determine what percentage of the weight being gained is muscle and fat. This will allow trainees to monitor the results of their experiments and make adjustments to calorie and carbohydrate intake.

Training

In terms of training, mass gains are best achieved with an emphasis on basic movements like squats, benches, deadlifts, pulldowns/chins, etc, with few isolation movements. Recall that the growth range is somewhere between 6-20 reps or about 20-60" per set. Emphasis should be placed on the negative (lowering) portion of the movement as this seems to be a primary stimulus for strength and mass gains.

Most advanced lifters find that training a muscle once every 5-7 days is an ideal frequency, although this depends on the intensity of loading. In general, it seems that larger muscles (quads, chest, back) take longer to recover than smaller muscle groups (shoulders and arms). However, trying to set up workout programs around individual bodypart recovery times leads to too many days in the gym and unrealistic schedules (such as training triceps the day before chest). Most lifters will get the best mass gains training 3-4 hours per week maximum.

In terms of sets and reps, no one prescription is ideal for everyone. Some lifters respond best to high rep (12-20) sets while others thrive on low rep sets (6-12). An ideal situation is probably a combination of varying rep ranges, either in the same workout or alternated as in the periodization scheme presented in chapter 26.

In a periodized scheme, a lifter might alternate between periods of 10-15 reps (roughly 40-60 seconds per set) and periods of 6-10 reps (roughly 20-40 seconds per set) every 4-6 weeks or so. An occasional (i.e. every 6-8 weeks or so) change to very low reps (1-5 reps, sets 20" or less) can help improve the neural aspects of training, raising strength thresholds for the higher rep brackets.

The primary issue that lifters must keep in mind is that they will be limited to a certain number of sets based on the length of the carb-up. To a great degree, that will ultimately determine the training structure which should be used. This is another reason why the CKD is probably not ideal for mass gains. The structure of the diet puts limitations on the types of training which can be done.

As calories are above maintenance, techniques such as forced reps and strip sets may be useful but care must be taken. Overuse of any high-intensity technique can lead rapidly to overtraining regardless of diet. It is best to pick one or two body parts per cycle (generally weak body parts for bodybuilders) for extra attention while working other body parts at maintenance with fewer sets.

Continual progress on all body parts at once is rare, especially in advanced lifters. While devoting extra intensity on one or two body parts, techniques such as forced reps should not be used more than every other workout for any given bodypart. The intervening workout should be taken only to the point of positive failure (straight sets).

The main problem with the CKD for mass gains is that only muscles trained on Friday will receive optimal super compensation and growth. This means that either a full-body workout should be performed or that a rotating schedule must be used (such as the Upper/Lower split in chapter 27). Each muscle group will be worked prior to the carb-up period once every two or three weeks depending on the rotation used. Alternately, weak body parts can be trained on Friday so they will receive the greatest super compensation and growth from the carb-up. Maintenance body parts can be trained Mon/Tue or Mon/Wed after the carb-up. Another alternative is to train weak body parts at a low rep range (6-8) on Monday when trainees are strongest from the carb-up and again on Fridays with higher reps (10-15) before the carb-up. Maintenance body parts can be trained on Wednesday with lesser volume.

An optional method is to use the four day Upper/Lower body split in chapter 27 but plan it so that one of the lifting days occurs during the carb-up. Table 1 gives an example sequence.

Table 1: Sample workout sequence for mass gains

Day	Workout	Diet
Mon:	Off	Lowcarb
Tue:	Upper body	Lowcarb
Wed:	Lower body	Lowcarb
Thu:	Off	Lowcarb
Fri:	Upper body	Begin carb-up
Sat:	Lower body	Continue carb-up
Sun:	Off	Continue carb-up

Aerobics

During mass gaining phases, aerobic training should generally be limited to 20-30' once or twice a week. This will contribute to maintenance of aerobic fitness and may help with recovery without detracting too much from mass gains. Many lifters, fearing fat gain, continue to do copious amounts of aerobics during their mass gaining phases. While generally preventing much of the fat gain, excess aerobics also tends to prevent muscle gain. Therefore, high amounts of aerobic training are emphatically not recommended.

Section 2: Strength/Power Athletes

As with mass gains for bodybuilders (previous section), the CKD is not ideal for powerlifters and other strength/power athletes (throwers, sprinters, Olympic lifters, etc). The extremely high intensity nature of training for these sports absolutely requires carbohydrates for optimal performance.

Additionally, the dehydration caused by ketogenic diets may compromise joint integrity, increasing the risk of injury. However, if a powerlifter or other athlete needs to maintain performance while losing body fat to make a weight class, the CKD may be a viable option.

Power lifters

Since the days following the carb-up are when individuals are typically strongest, it makes sense to put the power training days there. Possibly, the performance of a short tension workout (with higher reps) on Friday before the carb-up may allow a slight increase in muscle mass to support the next cycle of power training.

If muscle gain is not desired (for example, individuals close to the top of their weight class), performance of a high rep depletion workout or assistance exercises should be performed on Friday instead. A sample workout cycle appears in tables 2 through 4.

The inclusion of light squats and deadlifts is so that the movement pattern can be trained. Alternately, the light movement of the week can be trained on Friday prior to the carb-up. Sets/reps for the power lifts are typically cycled throughout a training period as indicated by the and no repetition guidelines are given in the following workouts. The example given in chapter 26 for undulating periodization gives a basic set/rep protocol for reaching a new 1RM. Typically, assistance exercises are worked for slightly higher reps, 6-8 or more. Assistance exercises should be chosen to improve the weak point of a given power movement (i.e. lockout problems on bench would require more triceps work, heavy partials in the rack or isometrics).

Table 2: Sample Monday workout: Squats and support exercises OR deadlifts and support exercises alternating week to week

Week 1: Sample Squat workout

Exercise	Sets	Reps	Rest
Squat	a	a	3-5'
Leg curl	3	6-8	2'
Calf raise	3	12-15	2'
Weighted crunch	3	8-10	2'
Cable row	2	6-8	2'
Barbell curl	2	6-8	2'
Light deadlifts	1	b	
OR Stiff legged DL	1	6-8	

Week 2: Sample Deadlift workout

Exercise	Sets	Reps	Rest
Deadlift	a	a	3-5'
Undergrip pulldown	3	6-8	2'
Shrug	3	6-8	2'
Low back	3	8-10	2'
Extension	2	12-15	2'
Grip work	Varies but 2-4 sets of 40-70 seconds each are recommended.		
Light squat	1	b	

a. Sets and reps are typically varied throughout the training cycle
b. Weight would be 80-85% of the previous weeks work weight for the same reps

---

Table 3: Sample Tuesday: Bench and support exercises and abdominals

Exercise	Sets	Reps	Rest
Bench press	a	a	3-5'
Bench assistance exercise (focusing on weak point)	3	6-8	2-3'
Shoulder press or dips	2	10-12	2-3'
Close grip bench	2	10-12	2-3'
Abdominals	3	6-8	1-2'

a. Sets and reps are typically varied throughout the training cycle

Wed/Thu: Off or low-intensity aerobics if fat loss is the goal

Table 4: Sample Friday workout: tension workout

Exercise	Sets	Reps(a)	Rest
Leg press	3	8-10	90"
Leg curl	1	10-12	60"
Calf raise	2	10-12	60"
Incline bench	3	8-10	90"
Wide grip row	3	8-10	90"
Shoulder press	1-2	10-12	60"
Pulldown	1-2	10-12	60"

a Set tempo should be such that failure occurs within 40 to 60 seconds.

Note: Direct arm work is dropped as the arms get considerable training from the compound chest, back, and shoulder movements. If trainees must perform arm work, they should perform 1-2 sets of 12-15 repetitions for one basic exercise (alternate DB curl, barbell curl, close grip bench press, etc).

Different exercises should be used during the Friday workout than on the Mon/Tue workouts to stress different muscle fibers. Additionally, using a higher rep bracket should help avoid problems with training a muscle heavily twice per week. That is, low rep sets on Mon/Tue will stress primarily Type IIb fibers (with some Type IIa stimulation) while the Friday workout, with higher reps will stress Type IIa fibers more (due to longer set times).

Other Power Athletes

Athletes such as volleyball players, etc. may wish to use the CKD for the same reasons as powerlifters: to drop body fat while maintaining anaerobic performance. The same guidelines apply to these athletes. During and following the carb-up is the time to perform skill work and weight training. Later in the week, when glycogen is depleted, metabolic conditioning such as aerobic exercise can be done. A sample workout schedule appears in table 5.

Table 5: Sample workout week for a volleyball player appears below		
Day	Workout	Diet
Mon:	Weight training,	Lowcarb
Tue:	Weight training (depending on split)	Lowcarb
Wed:	Metabolic conditioning (run, bike, intervals)	Lowcarb
Thu:	Metabolic conditioning (run, bike, intervals)	Lowcarb
Fri:	Depletion workout	Lowcarb
Sat:	Volleyball scrimmage or match	Continue carb-up
Sun:	Skills drills, interval training	Continue carb-up

For most power athletes, the CKD is probably best used during the off-season when relatively less high-intensity training is being performed. During the season, a moderate to high carb diet will provide better performance.

Summary

Although the ketogenic/CKD is not ideal for most strength and power sports, it is a viable option for use during the off-season by those athletes who need to lose bodyfat while maintaining high intensity exercise performance.

Section 3: Endurance athletes

Of all the types of exercise, low-intensity endurance exercise can be sustained by a ketogenic diet. Individuals who are involved in endurance activities can therefore use a ketogenic diet during their training. It should be recalled from chapter 18 that high-intensity aerobic exercise above the lactate threshold can not be optimally sustained without carbohydrates. As well, most individuals find that their overall performance is higher on a carb-based diet.

For optimal endurance performance, some combination of aerobic training below and near LT as well as high-intensity intervals will be necessary. In general, endurance athletes tend to emphasize lower-intensity training during the off-season, incorporating more high-intensity efforts as the racing season draws near. As it is impossible to outline an entire annual plan for different endurance sports, athletes should keep the following guidelines in mind.

1. A standard ketogenic diet (SKD) can only sustain exercise intensities of 75% maximum heart rate and below. Endurance athletes in their off-season, performing primarily long duration, low-intensity training may benefit from the SKD.

2. For exercise intensity above 75% of max. (interval training or races), carbs will absolutely be necessary and the CKD or TKD is suggested. Interval training can be performed during the carb-up or the day or two afterwards. The rest of the week's training sessions can be long-duration

endurance training. Pre-workout carbohydrates may substitute for the weekend carb-up if preferred.

3. Endurance athletes will benefit from heavy weight training and it should be performed 2-3 times per week (full periodization of strength for athletes is beyond the scope of this book). A sample week of training (assuming a 2 day carb-up) appears in table 6.

Table 6: Sample week of training for and endurance athlete

	Workout	Diet
Mon:	Weight training	Lowcarb
Tue:	Long slow distance	Lowcarb
Wed:	Off	Lowcarb
Thu:	Long slow distance	Lowcarb
Fri:	Weight training	Begin carb-up after weight workout
Sat:	Off or intervals	Continue carb-up
Sun:	Intervals/race	Lowcarb*

* For races, it will be necessary to consume pre and during workout carbs depending on the length of the race. For events less than 90', pre-workout carbs and water while racing are sufficient. For events longer than 90', pre-workout carbs as well as 45-60 grams of carbs/hour while racing should be consumed. Additionally, 8 oz. of water should be consumed every 15' during the race to prevent dehydration.

An alternate and probably superior dietary strategy for endurance athletes is to vary the diet based on performance needs. That is, during off-season training, when primarily low-intensity aerobic training and some weights are being done, the SKD or CKD can be used. During higher performance periods (preseason, competitive season), a higher percentage of carbohydrates should be consumed for optimal performance.

Chapter 30:
The pre-contest bodybuilder

Not everyone reading this book is a competitive bodybuilder, nor do they want to be one. Despite the title of this chapter, the following information applies to anyone trying to get into their best shape for any special event: family reunion, pool party, best-shape-of-your-life photos, etc.

The final week of preparation is questionable for individuals who are not competitive bodybuilders. It involves manipulations of water and electrolytes which are of limited importance for most dieters. Additionally, manipulating water levels in the body carries some risk and individuals must make their own choices as to how far they will go to reach a given level of physical development.

Pre-contest bodybuilders are an entirely different species when it comes to fat loss for a contest. Their desire to maintain a high level of muscle mass makes dieting more difficult in terms of their diet and workout schedules. Please note that most of the comments which appear below apply primarily to natural bodybuilders.

Section 1: Four rules for natural bodybuilders

A huge disservice has been done to natural bodybuilders by training concepts from drug-assisted competitors. With anabolic steroids and drugs which increase energy while decreasing recovery time (such as clenbuterol, thyroid, GH, etc) specifics of the diet and training structure become less critical. Without these drugs, natural bodybuilders risk losing considerable muscle preparing for a contest. There are several basic rules that should be followed by natural bodybuilders to avoid excessive muscle loss during a pre-contest diet.

Rule #1: Don't get too fat in the off season.

The longer a bodybuilder has to diet, the more they risk risk losing muscle. As a general guideline, male bodybuilders should go no higher than 10-12% body fat during the off season, women 13-15%. Keeping bodyfat to these levels accomplishes two things. First, it prevents the bodybuilder from having to diet for months to get ready. Not only does extended dieting increase the risk of muscle loss, but many bodybuilders seem to disappear from the gym for a month after their contest, engaging in a full-blown food binge. The less time a person has to diet, the less likely they are to blow the diet. Additionally, starting a diet from a low enough bodyfat prevents the bodybuilder from having to cut calories and/or increase aerobics so drastically that they lose too much muscle.

To accurately measure body composition, dieters must have their body fat measured regularly, preferably with skin fold calipers. Guidelines for measuring body composition on the CKD appear below. Using the mirror only works for experienced competitors and it is recommended that beginning bodybuilders use calipers. The mirror will tell trainees what they want to see and it's easy to put the fat blinders on during the off-season when strength and mass are increasing.

Many lifters underestimate their body fat percentage, thinking they are leaner than they really are. Despite the problems associated with calipers, they will give accurate measurements as long as certain guidelines are kept in mind. By charting individual skinfold measurements, athletes can track the changes occurring, either good or bad, during their diet. A skinfold reading of 3-4 millimeters indicates maximal leanness. If a bodybuilder allows an individual skinfold to approach 20 mm during the off season, they will have a problem when it is time to diet.

Rule #2: Do not change training radically before a contest.

A second mistake many bodybuilders make is switching to lighter weights and higher reps to 'cut up' the muscle for a contest, an idea that most likely came from drug-assisted bodybuilders. With steroids, lowering training weights doesn't cause muscle loss and higher reps will burn more calories, causing greater fat loss. For a natural bodybuilder, this will not maintain muscle mass optimally.

Trainees should not confuse weights with aerobics or vice versa. If a bodybuilder has acquired a certain level of muscle mass with heavy weights and low repetitions, they should continue to perform heavy sets (as much as their depleted body will allow) to maintain that mass. Fat loss will occur as a result of caloric deficit and aerobics. Genetics, as well as the ability to eliminate subcutaneous water, will determine to a great degree what kind of striations and cuts a competitor will have on contest day.

Obviously, expecting training weights to remain the same while dieting is a false hope. However, trainees shouldn't automatically start lowering their training weights until they absolutely have to. Rather, trainees should attempt to keep training heavy until the last two weeks before a contest. However, an extreme drop in training weights, or the number of reps which can be performed with a given weight, can be indicative of muscle loss. Keeping records of workouts is encouraged as another method of tracking progress during a diet.

Near the end of the pre-contest phase, many bodybuilders will have to switch to lighter weights as they become more and more depleted. As body fat levels decrease, the body's natural joint lubrication decreases as well and heavy weights can cause injury. However, weights should not be decreased until absolutely necessary to avoid muscle loss.

Rule #3: Start the diet early enough.

In addition to underestimating body fat levels, many bodybuilders start their diets too late giving themselves 8 weeks or less to get into contest-ready shape. Getting into contest shape 2 weeks early is preferable to getting into contest shape 2 weeks late.

Assuming a starting body fat of 10-12% for men (13-15% for women), beginning contest preparation 10-12 weeks before a contest should be sufficient for most bodybuilders. If an individual knows that their body is slow to drop body fat, they may start their diet 16 weeks prior to a contest. If a trainee is unsure of how quickly they will drop fat (i.e. preparing for their first contest), they should start earlier rather than later. Starting early has an additional benefit: it allows the possibility of taking a week off of the diet. This strategy, along with others to break fat loss plateaus, is discussed in chapter 13.

Rule #4: Know pre-diet calorie levels

This gives trainees a starting point to set calories for their diet. For those who do not know their pre-diet calorie intake, 15 cal/lb should be used as a starting point. Adjustments can be made based on changes in body composition. If a bodybuilder is already adapted to a CKD, they should start by reducing caloric intake by 250-500 calories per day. This should yield a fat loss of .5-1lb fat per week with no muscle loss as long as protein intake is sufficient. Based on changes in body composition, caloric intake should be adjusted. Additionally, changes can be made in terms of the quality and length of the carb-load.

If fat loss is less than .5 lbs, calories may be reduced an additional 250 per day. If fat loss is greater than 2 lbs (very rare), calories should be increased by 250-500 per lowcarb day. Remember that, in general, alterations in caloric intake will be made by manipulating fat intake, as protein should remain constant throughout the diet.

Calories and aerobics

A mistake many bodybuilders make, which is generally related to starting their diet too late and at too high a body fat level, is to excessively cut calories and add hours of aerobics every day in an attempt to 'catch up' in their contest preparation. Even though this increases fat loss, it also causes muscle loss.

With good preparation, and by starting a diet early enough, a bodybuilder shouldn't have to lose much muscle dieting down. It is not unheard of for competitors to gain a pound or two of lean body mass using the CKD while dieting. However, it should not be expected.

One easy modification to the pre-contest diet is during the carb-up. Controlling fat intake and shortening the carb-up to 30 hours or less (from Friday evening to Saturday bedtime) can help to maintain fat loss. See chapter 13 for more details on overcoming fat loss plateaus.

Section 2: Aerobics and the pre-contest bodybuilder

Aerobic exercise should not be necessary early in the contest diet except on Sunday after the carb-up to help reestablish ketosis. Reducing calories to maintenance levels or a slight deficit coupled with weight training should be sufficient to cause fat loss in the early stages of the diet.

Using the ephedrine, caffeine and aspirin (ECA) stack can help to kick-start fat loss as well as blunting hunger. However, some bodybuilders prefer to save the ECA stack for later when fat loss slows, relying on diet and training alone in the initial stages of the diet.

In general, bodybuilders are better off using only weight training plus caloric restriction until fat loss slows. The cardio done on Sunday to reestablish ketosis plus the cardio done as a warm-up and cool-down from training should be sufficient at the beginning of the diet.

Only when fat loss slows should small amounts of aerobic exercise be added. A maximum of four to five sessions of 20 to 40' is about the most a natural bodybuilder should perform although this will vary with the individual. Assuming that a bodybuilder has followed the rules presented above, much more than this should not be needed.

Contrary to recommendations for non-bodybuilders, intensity should be kept low. At higher aerobic intensities, fast twitch muscle fibers are recruited. Coupled with high-intensity weight training and no carbs, a high aerobic intensity increases the risk of overtraining and muscle loss. An intensity of 60% of maximum heart rate (or about 15 beats below lactate threshold) is the highest intensity any pre-contest bodybuilder should use. In practice, this means walking on an inclined treadmill, riding the bike, or doing the Stairmaster at low intensities. Interval training is one option that some individuals have found works well but intervals should be eliminated at the first signs of muscle loss or overtraining.

The only exception is the one hour of low-intensity aerobics after the carb-up. The purpose of this workout is to deplete liver glycogen and establish ketosis as quickly as possible and should be done from the beginning of the contest diet. Ideally, this workout should be done before breakfast on Sunday to ensure depletion of any remaining liver glycogen.

Bodybuilders have typically performed their aerobic training at one of two times: first thing in the morning on an empty stomach, or immediately after training. The rationale for this was that the lowered blood glucose and insulin would allow for better FFA utilization. Whether this strategy will have a benefit on a ketogenic diet is unclear. The nature of the ketogenic diet is that the body is relying on fat for fuel all day so it shouldn't make a difference whether cardio is performed prior to eating or not. However, morning cardio is a tried and true method for pre-contest fat loss, and may be a strategy worth trying, especially coupled with the herbal supplement yohimbe (see chapter 31). In theory, performing aerobics on an empty stomach first thing in the morning will maximize utilization of body fat, rather than using dietary fat.

Section 3: Measuring body composition

If possible, pre-contest bodybuilders should have body composition measured weekly so that adjustments can be made to the diet. Keep in mind that the prediction equations become less accurate as lower body fat percentages are reached. Pre-contest bodybuilders should pay more attention to total skin folds and overall appearance than trying to achieve an arbitrary body fat percentage. Ultimately, the judges are not judging skin fold measurements. If dropping another few millimeters of skinfolds results in the loss of several pounds of muscle, overall appearance will suffer. Guidelines for the pre-contest bodybuilder to track body composition changes appear below:

1. Weigh and take skin folds the morning of the last low-carbohydrate day of the week. This is when a bodybuilder should be their leanest and is most representative of overall body fat levels and appearance.

2. Weight should be taken again at the end of the carb-loading phase. This tells how much weight needs to be lost during the next low-carb cycle for fat loss to occur. If body weight increases 7 pounds from Friday morning (pre-carbup) to Sunday morning (after carbing has ended), body weight will have to drop more than 7 lbs by the following Friday for fat loss to have occurred (assuming similar levels of hydration, etc). Skin folds taken after the carb-up will tend to over-estimate true body fat due to an increase in water underneath the skin.

3. Finally, pre-contest bodybuilders should keep visual tabs on how long after the carb-load they look their absolute best. There will be some time point when the water underneath the skin has been lost but muscles are still full from the increased glycogen storage. This will help to plan the week immediately before the contest. For example, if a bodybuilder's physique is at its best 36 hours after ending the carb-up, this will be used to adjust the timing of the carb-up for the contest. The specifics of the pre-contest week are described below.

Section 4: Other Issues

Many competitors begin having muscle cramps as they reach excessively low body fat levels although the reason for this is unknown. Ensuring adequate calcium (up to 1200 mg/day), potassium (up to 1000 mg/day) and magnesium (up to 1000 mg/day) can help. All should be taken in divided doses with food to avoid stomach upset.

Also, some competitors suffer from insomnia late in their contest preparation. Various herbal sleep aids, such as Valerian root or melatonin, may be of help. Finally, female competitors may stop menstruating as their body fat reaches low levels. While the fat intake of the CKD seems to prevent this, supplementing with DHEA (25-50 mg/day max. for women) may help.

One advantage of the CKD is that it allows bodybuilders to practice the carb-up each week. Judging by their appearance each week, competitors can determine what food choices and timing works for them. If a bodybuilder has determined that they can only handle 30 hours of carbing and it takes them 3 days to drop the water, adjust the following schedule accordingly. Ideally, bodybuilders should record how their body responds to different types of carb-loads and at what time of the week they look their best.

Section 5: The pre-contest diet

Having discussed a variety of topics which pertain to the pre-contest diet, we can set up the details of the diet. During the first 2 weeks of a pre-contest diet, the only aerobics performed will be on Sunday, the day after the carb-up. This helps establish ketosis quickly without negatively affecting the Monday and Tuesday workouts. After the second week of the diet, aerobics can be gradually added as necessary. Although a maximum of forty minutes, four to five times a week is allowed, bodybuilders should gradually build up to this level to avoid putting too much stress on the body. Bodybuilders should begin with twenty minutes of aerobics done three times per week and increase each session by five to ten minutes per week and add sessions as necessary. A sample weekly schedule appears in table 1.

Table 1: Sample weekly schedule for a pre-contest diet

Day	Workout
Sun:	30-60 minutes of low intensity aerobics first thing in the morning
Mon/Tue:	2 day split of preferred training regime.
Wed/Thu:	*
Fri evening:	Full body workout and then begin the carb-up.
Sat:	No workout while carbing.
Sun:	Repeat cycle

* Wednesday and Thursday should be used for aerobic workouts. Alternately, calories may be reduced an additional 10%.

Section 5: The Final 2 weeks before the contest

The final two weeks prior to a bodybuilding contest differ from the rest of the pre-contest diet. Table 2 provides a fairly generic schedule for the two weeks before the contest. Unfortunately it is impossible to say what will work ideally for every competitor. Novice bodybuilders should not be surprised if they don't come in perfectly at their first contest. With practice and repetition, they can determine what type of contest carb-up schedule works best.

Table 2: Overview of the 2 weeks leading up to the contest

Day	Training	Diet	Water Intake
Mon	Normal Mon training	Lowcarb	Normal
Tue	Normal Tue training	Lowcarb	Normal
Wed	cardio optional	Lowcarb	Normal
Thu	cardio optional	Lowcarb	Normal
Fri	Last heavy day of training	Lowcarb	Normal
Sat	Cardio optional	Lowcarb	Normal
Sun	Cardio optional	Lowcarb	Normal
Mon	Cardio optional	Lowcarb	Normal
Tue	Depletion workout in morning	Start carb-up	High
Wed	None	2nd day of carb-up	High
Thu	Posing/none	Continue carb-up if necessary	1/2 of Wed
Fri	Posing	See below	1/2 of Thu
Sat	None	See below	As needed
Sun	None	Go eat	

- Monday/Tuesday: Monday and Tuesday are normal training and diet days. As always, pre-breakfast aerobics is optional, but will negatively affect the workouts.

- Wednesday/Thursday: Aerobics optional or debit calories an additional 10%

- Friday: last heavy training day, full body, no carb-up

The body needs at least a week (legs may require more) to recover and rebuild completely so this should be the last heavy training day. Lifters should do the full-body tension workout from chapter 29. Pre-workout carbs are optional, but bodybuilders should return to low-carb afterwards taking in only protein with the supplements of choice immediately after training. Aerobics are optional after training.

- Saturday: aerobics optional, low carb

Under ideal circumstances, bodybuilders should be nearly ready for the contest by this point. If they still have fat to lose, aerobics first thing in the morning may help but it is a mistake to panic and do 3 hours of aerobics today. If a bodybuilder comes into their first contest too fat, they will know to start their contest prep earlier next time.

If appearance is fine, calories should be increased back to maintenance levels (13-15 cal/b) while remaining on the ketogenic diet. No workout today except to practice posing. Most competitors begin to practice posing several weeks out from their contest and it should not be inferred that this is the first day you should practice. Water intake should remain high.

- Sunday: aerobics optional, low carb

Same as Saturday, aerobics and calorie restriction are both optional. Otherwise, eat at maintenance and take the day off except for posing. Water intake is still high.

- Monday: no training, low carb

Regardless of appearance, no training should be done and calories should be set at maintenance using the ketogenic diet. Again, continue to practice posing. Water intake is still high.

- Tuesday: The final depletion workout, begin carb-up

Begin the final carb-up for the contest. Early afternoon or evening is the time for a true depletion workout. Even if a bodybuilder has been using a tension workout up until this point, they must do a true depletion workout (meaning high reps, not to failure) to maximize glycogen depletion and supercompensation. Glycogen should be very low from the previous week's workouts, minimizing the number of circuits needed.

Approximately 5 hours prior to the depletion workout, 25-50 grams of carbohydrate with some protein should be consumed as discussed in chapter 12. About 1-2 hours before the final depletion workout, 50 grams of carbohydrates, including some fructose, with some protein should be consumed. The goal of this workout is to completely deplete glycogen and circuits should be performed until strength starts to drop. This indicates that glycogen is being fully depleted.

Since glycogen levels should be low from the previous 10 days of lowcarb dieting, only three to six sets per bodypart should be needed. Each set should be roughly 50% of 1 rep max. Sets should be 10-20 quick reps (about 1 second up, 1 second down) stopped several reps short of failure. Many athletes prefer to use machines for this workout for safety reasons (i.e. low body fat and general depletion/fatigue). Use a variety of movements (see chapter 28 for sample circuits) to hit all available muscle fibers. Don't forget often neglected body parts like forearms, traps, rear delts, etc.

Immediately after this workout, the final carb-up must begin. A liquid carb drink with 1.5 grams of carbs/kg lean body mass, 25-50 grams of protein and any supplements of choice (i.e. creatine, glutamine) should be consumed immediately after this workout and again 2 hours later to maximize glycogen storage. After that, bodybuilders should move to the normal carb-up and supplement schedule, consuming ~50 grams of carbs every 2 hours or so, for a total of 10 grams of carbs/kg of lean body mass (see chapter 12 for details).

Assuming that a bodybuilder has been on the CKD for a sufficient amount of time, they should have a pretty good idea how their body responds to carb-ups since they have practiced it every week. If they know that they do better with high GI carbs, those should be used. If they have found that anything but starches makes them bloat, go with what works. Now is not the time to experiment with anything new.

Water intake should be kept high to maximize muscle fullness and this is not the time to start experimenting with sodium and potassium levels. Optimal glycogen transport across the intestinal wall requires adequate sodium so reducing sodium intake will slow the carb-up.

- Wednesday: Continue carb-up

Into the second day of carbing, fats should be kept to 15% of total calories, primarily as essential fatty acids, and carbs should be limited to 5 g/kg lean body mass. Switching to starches and vegetables should ensure no fat spill over and chromium (up to 800 mcg per day), vanadyl sulfate (up to 120 mg per day), magnesium (at least 300 mg per day), alpha lipoic acid (600-2000 mg), and Citrimax (750 mg taken three times at least thirty minutes before meals) may be used. Some bodybuilders will start retaining water at this point but water intake should be kept high to avoid increasing the body's level of aldosterone, the hormone which causes water retention.

- Thursday: continue carb-up as necessary

Many athletes don't eat enough during carb-ups, whether from fullness or fear of gaining fat. This day is for those athletes. If a bodybuilder doesn't appear fully carbed after two days of carbing-up, they can continue to consume small amounts of carbs (mainly vegetables with some low GI starches) during the day with protein and some fat. Water intake should be curtailed somewhat, cutting back to half of what they've been drinking in the previous days. It's probably best to switch to distilled water so that mineral intake (notably sodium, potassium and calcium) can be monitored.

If a bodybuilder is fully carbed up by Thursday, they should switch back to ketogenic eating with small amounts of vegetables (30 grams of carbs maximum) throughout the day. This will allow the loss of any water being held beneath the skin.

• Friday: The day before the contest

Regardless of appearance, the ketogenic diet should be resumed on on Friday. Consume small amounts of carbs throughout the day (5-10 grams per meal, vegetables only) to keep blood glucose steady and muscle glycogen topped off. Calories should be set to maintenance or slightly (10%) below.

While the simple act of restricting carbohydrates will have a diuretic effect, most bodybuilders will need to take a herbal diuretic approximately 24 hours before prejudging. Although the use of prescription diuretics (i.e. Lasix, Aldactone, Aldactazide, etc) is banned because of the danger of severe dehydration and death, the diuresis caused by the herbal products is relatively minor but will improve appearance. Many health food stores stock various types of herbal diuretic which typically contain ingredients such as buchu leaves, dandelion, uva ursi, etc. Additionally, the simple restriction of carbohydrates has a diuretic effect. Some bodybuilders have used glycerol to pull water from underneath their skin as well.

While sodium loading is not recommended, sodium intake should be monitored from Friday through the evening show. While a bodybuilder need not avoid all sources of sodium, an effort should be made to consume very small amounts, approximately 1000 mg/day total. This means that the sodium content of foods will have to be checked. Additionally, three times as much potassium (i.e. 3000 mg) should be consumed in divided doses.

Friday night, competitors should consume a moderate carb meal (about 50 grams or so) with some protein (20-30 grams) and a small amount of healthy fats (i.e. olive oil). This last carb meal helps ensure normal blood glucose and liver glycogen, to improve vascularity at prejudging. Many competitors who skip this meal find that they aren't vascular until the evening show. By then it's too late.

Finally, an effort should be made to consume easily digested meals from this point on so that the stomach doesn't protrude from undigested food. Some competitors will use laxatives to help tighten the waist. Many herbal diuretics contain a light laxative, such as cascara sagrada, in them already.

• Saturday: prejudging

If a bodybuilder is still holding water the morning of the show, they will need to find a sauna to sweat out the last little bit of water from underneath the skin. There are no hard and fast rules for how long to stay in the sauna. Simply use appearance as a guide.

Breakfast should be a small meal containing easily digested carbs to keep blood glucose and liver glycogen normal. Prior experience will help determine the ideal time prior to prejudging to eat breakfast. Failing that, since most contests have pre-judging around 9 or 10 in the morning, a breakfast at 6 or 7 am should be sufficient.

Approximately an hour or so before prejudging, consume 25-50 grams of easily digested carbs similar to what is consumed before the Friday depletion workout. About 20-30' before prejudging, competitors should begin their pump-up routine to maximize vascularity. In general, pumping the legs seems to detract, rather than enhance vascularity.

- Saturday: Prejudging and the evening show

Between prejudging and the evening show is a nebulous area. Many people involved in bodybuilding feel that the competitors are placed at prejudging but occasionally an individual will move up at the evening show if they really tighten up or if another competitor really falls apart appearance wise.

It's probably best to continue eating small, easily digested meals with some carbs during this time period and many competitors use sodium-free carbohydrate drinks. Large meals should be avoided as this may cause the stomach to distend. The competitor wants just enough carbs to maintain fullness and vascularity.

Prior to the evening show, consume 25-50 grams of carbs about an hour out and then pumping up about 20-30' out. After the evening show, the competitor can finally go eat a real meal.

Section 6: A final comment

Don't panic. Many (probably most) competitors, even if they have done many contests, tend to panic right before their show. Regardless of their adherence to the diet plan or whether or not they are on schedule, bodybuilders tend to get a little crazy in those last few days, questioning whether they are truly ready or not. They may try untested methods, or do an extra three hours of cardio or a last workout before their contest. Invariably, they sabotage themselves and end up looking worse on stage than if they had left well enough alone.

If a competitor has not shown a given technique (such as sodium loading or glycerol) to work for them, they should not experiment in the few days before the show. Ideally novice bodybuilders should find an objective coach who will keep them on track and prevent them from panicking at the last minute. By the same token, a good coach can give a bodybuilder feedback on their condition and whether or not they should make changes to their pre-contest preparation. In contrast, listening to gym buddies can be a disaster. For fear of hurting a competitor's ego, many people will not tell them how they truly look. Rather they'll tell a competitor "You're looking ripped" rather than tell them that they are not going to be lean enough for the contest.

Part VIII:
Supplements

Chapter 31: General health
Chapter 32: Fat loss
Chapter 33: The carb-load
Chapter 34: Muscle/strength gain

With the exception of a basic vitamin/mineral supplement and calcium, there are no supplements which are required for a ketogenic diet. However there are additional supplements which may be helpful for a variety of goals while on a ketogenic diet. They are discussed in the following chapters.

Supplements should be chosen for specific goals, whether those goals are fat loss, muscle/strength gain, or improved endurance. A comprehensive guide to all available supplements would require an entire book. This chapter will only deal with those supplements which are specifically useful to the ketogenic diet, or which have an impact on ketosis that ketogenic dieters should be aware of. There is a great deal of individual response to the different supplements available. For this reason, it is recommended that supplements be added one at a time so that the effects can be noted.

Chapter 31: Supplements for the ketogenic diet

There are a number of supplements which can be useful on a ketogenic diet, depending on the goal of the dieter. This chapter discusses general supplements such as a basic multi-vitamin/mineral, anti-oxidants, fiber supplements, and fatty acid supplements.

Basic multi-vitamin/mineral

Any calorically restricted diet may not provide for all nutritional requirements and the limited number of food available on a ketogenic diet may cause deficiencies as discussed in chapter 7 (1).

At the very least, individuals on a ketogenic diet should take some form of sugar free vitamin and mineral supplement to ensure nutritional adequacy. Additionally, supplemental sodium, magnesium and potassium may be necessary, as detailed in chapter 7. Depending on dairy intake, a calcium supplement may also be necessary.

As a general rule, there is little difference between the vitamins sold in health food stores and those sold in the grocery store. Obviously if individuals wish to take higher doses of any given nutrient, a more expensive vitamin/mineral formulation is necessary.

Anti-oxidants

A great deal of recent research is currently focusing on the benefit of various anti-oxidant nutrients such as vitamin C, vitamin E and beta-carotene (2,3). These substances, as well as many others, may help to prevent tissue damage from substances called 'free radicals'. Free radicals are thought to damage cells causing the accumulation of toxic chemicals. Individuals involved in intense exercise appear to generate an excess of free radicals so supplementation may be indicated (4). Additionally, the few carbohydrates which are consumed on a ketogenic diet should come from a variety of vegetable sources whenever possible. Individuals on a CKD should try to consume vegetables during the carb-loading period. Dosing of anti-oxidant nutrients is highly individual and readers are encouraged to review one of the many books available on this subject.

Fiber supplements

As discussed in chapter 7, a common side effect of ketogenic diets is a decrease in bowel movements. At least part of this is caused by the general lack of fiber in the ketogenic diet. For this reason, a sugar-free fiber supplement may be useful to maintain regularity. Additionally, the inclusion of high fiber vegetables, such as a large salad, can help with regularity in addition to the nutrients they provide.

Essential fatty acids (EFAs)

As stated in chapter 9, EFAs are a special class of fatty acids which cannot be synthesized in the human body and must be obtained from the diet. The two EFAs are linoleic acid (LA) and alpha-linolenic acid (ALA). Both LA and ALA are found only in foods of plant origin such as nuts, seeds, and some vegetables. Since a great deal of the fat intake on an average SKD is from animal sources, a source of EFAs is needed.

One possible source is through supplementation. EFAs are found in varying degrees in most vegetable oils. In general, LA is more abundant than ALA as it occurs in a wide variety of vegetable oils. ALA occurs in high amounts in flax and pumpkin seeds oil as well as in soybean oil. Many individuals have also used flax seeds or flax meal as a source of both EFAs and fiber. It is difficult to determine EFA requirements for all individuals but many ketogenic dieters seem to do well consuming 1-3 TBSP of a concentrated EFA source, such as flax oil, per day.

Omega-3 and omega-6 fatty acids

Another class of fats which may have health benefits are the omega-3 and omega-6 fatty acids, also known as docosahexanoic acid (DHA) and eicosapentanoic acid (EPA) (5,6,7). Both occur naturally in fatty fish such as salmon, sardines, mackerel, and trout. and may provide cardioprotective effects. Since fatty fish can easily be consumed on a ketogenic diet, supplementation of these oils is probably unnecessary.

Olive oil

Although not an essential fatty acid, oleic acid, which is found in high concentrations in olive oil has been shown to have additional health effects, especially in terms of blood lipid levels. Studies have shown that consumption of oleic acid lowers blood cholesterol (8). Therefore, substituting olive oil for some of the saturated fats normally consumed on a ketogenic diet may be useful for those individuals who show a negative blood cholesterol response.

References cited

1. Stock A and Yudkin J. Nutrient intake of subjects on low carbohydrate diet used in treatment of obesity. Am J Clin Nutr (1970) 23: 948-952.
2. Diplock AT. Antioxidant nutrients and disease prevention: An overview. Am J Clin Nutr (1991) 53: 189s-193s.
3. Rock CL et. al. Update on the biological characteristics of the antioxidant micronutrients:

vitamin C, vitamin E and the carotenoids. J Am Diet Assoc (1996) 96: 693-702.

4. Dekkers JC et. al. "The role of antioxidant vitamins and enzymes in the prevention of exercise-induced muscle damage. Sports Med (1996) 21: 213-238.

5. Phillipson BE et. al. Reduction of plasma lipids, lipoproteins, and apoproteins by dietary fish oils in patients with hypertriglyceridemia. N Engl J Med (1985) 12: 1210-1216.

6. Herold PM et. al. Fish oil consumption and decreased risk of cardiovascular disease: A comparison of findings from animal and human feeding trials. Am J Clin Nutr (1986) 43: 566-598.

7. Leaf A and Weber PC. Cardiovascular effects of n-3 fatty acids. N Engl J Med (1988) 318: 549-557.

8. Mattson FH et al. Comparison of effects of dietary saturated. monounsaturated, and polyunsaturated fatty acids on plasma lipids and lipoproteins in man. J Lipid Res. (1985) 26:194-202.

Chapter 32: Fat loss aids

Although there is no magic pill which can cause fat loss without effort, there are supplements which can be combined with dietary changes and exercise to hasten fat loss and/or limit muscle loss. These types of supplements work through a variety of mechanisms including increasing caloric expenditure, preventing a drop in metabolic rate, decreasing the amount of lean body mass lost while dieting and decreasing hunger when calories are being restricted. Fat loss aids can generally be grouped into three categories: thermogenic agents, appetite suppressants, and 'fat burners'.

Section 1: Thermogenesis and adrenoreceptors

Thermogenesis refers generally to the burning of calories to generate heat which is then dissipated by the body. There are numerous types of thermogenesis including exercise-induced thermogenesis and dietary-induced thermogenesis. All forms ultimately cause the body to burn fuel to produce energy and heat.

To understand the mechanism by which thermogenic agents work, it is necessary to discuss some of the underlying physiology. This includes a brief discussion of adrenaline and noradrenaline as well as adrenoreceptors.

The catecholamines: adrenaline and noradrenaline

In response to stress, the body releases two hormones known generally as catecholamines. They are adrenaline (or epinephrine) and noradrenaline (or norepinephrine). Adrenaline is released from the adrenal glands and travels through the bloodstream to its target tissues while noradrenaline is released only from the nerve endings to act on its target tissues (1). Both work by binding to structures on the cell membrane called adrenoreceptors.

Adrenoreceptors

Generally termed, an adrenoreceptor is a specific receptor on a cell which binds to either adrenaline or noradrenaline (1). When binding occurs, the adrenoreceptor sends a signal into the cell causing several reactions to occur. There are two major types of adrenoreceptors: beta-receptors and alpha-receptors. As well, there are several subtypes of each receptor. They are discussed briefly below.

There are three primary types of beta receptors known as beta-1, beta-2, and beta-3. B-1 receptors are found primarily in the heart and increase heart rate and blood pressure when stimulated. B-2 receptors are found primarily on fat and muscle cells and cause the body to mobilize free fatty acids (FFA) for burning when activated. Additionally, the stimulation of B-2 receptors seem to help prevent muscle wasting during dieting. B-3 receptors are found primarily in brown adipose tissue (BAT, see below for details) and are also involved in calorie burning.

Overall, the activation of beta-receptors tends to accelerate certain processes in the body including heart rate, blood pressure, calorie burning, heat generation and fat breakdown (1). In a sense they can be thought of as 'accelerators' similar to the one in a car. Therefore, substances which stimulate beta-receptors will increase these processes. Although there are numerous beta-agonists, the most commonly known one is ephedrine, which is discussed shortly.

There are two types of alpha receptors: alpha-1 and alpha-2. A-1 receptors are found primarily in the heart while a-2 receptors occur primarily in fat cells. When stimulated, A-2 receptors inhibit FFA mobilization (2,3) making them a 'bad' receptor from a fat loss point of view. Additionally, research has found that body fat in women's legs and buttocks has a preponderance of a-2 receptors compared to b-2 receptors (4-6). It is not uncommon to see women whose upper body is very lean, but whose lower body still appears fat. This may be partially explained by differences in receptor density.

Overall, the activation of alpha receptors tends to slow certain processes in the body including heart rate, blood pressure, calorie burning and fat breakdown. In a sense they can be thought of as 'brakes' similar to those in a car. Since alpha receptors inhibit fat mobilization, a substance which inhibits these receptors will increase fat mobilization (2). By inhibiting the inhibitors, the overall response is an increase. The primary substance which can be used to inhibit alpha-receptors is an herb called yohimbe, discussed below.

Brown adipose tissue (BAT) and white adipose tissue (WAT)

There are two different types of adipose tissue in the body. White adipose tissue (WAT) is the primary storage site for bodyfat, containing mostly stored triglycerides, some water, and a few mitochondria (which are used to burn fat for energy). In contrast, brown adipose tissue (BAT) contains little triglyceride but relatively more mitochondria (7). This makes BAT a type of fat which burns FFA generating heat in the process.

Initially, humans were not thought to have much BAT but recent research documents its existence, primarily in the back of the neck and between the ribs (7). Some research has suggested that BAT, like any other tissue, can grow larger if chronically stimulated by such things as ephedrine, cold, etc (8). An increase in BAT would increase the thermogenic response (amount of calories burned) to those same stimuli.

Section 2: Ephedrine and related compounds

Probably the most common, and perhaps the most effective, fat loss compound currently available over the counter is ephedrine, also known by its herbal name MaHuang. Ephedrine is sold as asthma medication and is known as a non-specific beta-agonist, meaning that it stimulates the all of the beta-receptors to one degree or another.

Ephedrine may work through both direct and indirect methods. Directly it can attach to beta receptors itself. However at the concentration seen with therapeutic doses, ephedrine does not appear to bind well to beta-receptors (8). Indirectly ephedrine causes a release in the body of adrenaline and noradrenaline both of which have potent effects at both beta and alpha receptors in the body (8). It seems that most of ephedrine's thermogenic effect is through the indirect mechanism of adrenaline and noradrenaline release, rather than through direct binding to fat cell adrenoreceptors (8).

There have been numerous research studies done on ephedrine as an adjunct to low calorie diets for the treatment of obesity (9,10). Through this research, it was found that the combination of ephedrine and caffeine gave better results than ephedrine alone (8,9). One study suggests that the combination of ephedrine and caffeine is more effective than the appetite suppressant dexfenfluramine (11). Some research suggests that adding aspirin to the combination of ephedrine and caffeine may provide even greater results (8,12,13). Side effects from ephedrine include jitters, hand tremor, increased heart rate/blood pressure, and insomnia (9,.

In general, the side effects from ephedrine use typically go away in several weeks (9), while the thermogenic effects may increase with time (8,10). Thus, unlike most diet compounds which have a positive tolerance curve, meaning that dieters must take more to get the same effect, ephedrine appears to have a negative tolerance curve, meaning that the same amount gives a greater effect. Additionally, the addition of ephedrine to a calorically restricted diet appears to prevent some of the muscle loss which would otherwise occur.

Caffeine

When ephedrine increases thermogenesis in the body, the body attempts to return itself to homeostasis through various mechanisms. One is to increase activity of an enzyme called phosphodiesterase (PDE). When noradrenaline attaches to the beta receptors, it causes an increase in a substance called cAMP which is involved in regulating fat burning. The body raises levels of PDE to inhibit the cAMP from doing its job (8,15). Caffeine indirectly blocks PDE by attaching to adenosine receptors on the cell, preventing the decrease in cAMP levels (8). Thus, caffeine inhibits the enzyme which inhibits fat burning. The net result is an increase in use of fat for fuel.

Dieters who do not wish to use ephedrine, or cannot tolerate its effect, may still derive some benefit from caffeine taken by itself as this increases thermogenesis and enhances fat utilization (16,17). Consuming caffeine prior to exercise increases the use of FFA for fuel and may be useful for fat loss (18). In fact, this occurs to a greater degree when carbohydrates are restricted (18).

Aspirin

Another mechanism the body uses to reduce the increase in metabolic rate is through the release of prostaglandins, specifically the PGE2 type, which accelerates the breakdown of noradrenaline (15). Aspirin generally inhibits prostaglandin release further potentiating the effects of ephedrine (8). The effects of aspirin on ephedrine appears to occur primarily in obese, but not lean individuals (12,13).

The combination of ephedrine, caffeine and aspirin has become known as the ECA stack in sports nutrition. It can be consumed in synthetic form or by taking the herbal equivalents of MaHuang (herbal ephedrine), kola nut or guarana (herbal caffeine), and white willow bark (a herbal form of aspirin). At least one popular author feels that white willow bark is not a suitable substitute for aspirin (19).

Important note on the ECA stack

The ECA stack is a potent stimulant for the central nervous system (CNS) making it a potentially dangerous compound, especially if used indiscriminately. There are an increasing number of individuals reporting negative responses to ephedrine, and a handful of deaths have been attributed to the combination of ECA. While details of all of these negative reactions are not available, there is an increasing use of herbal ephedrine (MaHuang) in a variety of nutritional supplements. The risk of overdose, especially in herbal products which are not standardized, is a possibility. In general, the studies show good tolerance among subjects taking the ECA stack at the recommended dose (11,14,20).

Under no circumstances should the recommended dose of ECA be exceeded. Any negative reactions beyond the normal stimulant effect indicates that the ECA stack should not be taken. Additionally, as a potent CNS stimulant, individuals with any type of preexisting heart condition should not use this combination of compounds. Also, individuals with thyroid or prostate problems should not use ECA. Individuals taking monoamine oxidase inhibitors (MAOI) should not use ECA.

Dosing and the ECA stack

Most of the available research points to the following combination of doses as optimal for the ECA stack (9,12-14,20,21):
ephedrine: 20 milligrams
caffeine: 200 milligrams (the amount of caffeine should be 10 times the amount of ephedrine)
aspirin: 80-325 milligrams

There is some debate over the amount of aspirin necessary to potentiate the effects of caffeine and ephedrine. While 300 mg has been used in research (13,14), this much aspirin three times daily can have potentially negative effects on the gastrointestinal tract, and can not be recommended. Some popular authors have suggested as little as 80 milligrams for positive effects (19).

This ECA stack is typically taken three times daily, with one dose in the morning, a second dose four to five hours later, and a third dose taken in the afternoon no later than 4 pm (to avoid problems with insomnia). Individuals who are sensitive to the side effects of ECA should begin with one dose in the morning for several days, adding a second dose as tolerance increases, and finally the third dose. Some authors suggest a 5 day on, 2 days off dosing pattern although no research exists to support this recommendation (19). Individuals on a CKD may wish to discontinue ephedrine during the carb-up.

Other compounds to enhance the ECA stack

The ECA stack can be potentiated by at least one other compound: the amino acid L-tyrosine. This may allow less ephedrine to be taken, further minimizing side effects, while maintaining the thermogenic effects. Although the addition of yohimbe to the ECA stack has been suggested, the potential for a negative reaction (discussed below) from this combination contraindicates using them together.

L-tyrosine

L-tyrosine is an amino acid used in the synthesis of adrenaline and noradrenaline. Additionally L-tyrosine is important for synthesis of the thyroid hormones (1). In theory, adding it in supplemental form could further improve the thermogenic effect of the ECA stack. In animal models, injection of ephedrine and L-tyrosine improves the thermogenic effect over ephedrine alone but it remains to be seen if the same synergistic effect will be seen in humans (22). Anecdotally most individuals report a greater 'kick' from the ECA stack when L-tyrosine is added. The typical dose of L-tyrosine is 500-1000 milligrams taken with the ECA stack.

Section 3: Yohimbe

As discussed in section 1, one approach to fat loss is to block the alpha-adrenoreceptors, specifically the alpha-2 adrenoreceptors (2). The herb yohimbe may act in this fashion, giving it a potential role in aiding fat loss (2). Like ephedrine, yohimbe may work through both direct and indirect methods. Directly, it may inhibit the effects of alpha-2 receptors, enhancing fat loss. Indirectly, it may stimulate the release of noradrenaline from nerve endings, stimulating fat breakdown (23-25). It appears that, at the doses seen in humans, most of the effects of yohimbine are through the indirect mechanism of increased adrenaline release, rather than by direct binding to alpha-2 receptors (23-25).

Yohimbe by itself

The primary use of yohimbe for fat loss has been in women although some men have reported good results. Since the combination of yohimbe with ECA cannot be recommended because of the potential for side effects, the use of yohimbe by itself is discussed here.

As mentioned above, yohimbe blocks alpha-2 receptors with the ultimate result of increased fat breakdown and dosing yohimbe has been shown to increase fat loss on a diet (24-27). Since the presence of insulin blocks the effects of yohimbe, it cannot be taken with or around carbohydrate containing meals. Additionally, the consumption of yohimbine with food increases the insulin response over what would normally be seen (23). This suggests that the best time to take yohimbe (along with caffeine to increase fat breakdown) would after an overnight fast, first thing in the morning, prior to aerobic exercise (23). In addition, the combination of yohimbine and exercise leads to increased energy expenditure compared to aerobic exercise done alone (25,26). However, this also causes an increased heart rate response to exercise.

By exercising prior to eating any food, the body should draw on bodyfat stores for fuel and the yohimbe and caffeine should increase FFA release from stubborn fat depots. Anecdotally, this strategy seems to help with the loss of hard to remove fat deposits, such as women's hips and the abdominals in men.

If individuals choose to use yohimbe in this fashion, and also wish to use ECA during their diet, there are two options. The first is to alternate days, using yohimbe on one day, and ECA the next. An alternate approach is to use yohimbe first thing in the morning prior to aerobic exercise, and then use the ECA stack later in the day (with the first dose approximately four to five hours after the yohimbe has been taken, to avoid potential interactions). Once again, individuals should monitor their heart rate and blood pressure responses to avoid negative reactions. If an individual is sensitive to yohimbe, its use should be discontinued.

Dosing of yohimbe

The optimal dose of yohimbe is thought to be 0.2 milligrams of active ingredient/kilogram of bodyweight (2,24,25). Thus a 68 kilogram individual (150 lbs) would require 13 milligrams to increase fat breakdown. Individuals should start with a lower dosage to assess their tolerance and increase dosage only when no negative heart rate or blood pressure responses occur.

A significant problem with most yohimbe on the market is a lack of standardization, making it difficult to know how much of the active compound is present. Additionally, there are compounds present in herbal preparations, that appear to cause greater side effects for herbal yohimbine, compared to prescription yohimbine hydrochloride. As with ephedrine, yohimbe should not be taken with any medication which acts as a MAOI.

Combining yohimbe with the ECA stack

As mentioned above, ephedrine has non-specific beta receptor agonist effects which are generally geared towards increasing fat burning. However, some of its effects are also felt at the alpha receptor, specifically the alpha-2 receptor. Recall from above that the alpha-2 receptor inhibits the use of fat for fuel when it is stimulated. So by stimulating alpha-2 receptors, ephedrine is limiting some of its fat burning potential.

Adding an alpha-2 antagonist could conceivably increase fat loss when used with the ECA stack. However an important cautionary note is needed. Recall from above that beta-receptors are in essence an 'accelerator' for certain metabolic processes while alpha-receptors are the 'brake'. Combining ECA with yohimbe is similar to pressing on the accelerator while releasing the brake at the same time which should enhance fat loss. While this may occur, the combination of ECA and yohimbe can cause profoundly negative effects on heart rate and blood pressure. Therefore the combination of ECA and yohimbe is not recommended.

Section 4: Appetite suppressants

A second class of potential fat loss aids are appetite suppressants. In general, these types of supplements are probably not needed on a ketogenic diet as the diet tends to blunt appetite in and of itself. However for those individuals who find themselves hungry on a ketogenic diet, appetite suppressants may be useful.

The ECA stack and yohimbe

The ECA stack is quite potent as an appetite suppressant in and of itself, especially when it is first used (9). Typically any anorectic effects of ECA go away within a few weeks of use. However, animal research suggests that combining ECA with the amino acid L-tyrosine may maintain the appetite blunting effect of ECA for longer periods of time (22). Individuals who find it hard to control their hunger on a ketogenic diet, may want to consider this combination. Yohimbe may also suppress appetite (2).

Fiber supplements

Although fiber has already been discussed within the context of regularity, it can also be used to suppress appetite on a diet. Fiber has many effects in the body, one of which is to slow digestion and gastric emptying (how quickly food exits the stomach). This would be expected to increase fullness, decreasing food intake. There are various types of fiber supplements available from basic psyllium husk fibers to substances like guar gum. No one fiber supplement appears to be superior to any other and most likely a combination of different types of fibers is optimal for health. Dieters should ensure that their fiber supplement is sugar free and does not contain any hidden carbohydrates that might affect ketosis.

Section 5: Other 'fat burners'

At any given time, there are any number of 'fat burners' being marketed to dieters. In almost all cases, these supplements are based on hype rather than science. The only two which are discussed here are the amino acid L-carnitine and pyruvate.

L-carnitine

L-carnitine is an amino acid involved in the burning of FFA for energy (28). Previous chapters have detailed how the carnitine palmityl transferase-1 system is intimately involved in ketone body formation and fat oxidation in the muscle. Because of its role in fat oxidation, many authors have suggested that supplemental L-carnitine might hasten fat loss. While this makes sense from a theoretical standpoint, most studies have not shown the expected results (28). Additionally, supplementation of L-carnitine under conditions of glycogen depletion, when it would be expected to have the greatest impact (since fat oxidation is at its highest), shows no benefit (29). Considering the high cost of L-carnitine, its use is not recommended.

Pyruvate

Supplemental pyruvate is a new supplement which has entered the fat burner market. Studies have shown that pyruvate slightly enhances fat loss on very low calorie diet (30,31). However, the doses necessary, 30 or more grams per day, to achieve this fat loss are cost prohibitive. Additionally, since commercially available pyruvate supplements typically contain half their weight as sodium or calcium, the risk for overload exists. Finally, pyruvate can inhibit ketosis. Pyruvate supplements are not recommended.

Conclusion

There are a number of supplements which may be beneficial to hasten fat loss, spare muscle loss, and blunt appetite while on a diet. These include the combination of ephedrine, caffeine and aspirin ; yohimbe ; as well as a variety of fiber supplements that can be used while dieting. Additionally, there are at least two popular 'fat burning' supplements, L-carnitine and pyruvate, which are not recommended.

References cited

1. "Textbook of Medical Physiology" Arthur C. Guyton. W.B. Saunders Company 1996.
2. Lafontan M and Berlan M. Fat cell alpha-2 adrenoreceptors: The regulation of fat cell function and lipolysis. Endocrine Rev (1995) 16: 716-738.
3. Lafontan M and Berlan M. Evidence for the alpha-2 nature of the alpha-adrenergic receptor inhibiting lipolysis in human fat cells. Eur J Pharmacology (1980) 66: 87-93.
4. Wahrenberg H et. al. Adrenergic regulation of lipolysis in human fat cells during exercise. Eur J Clin Invest (1991) 21: 534-541.
5. Wahrenberg, H et. al. Mechanisms underlying regional differences in lipolysis in human adipose tissue. J Clin Invest (1989) 84: 458-467.
6. Arner P. Adrenergic receptor function in fat cells. Am J Clin Nutr (1992) 55: 228S-236S.
7. Strosberg AD. Structure and function of the b3-adrenergic receptor. Annu Rev Pharmacol

Toxicol 1997; 37:421-450.

8. Dulloo AG. Ephedrine, xanthine, and prostaglandin-inhibitors: actions and interactions in the stimulation of thermogenesis. Int J Obes (1993) 17 (suppl. 1): S35-S40.

9. Astrup A and Toubro S. Thermogenic, metabolic and cardiovascular responses to ephedrine and caffeine in man. Int J Obes (1993) 17 (suppl 1): S41-S43.

10. Astrup A et. al. Enhanced thermogenic responsiveness during chronic ephedrine treatment in man. Am J Clin Nutr (1985) 42: 83-94.

11. Breum L et. al. Comparison of an ephedrine/caffeine combination and dexfenfluramine in the treatment of obesity. A double-blind multi-centre trial in general practice. Int J Obes (1994) 18: 99-103.

12. Horton TJ and Geissler CA. Post-prandial thermogenesis with ephedrine, caffeine and aspirin in lean, pre-disposed obese and obese women. Int J Obes (1996) 20: 91-97.

13. Horton TJ and Geissler CA. Aspirin potentiates the effect of ephedrine on the thermogenic response to a meal in obese but not lean women. Int J Obes (1991) 15: 359-366.

14. Daly PA et. al. Ephedrine, caffeine and aspirin: safety and efficacy for treatment of human obesity. Int J Obes (1993) 17 (suppl. 1): S73-S78.

15. Arner P. Adenosine, prostaglandins and phosphodiesterase as targets for obesity pharmacotherapy. Int J Obes (1993) 17 (suppl. 1): S57-S59.

16. Acheson KJ et. al. Caffeine and coffee: their influence on metabolic rate and substrate utilization in normal weight and obese individuals. Am J Clin Nutr (1980) 33: 989-997.

17. Astrup A et. al. Caffeine: a double-blind, placebo-controlled study of its thermogenic, metabolic, and cardiovascular effects. Am J Clin Nutr (1990) 51: 759-767.

18. Weir J et. al. A high carbohydrate diet negates the metabolic effects of caffeine during exercise. Med Sci Sports Exerc (1987) 19: 100-105.

19. "Fat Management! The Thermogenic Factor." Daniel B. Mowery, PhD. Utah: Victory Publications, 1994.

20. Toubro S et. al. Safety and efficacy of long-term treatment with ephedrine, caffeine and ephedrine/caffeine mixture. Int J Obes (1993) 17 (suppl. 1) S69-S72.

21. Astrup A et. al. Thermogenic synergism between ephedrine and caffeine in healthy volunteers: a double-blind, placebo-controlled study. Metabolism (1991) 40: 323-329.

22. Hull KM and Maher TJ. L-tyrosine potentiates the anorexia induced by mixed-acting sympathomimetic drugs in hyperphagic rats. Journal of Pharmacology and Experimental Therapeutics (1990) 255: 403-409.

23. LaFontan M et. al. Alpha-2 adrenoreceptors in lipolysis: alpha-2 antagonists and lipid-mobilizing strategies. Am J Clin Nutr (1992) 55: 219S-227S.

24. Berlan M et. al. Plasma catecholamine levels and lipid mobilization induced by yohimbine in obese and non-obese women. Int J Obes (1991) 15: 303-315.

25. Galitzky, J et. al. Alpha-2 antagonist compounds and lipid mobilization: evidence for a lipid mobilizing effect of oral yohimbine in healthy male volunteers. Eur J Clin Invest (1988) 18: 587-594.

26. Zahorska-Markiewicz B et. al. Adrenergic control of lipolysis and metabolic responses in obesity. Horm Metab Res (1986) 18: 693-697.

27. Kucio C et. al Does yohimbine act as a slimming drug? Isr J Med Sci (1991) 27: 550-556.

28. Brass EP and Hiatt WR. The role of carnitine and carnitine supplementation during exercise in man and in individuals with special needs. J Am Coll Nutr (1998) 17: 207-215.

29. Decombaz J et. al. Effect of L-carnitine on submaximal exercise metabolism after depletion of muscle glycogen. Med Sci Sports Exerc (1993) 25: 733-740.

30. Stanko RT et. al. Body composition, energy utilization, and nitrogen metabolism with a 4.25 MJ/d low-energy diet supplemented with pyruvate. Am J Clin Nutr (1992) 56: 630-635.

31. Stanko RT et. al. Body composition, energy utilization, and nitrogen metabolism with a severely restricted diet supplemented with dihydroxyacetone and pyruvate. Am J Clin Nutr (1992) 55: 711-776.

Chapter 33:
The carb-load

The carb-up section of the CKD is one area where specific supplements can help to maximize glycogen synthesis while minimizing fat regain. There are three major ways that supplements may improve the quality of the carb-up. The first is by improving insulin sensitivity, which is an index of how well or poorly a given tissue can utilize insulin. By keeping muscle insulin sensitivity high, there is less likelihood that fat cells will be stimulated to store fat. The three main insulin sensitizers are chromium picolinate, vanadyl sulfate, and alpha lipoic acid.

The second way that supplements may help the carb-up is by preventing the conversion of carbohydrate to fat, a process called de novo lipogenesis (DNL, discussed in more detail in chapters 3 and 12). The only supplement which may have this capacity is hydroxycitric acid (HCA).

The final mechanism by which supplements may improve the carb-up is by increasing glycogen storage in the muscles. Supplements which improve glycogen storage are creatine and glutamine, which are discussed in section 4 of this chapter.

Section 1: Insulin sensitizers

In general terms, insulin sensitivity refers to how well or how poorly a given tissue responds to the presence of insulin. There are a number of supplements which may improve insulin sensitivity, meaning that less insulin is needed to elicit the same effect.

Chromium

Chromium picolinate is a supplement which has been popularized in the media. Early studies suggested that it had a profound impact on body composition, but not all studies have found this to be the case (1). Chromium has been suggested to be part of a glucose tolerance factor (GTF) and may regulate how well or how poorly the body handles carbohydrates (1,2).

Chromium is thought to improve insulin sensitivity, which means that less insulin is necessary to have the same effect (2). For this reason chromium may play a role in the treatment of Type II diabetes (2,3). It has also been suggested that chromium may establish ketosis by helping to remove glucose from the bloodstream at the beginning of the low carb phase of the CKD. Anecdotally, it has shown only minimal effects in this regard. Individuals who suffer from insulin resistance may find that chromium supplements are useful during a SKD (2-4).

Due to the high carbohydrate intake during the carb-up, and considering that exercise is known to increase chromium excretion, supplementation with chromium may be beneficial (5). Typical doses vary from 200 to 800 micrograms per day. Although a recent concern was raised that chromium may cause chromosomal damage (6), the dosage necessary to cause toxicity problems is far in excess of what could be reasonably consumed (1).

Vanadyl sulfate

Vanadyl sulfate is a specialized form of the mineral vanadate. Although this seems a minor distinction, it becomes important when considering the issue of toxicity. While vanadate (a heavy metal) can be extremely toxic, vanadyl sulfate (the mineral salt) has not shown as great of toxicity.

Vanadyl has been suggested to work similarly to chromium picolinate, by improving insulin sensitivity in tissues of the body. It has shown some benefit in the treatment of Type II diabetes in this regard (7-9).

Because of its effects, vanadyl may have some benefit during carb-ups by keeping insulin sensitivity high. Additionally, vanadyl appears to improve glycogen storage in muscle tissue. Vanadyl has also been suggested to help establish ketosis, similar to chromium picolinate. However, vanadyl appears to keep some people out of ketosis, and this may occur from an effect on liver glycogen. The use of vanadyl sulfate is not recommended on a ketogenic diet.

Alpha lipoic acid

Alpha lipoic acid is a substance which acts as an anti-oxidant (10) as well as improving insulin sensitivity and the removal of glucose from the bloodstream (11, 12). Although human data on the effects of alpha lipoic acid is limited, anecdotal evidence suggests that lipoic acid is far more potent than either chromium or vanadyl. In this respect it is considered one of the best supplements to use on a carb-up, although it is somewhat expensive. Typical dose for lipoic acid during carb-ups are 1.2-2 grams total taken in divided doses. Considering the high cost of lipoic acid, individuals may wish to start with lower doses, and increase only if no noticeable effect is seen.

Section 2: Supplements to block De Novo Lipogenesis

The second mechanism by which supplements may improve the carb-up is by blocking the conversion of carbohydrates to fat. This process is called de novo lipogenesis (DNL) and is discussed in chapter 3 and 12. The only supplement which may have this effect is hydroxycitric acid.

Hydroxycitric acid

Hydroxycitric acid (HCA) has been found, in animal models only, to inhibit the conversion of excess carbohydrates to fat in the liver, a process called de novo lipogenesis (DNL) (13). The process of DNL is determined by the activity of an enzyme called ATP lyase, which HCA may inhibit. Additionally, it may enhance fat utilization and blunt appetite (13,14). Some authors have suggested that HCA will have similar effects in humans and may have a role in fat loss and exercise performance (15-17).

The problem with HCA is the lack of human research to show its effectiveness. The biggest argument against HCA is that DNL is not active in humans under normal conditions (18). As discussed in chapter 12, DNL can occur under one specific situation: severe carbohydrate overfeeding, as might occur during the carb-up phase of a CKD (19).

Although no research exists on this topic, anecdotal evidence suggests that the use of HCA can improve the carb-up, giving better muscle glycogen resynthesis with less spillover of water and fat. Additionally, in some people HCA blunts appetite, which may be good or bad during a carb-up. For those individuals who tend to over consume calories during a carb-up, HCA may be of benefit. For those individuals who find it difficult to consume sufficient carb calories during the carb-up, HCA may not be a good supplement to try.

The typical dose of HCA is 750-1000 mg of active ingredient taken three times per day. Since HCA comes in 50% standardization in most products, this means that 1500-2000 mg will need to be taken. An important aspect of making HCA effective is that it must be in the liver prior to the consumption of carbohydrates. This generally means that HCA should be taken at least thirty minutes before a meal is consumed.

Finally, in some individuals HCA seems to inhibit ketosis during the week although the exact mechanism is unknown. Beyond a potential effect on ketosis, as no carbohydrates are being consumed during the low-carbohydrate week of a CKD, HCA is unnecessary. Some products containing the ECA stack include HCA in them. These products are inappropriate for use during the lowcarb week.

Section 3: Supplements that increase glycogen storage

The final mechanism by which supplements may improve the carb-load is by increasing glycogen storage. The two major supplements which may increase glycogen storage during the carb-load are creatine and glutamine. Both are discussed in greater detail in the next chapter.

Glutamine is an amino acid which has been found to increase glycogen storage when consumed with carbohydrates (20). Additionally, creatine has also been found to increase glycogen synthesis when taken with carbohydrates (21). Therefore individuals may wish to experiment with one or both during the carb-load phase, to see if it gives them noticeably better glycogen supercompensation. As mentioned in the next chapter, glutamine supplementation can keep some people out of ketosis. If individuals find it difficult to establish ketosis after having used glutamine during the previous carb-load, they should try carb-loading without the glutamine to see if there is any difference.

References cited

1. Anderson R. Effects of chromium on body composition and weight loss. Nutr Rev (1998) 56: 266-270.
2. Anderson RA. Chromium, glucose tolerance and diabetes. Biol Trace Elem Res (1992) 32: 19-24.
3. Lee NA and Reasner CA. Beneficial effects of chromium supplementation on serum triglyceride levels in NIDDM. Diabetes Care (1994) 17: 1449-1452.
4. Anderson R et. al. "Supplemental-chromium effects on glucose, insulin, glucagon, and urinary chromium losses in subjects consuming controlled low-chromium diets. Am J Clin Nutr (1991) 54: 909-916.
5. Kozlovsky AS et. al. Effects of diets high in simple-sugars on urinary chromium losses. Metabolism (1986) 35: 515-518.
6. Stearns DM et. al. Chromium (III) picolinate produces chromosome damage in Chinese hamster ovary cells. FASEB Journal (1995) 9: 1643-1648.7.
7. Boden G et. al. Effects of vanadyl sulfate on carbohydrate and lipid metabolism in patients with non-insulin-dependent diabetes mellitus. Metabolism: Clinical and Experimental (1996) 45: 1130-1135.
8. Halbertstam M et. al. "Oral vanadyl sulfate improves insulin sensitivity in NIDDM but not in obese nondiabetic subjects. Diabetes (1996) 45: 659-666.
9. Cohen N et. al. Oral vanadyl sulfate improves hepatic and peripheral insulin sensitivity in patients with non-insulin-dependent diabetes mellitus. J Clin Invest (1995) 95: 2501-2509.
10. Packer L et. al. Alpha-lipoic acid as a biological antioxidant. Free Rad Biol Med (1995) 19: 227-250.
11. Jacob, S. et. al. "The antioxidant alpha-lipoic acid enhances insulin-stimulated glucose metabolism in insulin-resistant rat skeletal muscle" Diabetes (1996) 45: 1024-1029.
12. Jacob S et al. Thiotic acid enhances glucose disposal in patients with type 2 diabetes. Drug Res (1995) 45: 872-874.
13. Sullivan AC et. al. Effect of (-)-hydroxycitrate upon the accumulation of lipid in the rat. I. Lipogenesis. Lipids (1974) 9: 121-128.
14. Sullivan AC et. al. Effect of (-)-hydroxycitrate upon the accumulation of lipid in the rat. II. Appetite. Lipids (1974) 9:129-134.
15. McCarty MF. Optimizing exercise for fat loss. Med Hypotheses (1995) 44: 325-330.
16. McCarty MF. Promotion of hepatic lipid oxidation and gluconeogenesis as a strategy for appetite control. Med Hypotheses (1994) 42: 215-225.
17. McCarty MF. Inhibition of citrate lyase may aid aerobic endurance. Med Hypotheses (1995) 45: 247-254.
18. Hellerstein MK. Synthesis of fat in response to alteration in diet: insights from new stable isotope methodologies. Lipids (1996) 31 (suppl): S117-S125.
19. Acheson KJ et. al. Glycogen storage and de novo lipogenesis during massive carbohydrate overfeeding in man. Am J Clin Nutr (1988) 48: 240-247.
20. Varnier M et.al. Stimulatory effect of glutamine on glycogen accumulation in human skeletal muscle. Am J Physiol (1995): E309-315
21. Green AL et. al. Creatine ingestion augments muscle creatine uptake and glycogen synthesis during carbohydrate feeding in man. J Physiol (1996) 491: 63-64.

Chapter 34:
Mass Gains

There are a number of supplements used by weight trainers in an attempt to increase either strength or mass gains. Although the CKD is probably not the optimal mass gaining diet, many individuals choose to use these supplements to maintain strength and muscle mass while dieting and they are discussed here.

Glutamine

Glutamine is one of the most popular supplements on the market right now. Glutamine is typically considered a non-essential amino acid (AA) since it can be made within the body. However, in times of high stress, it may become essential (2). Glutamine is involved in maintaining the immune system (1) and low glutamine levels have been linked to overtraining in endurance athletes (1). Weight training is a form of stress and, although not directly studied, glutamine supplements have been suggested to help deal with the stress of training.

A majority of glutamine research has focused on its effect in critically ill individuals and burn patients. It is a major mistake to extrapolate from pathologically ill patients to healthy, weight training athletes although many authors in the field of nutrition have made that mistake.

Outside of its effects on immune system function, oral glutamine has also been shown to elevate growth hormone levels in the bloodstream, which may be useful for fat loss (1). The primary problem with oral glutamine supplementation is that glutamine is a major metabolic fuel for the small intestine. As well, high doses of glutamine tend to be absorbed by the kidney with the end result being that little of the glutamine ingested actually gets into the muscles (2).

A possible solution is to take glutamine in small doses throughout the day. Doses of 2 grams may not activate absorption by the kidney (1) and it should be possible to keep blood glutamine levels high by taking it in this fashion.

However, a little known effect of glutamine is that it inhibits ketogenesis in the liver (2). Many individuals have found that glutamine supplementation prevents them from establishing ketosis. However others have not found this to be the case and, as with many supplements, experimentation is the key. Glutamine probably has its greatest potential during the carb-up period of the CKD.

Creatine Monohydrate

If there is a single sports supplement that has been shown to work under a variety of conditions, it is creatine. Recall from chapter 19 that creatine phosphate (CP) is used to provide short term energy for exercise lasting approximately 20-30 seconds. Numerous studies have shown that supplementing with creatine monohydrate can increase muscular stores of CP and enhance high intensity exercise performance (for recent reviews of the effects of creatine, see references 3-5).

Improvements are primarily seen in short duration, high-intensity activity such as sprint performance as well as weight lifting (3). However, creatine has not consistently been shown to improve longer events, which rely on other energy systems. The improvements range from the ability to maintain a higher performance level prior to fatigue, the ability to perform more repetitions with a given weight, and some studies suggest that creatine supplementation may increase maximal strength (1 repetition maximum). Additionally, creatine typically causes a large initial weight gain of 5 or more pounds, although the majority of this weight is water. Whether long-term creatine supplementation causes significantly greater gains in lean body mass is still under research.

Creatine is typically loaded first to saturate muscular stores. Although the optimal dosage can vary, most studies suggest consuming 20 grams of creatine in divided doses (typically 5 grams four times a day) for 5 days to saturate muscular stores. An alternate method is to take small (3 grams) daily doses of creatine, which results in similar loading over a period of a month. Some individuals find that high doses of creatine cause stomach upset, and lower doses may make loading possible while avoiding this problem.

Although maintenance doses have been suggested, there is some debate as to whether or not this is truly necessary . As long as red meat is an integral part of the diet, as it will most likely be on any form of ketogenic diet, muscular CP stores will stay elevated for long periods of time.

One concern regarding creatine and the ketogenic diet is that research suggests that creatine is absorbed most efficiently if it is taken with a high glycemic index carbohydrate (6,7). Thus the low-carbohydrate nature of the ketogenic diet raises the question of whether creatine supplementation is useful. What should be remembered is that the early creatine studies used coffee or tea, without carbohydrates, and creatine uptake was still fairly high. Simply more creatine is absorbed if it is taken with a carbohydrate.

There are several strategies to get around this problem. The first is to load creatine before starting a ketogenic diet, so that it can be taken with a high glycemic carbohydrate. Once loaded, the high intake of meat on a ketogenic diet should maintain muscular stores. Additionally, creatine uptake is higher following exercise so that a maintenance dose could be taken immediately after training. Finally, many individuals have had success taking high dose of creatine (10-20 grams) during the carb-load of the CKD. As well, creatine could be taken around workouts on a TKD.

Creatine has no known effects on ketosis, nor would it be expected to affect the establishment or maintenance of ketosis.

Other mass gaining supplements

Weight trainers and bodybuilders are bombarded daily with advertisements for new supplements purported to increase strength and mass. As a general rule, there is little human data to suggest that these substances offer a significant advantage in terms of strength or mass gains.

Along with this, individuals constantly want to know if a given supplement will work on a ketogenic diet, or how it will affect ketosis. In all of these cases, there is simply no data available, and individuals will have to experiment to find what does and does not affect the diet.

References cited

1. Welbourne TC. Increased plasma bicarbonate and growth hormone after an oral glutamine load. Am J Clin Nutr (1995) 61: 1058-1061.
2. Lacey J and Wilmore D. Is glutamine a conditionally essential amino acid? Nutr Rev (1990) 48: 297-309.
3. Williams, MH and Branch D. Creatine supplementation and exercise performance: an update. J Am Coll Nutr (1998) 17: 216-234.
4. Balsom PD et. al. Creatine in humans with special reference to creatine supplementation. Sports Med (1994) 18: 268-280.
5. Volek JS and Kraemer WJ. Creatine supplementation: its effect on human muscular performance and body composition. J Str Cond Res (1996) 10: 200-210.
6. Green AL et. al. Carbohydrate ingestion augments creatine retention during creatine feeding in humans. Acta Physiol Scand (1996) 158: 195-202.
7. Green AL et. al. Carbohydrate ingestion augments skeletal muscle creatine accumulation during creatine supplementation in man. Am J Physiol (1996) 271: E821-826.

Appendix 1: Partial glycemic index

The glycemic index (GI) is a measure of how much a given carbohydrate food will affect blood glucose and insulin. Its primary use for ketogenic dieters is to pick carbohydrate sources while on a low-carbohydrate diet (where low GI carbs should be consumed) and also to make carb choices during the carb-up or around exercise (where high GI carbs are traditionally used). The following list uses white bread as a reference (given a value of 100) but some lists use glucose as the reference. To convert from the white bread GI to the glucose GI, divide by 0.7. To convert from the glucose GI to the white bread GI, multiply by 1.42. For ease of reference, foods are grouped by their GI, rather than by category. Therefore if individuals are looking for relatively higher or lower GI foods, it should be easier to make food choices.

Glucose	138	Bananas	76
Instant rice	128	Orange juice	74
Baked potatoes	121	Lactose	65
Corn Flakes	119	Mixed grain bread	64
Instant potatoes	118	Grapes	62
Rice Crispies	117	Oranges	62
Rice cakes	117	All Bran cereal	60
Jelly beans	114	Spaghetti	59
Honey	104	Apple juice	58
Carrots	101	Apples	52
White bread	100	Chickpeas	47
Cream of wheat	94	Skim milk	46
Sucrose	92	Lentils	41
Ice cream	87	Full fat milk	39
White rice	81	Grapefruit	36
Brown rice	79	Fructose	32
Popcorn	79	Peas	32
		Peanuts	21

Source: Foster-Powell K and Miller JB. International tables of glycemic index. Am J Clin Nutr (1995) 62: 871S-893S.

Appendix 2: Resources

Note: The author does not have any financially vested interest in any of the following companies. They simply represent good sources of products which may interest ketogenic dieters.

1. Creative Health Products: CHP is an excellent source for body fat calipers and heart rate monitors. For calipers, the Slimguide calipers can't be beat for cost or accuracy. They have some of the best prices anywhere.
1-800-742-4478

2. Beyond A Century: BAC sells many nutritional supplements that can be useful on a ketogenic diet. They have both an in-house brand as well as selling many well-known products from other companies. They also carry unique products (such as DMSO and Guar Gum) that are difficult if not impossible to find elsewhere.
1-800-777-1324
email: beyacent@aol.com.
Http://www.beyondacentury.com

3. Dave's Power Store: The Power Store offers the best prices on nutritional products around from all the major companies as well as their own in-house brand. They also publish an excellent newsletter (both hardcopy and online) to help individuals keep up to date on cutting edge nutrition and supplementation.
1-800-382-9611
email: dpower@essex1.com
http://www.thepowerstore.com/

4. The Scientific Bodybuilding Journal: The SBJ is a bimonthly magazine that the author contributes to regularly. It is pro-ketogenic and focuses on training and supplementation for the natural bodybuilder.
Contact Vince Martin at:
vinnie@mail.io.com for information about subscriptions.
http://www.io.com/~vinnie/index.html

5. The Lowcarb-l mailing list: For individuals with access to the internet, there is a mailing list dedicated to exercising on a low-carbohydrate diet. To subscribe, send email to:
majordomo@solid.net
with the message.
subscribe lowcarb-l
in it.

6. The Low carb technical list: This mailing list exists for the dissemination of technical information regarding low-carbohydrate diets. To subscribe, send email to:
majordomo@maelstrom.stjohns.edu
with the message
subscribe lowcarb
in it.

7. "Everyday Low Carb Cookery" by Alex Haas is a collection of lowcarb recipes for use with any of the popular lowcarb diets.

The price for each book is $19.95 (American dollars) plus Shipping and Handling (priority mail insured within the U.S.). Note that I take personal checks and money orders.

Shipping and handling (within the U.S.) - $5.00 (American) per book
Shipping and handling (to Canada) - $8.00 (American) per book
Shipping and handling (anywhere else) - $12.00 (American) per book

For gifts for the holidays, there is a 10% discount on orders of 3 or more books.
Send orders to:
Alex Haas
P.O. Box 7802
Talleyville, DE   19803-7802
U.S.A.

Glossary

Acetyl-CoA: An intermediate in energy metabolism, produced from the breakdown of free fatty acids, glucose and protein.

Adenosine Diphosphate: The by-product of the breakdown of adenosine triphosphate.

Adenosine Monophosphate: The by-product of the breakdown of adenosine diphosphate.

Adenosine Triphosphate (ATP): The principle form of stored energy in the body. Composed of an adenosine molecule and three phosphate molecules.

Amino acids (AAs): The building blocks of proteins of which there are 20.

Anabolic: A general term which refers to the building of larger substances from smaller substances.

Branch chain amino acids (BCAAs): The amino acids valine, leucine, and isoleucine.

Carbohydrate (CHO): Organic substances made up of carbon, hydrogen and oxygen, which provide energy to the body.

Carnitine Palmityl Transferase 1 (CPT-1): Carries free fatty acids into the mitochondria of cells for burning.

Catabolic: A general term which refers to the breaking down of larger substances into smaller substances.

Cholesterol: A steroid compound most often associated with triglycerides. Cholesterol is used in the body for the synthesis of cell membranes.

Cyclical ketogenic diet (CKD): A diet which alternates periods of ketosis with periods of high carbohydrate intake.

De Novo Lipogenesis (DNL): A process by which excess carbohydrate is converted to triglycerides in the liver.

Diabetic ketoacidosis: A potentially fatal condition occurring only in Type 1 (insulin dependent) diabetics as a consequence of high blood glucose but low insulin concentrations.

Fat mass (FM): Bodyfat stored in adipose tissue under the skin.

Glucagon: A hormone released from the pancreas which raises blood glucose when it drops too low.

Glucose: A single chain carbohydrate molecule, found circulating in the bloodstream.

Gluconeogenesis: An anabolic process where amino acids, lactate, pyruvate and glycerol are converted into glucose in the liver.

Glycogen: A storage form of carbohydrates in the body, found in muscle and liver.

Glycogenesis: An anabolic process where glucose is formed into glycogen. This occurs in muscle or in the liver.

Glycolysis: A catabolic process where glycogen is broken down into glucose.

Insulin: A hormone released from the pancreas which lowers blood glucose when it raises too high.

Ketone body (KB), also ketone: Ketone bodies are water-soluble substances which can be used by most tissues of the body as an alternative fuel to carbohydrate.

Ketogenesis: The production of ketone bodies in the liver from the incomplete breakdown of free fatty acids.

Ketogenic diet (KD): Any diet which causes the accumulation of ketone bodies in the bloodstream. Generally defined as any diet containing less than 100 grams per day of carbohydrate.

Ketonemia: Ketonemia refers to the buildup of ketones in the bloodstream to such a point that a metabolic state of ketosis occurs.

Ketonuria: Ketonuria refers to the buildup and subsequent excretion of ketones in the urine.

Ketosis: A metabolic state where ketone bodies have built up in the bloodstream to a point that the body changes its overall metabolism from one based primarily on carbohydrate to one based on fat.

Lactate threshold (LT): The exercise intensity above which lactic acid accumulates rapidly, causing fatigue.

Lactic acid: A by-product of high-intensity exercise.

Lean body mass (LBM): Everything in the body except adipose tissue. LBM includes muscle, bone, organs, the brain, water, glycogen, minerals, etc.

Lipogenesis: An anabolic process where free fatty acids and glycerol are made into triglyceride.

Lipolysis: A catabolic reaction which refers to the breaking down of triglycerides into free fatty acids and glycerol.

Macronutrients: Protein, carbohydrate and fat.

Malonyl-CoA: An intermediate in fat synthesis. Malonyl-CoA regulates free fatty acid use in the liver and muscle and is the determining factor in ketone body formation in the liver..

Micronutrients: Vitamins and minerals.

Mitochondria: The powerhouse of the cell, where free fatty acids are burned to produce energy.

Protein: Substances used in the body primarily for tissue repair. Proteins are made up of amino acids.

Protein synthesis: An anabolic process where amino acids are formed into larger proteins.

Proteolysis: A catabolic process where proteins are broken down into amino acids.

Targeted Ketogenic Diet (TKD): A compromise approach for those who can not use the CKD (for a variety of reasons) but who need to sustain high intensity activities (such as weight training).

Triglyceride (TG): Organic substances composed of three free fatty acid (FFA) molecules and a glycerol molecule.

Total body mass (TBM): The total weight of the body, including fat and lean body mass.

Index

Order Form

To obtain more copies of this book, please copy and mail the following order form to:

Lyle McDonald
PMB 314
8760-A Research Blvd.
Austin, Tx 78758

Please send me _____ copy (ies) of "The Ketogenic Diet: A Complete Guide for the Dieter and Practitioner" at $29.95 (US) per copy.

Please include $5/copy shipping and handling. All orders are sent insured US Priority Mail (3-4 day delivery after order is received).
For Canadian orders, include $8 shipping and handling per book.
Other international orders can not be taken at this time.

There is a 10% discount for orders of 3 or more books. Please subtract 10% from the total book cost not including shipping and handling.

Personal checks may be held for 7 days until they have cleared the bank.
Individuals who desire faster service should pay by money order.
Credit card orders can not be taken at this time.

Checks and money orders should be made payable to: Lyle McDonald

Enclosed is a ( ) check ( ) money order in the amount of $ _____

Please print your adress clearly:

Name _____
Adress _____
City/State/Zip _____
Telephone# _____
email _____

Note: the above information will not be released in any way, shape or form. Telephone and email will only be used if there is a problem with filling your order.